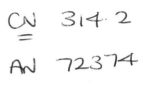

British Social Attitudes

Attitudes The 19th REPORT

The *National Centre for Social Research* (NatCen) is an independent, non-profit social research institute. It has a large professional staff together with its own interviewing and coding resources. Some of NatCen's work – such as the survey reported in this book – is initiated by the institute itself and grant-funded by research councils or foundations. Other work is initiated by government departments, local authorities or quasi-government organisations to provide information on aspects of social or economic policy. NatCen also works frequently with other institutes and academics. Founded in 1969 and now Britain's largest social research institute, NatCen has a high reputation for the standard of its work in both qualitative and quantitative research. NatCen has a Survey Methods Centre and, with the Department of Sociology, University of Oxford, houses the Centre for Research into Elections and Social Trends (CREST). It also houses, with Southampton University, the Centre for Applied Social Surveys (CASS), an ESRC Resource Centre, two main functions of which are to run courses in survey methods and to establish and administer an electronic social survey question bank.

The contributors

Catherine Bromley
Senior Researcher at NatCen, Scotland and Co-Director of the *British Social Attitudes* survey series

Alex Bryson
Principal Research Fellow at the Policy Studies Institute and Research Associate at the Centre for Economic Performance at LSE

Ian Christie
Associate Director of The Local Futures Group and associate of the New Economics Foundation and the Centre for Environmental Strategy, University of Surrey

John Curtice
Head of Research at NatCen, Scotland, Deputy Director of CREST, and Professor of Politics at Strathclyde University

Geoffrey Evans
Official Fellow in Politics, Nuffield College Oxford and Professor of the Sociology of Politics

Sonia Exley
Researcher at NatCen and Co-Director of the British Social Attitudes survey series

Raphael Gomez
Lecturer at the Interdisciplinary Institute of Management and a Research Associate at the Centre for Economic Performance at LSE

Arthur Gould
Reader in Swedish Social Policy at Loughborough University

Charlotte Hastie
Research Assistant in Social Policy at the University of Kent

Anthony Heath
Professor of Sociology at the University of Oxford and Deputy Director of CREST

Lindsey Jarvis
Research Director at NatCen and Co-Director of the *British Social Attitudes* survey series

Stephen McKay
Deputy Director of the Personal Finance Research Centre at the University of Bristol

Alison Park
Research Director at NatCen and Co-Director of the *British Social Attitudes* survey series

Ceridwen Roberts
Senior Research Fellow at the Department of Social Policy and Social Work at the University of Oxford

Catherine Rothon
Research Officer for CREST at the University of Oxford

Karen Rowlingson
Lecturer in the Department of Social and Policy Sciences at the University of Bath

Nina Stratford
Research Director at NatCen

Peter Taylor-Gooby
Professor of Social Policy at the University of Kent

Katarina Thomson
Research Director at NatCen and Co-Director of the *British Social Attitudes* survey series

Ted Wragg
Professor of Education at Exeter University

British Social Attitudes

The 19th REPORT

EDITORS

Alison Park
John Curtice
Katarina Thomson
Lindsey Jarvis
Catherine Bromley

SAGE Publications
London · Thousand Oaks · New Delhi

 National Centre *for* Social Research

First published 2002

 SAGE Publications Ltd
6 Bonhill Street
London EC2A 4PU

SAGE Publications Inc.
2455 Teller Road
Thousand Oaks, California 91320

SAGE Publications India Pvt Ltd
B-42, Panchsheel Enclave
Post Box 4109
New Delhi 100 017

British Library Cataloguing in Publication data

A catalogue record for this book is available from the British Library

ISSN 0267 6869
ISBN 0 7619 7454 7

Library of Congress Control Number 2002106571

Printed in Great Britain by The Cromwell Press Ltd, Trowbridge, Wiltshire

This book is dedicated to
the memory of
Sheila Vioche

Contents

List of tables and figures

Chapter 4

Chapter 5

Chapter 6

Chapter 7

Chapter 8

Chapter 9

Introduction

This volume, like each of its annual predecessors, presents results, analyses and interpretations of the latest *British Social Attitudes* survey – the 19th in the series of reports on the studies designed and carried out by the *National Centre for Social Research*.

The series has a widely acknowledged reputation as the authoritative map of contemporary British values. Its reputation owes a great deal to its many generous funders. We are particularly grateful to our core funder – the Gatsby Charitable Foundation (one of the Sainsbury Family Charitable Trusts) – whose continuous support of the series from the start has given it security and independence. Other funders have made long-term commitments to the study and we are ever grateful to them as well. These include the Department of Health, the Department for Work and Pensions, and the Department of Transport, all of whom funded the 2001 survey. Thanks are also due to the Health and Safety Executive[1] and the Institute of Community Studies.

We are particularly grateful to the Economic and Social Research Council (ESRC) who provided funding for three modules of questions in the 2001 survey. These covered: attitudes towards, and knowledge about, public policy; illegal drugs; and devolution and national identity (funded as part of the ESRC's Devolution and Constitutional Change Programme). The ESRC also supported the *National Centre*'s participation in the International Social Survey Programme (ISSP), which now comprises 38 nations, each of whom help to design and then field a set of equivalent questions every year on a rotating set of issues. The topic in 2001 was social networks.

We are also very grateful to the ESRC for its funding of the *Centre for Research into Elections and Social Trends* (*CREST*), an ESRC Research Centre that links the *National Centre* with the Department of Sociology at Oxford University. Although *CREST*'s funding from the ESRC sadly ended in autumn 2002, we will endeavour to continue its role in uncovering and investigating long-run changes in Britain's social and political complexion

One recent spin-off from the *British Social Attitudes* series has been the development of an annual *Scottish Social Attitudes* survey. This began in 1999 and is funded from a range of sources along similar lines to *British Social Attitudes*. It is closely associated with its British counterpart and incorporates many of the same questions to enable comparison north and south of the border,

while also providing a detailed examination of attitudes to particular issues within Scotland. Two books have now been published about the survey (Paterson *et al.*, 2000; Curtice *et al.*, 2001) and a third is due to be published early in 2003.

The *British Social Attitudes* series is a team effort. The researchers who design, direct and report on the study are supported by complementary teams who implement the sampling strategy and carry out data processing. They in turn depend on fieldwork controllers, area managers and field interviewers who are responsible for getting all the interviewing done, and on administrative staff to compile, organise and distribute the survey's extensive documentation. In this respect, particular thanks are due to Kerrie Gemmill and her colleagues in the *National Centre*'s administrative office in Brentwood. Other thanks are due to Sue Corbett and her colleagues in our computing department who expertly translate our questions into a computer-assisted questionnaire. Meanwhile, the raw data have to be transformed into a workable SPSS system file – a task that has for many years been performed with great care and efficiency by Ann Mair at the Social Statistics Laboratory in the University of Strathclyde. Many thanks are also due to Lucy Robinson and Vanessa Harwood at Sage, our publishers.

Unfortunately, this year the *British Social Attitudes* team has had to bid farewell to a much loved colleague, Sheila Vioche, who died in August. Among countless other things, Sheila played an invaluable role in organising, formatting and checking the content of our previous five reports. Her calm presence, style and wit will be sorely missed by all of us, as will her fantastic poems.

Finally, we must praise the anonymous respondents across Britain who gave their time to take part in our 2001 survey. Like the 46,000 or so respondents who have participated before them, they are the cornerstone of this enterprise. We hope that some of them will one day come across this volume and read about themselves with interest.

The Editors

Notes

1. This funding supported a module of questions about health and safety in the workplace. Although its findings are not discussed in this report, they are explored at www.hse.gov.uk/statistics/bsahs01.pdf.

References

Paterson, L., Brown, A., Curtice, J., Hinds, K., McCrone, D., Park, A., Sproston, K. and Surridge, P. (2000), *New Scotland, New Politics?*, Edinburgh: Edinburgh University Press.

Curtice, J., McCrone, D., Park, A. and Paterson, L. (eds.) (2001), *New Scotland, New Society? Are social and political ties fragmenting?*, Edinburgh: Edinburgh University Press.

1 Off the buses?

Sonia Exley and Ian Christie [*]

The quality of public transport, and the question as to how to manage growing demand for mobility in a crowded country, have become central issues for the Labour government. Transport has become a priority as ministers strive to show that public services can be revitalised and improvements in quality of service 'delivered' to the public. A whole range of issues, from railway safety and reliability, to road congestion and the pressure for more airport capacity, have come together to put transport higher up the policy agenda than it has been for decades.

The reasons for this are well known. The botched privatisation of the rail system has led to many problems, especially relating to safety and maintenance of the network, and has increased the costs of operation. The deregulation of bus services outside London in the 1980s failed to halt a long-running decline in bus use (DETR, 2001a). Demand for car use continues to rise, creating serious problems of congestion. Air travel continues to boom, despite September 11th, causing concern about safety in the skies, and adding to pressures on roads and rail connections around airports. And the neglect of investment in the rail and road networks over decades – especially serious in relation to inter-city rail links and many commuter lines – means that modernising the transport system will take many years and cost billions of pounds. The UK seems to be among the worst-off countries in Europe for quality of public transport and trouble with road congestion (Commission for Integrated Transport, 2001).

However, the challenges in transport policy are not simply about finding the resources to upgrade services and infrastructure. Upgrading the supply of transport services is not enough: the government is also concerned with changing the *pattern of use* of transport modes, for environmental reasons above all. This imperative points to the need for measures to change people's long-established habits and transport choices. A key part of this will have to

---

[*] Sonia Exley is a Researcher at the *National Centre for Social Research* and Co-Director of the *British Social Attitudes* series. Ian Christie is associate director of The Local Futures Group, and an associate of the New Economics Foundation and the Centre for Environmental Strategy, University of Surrey.

attempt to change *attitudes* towards different modes of travel. In particular, if the Labour government is going to achieve the policy goals it has set itself, a fundamental part of their task will be to change the way people feel about their cars and the way they view public transport alternatives. In this chapter, we explore public attitudes towards transport in general; towards a range of policies intended to promote changes in use of modes, especially to reduce dependency on cars; and in particular towards *buses*, which could be a vital ingredient in a more environmentally sustainable and socially equitable transport system. In an effort to examine the degree to which Labour has been successful in changing views since their election in 1997, we will focus particularly on identifying any change over time in people's views on these matters.

Transport policy challenges: expanding supply and managing demand

The government faces two main challenges with regards to transport policy, and cannot afford to deal with one and not the other. Their first challenge is to improve the supply of transport services – both in terms of quality and quantity. And the second is to change the nature of demand, in order to reduce both environmental damage and the harmful social and economic effects of congestion and car dependence. Neither approach offers any political 'quick wins' and both are certain to alienate voters in different ways.

  This is a predicament bequeathed by decades of under-investment in public transport and by the great post-war increase in car ownership. The growth in travel by car has produced a ratchet effect: more use of the car, more demand for road-building, less resources for public transport, more scope for car use, less demand for public transport, less safe roads for cyclists and pedestrians, and consequently more reason for people to switch to cars instead of trains and buses, cycling and walking. Two factors have made it imperative to break this vicious circle: the impossibility of meeting potential demand for car use, and the impact of the ratchet effect on the environment.

  There is good evidence that, when it comes to coping with demand for road transport, the policy of 'predict and provide' is unsustainable. This approach, used since the 1950s, involves measuring the growth in car ownership and use, and in demand for road freight, and providing the extensions in the road network to meet it. But experience indicates that growth in car traffic tends to outstrip provision of new road capacity and so any alleviation in congestion afforded by road-building is only temporary (Whitelegg, 1997; DETR, 1998; Goodwin, 1998).

  As for the environmental effects, these are now a major influence on policy. Congestion in cities, suburbs and towns has grown more severe, with accompanying pollution, noise and impacts on pedestrians. Although cars have become *individually* less polluting thanks to regulation and technical improvements, air quality still suffers because of the sheer volume of exhaust emissions. And, more threateningly for the longer term, the transport sector has

become the fastest growing source of greenhouse gas emissions which are linked to the threat of global warming and climate disruption (DETR, 2000).

The government has sought to meet these two challenges in its transport policy, with mixed results. The 'integrated transport strategy' heralded in the 1998 White Paper on Transport recognised that there must be limits to car use, and placed a high priority on making alternatives to the car – not only public transport, but also walking and cycling – much more attractive and accessible (DETR, 1998). But, in practice, the government has made concessions to the 'predict and provide' model of the past, promising some more road-building to alleviate congestion and abandoning the idea that the success of government should be judged by reductions in car use levels. Now, reducing the *rate* of increase in car use would count as an achievement.

What has happened to the aims of changing travel habits and reducing car dependency? Policy now focuses on an extremely expensive ten-year strategy to improve public transport, in the hope that greatly enhanced facilities will attract more people to use it. However, the current scale of road use makes it impossible to imagine that a supply-side approach alone can make much difference to congestion and the environmental impacts of the car. While improving public transport is important, finding ways to manage and reduce demand for car use is vital too.

In official planning guidance (DETR, 2001b), this combination of supply- and demand-side measures is held to be the key to integrated transport policy. In the guidance, the government calls for promotion of "more sustainable transport choices for both people and for moving freight" and greater "accessibility to jobs, shopping, leisure facilities and services by public transport, walking and cycling". But it includes a third goal which is "to reduce the need to travel, especially by car", and it is here that the political difficulties mount up.

As concern about environmental pollution in general, and climate disruption in particular, have grown in recent years in Britain and Europe as a whole (Dalton and Rohrschneider, 1998), it has become clear that the issue of managing demand for road use is acutely sensitive for politicians and the public. The recognition of the environmental problems created by 'hyper-mobile' lifestyles (Adams, 2000) is accompanied by great resistance among consumers to curb car use and shift to public transport, and by reluctance among policy makers to discuss limits to car use. This is a familiar theme from previous *British Social Attitudes* surveys (Taylor, 1997; Christie and Jarvis, 1999). The problem for the government is that it needs to offer major improvements in the supply of public transport services *and* also find ways to reduce demand for car use. Improving trains and buses at the same time as enhancing conditions for drivers might bring more people onto public transport but will also put new car traffic on the roads.

Both ambitions – improving transport supply and constraining demand for road use – run up against serious opposition. One of the factors in the gradual abandonment of 'predict and provide' as a strategy for road network expansion was the growth in costly and damaging public protests, in which anti-road Green guerillas (symbolised by the famous Swampy) and well-heeled home owners joined forces to block road schemes. (This kind of alliance seems ready

to be revived for protests against planned expansions in airports around the UK.) But the problems on the demand side are just as daunting. The 'fuel crisis' or 'petrol revolt' of September 2000 was sparked by anger among haulage drivers over increases in road fuel costs, and led to a scaling back of government rhetoric and action on policies to deter car use through charging and new taxes on the motorist. And the bitter controversy over the introduction of congestion charging in London in 2003 indicates how sensitive the issue of managing demand can be. While a successful road-pricing scheme in London could lead to similar initiatives in cities around the UK, policy makers are nervous of enraging motorists and businesses.

As we argued in *The 16th Report* (Christie and Jarvis, 1999), here is a dramatic illustration of the economist Fred Hirsch's analysis of the "social limits to growth" (Hirsch, 1977): free use of the road is a classic 'positional good', producing satisfaction and status which *decline in quality the more that others have access to them*. Expanding supply indefinitely is not possible; but restricting access to such goods produces sharp political conflicts and pits people's awareness of the need for collective action against their self-interest as consumers. The politics of positional goods, as played out in transport policy, involves not just attempts to improve provision but also to change people's *habits and aspirations*, and thus involves social and cultural issues.

The following sections begin by considering transport use and trends in attitudes towards various options for improving services and reducing reliance on cars. We then look in detail at the factors affecting use of, and attitudes towards, bus services. We identify a range of important social factors which influence both willingness to use the bus, and levels of satisfaction with bus services. What emerges is the major policy challenge of changing a culture of resistance towards the bus, reversing a decline in use, and persuading people that they should switch to using buses more often. Moreover, it is also clear that improving services will need to be accompanied by other measures to provide incentives for use, and to deter car use.

Transport use: patterns and attitudes

Labour's inheritance in 1997 was a public transport system that had been subjected to major reorganisations – bus deregulation outside London, rail privatisation – accompanied by well-publicised service failures, management problems, accidents and political rows. At the end of 2000, there were over 24 million cars registered in the UK, twice the total for 1975, and over 70 per cent of households had regular use of a car. The proportion of households with use of two or more cars doubled over the last 20 years reaching 28 per cent (ONS, 2001). Car use dominates our travel patterns, accounting for 85 per cent of all passenger kilometres in 2000; buses and coaches account for six per cent; trains for seven per cent; and motorcycles and cycles for one per cent (ONS, 2001).

There is a powerful incentive for car users to keep on driving: while the costs of motoring have more or less kept up with inflation over the past two decades, the price of using public transport has gone up well above the rate of inflation.

The Commission for Integrated Transport (2001) has found that bus subsidy levels in the UK are far lower than in other member states, and that public transport trips by any mode cost significantly more (15 per cent more than in Germany, and 60 per cent more than in France).

In spite of this, the long decline from 1950 to the mid-1980s in the distance travelled by bus has been arrested in recent years, and use has actually increased in London, if not outside. Even numbers of train journeys have increased, despite the problems of the rail networks, as well as the distance travelled by train. However, as journeys have proliferated and travel distances have risen by car, the proportion of trips made by public transport has remained very low. Let us now examine Labour's record in terms of different transport modes in 2001. Has the government managed to make any sort of difference in the face of the legacy it inherited? The next table sums up changes in transport use since 1997, the year Labour arrived in government armed with a vision of a more integrated transport strategy and a less car-dependent society. It shows that, far from seeing a decrease in car dependency, there has been an increase of seven percentage points since 1997 in the proportion of people saying that they travel by car at least twice a week. Now nearly two-thirds of respondents count as habitual drivers. Since the proportions travelling as car passengers have stayed much the same over this time, we can conclude that the number of single-person car journeys – an energy-inefficient mode of travelling that maximises congestion – has gone up. This is confirmed by National Travel Survey data, which show that average car occupancy (the average number of people per car) has declined from 1.64 in 1985/86 to 1.59 in 1999/2001 (DETR, 2001a). While the proportion of regular train travellers has been stable at around four per cent since 1997, the story for bus use is a troubling one for policy makers. One in five used buses regularly in 1997 but there has been a steady decrease since. This decline is again confirmed by the figures for the National Travel Survey about the number of journeys made by bus outside London (DTLR, 2001).

Table 1.1 Patterns of transport use, 1997–2001

% who travel by the following form of transport at least two days a week	1997	1998	1999	2000	2001
By car as a driver	56	62	60	63	63
By car as a passenger	35	34	35	35	35
By local bus	20	17	19	18	16
By train	4	4	5	4	4
Base	*1355*	*1075*	*1031*	*1133*	*1099*

How serious is the transport problem?

The decline of public transport and the rise of the car has produced a general sense of crisis in political circles over recent years. Congestion has become a major political issue in London and headlines about 'gridlock Britain' have proliferated. But how serious a problem is congestion for the public? The next table shows that perceptions of congestion on motorways have not changed much since 1997 but, on the face of it, perceptions of traffic congestion in towns and cities could be seen as one of Labour's success stories. In 1997, seven in ten felt this to be a "very serious" or at least "a serious problem", compared with only a half in 2001 – a big improvement in perceptions of urban congestion in a very short time. So, in some areas, there appears to have been real progress in reducing congestion, through better public transport and (perhaps more likely) diversion of traffic elsewhere. But this is hard to square with the increase in road use we have seen. An alternative interpretation is that in many areas people have simply become *accustomed* to the level of congestion they experience daily, and that perceptions of what is excessive and normal have adjusted accordingly. However, it is also possible that the change is partly artificial and reflects questionnaire context effects. The order in which these questions were asked was altered in 2001; previously, it was asked directly after a comparable question about congestion in the countryside and it is possible that, by thinking about the countryside first, respondents then overstated congestion in towns. Nevertheless, similar levels were found in July 2001 on ONS's Omnibus survey.

Table 1.2 How bad is congestion?

	1997	1998	1999	2000	2001
Traffic congestion on motorways is ...	%	%	%	%	%
... a very serious/serious problem	32	32	36	35	31
... not very serious/not a problem	67	66	63	64	69
Traffic congestion in towns and cities is ...	%	%	%	%	%
... a very serious/serious problem	70	67	71	72	52
... not very serious/not a problem	29	32	28	27	47
Base	*1355*	*1075*	*1031*	*1133*	*1099*

Attitudes to transport policies

The backdrop to our story is thus one of rising car use, concern about traffic congestion and stable (or declining) use of public transport. This provides policy makers with a number of challenges, particularly in relation to reducing

car dependency. So we now turn to assess the likely impact that people think particular policies might have on their own car use. While it is important to be tentative in drawing conclusions from these data since the policies in question have not been implemented (yet), the attitudes revealed are of interest given the growth in concern over congestion and the rising profile of road pricing, particularly in London. We asked about measures that fit into two general approaches to policy – attempts to manage demand by making driving more expensive and difficult, and policies to improve the quality of alternatives to the car. Car drivers were asked the following question:

> *I am going to read out some of the things that might get people to* **cut down** *on the number of car journeys they take. For each one, please tell me what effect, if any, this might have on how much* **you yourself** *use the car to get about.*

The next table shows the percentage who said they might use their car "a little less", "quite a bit less" or "give up using" their car if a particular measure was adopted. The most dramatic results relate to doubling the cost of petrol over the next ten years. Nearly two-thirds (63 per cent) say their car use would fall, up from 54 per cent in 1997. This might sound to many the most 'draconian' of the policies mentioned, accounting for the greater sensitivity reported to this option than to the others. The increase in deterrent effect here might also reflect increases in the relative price of petrol in recent years (because, as petrol costs increase, so of course does the severity of its cost doubling). Attitudes towards road pricing and more severe parking penalties and restrictions show a less positive pattern. Although the prospect of a £2 city centre congestion charge seemed to be making a difference in figures up to 2000, the proportion who said this would change their driving behaviour dropped back to 1997 levels in 2001. Perhaps this drop in some ways reflects the changing political climate as congestion charging in Britain gradually becomes more of an impending reality than a hypothetical situation. Lastly, the majority said that motorway charges and more severe parking regimes would make no difference – with slight *increases* in the proportion since 2000.

  So, if anything, there has been a modest hardening of opinion against policies that aim to shift us from our cars. How can this be explained? It seems likely that the experience of, and reporting of, transport alternatives between 2000 and 2001 will have played a part. In this period Railtrack more or less collapsed, the Hatfield crash paralysed train services for many weeks, and the government began to admit that it would take decades for under-investment in public transport to be made good. Given a powerful and widely reported set of problems for rail, touted as an alternative to the car, many respondents might conclude that they would prefer to soak up the higher costs of driving rather than drive less.

Table 1.3 Measures to curb demand for car use: will they affect drivers' habits?

% who say the following measures might mean they would use their car less	1997	1998	1999	2000	2001
Doubling the cost of petrol over the next ten years	54	59	61	61	63
Introducing a £2 city centre peak-time congestion charge	49	52	55	61	48
Charging £1 per 50 miles on motorways	36	39	40	41	39
More severe parking penalties and restrictions	32	42	43	44	39
Base	*768*	*639*	*620*	*689*	*686*

Improving public transport has consistently been supported by over nine in ten (94 per cent in 2001) since Labour came to power in 1997. But how do people think the revenue to fund improvements in public transport should be raised? To assess this, we asked people whether they supported or opposed various ways of finding money to improve public transport. Unfortunately for politicians, although the vast majority agree that improving public transport is a matter of national importance, this finding is not matched by public support for various policy measures which might be used in order to fund improvement. In fact, as the next table shows, support for the various policy measures asked about on the survey *has not increased at all since 1997* – either remaining stable or declining. Particularly striking examples of this can be seen in the drop in support for cutting spending on new roads and road maintenance.

There is strong opposition to *general* measures that would affect all drivers in all places – doubling the cost of petrol, increasing VAT on goods and services and cutting funds for road maintenance. Opposition to more *targeted* measures that would affect particular road users at the point of use – taxes on employers, motorway pricing and congestion charging – is much less vehement, and substantial minorities are in favour (support presumably coming from those who are less likely to be affected). However, in all these areas there is still a clear majority against the proposed measure. One interpretation of this is that less discriminate policies are seen as 'anti-car', a fundamental attack on a basic item of modern life, whereas targeted measures focused on obvious problems – congestion at particular times and places – are seen as appropriate and less threatening.

Table 1.4 Paying for better public transport

% who support the following ways of funding improvements in public transport	1997	1998	1999	2000	2001
Introducing a £2 city centre peak-time congestion charge	30	31	25	29	30
Charging £1 per 50 miles on motorways	30	27	24	25	26
Taxing employers for employee car parking	–	–	26	24	22
Cutting in half spending on new roads	30	30	21	19	18
Doubling the cost of petrol in the next ten years	12	12	8	7	6
Increasing taxes like VAT on goods and services	11	11	9	7	9
Cutting in half spending on road maintenance	10	8	7	5	5
Base	*1080*	*877*	*813*	*972*	*912*

Regardless of how improvements are to be financed, what effect might they have on travel habits? The next table sums up the attitudes of car drivers over the last five years. The pattern here is not too surprising: people prefer 'carrot' policies to the 'stick' of higher charges of different kinds. Although the prospect of improved provision of cycle lanes leaves nearly 80 per cent of car drivers cold, with a hardening of opinion since 2000, the majority say that better long-distance and local public transport would induce them to use their cars less. Nearly two-thirds say that better local public transport would reduce their car use, up by 11 percentage points since 1997. So, overall the results are more encouraging for policy makers concerned about reducing car dependency. If the government's planned investment programme over the next decade bears fruit, there would appear to be many people who say they are willing to make more use of a much improved public transport system.

However, sceptics would respond to these results by arguing that drivers might be influenced by a pressure to give a socially desirable answer. But we can make some assessment of what individuals would in fact do by measuring their perception of how *inconvenient* it would be to reduce their car use.

Table 1.5 Will improvements in alternative forms of transport change patterns of car use?

% who say the following measures might mean they would use their car less	1997	1998	1999	2000	2001
Greatly improving the reliability of **local** public transport	54	61	63	65	65
Greatly improving **long-distance** rail and coach services	45	51	53	57	56
Introducing special cycle lanes on roads	22	24	27	28	21
Base	768	639	620	689	686

The results shown in the next table place our earlier findings into perspective. Here we see a very stable pattern of car dependency, with over eight in ten saying it would be inconvenient to cut their car driving. It should be noted here that attitudes reflect car dependency in light of the current policy context and perhaps the findings might change were there to be substantial improvements in public transport.

Table 1.6 Car dependency: how inconvenient would less car use be? 1997–2001

Inconvenience of cutting a quarter of regular car trips	1997	1998	1999	2000	2001
	%	%	%	%	%
Very inconvenient	53	50	48	50	55
Fairly inconvenient	28	29	34	32	28
Not very/not at all inconvenient	17	19	17	18	16
Inconvenience of cutting half of regular car trips					
	%	%	%	%	%
Very inconvenient	74	66	69	71	74
Fairly inconvenient	16	20	20	21	16
Not very/not at all inconvenient	10	11	9	8	10
Base	518	463	429	476	467

These findings together suggest that the British love affair with the car is going to be hard to break, regardless of how much effort is put into improving public

transport. But are there particular *attitudinal* barriers at work, not perhaps reflected in the answers given so far? To assess this, the following sections examine the social dimension of use of different travel modes, and attitudes to bus use in particular.

Car and bus users

We have already seen that government is not yet succeeding in scaling back demand for car use and in encouraging more use of public transport, especially buses. This is partly a matter of infrastructural investment, but also concerns attitudes towards different modes of transport. If dependency upon everyday car use is to be tackled, a better understanding of attitudes towards public and private transport will be required in order to inform thinking about where efforts should be channelled to improve policies and what incentives might be necessary to encourage people to switch to public transport. Who are the groups that are so attached to their cars? What kinds of characteristics do they have? It has often been argued that buses are considered to be the poor person's public transport mode, mainly used by those who are socially marginalised or 'excluded' – people on low incomes, those who are economically inactive or retired, those with low levels of education and those in 'routine' occupations. By contrast, cars and trains are largely the preserve of the affluent. In this section we explore the social dimension of bus and car travel, in an effort to identify key target groups for policy action.

The following table gives an outline of regular car and local bus users (defined as those using a car or bus at least twice week), broken down by key demographic characteristics. It shows that those who are more likely to drive a car are people in paid work, those in 'higher' occupations (such as managerial and professional occupations), with higher household incomes and levels of education, and those in middle age groups (34–49 and 50–64). Men are substantially more likely than women to drive regularly (three-quarters of men compared with a half of women). Not surprisingly, those with children under 16 living in the home were more likely to drive than those without.

The converse of middle-class car dependency can be seen (albeit less starkly) in the corresponding figures for regular bus travel. Those in the middle age groups (34–49 and 50–64), men, those in paid work, those on higher incomes and levels of education are substantially *less* likely to take the bus regularly than other groups. The most obvious example of this can be seen for occupational categories – one in four of those in semi-routine/routine occupations is a regular bus user, compared to just one in ten of those in the professional and managerial category.

The numbers who take the train on a regular basis are so small (just four per cent of respondents) that clear patterns between subgroups cannot be seen clearly in the data. However, it is worth noting that, within this small proportion, users did tend to be similar to those who drive, that is in professional and managerial occupations, with higher incomes and education

levels. This perhaps reflects the relatively steep cost of train use (Commission
for Integrated Transport, 2001).

Table 1.7 Regular car and bus use

	% who drive car at least two days a week	% who take bus at least two days a week	Base
Managerial/professional occupations	79	9	355
Intermediate occupations	65	22	155
Small employers/own account workers	78	2	88
Lower supervisory/technical occupations	69	9	127
Semi-routine/routine occupations	42	26	350
Men	77	12	470
Women	52	19	629
18–33	58	19	252
34–49	72	8	348
50–64	72	14	249
65+	42	29	248
Income less than £9,999	39	29	293
Income £10,000–£17,999	52	18	183
Income £18,000–£31,999	75	10	221
Income £32,000 and above	85	8	253
In paid work	76	10	578
Economically inactive	44	24	246
Retired	48	25	271
Higher education including degree	78	10	309
A level or equivalent	77	19	131
GCSE level or equivalent	72	12	203
Below GCSE level	43	21	423
Children under 16 living in household	72	12	289
No children under 16 living in household	60	18	810

Findings in Table 1.7 were largely affirmed by multivariate analyses (see
models 1 and 2 in the appendix), which took account of all these characteristics
simultaneously, as well as additional factors such as the type of area in which a
person lives (as clearly the patchy distribution of public transport services in
different parts of the country is bound to affect the travel choices that people
make). All this confirms everyday observation – poorer people are more likely
to be bus users. But has this social divide changed since 1997? Is there any
evidence that Labour has succeeded at all in appealing to those who are wedded
to their cars and tempting them onto buses? To assess this we can look at the
social composition of bus users over the last five years, measured in terms of
economic activity and household income level. As the next table shows, the
clear divide in bus use has remained pretty much consistent across the time

period, with the proportions who take the bus dropping in all social groups. This general picture confirms the earlier trend we noted of declining bus use and increasing car use in the last five years, undermining the government's policy goals for 'integrated transport'.

Table 1.8 Changing patterns of bus use, 1997–2001

% who take bus	1997	1998	1999	2000	2001	Base (smallest)
In paid work	13	15	15	11	10	528
Economically inactive	28	22	22	26	24	243
Retired	28	20	25	25	25	248
Income less than £9,999	32	29	29	27	29	293
Income £10,000–£17,999	19	21	18	19	18	191
Income £18,000–£31,999	14	12	17	16	10	216
Income £32,000 and above	10	5	4	6	8	155
Total	20	17	19	18	16	195

Who supports what?

How does the attachment of the middle classes to their cars relate to their views about 'controversial' transport policy measures designed to reduce car dependency and promote alternatives such as bus use? One measure, to be introduced to London in early 2003, is that of congestion charging in city centres. We saw earlier that the *overall* popularity of this measure as a means of raising revenue with which to pay for public transport improvements has remained relatively stable since 1997; we turn now to examine how attitudes towards it, and other policies, differ between social groups.

The next table shows what might seem to be a contradictory finding – that those in the highest income quartile, who are the most likely to drive a car regularly, are the *most* likely to support congestion charging. Thirty-eight per cent were in support, compared with just 19 per cent of those in the lowest quartile. When multiple regression was used here to untangle the effects of different factors, although occupational category proved less important than might have been suspected, high levels of education and high levels of income were key predictors of agreement with the measure.

Table 1.9 Support for congestion charging by income

	Strongly support	Support	Neither support nor oppose	Oppose	Strongly oppose	Base
Income	%	%	%	%	%	
Less than £9,999	3	16	9	33	31	236
£10,000–£17,999	3	25	13	25	29	156
£18,000–£31,999	6	32	13	30	13	200
£32,000 and above	7	31	13	26	21	224

This finding reflects a wider pattern of interesting social divisions in attitudes towards measures which raise revenue to pay for public transport improvements. Using logistic regression, we found that those on higher incomes and in higher occupational categories were also more likely to support measures such as charging motorists £1 for every 50 miles they travel on motorways and increasing taxes like VAT on goods and services. However, although such high levels of support among the groups who are most likely to drive might appear contradictory, they may well reflect nothing more than enthusiasm for any measure that might cut down on other people's car use (as, after all, richer groups will be better able to pay congestion charges or road tolls than poorer ones).

The same groups were also more likely to think that public transport needs more money. We asked respondents to choose between two contradictory statements:

> *Changing the way public transport is run would do a great deal to improve it;*

> *Changing the way it is run is not enough, public transport needs a lot more money*

Those on higher incomes and the better educated were substantially more likely to agree with the latter statement that public transport needs more money. They were also more likely to agree that car users should pay higher taxes for the sake of the environment, confirming past research which indicates that those with higher education levels are more likely to espouse pro-environmental views (see, for example, Christie and Jarvis, 2001). However, what is interesting about these seemingly pro-public transport views among the affluent is that they are *not* supported by a corresponding support for measures which might inconvenience their everyday car use in ways that are *not* financial (such as "having speed bumps to slow down traffic" and "speed limits of 20 miles per hour in residential streets"). Indeed, in some cases, the affluent stand out as being less likely to support these measures than those in lower social groups.

For example, our analyses showed that those with high levels of education and income are significantly *less* likely to agree with "making cars stop for people to cross residential streets even if they are not at pedestrian crossings", whereas those in routine/semi-routine occupations stood out as significantly *more* likely to agree. Additionally, those with high incomes were less likely to agree that 'building roads just encourages more traffic'.

So the affluent tend to back both increased investment in public transport and also demand measures targeted on *specific* areas of road use, particularly those which use financial penalties (like congestion charging). But their support for other, less tax-orientated, measures is more qualified, suggesting that their enthusiasm is restricted to measures which they believe will reduce the number of other drivers on the roads, rather than affecting their own everyday journeys.

Of course, attitudes to policy are one thing; *personal action* in response to policies is quite another. Would the car-driving classes consider using their cars less if certain policies were brought in to fund improvements in the way public transport in Britain is run? When asked if congestion charging would make any difference to their *personal* car use habits, over half (53 per cent) of those in professional and managerial occupations with access to a car said it would make no difference, making them as reluctant as any other group to break away from car use. So, as we noted earlier, this appears to confirm the widely-held view that many citizens are liable to support measures to get other people out of their cars, while regarding their own car use as essential – a finding that has remained consistent in the *British Social Attitudes* series in recent years (Christie and Jarvis, 1999).

Attitudes towards buses

In this section we consider the attitudes surrounding bus use, which we take as a key issue for public transport policy. We have focused on buses for a number of reasons:

- Bus use accounts for the largest proportion of public transport use in the UK.
- Improvements in bus services are in general easier to make than those in more complex rail services.
- Buses can offer a more flexible service than rail and thus compete better in some respects with the car.
- There seems to be more scope overall to shift people from car use to bus use, than from cars to trains, given the comparative costs and accessibility of services.

Buses, in short, are the great hope of the public transport sector. How they are used and viewed is a key issue for policy makers concerned with reducing car dependency and improving the take-up of public transport. So we turn now to look at perceptions of bus services in Britain.

As with British railways, bus services have been the butt of jokes for decades. The 1970s TV comedy *On the Buses* helped portray the bus service as an emblem of British decline – conjuring up images of tattiness, public sector incompetence and buffoonery. There was relatively little outrage in response to the prejudices of the Conservative governments of the 1980s and 1990s about bus users: Mrs Thatcher is said to have remarked that anyone over the age of 30 using a bus must be a failure. Recent attitude research on bus services in urban areas outside London reveals patterns of dissatisfaction that echo this disparaging remark: many bus users regard buses as transport to be used only because they have no alternative, and see the service as unreliable, insecure and unpleasant (Audit Commission, 1999).

It is important to explore fully the notion of resistance concerning bus use. Do car users reject the bus as a transport option without giving it a fair chance? Do bus users feel that they are using a service they would reject if they could? The next table shows findings from two questions which test levels of general resistance towards taking the bus. While two-thirds agree they would only take the bus if they had "no other way of getting there", only one in five agrees that the bus is for those who "can't afford anything better".

Table 1.10 Attitudes towards bus travel

	Agree strongly	Agree	Disagree	Disagree strongly	Varies too much to say
Travelling by bus is mainly for people who can't afford anything better %	5	14	16	44	15
I would only travel some-where by bus if I had no other way of getting there %	23	44	9	19	3

Base: 912

Responses to the idea that buses are for those "who can't afford anything better" did not vary to any significant degree between those in different occupational categories, nor was there any clear pattern between those in different income brackets – the main message was one of general disagreement with the statement. However, there were some interesting findings with respect to gender and age. Men were significantly more likely than women to agree (23 per cent compared with 15 per cent). This fits with women's lower likelihood of being regular car drivers and higher likelihood of being bus users. Even more interestingly, those in the 65-plus age group stood out as being *more* likely to agree with the statement. However, it might be the case that, for those falling into this category, agreement with such a statement is less an indication of prejudice towards bus travel, more an issue of personal identification – after all,

those aged 65 and over *do* have an increased likelihood of living on a low income, and *do* have an increased likelihood of taking the bus. This theory is supported by the fact that economic activity plays an important role in determining attitudes – those who are in paid work are significantly less likely to agree with the statement than those who are retired and those who are economically inactive (see model 3 in the appendix to this chapter for full results).

Responses to the second statement, "I would only travel by bus if I had no other way of getting there", provide an interesting contrast to the patterns outlined above. People are much more likely to back this view than admit to thinking that buses are the preserve of poor people. However, some common themes emerged between the two statements in terms of social divisions in attitudes. Again, proportions in agreement were higher for men than for women (71 per cent compared with 63 per cent) and for those with higher incomes. Those in the 18–33 age group stood out as more likely to agree with the statement, providing some support for theories that young people – although more likely to use the bus and less likely to drive cars than older age groups – tend to view their years of reliance on buses as a 'temporary measure' which will end as soon as they earn enough to buy a car. Recent survey research on young people and transport in rural areas in South West England shows that young bus users tend to be alienated by their experience of depending on restricted bus services and their experience of hostile drivers (Storey and Brannen, 2000).

Looking at the differing patterns in attitudes towards the two statements described in Table 1.10, it is perhaps less the case that people have *no* prejudice against the bus as a viable alternative, and more the case that such prejudice is not something to which they would readily admit. This all reinforces the point that attitudes 'in principle' towards bus use in modern Britain are quite positive, but that the story becomes rather different when it comes to personal action. But do the car-driving classes have any basis for their resistance towards using the bus? We know that car drivers are much more likely than those who actually use the bus to view it as something of a 'last resort', but do they hold strong opinions on the quality of bus services that might help justify this view? The next section explores satisfaction with bus services, and any social divisions within this.

Satisfaction with bus services

Overall reactions to questions about aspects of bus services are shown in the next table. People are generally satisfied with the proximity of bus stops to their home, their ability to go by bus to places they want to reach, buses' cleanliness and the cost of bus use. More people feel unsafe than secure in buses after dark, and women and older people are more likely to feel this. Similarly, there is cynicism about buses generally running on time. But in all of these respects, except cost, there has been a decline in satisfaction since 1998.

Table 1.11 Levels of satisfaction with features of bus services, 1998 and 2001

% who agree that buses generally ...	1998	2001
... will take you where you mostly need to go	67	60
... are clean and tidy	62	59
... are safe to travel in after dark	51	46
... cost too much	57	46
... do not run often enough	42	45
... stop too far away from your home	13	17
... do the journey quickly enough	n.a.	53
... generally run on time	n.a.	45
Base	*804*	*912*

n.a.=not asked

Reassuringly, bus users are more likely to have positive views about buses than those who do not go on buses regularly. They are substantially more likely to *disagree* that buses do not run often enough and to agree that they are punctual. Meanwhile, regular car users are more likely to say buses *would not* take them mostly where they need to go, while regular bus users are more likely to say buses *do* meet their needs. Of course, care is needed here in assessing the direction of cause. Being a regular car driver means that prejudices about buses are not often put to the test (if at all), reinforcing preferences for the car. And being a regular bus user might well expose people to a reality of reasonable or good service, or accustom them to accept services that others would reject.

Conclusions

British Social Attitudes research over recent years confirms what policy makers and politicians know all too well – transport policy is a minefield. People are concerned about transport problems, and want to see major improvements in public transport. On the other hand, they show much less consensus when it comes to decisions about how such improvements should be funded, and about how measures to curb car use might be devised. Overall, people are in favour of 'carrot' policies to make public transport more attractive, and much less enthusiastic about 'stick' policies to make motoring more costly and inconvenient. Opposition is particularly high to policies that appear to be 'anti-car' in general – such as large rises in petrol costs or reductions in spending on road maintenance. There is less opposition to more targeted measures to make car use more expensive in specific contexts – as with forms of road pricing – but here too there is considerable resistance. Levels of dependency on car use are high – large majorities among car users claim that significant reductions in their driving would be inconvenient. Perhaps the most worrying finding in this chapter is that attitudes in recent years towards the key issues do not seem to

have changed to any great degree, meaning that the government's task of reducing car use is not becoming any easier. Taking decisive policy measures to make us less dependent on our cars, whether through costly supply-side measures or varieties of demand-side management, will call for considerable political courage. Much will depend on the outcomes of experiments such as the introduction of road pricing in central London in 2003, a measure which has already aroused furious controversy.

But there are social divisions in attitudes to be tackled too. Our findings indicate clear differences in views between car users and those dependent on public transport. Attracting many more people onto bus services will need to be a key component of a more integrated and sustainable transport strategy for the UK, but we have seen that social segmentation plays a significant part in reinforcing particular travel patterns. If more people are to switch to bus travel, not only will car use need to become more costly, but major efforts will also be needed both to improve services and to change the negative perception of buses that non-users tend to have. So Britain's transport problems are likely to continue to preoccupy both policy makers and citizens, offering neither group any easy answers.

References

Adams, J (2000), *The Social Implications of Hypermobility*, Paris: OECD.

Audit Commission (1999), *All Aboard: a review of local transport and travel in urban areas outside London*, London: Audit Commission.

Christie, I. and Jarvis, L. (1999), 'Rural spaces and urban jams' in Jowell, R., Curtice, J., Park, A. and Thomson, K. (eds.), *British Social Attitudes: the 16th Report –- Who Shares New Labour Values?*, Aldershot: Ashgate.

Christie, I. and Jarvis, L. (2001), 'How green are our values?' in Park, A., Curtice, J., Thomson, K., Jarvis, L. and Bromley, C. (eds.), *British Social Attitudes: the 18th Report – Public policy, Social ties*, London: Sage.

Commission for Integrated Transport (2001), *European Best Practice in the Delivery of Integrated Transport*, London: Department for Transport, Local Government and the Regions.

Dalton, R. and Rohrschneider, R. (1998), 'The Greening of Europe', in Jowell, R., Curtice, J., Park, A., Brook, L., Thomson, K. and Bryson, C. (eds.), *British – and European – Social Attitudes: the 15th Report – How Britain differs.* Aldershot: Ashgate.

Department for the Environment, Transport and the Regions (DETR) (1998), *A New Deal for Transport: the Government's White Paper on the future of transport*, London: The Stationery Office.

Department for the Environment, Transport and the Regions (DETR) (2000), *Climate Change: The UK Programme*, London: The Stationery Office.

Department for the Environment, Transport and the Regions (DETR) (2001a), *Transport Trends,* London: The Stationery Office.

Department for the Environment, Transport and the Regions (DETR) (2001b), *Planning Policy Guidance Note 13: Transport*, London: The Stationery Office.

Department for Transport, Local Government and the Regions (DTLR) (2001), *Focus on Personal Travel (including the report of the National Travel Survey 1998–2000)*, London: The Stationery Office.

Goodwin, P. (1998), 'We are at a historic crossroads', in Taylor, J. (ed.), *Can Prescott steer us through a transport revolution? Special supplement, New Statesman*, 22nd May 1998.

Hirsch, F. (1977), *The Social Limits to Growth*, London: Routledge and Kegan Paul.

Office for National Statistics (ONS) (2001), *Social Trends 2001*, London: The Stationery Office.

Storey, P.and Brannen, J. (2000), *Young People and Transport in Rural Areas*, Leicester: Joseph Rowntree Foundation/National Youth Agency.

Taylor, B. (1997), 'Green in word', in Jowell, R., Curtice, J., Park, A., Brook, L., Thomson, K. and Bryson, C. (eds.), *British Social Attitudes: the 14th Report – The end of Conservative values*, Aldershot: Ashgate.

Whitelegg, J. (1997), 'Finding an Exit from the Mobility Maze: non-conventional approaches to mobility in urban areas', IPTS Report, No. 11, February 1997, Seville: IPTS-JRC-European Commission.

Acknowledgements

The *National Centre for Social Research* is grateful to the Department for Transport for their financial support which enabled us to ask the questions reported in this chapter.

Appendix

Multivariate analysis

Models referred to in the chapter follow. Two multivariate techniques were used: multiple regression (models 3 and 4) and logistic regression (models 1 and 2). These are explained in more detail in Appendix I to this Report.

For the multiple regression models, it is the coefficients (or parameter estimates) that are shown. These show whether a particular characteristic differs significantly from its 'comparison group' in its association with the dependent variable. Details of the comparison group are shown in brackets. A positive coefficient indicates that those with the characteristic score more highly on the dependent variable and a negative coefficient means that they are likely to have a lower score. For the logistic regression models, the figures reported are the odds ratios. An odds ratio of less than one means that the group was less likely than average to be in the group of interest on the dependent variable (the variable we are investigating), and an odds ratio greater than one indicates a greater than average likelihood of being in this group. For both methods, those variables which were selected as significant in predicting this are shown in order of the importance of their contribution. Variables which proved to be non-significant in the models have been dropped from the tables.

Two asterisks indicate that the coefficient or odds ratio is statistically significant at a 99 per cent level and one asterisk that it is significant at a 95 per cent level.

Regression analyses

The independent variables used in the following regression analyses were:

Age
1. 18–33
2. 34–49
3. 50–64
4. 65+

Sex
1. Men
2. Women

Highest educational qualification
1. Degree or other higher education
2. A level or equivalent
3. GCSE level or equivalent
4. Lower than GCSE level

Household income
1. Less than £9,999
2. £10,000–£17,999
3. £18,000–£31,999

4. £32,000 and above
5. Unknown

Economic activity
1. Paid work
2. Economically inactive
3. Retired

Socio-economic group
1. Managerial/Professional
2. Intermediate
3. Small employer/own account worker
4. Lower supervisory/technical
5. Semi-routine/routine

Children under 16 living in household
1.   No children.
2.   Children

Type of area
1.   A big city
2.   The suburbs/outskirts of a big city
3.   A small city or town
4.   A country village/farm/country home

Party identification
1.   Conservative
2.   Labour
3.   Liberal Democrat
4.   Other party
5.   None
6.   Green party

Regular car use
1.   Does not use car at least 2–5 times a week
2.   Uses car at least 2–5 times a week

Regular bus use
1.   Does not use bus at least 2–5 times a week
2.   Uses bus at least 2–5 times a week

Model 1: Predictors of regular car use

Logistic regression with dependent variable: Driving a car at least twice a week. Independent variables: Socio-economic group, age, household income, highest educational qualification, type of area, party identification, economic activity, sex, children under 16 living in household.

Category	B	S.E.	Wald	Odds ratio (Exp(B))	Sig
Baseline odds	.880	.143	37.789	2.412	**
Socio-economic group			20.253		
Managerial /Professional	.170	.165	1.064	1.185	
Intermediate	.274	.195	1.979	1.316	
Small employer/own account worker	-.188	.250	.564	.829	
Lower supervisory/technical	.296	.208	2.032	1.345	
Semi-routine/routine	-.553	.142	15.149	.575	**
Sex					
Men	.561	.087	41.082	1.752	**
Women	-.561	.087	41.802	.571	**
Age			29.955		**
18–33	-.681	.177	14.808	.506	**
34–49	-.076	.170	.197	.927	
50–64	.720	.155	21.542	2.054	**
65+	.036	.263	.019	1.037	
Income			22.930		
Less than £9,999	-.253	.175	2.102	.776	
£10,000–£17,999	-.478	.162	8.752	.620	**
£18,000–£31,999	.251	.160	2.459	1.285	
£32,000 and above	.701	.173	16.346	2.016	**
Unknown	-.221	.171	1.663	.197	
Highest educational qualification			34.121		**
Degree or other higher education	.149	.152	.968	1.161	
A level or equivalent	.465	.190	5.999	1.591	*
GCSE level or equivalent	.227	.157	2.078	1.254	
Lower than GCSE level	-.841	.144	34.013	.431	**
Economic activity			13.769		**
In paid work	.477	.156	9.347	1.610	**
Economically inactive	-.322	.156	4.276	.724	*
Retired	-.154	.222	483	.857	
Type of area			18.720		**
A big city	-.698	.222	9.878	.497	**
The suburbs/outskirts of a big city	-.092	.148	.390	.912	
A small city or town	.111	.126	.779	1.118	
A country village/farm/country home	.679	.167	16.584	1.973	**
Children under 16					
Children under 16 in household	.318	.109	8.505	1.374	**
No children under 16 in household	-.318	.109	8.505	.728	**

Number of cases in model: 1010

Model 2: Predictors of regular bus use

Logistic regression with dependent variable: Taking a local bus at least twice a week. Independent variables: Socio-economic group, age, household income, highest educational qualification, type of area, party identification, economic activity, sex, children under 16 living in household.

Category	B	S.E.	Wald	Odds ratio (Exp(B))	Sig
Baseline odds	-1.980	.194	104.529	.138	**
Socio-economic group			30.480		**
Managerial/Professional	-.096	.237	.165	.908	
Intermediate	.825	.246	11.265	2.281	**
Small employer/own account worker	-1.528	.636	5.679	.217	*
Lower supervisory/technical	-.118	.301	.153	.889	
Semi-routine/routine	.917	.211	18.864	2.502	**
Age			14.701		**
18–33	.134	.183	.534	1.143	
34–49	-.680	.201	11.428	.507	**
50–64	-.126	.170	.555	.881	
65+	.673	.260	6.724	1.960	*
Economic activity			9.307		*
In paid work	-.318	.170	3.525	.727	
Economically inactive	.399	.162	6.095	1.491	*
Retired	-.081	.230	.124	.922	
Type of area			22.069		**
A big city	.428	.244	3.074	1.534	
The suburbs/outskirts of a big city	.482	.158	9.331	1.620	**
A small city or town	-.350	.153	5.200	.705	*
A country village/farm/country home	-.561	.209	7.202	.571	**

Number of cases in model: 1010

Model 3: Correlates of agreeing that 'travelling by bus is mainly for people who can't afford anything better'

Multiple regression with dependent variable: Agreement with the view that 'travelling by bus is mainly for people who can't afford anything better'. Independent variables: Socio-economic group, age, household income, highest educational qualification, type of area, party identification, economic activity, sex, children under 16 living in household.

Individual characteristics (comparison group in brackets)	Standardised Beta coefficient
Sex (men)	
Women	-.153 **
Income (lowest quartile)	
£10,000–£17,999	-.010
£18,000–£31,999	-.091 *
£32,000 and above	-.004
Unknown	-.016
Economic activity (retired)	
In paid work	-.086 *
Economically inactive	-.055

Model 4: Correlates of agreeing that 'I would only travel by bus if I had no other way of getting there'

Multiple regression with dependent variable: Agreement that 'I would only travel by bus if I had no other way of getting there'. Independent variables: Socio-economic group, age, household income, highest educational qualification, type of area, party identification, economic activity, sex, children under 16 living in household.

Category	Standardised Beta coefficient	
Socio-economic group (Managerial/Professional)		
Intermediate	-.006	
Small employer/own account worker	.069*	
Lower supervisory/technical	-.015	
Semi-routine/routine	.040	
Age (65+)		
18–33	.078	*
34–49	-.001	
50–64	.009	
Highest educational qualification (lower than GCSE level)		
Degree or other higher education	-.029	
A level or equivalent	-.002	
GCSE level or equivalent	-.091	**
Regular car use (does not use car at least 2–5 times a week)		
Uses car at least 2–5 times a week	.161	**
Regular bus use (does not use bus at least 2–5 times a week)		
Uses bus at least 2–5 times a week	-.150	**

2 Buy now, pay later?

Karen Rowlingson and Stephen McKay *

Recent governments of all political hues have encouraged people to save for the future, and new products like the stakeholder pension and Individual Savings Account (ISA) have been designed to encourage individual saving. The current government (as of August 2002) has emphasised the importance of saving with the development of the Saving Gateway, Child Trust Funds ('baby bonds') and the rules for the new Pension Credit. But, despite these government initiatives, it appears that messages about saving are not getting through to people and affecting their saving habits. In particular, there is increasing concern that people are not saving enough money during their working lives to fund the kind of retirement lifestyle that they say they want (Rowlingson, 2002; Thomas *et al.*, 1999; Hedges, 1998). In fact, rather than saving, people appear to be borrowing and spending instead. The household saving ratio (the proportion of household net income that is saved as opposed to spent) more than halved during the late 1990s (Office for National Statistics, 2002) and the level of consumers' unsecured borrowing more than doubled, according to the market analyst, Datamonitor (quoted in *The Guardian*, 20th February 2002). And despite the events of 11th September 2001 (including large drops in the value of stocks and shares), there are no signs, in Britain at least, that consumers are cutting back on their spending. According to the Credit Card Research Group, spending on debit and credit cards increased by 15 per cent and 14 per cent respectively from 2001 to 2002 (Guardian Unlimited Money, 2002). Moreover, mortgage lending in April 2002 was 47 per cent up on the previous April (British Bankers' Association, 2002). It seems as though the old saying, "live within your means, even if you must borrow to do so"[1] might still apply in force.

Culturally, views about saving, spending and borrowing are complex and ambiguous (see Lea *et al.*, 1987). In line with Victorian values, saving is

* Karen Rowlingson is a Lecturer in Social Research in the Department of Social and Policy Sciences at the University of Bath and Stephen McKay is Deputy Director of the Personal Finance Research Centre at the University of Bristol.

generally regarded positively, as a sign of responsible behaviour and self-reliance. That said, people who save excessively are at risk of being labelled as being 'mean' or 'tight' with their money. Take, for instance, Dickens's *A Christmas Carol* and its character Scrooge who saw saving as a goal in itself, something Keynes referred to as "the instinct of pure miserliness". Likewise when it comes to spending, attitudes are somewhat paradoxical. On the one hand, modern consumer culture bombards people with opportunities to spend money, and a certain level of spending and generosity is applauded. People are encouraged to buy designer brands and the latest technology, almost regardless of whether they really 'need' these items. Credit is widespread, from credit cards to mortgages, and the stigma of buying on the 'never-never' appears to have declined. But, on the other hand, *excessive* spending is seen as irresponsible extravagance and views about credit are often negative. And some cultural stereotypes exist about the tendency of certain groups, particularly the young, and those on low incomes, to be 'feckless' in their spending habits and insufficiently worried about getting into debt.

Our first task in this chapter will be to examine whether we are a nation of spenders and borrowers, revelling in consumer culture. Are we a 'must have now' society? Or are we a nation of savers? To what extent are attitudes affected by people's ability to spend, save and borrow. Is there a group of 'feckless' individuals who are especially keen on spending *and* borrowing? Wherever possible, we will compare our findings with previous research, to assess the extent to which views might have changed over time. Although the *British Social Attitudes* survey has not previously asked questions about saving, spending and borrowing, other surveys have covered similar areas. In particular, a study by Berthoud and Kempson (1992) identified three groups in the population: a quarter with favourable attitudes towards credit; another quarter with negative attitudes; and the remaining half with mixed views. However, the same study also found that 43 per cent of people thought "credit was never a good thing". This was much higher than had been found in a previous survey in 1979 (31 per cent), and it is likely that attitudes to credit had hardened over the 1980s as the recession and negative equity caused a consumer bust to follow on from the consumer boom.

Previous research has found marked age differences in attitudes towards personal finances. For example, younger people are less likely than older people to say that they save for a 'rainy day' (Financial Services Authority, 2000). And recent research from the Henley Centre (quoted in *The Guardian*, 20th February 2002) suggests that debt is seen as inevitable among the majority of 16–34 year olds. So our second task will be to assess the extent to which our findings back up the strong link that seems to exist between age and attitudes towards credit and debt.

There are two particularly plausible reasons as to why we might expect to find marked age differences in attitudes and practice; the first relating to the stage a person has reached in their 'lifecycle', and the second to the experiences of particular 'generations' of people during their formative years. For example, a lifecycle explanation might argue that, while people are young and on low incomes, they are likely to borrow money against the prospect of future income,

but that, as they get older and their income rises, they will repay their loans and start to save (Friedman, 1957; Atkinson, 1971). Finally, when their income falls in retirement, people will begin to spend their savings. Of course, this theory has a number of limitations; people may not be able to borrow as much as they wish, for example. And after decades of saving it might be difficult for people to spend when they are older.

Age differences might also reflect different generational experiences. Many of today's retired generation lived through less affluent times when home-ownership and mortgages were reserved for the rich. Although hire purchase (the 'never-never') was just becoming available, credit was seen as synonymous with debt, and highly stigmatised. By contrast, today's middle-aged generation are much more likely than their predecessors to be home-owners and credit-users, having experienced the 1980s personal credit boom. Meanwhile, the youngest generation have not only come of age while watching their parents use credit cards, but may also have considerable personal experience of debt, particularly that incurred to fund higher education.

Unfortunately, we will not be able to provide a definitive answer to the 'lifecycle' versus 'generation' debate (to do so would require a longitudinal panel study which follows the same people over time or at least several readings on the same questions over a fairly long period of time), although we will be able to speculate about the factors that underpin any age differences we find.

Finally, we will examine the implications of our findings on government social policy. How do people's own views about spending, credit and debt relate to their views about state welfare? In particular, do people expect to be able to spend and borrow throughout their lives and then rely on the state in times of need? Answering these question will help us ascertain whether the government is fighting a losing battle in its attempt to encourage people to save for their own welfare (and replace potential state welfare).

Attitudes to saving and borrowing

We begin by examining the extent to which people prefer spending and borrowing rather than saving. We then discuss attitudes to consumer credit, the litmus test for any 'must have now' society.

Respondents were asked to choose which of two statements, shown in the next table, came closest to their own views on, firstly, borrowing and then saving. Their answers provide little support for the view that the British psyche is one based upon instant gratification. True, only one in ten believed that people should *never* borrow money, and almost nine in ten said that there was nothing wrong with borrowing money so long as people can pay it back. But this simply suggests that attitudes to borrowing are contingent rather than fixed; they depend on a number of factors, including whether people can manage the repayments. Meanwhile, two-thirds felt that young people should start saving for their retirement as soon as possible, even if this means they have to cut back on their spending. However, a significant minority – one in five – took a quite different approach and thought that young people should spend their money

while they were young and put off worrying about retirement until they were older.

Table 2.1 Views on saving and borrowing

Borrowing	%
People should never borrow money	11
There is nothing wrong with borrowing money as long as you can manage the repayments	87
Can't choose	2
Saving	**%**
Young people should spend their money while they are young and worry about saving for retirement when they are older	19
Young people should start saving for their retirement as soon as they can even if they have to cut back on other things	66
Can't choose	14

Base: 2795

It is sometimes assumed that people who are fond of spending will also be keen to borrow, but this is not necessarily the case. Some people may like to spend but never wish to borrow. Other people may both save and borrow at the same time. While this may not seem rational in strict economic terms, people's financial behaviour does not always conform to a simple economic model. However, further analysis of the previous table shows that views about borrowing and saving do overlap somewhat. Among those who think that young people should spend, rather than save, their money, 93 per cent think it is all right for people to borrow money if they can afford the repayments. An accepting view of credit is more likely among those who advocate people saving for retirement from a young age (85 per cent hold this view). Still, in both cases, the vast majority are accepting of credit.

To explore attitudes towards spending and borrowing in more detail we asked respondents to consider what a person should do if they needed a particular item but did not have the money to pay for it. Should they save for the item beforehand, or borrow money and pay it back later? Respondents were asked in turn about three items: a holiday, a replacement sofa and a replacement for a broken cooker. If Britain has become a 'must have now' society we might expect to see strong support for borrowing in all circumstances but this is not what we found. As the next table shows, fewer than one in ten said that people should borrow money to pay for a holiday, and only two in ten supported borrowing to replace a sofa. In both cases, the overwhelming majority thought that people should save first and then spend. However, there was considerably more support for borrowing in order to replace a broken cooker, with most

thinking it was all right to borrow money for this purpose. Nevertheless, one in five still thought that people should save rather than borrow.

Table 2.2 Decisions to save or borrow

	What should a person do if they don't have the money to pay for it but they want to …		
	… go on holiday %	… replace a sofa %	… replace a broken cooker %
Save up the money beforehand	90	76	21
Borrow the money and pay it back later	7	21	77
Base: 3287			

This evidence suggests two things. Firstly, people generally support the idea of saving rather than borrowing. And, secondly, attitudes to borrowing depend on the perceived need for a particular item. Holidays are generally considered to be more of a luxury than a necessity, and so there seems less justification for borrowing money to fund them. Similarly, it is possible to live with an old sofa for a while until there is money saved to buy a new one. By contrast, a cooker is usually considered a necessity, and so people are more likely to support borrowing money for this purpose.

We now examine whether the positive views of saving we have seen so far are reflected in negative views about credit. Of course, cultural views of consumer credit may also be riddled with inconsistencies; credit could be seen at times as a useful and indeed necessary aid to consumption (particularly in relation to larger purchases such as houses and cars) but, on the other hand, there may also be concern that credit encourages people to spend too much money and is too readily available.

Respondents were asked how strongly they agreed or disagreed with the three statements about credit shown in the next table. The results suggest that attitudes towards credit are ambivalent. True, just over a third agreed with the most positive statement about credit – that it makes it easier to plan finances – but the same proportion disagreed. There was greater consensus that credit should be harder to obtain, even if this meant it moved beyond some people's reach, with almost a half of respondents agreeing. But there were still some people – a quarter in this case – who disagreed. Finally, a large majority, more than eight in ten, agreed that credit encourages people to spend much more money than they can really afford.

72374

Table 2.3 Attitudes to credit

		Agree strongly	Agree	Neither	Disagree	Disagree strongly
Credit makes it easier for people to plan their finances	%	3	33	25	28	6
It should be made much harder to borrow money even if this means that more people can't get credit	%	8	39	21	24	2
Credit encourages people to spend far more money than they can really afford to	%	32	51	10	4	1

Base: 2795

Of course, so far we have merely found strong support for the *principle* of saving, as opposed to borrowing, but this does not necessarily mean that people will always carry this out in practice. Perhaps, instead, they are only reflecting the principles that seem culturally acceptable, the normative frameworks around financial behaviour? Consequently, in the next section we compare support for the principle of saving with actual practice.

Saving and spending: words and deeds

Although we have so far uncovered little evidence to support the notion that there is a 'must have now' society in Britain today, there does appear to be a minority group whose views tend more towards immediate gratification. But to what extent do people's actions match their words? To what extent does practice in spending and saving reflect people's attitudes?

We asked respondents to choose between two statements about their own spending behaviour. A quarter (24 per cent) chose "if the money is there, I find it just goes" but three times more (73 per cent) opted for "I always try to keep some money in hand for emergencies". So, when it comes to actual behaviour, people again generally tend towards saving rather than spending. These results are almost identical to those obtained by Berthoud and Kempson (1992) who, in 1989, found 26 per cent of people said that their 'money just goes', compared with 74 per cent who said that they always tried to keep some money in hand for emergencies.

How do these spending characteristics link with attitudes towards saving? The next table categorises people into one of four groups depending on their behaviour and attitudes. The smallest group, only seven per cent of the sample, are those who are both spenders in practice (their money "just goes") and in principle ("young people should spend when young"). These are the hard core of any 'must have now' society. However, the greatest proportion, more than

half of the sample, supported the principle of saving, both in their actions and their words.

Table 2.4 The principle and practice of saving or spending

	In practice ...	
In principle ...	Money just goes	Try to keep some in hand
Spend when young	7	11
Save for retirement	12	53

Base: 2795

Note: the percentages in the table do not add up to 100 per cent because a significant minority of respondents could not choose from at least one of the options presented to them.

Differences between rich and poor

We might expect to find notable income differences in people's attitudes and behaviour when it comes to saving and spending. Perhaps, for instance, those on lower incomes are more likely to have problems managing their money – and to have a particularly tolerant attitude towards borrowing as a result? Or, conversely, perhaps the most accepting of borrowing are those wealthier groups who can afford to pay back their loans? In fact, as the next table shows, there is remarkable consistency in behaviour from one income group to the next, with around a quarter to a fifth of each income group reporting that their money 'just goes'. And there is little to suggest the existence of a 'feckless' poor who have particularly casual attitudes to debt; in fact, those on lower incomes were the most likely to take the view that "people should never borrow money" at all. Nearly a quarter of those living in households with an annual gross income of under £8,000 took this view, compared with only three per cent of those in households taking home £38,000 per annum. So perhaps attitudes to borrowing, above all, are linked to a person's ability to afford credit. Finally, there is very little difference between income groups in their attitudes to spending *versus* saving while young. Those on low incomes were no more likely to advocate spending than those on high incomes.

Table 2.5 Attitudes towards personal finance, and behaviour, by household income

	Household income groups				
	Less than £7,999	£8,000– £14,999	£15,000– £25,999	£26,000– £37,999	£38,000 or more
	%	%	%	%	%
Money just goes	24	22	25	29	21
Never borrow money	24	17	6	6	3
Spend when young	20	15	19	20	21
Base	*543*	*501*	*556*	*436*	*484*

This lack of variation between different income groups is also apparent when we consider attitudes towards credit. All income groups adopt a fairly unanimous stance on the question of whether credit makes it easier for people to plan their spending, and whether it encourages people to spend more money than they have. However, lower income groups are slightly more likely than higher income groups to think that it should be made *much* harder for people to borrow money – even though such a change might be expected to have the greatest impact on lower income groups. Just over a half (52 per cent) of those living in households with a gross annual income of under £15,000 took this view, compared with 44 per cent of those whose gross annual income was £15,000 or more.

Spendthrift youth?

There are a variety of reasons, explored in the introduction to this chapter, as to why we might expect to find notable age differences in attitudes towards borrowing, spending and saving, and in their associated behaviour. That age differences *do* exist is clearly borne out by the next table. This shows younger people to be consistently more supportive of borrowing than older people, as well as being more likely to report that the money they have "just goes" (as opposed to some being saved for emergencies).

First, we consider saving behaviour. Here the marked tendency is for each age group to be progressively less and less likely to say that their money "just goes". Consequently, if we compare the extremes of the age range we find that, whereas 44 per cent of 18–24 year olds describe their personal finances in this way, only six per cent of those aged 65 and over do so. A similar pattern exists in relation to attitudes towards spending rather than saving when one is young, with the proportion thinking that young people should "spend their money while they are young" gradually falling as we move from younger age groups to older ones.

A quite different pattern emerges in relation to general attitudes towards borrowing. Between the ages of 18 and 44 people have similar views, with few thinking that people should never borrow. Attitudes to borrowing then hardened progressively, if gradually, up to the age of 64. Those aged 75 and over are the most negative about borrowing – with almost one in three stating that people should "never" borrow.

Table 2.6 Personal finance attitudes and behaviour, by age

	Age						
	18–24	25–34	35–44	45–54	55–64	65–74	75+
	%	%	%	%	%	%	%
Money just goes	44	37	32	20	11	6	6
Never borrow money	6	4	6	8	11	20	32
Spend when young	34	24	21	19	17	7	8
Base	*182*	*469*	*618*	*482*	*216*	*348*	*280*

Given these findings, it is not surprising that there are marked age differences in responses to our questions about borrowing or saving in order to fund different purchases. As the next table shows, the youngest group (aged between 18 and 24) were no less than *six* times more likely than those aged 65 or more to advocate borrowing money to replace an old sofa. However, the relationship between age and attitudes to borrowing is not linear; rather, there is a remarkable similarity of views between those aged 18 to 54, and then a different set of attitudes among the 55-plus age group. So the idea that 'young' people are the most in favour of credit can only be supported if one's definition of 'young' extends to people in their early 50s!

Table 2.7 Saving and borrowing, by age

% who support	Age						
borrowing for ...	18–24	25–34	35–44	45–54	55–64	65–74	75+
	%	%	%	%	%	%	%
Holiday	8	10	9	8	5	4	4
Replacement sofa	23	25	25	26	18	4	4
Replacement cooker	81	81	81	79	73	71	63
Base	*226*	*567*	*712*	*555*	*467*	*396*	*359*

There were fewer age-related differences in attitudes to credit. As the next table shows, there is no simple pattern in views about the extent to which credit makes it easier to plan. There is a more predictable pattern when it comes to restricting the ease with which people can borrow money, with older age groups being much more likely than younger ones to agree. In fact, the 65-plus age group were over twice as likely as under-25 year olds to think that obtaining credit should be made harder. However, all age groups were united in their agreement that 'credit encourages people to spend far more than they can really afford to'.

Table 2.8 Attitudes to credit, by age

	Age						
	18–24	25–34	35–44	45–54	55–64	65–74	75+
% who agree that ...	%	%	%	%	%	%	%
Credit makes it easier to plan	44	34	35	37	39	32	33
Should be harder to borrow	27	40	40	53	57	61	55
Credit encourages too much spending	78	85	80	83	86	88	85
Base	*182*	*469*	*618*	*482*	*216*	*348*	*280*

As we have discussed, one of the possible explanations for this apparent link between attitudes and age is the stage that a person has reached in his or her lifecycle. To some extent, age is a proxy for this (because many people go through particular stages – such as parenthood – at a particular age). However, it is an imprecise proxy, because obviously some will experience different life events at different ages, if at all. So, in order to examine the extent to which lifecycle might influence attitudes towards personal finance, and spending behaviour, we now look specifically at people in a range of different lifecycle groups. There are many potential ways of dividing people into lifecycle groups (see Rowlingson *et al.*, 1999 for a review). Here we have chosen a fairly simple method which divides people into eight lifecycle groups in terms of their living arrangements (single versus in a couple), whether or not they have dependent children, and their age (under 35, 35 to state pension age and over state pension age). It is important to note, however, that the number of people in some of these groups is relatively small, so we must approach our findings with caution.

The responses of our different groups to some of the questions considered earlier are shown in the next table. This suggests that some, but by no means all, of the age differences we have found do reflect the stage a person is at in their lifecycle. For example, single people aged under 65, presumably getting by on one salary, are more likely than those living as a couple to report that their money "just goes". This applies to 42 per cent of single people aged under 35

(group 1), compared with 34 per cent of those living with a partner (group 2), and 25 per cent of those aged between 35 and state retirement age (group 5), compared with 16 per cent of those in the same age group who are living with a partner (group 6).

As the next table shows young single people and lone parents were the groups most likely to say that their money just goes. Not surprisingly, given our earlier findings, those over the stage pension age – whether single or not – are the least likely to report this.

When it comes to attitudes towards spending and borrowing money, we see a familiar pattern whereby those aged over the state pension age take by far the most negative view. Although this might reflect lifecycle influences, these differences might just as easily relate to profound differences between the experiences of particular generations of people during certain formative periods of their youth. Perhaps those who grew up with the consumer credit boom from the 1980s onwards will always be more positive towards credit than those over state pension age, for whom credit and debt are synonymous and equally stigmatising.

Table 2.9 Personal finance attitudes and behaviour by lifecycle group*

	Lifecycle group							
% who say ...	**1**	**2**	**3**	**4**	**5**	**6**	**7**	**8**
Money just goes	42	34	33	45	25	16	5	8
Never borrow money	7	4	5	4	11	7	21	29
Spend when young	30	24	22	34	17	18	8	7
Base	*266*	*150*	*533*	*176*	*400*	*537*	*338*	*393*

* Lifecycle groups:

1	Single people under 35, no dependent children
2	Couple under 35, no dependent children
3	Couple with dependent children, all ages
4	Lone parents with dependent children, all ages
5	Single people aged 35 to state pension age, no dependent children
6	Couple aged 35 to state pension age, no dependent children
7	Couples over state pension age
8	Single people over state pension age

Funding retirement

We conclude by examining whether there is a link between attitudes to personal finance and attitudes to state welfare. In particular, is there a group of people who are happy to spend and borrow during their working years, and then expect the state to look after them in retirement?

Our findings here are mixed. The next table shows people's expectations about their main source of income when they are retired, broken down both by their

views on whether one should spend or save when one is young (we shall refer to these groups as 'spenders' and 'savers'), and by their views about credit. As it shows, 'spenders' were indeed more likely than 'savers' to think that the state retirement pension will be their main source of income when they retire (33 and 21 per cent respectively). However, even among 'spenders', the majority (55 per cent) expected their main source of income on retirement to be an occupational or personal pension. This suggests that, even among those taking the most 'spendthrift' view, the majority expected to make their own provision for retirement.

The table also shows that those most in favour of borrowing money were *less* likely to expect to have to rely on the state retirement pension. So there is no link between, on the one hand, a credit-based culture and, on the other hand, the expectation that one will rely solely on the state at retirement. This no doubt partly reflects the fact that the most positive about credit also tend to be those on higher incomes, who are also the most likely to be able to save towards their retirement. But it will also reflect the marked age differences we saw earlier, with younger people being more likely than older ones to have positive views about credit and to have come of age during a period in which there has been considerable discussion about the extent to which a person will be able to rely on the state pension when they retire.

Table 2.10 Expected source of retirement income by attitudes to saving and credit

Expect main source of income when retired to be ...	Spend or save when young?		Attitudes to credit	
	Spend	Save	OK to borrow	Should never borrow
	%	%	%	%
State pension	33	21	24	38
Occupational pension	28	39	37	21
Personal pension	27	29	29	24
Other savings or investments	7	9	8	13
Elsewhere	1	*	1	1
Base	*444*	*1224*	*1818*	*134*

We explore this issue further in the next table. This examines people's views about who should 'mainly' be responsible for people's income when they are retired. As before, it contrasts the views of 'spenders' with those of 'savers', and the views of those who consider it acceptable to borrow with those who think that people should *never* borrow. It shows that 'spenders' were more likely than 'savers' to think that the government should mainly be responsible for pensions. But the difference between the views of these two groups was not

vast on this particular issue (66 per cent of spenders compared with 60 per cent of savers). More marked was the distinction between those who oppose credit and those who do not. Those with an 'anti-credit' stance were the most likely to think that the government should mainly be responsible for looking after people financially when they retire. Conversely, the more pro-credit were more likely to think that individuals and their families should be responsible. So, once again, we find little evidence that 'borrowers' are expecting government to bail them out in their retirement. As before, this is likely to reflect both their age and their income profile.

Table 2.11 Responsibility for pensions by attitudes to saving and credit

Who should mainly be responsible for ensuring people have enough money to live on in retirement?	Spend or save when young?		Attitudes to credit	
	Spend	Save	OK to borrow	Should never borrow
	%	%	%	%
Mainly the government	66	60	60	71
Mainly a person's employer	9	7	8	5
Mainly a person themselves and their family	25	31	30	23
Base	*514*	*1870*	*2394*	*335*

Conclusions

These findings demonstrate strong support for the principle of saving. Three-quarters of people support saving rather than borrowing in order to make non-essential purchases, and a similar proportion try to save in practice – a finding consistent with earlier research. The majority think that young people should start saving for retirement as soon as they can. Support for borrowing was rather mixed, and depended both on the need for a particular item and on whether people could afford the repayments. There was widespread support for the idea that credit encourages people to spend too much, and almost half of all respondents thought that credit should be harder to obtain. Although around one in ten said that people should never borrow, more than a third could see a positive side to credit, as a tool to make money management easier.

  We found that 'spenders' and 'borrowers' are not necessarily the same people. In particular, those who are favourable towards credit tend to come from higher income groups whereas 'spenders' are spread throughout all income groups. We also found that, while spenders were more likely to expect to be able to rely on the state in old age, borrowers were less likely to take this view. Whether this means that they will be financially prepared when they reach old age is, of course, another question.

All this provides very little support for the notion that Britain is a 'must have now' society, although we did identify a small minority who adhere to just such a philosophy, saying both that their 'money just goes' and advocating that young people should spend their money when they are young rather than save it. There is no evidence at all to suggest that this group is predominantly drawn from those on lower incomes, although they are more likely to be young rather than middle-aged or old.

These findings present us with something of a conundrum, given that we began our chapter by presenting various statistics which suggest that people are keener on spending and borrowing rather than saving. Why is it that our findings suggest so much support for saving, and only contingent support for credit, while other statistics point towards a credit boom? One possibility is that people are responding to the survey questions in ways that they think sound most respectable, perhaps reflecting social norms about the importance of saving? While, to a limited extent, this may be the case, it is unlikely to explain such an apparent gap between attitudes and behaviour.[2] A more plausible explanation is likely to be the fact that many of the main factors that underpin low savings levels are not related to attitudes at all, but reflect a number of other issues including low income levels (which will impose a financial constraint on saving), the complexity that can surround choosing between different financial products, insecurities about the long-term future, high house prices, and the possibility of tempting fate by planning too far ahead (Rowlingson et al., 1999; Rowlingson, 2002 forthcoming).

Clearly, government messages about the value of saving are working with the grain of public opinion. So the reason why people do not appear to be responding to these messages is unlikely to reflect their views about saving and borrowing. Rather, it is likely to stem from more concrete problems such as lack of money, insecurity, and the complexity that surrounds some savings and pension products. People *want* to save – the government needs to make it easier for them to do so.

Notes

1. This saying has been variously attributed to Josh Billings, Artemus Ward and Oscar Wilde.
2. For instance, the questions were carefully worded in order to ensure that less 'socially acceptable' responses were as easy as possible to give, and the majority were administered using a self-completion questionnaire as opposed to a face-to-face interview.

References

Atkinson, A. (1971), 'The distribution of wealth and the individual life-cycle', *Oxford Economic Papers 23*, Oxford: Oxford University Press.

Berthoud, R. and Kempson, E. (1992), *Credit and Debt: the PSI Survey*, London: Policy Studies Institute.

British Bankers' Association (2002), 'Easter stimulus for mortgages and credit cards', 28th May 2002, http://www.bba.org.uk/public/newsroom/pressreleases/52646.

Financial Services Authority (2000), *Better Informed Consumers*, London: Financial Services Authority.

Friedman, M. (1957), *A Theory of the Consumption Function*, Princeton: Princeton University Press.

Guardian Unlimited Money (2002), 'Consumer debt still rising', 3rd May, http://money.guardian.co.uk/creditanddebt/creditcards/story/0,1456,709405,00.html.

Hedges, A. (1998), *Pensions and Retirement Planning*, DSS Research Report No. 3, Leeds: Corporate Document Services Ltd.

Lea, S., Tarpy, R. and Webley, P. (1987), *The Individual in the Economy*, Cambridge: Cambridge University Press.

Office for National Statistics (2002), *Quarterly National Accounts*, 28th June, London: National Statistics.

Rowlingson, K. (2002, forthcoming), 'Private Pension Planning: the Rhetoric of Responsibility, the Reality of Insecurity', *Journal of Social Policy*.

Rowlingson, K., Whyley, C. and Warren, T. (1999), *Wealth in Britain*, London: Policy Studies Institute.

Thomas, A., Pettigrew, N. and Tovey, P. (1999), *Increasing Compulsory Pension Provision: Attitudes of the General Public and the Self-employed*, London: HMSO.

Acknowledgements

The *National Centre for Social Research* is grateful to the Department for Work and Pensions for their financial support which enabled us to ask the questions reported in this chapter.

3 Marching on together? Recent trends in union membership

Alex Bryson and Raphael Gomez[*]

It is often asserted by commentators that trade unions are outmoded institutions, shunned by employers and unable to reach a new generation of workers imbued with individualist values that are at odds with the solidaristic ethos underpinning unionism. They cite as evidence declines in union membership, observable across most of the western industrialised world (Western, 1995). Yet, at the beginning of the 21st century, after two decades of union decline, Britain remains a heavily unionised society. As we shall see, almost one-third of employees are union members: this makes trade unions the largest voluntary organisations in Britain. Nearly half (47 per cent) of workplaces contain at least some union members, with 36 per cent recognising one or more unions for pay bargaining.[1]

The sheer scale of unionisation might be a reason in itself for trying to understand patterns in union membership, but the main motivation is the influence that unions wield, even now. A raft of studies based on British evidence for the 1990s shows that unions have a significant impact on a variety of outcomes central to workers' quality of life and Britain's economic well-being. They improve employees' terms and conditions of work, including wages (Forth and Millward, 2000; Bryson, 2002) and fringe benefits, such as pension provision and sick pay (Forth and Millward, 2000). They also improve employees' working environment, for example by reducing accidents at work (Metcalf *et al.*, 2001). They operate as a 'sword of justice', tackling pay inequality, pay discrimination and low pay by altering procedures governing the contract of employment and challenging the ways in which employers set pay (Metcalf *et al.*, 2001). Moreover, unions influence the way that workers (both union members and non-members) feel about various aspects of their jobs, such as job satisfaction (Bryson *et al.*, 2002), perceived job insecurity, and the influence employees think they have over decisions which affect their jobs (Bryson and McKay, 1997). They affect the quality of workplace governance,

[*] Alex Bryson is a Principal Research Fellow at the Policy Studies Institute and Research Associate at the Centre for Economic Performance at the London School of Economics. Raphael Gomez is a Lecturer at the Interdisciplinary Institute of Management and a Research Associate at the Centre for Economic Performance, both at the London School of Economics.

as indicated by employee perceptions of managerial performance (Bryson, 2001a), trust in management (Bryson, 2001b) and the climate of employee relations (Bryson, 2001c). And, finally, they affect workplace performance: a recent review indicated that, during the 1990s, unions continued to influence productivity, workplace closure and employment growth (Bryson, 2001d). So – love them or hate them – unions cannot be ignored.

Nevertheless, the rapid decline in the proportion of employees who are union members (so-called 'union density') does raise questions about the long-term survival of trade unions in Britain. More immediately, the decline in union density weakens unions. This weakness can affect not only the degree of union influence on the ground, but its direction – weak unionism can actually have a *negative* effect on workplace performance and employee perceptions of their working environment (Bryson, 2001d).

In this chapter, we start by examining the evidence for a decline in union density. We then survey the literature to identify the main issues in the debate. These revolve around the role played by changes in the composition of the workforce and – given that this cannot explain the whole of the decline – what other factors might be involved, in particular, the costs and benefits to the employee of union membership and problems associated with union organisation and recruitment. Using data from the *British Social Attitudes* survey we can make an input into this debate. First, we shed new light on how much of the decline in union density is due to compositional change in the workforce and what implications this has for the future. Second, we consider individual entry to and exit from union membership. We show that the decline in union density is almost wholly accounted for by a decline in the rate of in-flow, resulting in a rise in the proportion of all employees who never become union members – people we term 'never-members' (Bryson and Gomez, 2002a). And, third, we consider whether the value of union membership to employees has declined by examining attitudinal data and calculating changes in the union wage premium.

Trends in union membership

As Figure 1 illustrates, figures from the *British Social Attitudes* survey series show that the percentage of employees who were union members fell by over a third between 1983 and 2001, from a half (49 per cent) to just under a third (31 per cent). A similar trend is apparent in the *Labour Force Survey*, which has collected union membership status since 1989.[2] In both series, density stabilises between 1998 and 2000. During this period, there was a net rise in the absolute number of union members but employment also grew (Sneade, 2001). However, the *British Social Attitudes* and *Labour Force Survey* figures both indicate that density fell once again between 2000 and 2001.

Figure 3.1 Union density among employees in Britain, 1983–2001

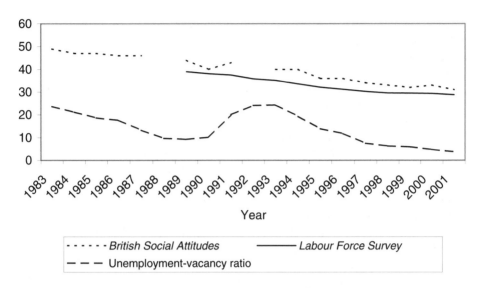

Source: The *Labour Force Survey* figures are taken from Sneade (2001) and DTI calculations for 2001.

Without controlling for other factors, the probability of being a union member fell by 19 percentage points between 1983 and 2001. Multivariate analyses (not shown here but available from the authors on request), controlling for demographic, job and workplace changes, also indicate a significant decline in union density in the 1990s relative to the 1980s, with the trend accelerating in the second half of the 1990s.[3] The trend is unaffected by the business cycle, as indicated by the lack of relationship between union density and the unemployment-vacancy ratio shown in Figure 1. The unemployment-vacancy ratio shows the seasonally-adjusted number of unemployed people per vacancy in the economy[4] (the lower the number, the tighter the labour market) and is thus a rough indicator of the business cycle.

Explanations for declining union density

Many reasons have been given for the decline in union membership in Britain. We group these reasons into five broad areas pertinent to the analysis presented later: changes in workforce composition; changes in the desire for union membership; the costs of membership; the benefits of membership; and difficulties in organising workers.

Changes in workforce composition

Since the early 1980s, there has been substantial change in the composition of the workforce: more women, a better qualified workforce, a growing service sector and contracting manufacturing sector, more non-manual jobs and fewer manual jobs, more private sector and less public sector employment, more part-time work. These changes have contributed to the decline in union density because traditional union strongholds have seen their share of employment decline in relative, and in some cases absolute, terms. However, there is considerable disagreement about the extent to which such compositional change alone can account for union decline. Some commentators find its effect to be relatively large: Booth (1989) attributes 42 per cent of the density decline from 1979 to 1987 to compositional change, while Green (1992) found compositional change accounted for just under one-third of the density decline between 1983 and 1989. Others show relatively little impact from compositional change for the first half of the 1980s (Carruth and Disney, 1988; Freeman and Pelletier, 1990). We return to this with our own estimates using *British Social Attitudes* data later in the chapter

  None of these studies find that compositional change in the workforce tells the *whole* story of union decline. Union density would have declined markedly even without it, because the probability of being a union member has fallen in the past two decades for most types of worker. Why is it that workers of almost any type are less likely to be members now than they used to be? There are two possibilities: either the desire for unionisation has fallen, or else the costs of membership have risen relative to their benefits, making even those employees who want membership less inclined to 'purchase' it. Let us look at each possibility in turn.

Changes in the desire for union membership

What do we know about employees' desire for union membership? Unfortunately, the answer is not very much. There are no British data over time measuring employees' desire for membership. However, some analysts argue that there has been a move towards individualism and away from the collectivist forms of industrial relations which underpin unionism (Phelps Brown, 1990; Bacon and Storey, 1996). This, in turn, may affect workers' attachment to unionism. There are two pieces of evidence that indicate such a shift in attitudes has occurred.

  First, as we show later, those on the political 'left' are a shrinking proportion of all employees. Since these workers are more likely than others to be union members this has reduced union density. Second, most of the decline in union density during the 1990s was due to declining membership within unionised workplaces (Millward *et al.*, 2000). Asked why union density was falling in unionised workplaces, the main reason cited by managerial respondents to the *Workplace Industrial Relations Survey* was "a decline in employee support for

their union" (Millward *et al.*, 2000: 92). When trying to quantify this effect, it has been estimated that around 10 percentage points of the 12–13 percentage point decline in mean union density in unionised workplaces between 1990 and 1998 "can be attributed to a reduced propensity among employees to join trade unions, even when encouraged to do so [by management]" (Millward *et al.* 2000: 149–151).

Another possibility is that employees' desire for union membership is as strong as ever, but the costs of union membership have risen relative to the benefits. This would manifest itself in non-members expressing a desire for unionisation – what we might call 'frustrated demand'. Without measures of the demand for union membership over time it is not possible to estimate the extent to which declining membership is accounted for by rising frustrated demand. However, there is clear evidence of a high degree of frustrated demand for unionisation in the late 1990s (Bryson and Gomez, 2002b).

The costs of union membership

The propensity of individuals to join unions is not simply a question of 'desire' or ideological commitment. More broadly, one can think of union membership as a good – a product or service to be purchased. Employees derive utility from this good, as they would other services or products. In the case of union membership, this utility can be psychological. For example, the decision to purchase membership may be due to the desire to conform to a social norm and thus maintain one's reputation among co-workers (Booth, 1985). It may also be driven by instrumentalism, wherein employees think they have something tangible to gain from membership, either in terms of better wages, better non-pecuniary terms of employment, or they may see it as insurance against arbitrary employer actions. So, benefits may accrue to the individual, but they come at a cost. Employees will purchase membership if the benefits outweigh the costs. A shift in the propensity to purchase union membership may reflect a shift in individuals' perceptions of the costs and benefits attached to membership.

The costs faced by workers in organising a union may indeed be rising in the following ways. First, management endorsement of unions declined dramatically in the 1990s, especially in the private sector and among larger unionised workplaces (Millward *et al.*, 2000) and employees are well aware of this (Bryson, 2001a). Dwindling employer support for unionisation may raise employee concerns about joining the union, and may raise uncertainty about the potential benefits. Second, the decline in the percentage of workplaces that are unionised (Millward *et al.*, 2000) means those wishing to become members are increasingly required to organise non-union workplaces, rather than simply join an existing union – a much more onerous task. Third, the costs of *not* being a member have fallen. This is partly due to policy changes, such as the outlawing of the closed shop, which used to make it difficult for employees in some workplaces to 'opt out' of membership, and partly because the reduction in

union density means there is less pressure on workers to conform with unionised co-workers (Belfield and Heywood, 2002).

A further cost is the fee required for membership. This is low: Reynolds *et al.* (1999) estimate that it is equivalent to roughly two hours' pay per month while the cost of industrial action accounts for less than one per cent of working time for the typical union worker – and it has not risen substantially over time. Nevertheless, the cost is substantial enough to deter some workers from joining. In 2001, roughly one in six (17 per cent) employees were non-members in workplaces with a union that they could join. Of these non-members, almost a third (30 per cent) said the fact that membership fees were too high was important in their decision not to join.[5] This is most likely an issue where the decision to join or not is a marginal one. Furthermore, less than a third (30 per cent) of union members think membership is "good value for money", with about half (53 per cent) saying it is "reasonable value" and a sixth (16 per cent) saying it is "poor value for money" (Diamond and Freeman, 2001). On this evidence, the costs of membership relative to the benefits may weigh in employees' decisions to remain union members, as well as the decision to become a member.

The benefits of union membership

What of the benefits of membership? Unionisation confers certain benefits to workers. Some of these, like the union wage premium, are fairly visible to both members and non-members alike. Since they are clearly visible, employees may decide whether or not to join with those benefits in mind. Most other benefits, such as the enforcement of procedural justice or the establishment of family-friendly policies, are harder to identify prior to entering the labour market and near impossible if one has never sampled union membership. It is only when a worker has actually been employed in a unionised job for long enough, or when a worker has access to reliable information about the nature of union membership, that he or she can form an accurate opinion about the value of unionisation and whether the benefits outweigh any of the potential costs (namely membership dues, industrial action and so on). In other words, the employee must be able to experience union membership to know its true benefits (Gomez and Gunderson, 2002; Bryson and Gomez, 2003). So, with this in mind, what has happened to these benefits in recent times?

The most obvious way of measuring the value of union membership to employees is to estimate the extent to which members' wages are higher than those of similar non-members. This 'union wage premium' arises because unions bargain on members' behalf for wages that are above the market rate. There has been speculation that the intensification of competition since the 1980s, coupled with a diminution of union bargaining strength, has prevented unions from obtaining the sort of wage premium they achieved in the past. Recent empirical evidence points to a premium which is significantly lower than the 10 per cent or so typical in earlier studies (Booth and Bryan, 2001; Machin, 2001; Bryson, 2002).[6] We return to this question later in the chapter

and do our own calculations of the union wage premium on the basis of *British Social Attitudes* data.

It is more difficult to assess the benefits of unionisation in other areas. Labour's programme of labour market re-regulation, which offers statutory protection to workers on wages, hours worked and family-friendly policies, may be a substitute for union protection in the eyes of some workers, lowering the perceived benefits of membership. Alternatively, these policies may highlight the benefits of unionisation where unions can improve on minimum legal protections through collective bargaining.

Difficulties in organising workers

Quite apart from the costs and benefits of union membership, unions have difficulties organising workers for two further reasons. First, they have had problems getting those starting a new job to join the union. This was cited by managers as one of the main reasons for density decline in unionised workplaces between 1990 and 1998 (Millward *et al.*, 2000). Union membership rates have always been lower among employees who have not been so long at their present workplace, but the gap is increasing.[7] One reason for this is the inadequacy of union organisation on the ground, as the 2001 *British Worker Representation and Participation Survey*[8] indicates. Over half (56 per cent) of non-members eligible to join the union at their workplace said they had never been asked to join the union. Yet, more than a third (36 per cent) of these employees said that, if they were asked, it was likely that they would join (10 per cent saying "very likely" and 26 per cent saying "quite likely").

The other problem unions face, of course, is membership retention. Waddington (cited in TUC, 2001) suggests 70 per cent of members leave because of a change in their job situation – a change in employer, or leaving employment for retirement, child-rearing or unemployment. This suggests unions often lose track of these leavers, resulting in lapsed memberships.

The biggest problem is that, in a growing number of cases, there is simply no union to join because fewer workplaces are unionised (Millward *et al.*, 2000: 83–108). The absence of workplace-level unionisation may affect individual employees' decisions to join a union because the cost of starting a union in an unorganised workplace is higher than the cost of becoming a member in an already unionised workplace (Green, 1990; Farber, 2001; Bryson and Gomez, 2002b). The growth in non-unionised workplaces is not due to unionised employers derecognising unions at a faster rate – derecognition remains rare (Millward *et al.*, 2000). Rather, the rise in non-union workplaces is due to new workplaces being less likely to unionise than 'dying' workplaces. Only one-tenth of the lower rate of unionisation among new workplaces is due to the fact that they differ in their characteristics from older workplaces; nine-tenths is a cohort effect – they are simply less likely to unionise regardless of the type of workplace (Millward *et al.*, 2000). This process has been going on for some time, with the height of union organising being shortly after the Second World

War (Machin, 2000; Millward *et al.*, 2000). In addition, the unionised sector is shrinking because employment growth in unionised workplaces is slower than growth in non-unionised workplaces (Bryson, 2001e) and, during the 1990s, unionised workplaces were more likely to close than non-unionised workplaces (Bryson, 2003).

Unions' reduced capacity to organise is partly due to diminishing resources available and the increasing costs that successful organising entails. These additional costs are due to difficulties in reaching a flexible and more mobile workforce, often located in smaller workplaces than would have been the case in the past. The decline in permanent employment and the demise of easy-to-organise larger workplaces raise the marginal costs of recruitment. Growing employer opposition to union membership also raises the costs of organising.

Similar trends are apparent in the United States. Analysts there have calculated that the rate of job creation and destruction is such that, even if union organising activity occurred at the high levels last witnessed in the 1950s, it would do little to reverse the decline in union density (Farber and Western, 2000). The organisation of non-union jobs in the American private sector would need to rise six-fold simply to maintain steady-state density (currently at 12 per cent), an effort which would entail financial resources which exceed current total union incomes. Although similar research has yet to be conducted for Britain, it is likely that unions here would face a similar uphill struggle due to the rate of employment decline in the union sector (Charlwood, 2000).

Another factor contributing to British unions' difficulties in organising is the political climate facing unions and, in particular, union legislation passed in the 1980s and 1990s. This may have directly affected unions' organising costs by making it more difficult for unions to engage in activities which helped unions recruit in the past, such as the enforcement of the closed shop, unofficial strike action and secondary picketing.[9] It also reduces the costs employers face in opposing unionisation.

New Labour has sought to address this issue, believing that unions can foster better industrial relations and assist in productivity improvements. Although they have not met union demands to repeal the legislation of the 1980s, they introduced a statutory union recognition procedure in 1999 (effective from 2000) which, for the first time since the early 1970s, requires employers to recognise trade unions where a majority of employees so wish. This may have a direct impact on unions' organising ability by helping unions overcome practical organisational difficulties, such as employer opposition. It may also have a more general impact on unionisation rates, by signalling to employers that, under the new political climate, government wishes employers to do business with unions where there is support among employees for this to happen. In effect, this lowers union organising costs and raises the cost to employers of opposing union organising.

Early evidence indicates that the direct effects of the legislation are small and limited to actions such as helping unions regain a foothold in industries like printing where employers exhibited strong anti-union sentiments in the 1980s. However, there has been a proliferation of voluntary recognition agreements suggesting that favourable public policy towards unions may influence workers'

willingness to join unions, as well as employer attitudes to unionisation (Wood *et al.*, 2002).[10] More time must elapse to allow the effects of these political and legal changes to come through, at which point it will be possible to evaluate their full impact on union density.

Implications

To summarise, at a time when unions are finding it more costly to organise, they have fewer resources to do so. This has prompted an innovative recruitment strategy by unions including the setting up of a TUC Organising Academy and increased use of the internet to galvanise support for unions in non-unionised workplaces (Heery, 2002; TUC, 2001). The government has also responded by creating conditions that are more conducive to union organising. But, with lower employment growth rates in the unionised sector and the birth of predominantly non-union workplaces and jobs there are serious doubts as to whether the fate of unions is in their hands.

What contribution can this chapter make to our understanding of trends in union membership? First, we quantify the impact of compositional change on density change over the whole period between 1983 and 2001. This is important since existing studies differ in the importance they attach to compositional change in explaining union decline since the early 1980s. We also consider whether membership is still declining for most types of worker. Second, we track the rise in the proportion of employees who have never experienced union membership, identify the determinants of 'never-membership' and discuss its implications. Third, we consider trends in members' and non-members' perceptions of how well they think unions are doing at their workplace. This is a measure of how employees experience unions and a proxy for the value attached to membership. We consider its relationship with union membership to see what impact the perceived effectiveness of the union has on membership status. Fourth, we consider whether the value of union membership, as measured by the union wage premium, has declined over time. In concluding, we discuss the implications of the analysis for union organising.

The impact of change in the composition of the workforce on union density

Since the early 1980s, there has been substantial change in the composition of the workforce. There is no doubt that these changes have contributed to the decline in union density because traditional union strongholds, such as manufacturing and manual occupations, have seen their share of employment decline.

This is illustrated in the next table. The middle columns show that throughout the period 1983–2001, full-timers have been more likely to be union members than part-timers, as have older workers relative to young workers, those

working in the public sector compared to those working in the private sector, and those on the 'left' of the political spectrum compared to those on the 'right'. This latter group could be described as those who espouse the ideas of distributive justice which chime with the collectivist ideals of the trade union movement, suggesting that changing ideological orientations may have played some part in the decline of unions. (For an explanation of the left–right scale, see Appendix I to this Report).

The first two columns in the table show that women, older workers, part-timers, non-manual workers, those in services, those in the private sector, and the higher paid have all increased their shares in employment by five percentage points or more. With the exception of older workers and the higher paid, the workforce segments that have increased their employment share are all among those where membership is traditionally lower. There has also been a reduction in the share of employment taken by those on the 'left' of the 'left–right' scale.

The other big compositional change in the workforce – the rise in qualified workers – has not had a substantial overall effect on union density. This is because the growth in workers with university or higher education qualifications (who are more likely to be union members than those without qualifications) has been largely cancelled out by the parallel growth in workers with middle-level qualifications (A levels, O levels, GCSEs etc.) who are no more likely to be union members than those without qualifications.

The last set of rows of the table reveals the extent to which the percentage of employees in unionised workplaces has declined – from around two-thirds in the early 1980s to a half in the late 1990s. Not surprisingly, since workplace-level unionisation is associated with membership rates that are over ten times higher than those in non-unionised workplaces, this compositional shift has also contributed to the decline in membership.

Irrespective of changes in the composition of the workforce, union density would have declined anyway because every type of worker had a lower probability of being a union member at the turn of the 21st century than they did two decades earlier. The middle columns show that union density declined in every segment of the workforce over the period, except in non-unionised workplaces where members continued to account for around one in twenty employees. The decline was particularly pronounced among young workers, manual workers, men, those with medium-earnings, and those with low or no qualifications.

The last two columns of the table quantify the relative contributions of workforce compositional change and within-group propensities for membership using a technique known as 'shift-share' analysis. By 'within-group' propensities for membership we mean membership rates for each type of worker. The shift-share technique, which is described more fully in the appendix to this chapter, separates out the decline in density that would have occurred through within-group density change with employee composition fixed at its 1983–1985 level, and the decline that would have occurred through change in employee composition if within-group density had stayed at its 1983–1985 level.[11]

Table 3.1 Shift-share analysis of the changing composition of the workplace and of union membership, 1983–2001

	% all employees		% who are members		Shift share analysis	
	1983–1985	1999–2001	1983–1985	1999–2001	% due to within-group density change	% due to change in composition of workforce
Gender						
Male	56	49	52	32		
Female	44	51	42	32	-94	-6
Age						
18–24	17	12	38	15		
25+	83	88	50	34	-106	+6
Ethnicity						
White	97	94	48	32		
Non-white	3	6	50	33	-101	+1
Qualifications						
Degree/HE	25	36	48	38		
A or O Level	32	39	44	28		
CSE/None	42	25	49	29	-104	+4
Region						
Scotland/Wales	13	14	59	42		
Midlands/North	43	41	54	35		
South	45	45	39	26	-100	0
Left–right scale						
Right	37	41	36	28		
Centre	29	31	49	35		
Left	35	27	53	39	-83	-17
Hours						
Full-time	83	76	52	34		
Part-time	17	24	27	24	-93	-7
Occupation						
Manual	46	37	54	31		
Non-manual	54	63	43	33	-98	-2
Earnings						
High	37	50	55	40		
Average	23	22	57	33		
Low	40	28	36	18	-116	+16
Workplace size						
<25 employees	32	32	25	17		
25+ employees	68	68	58	41	-97	-3
Sector						
Public	36	29	77	62		
Private	61	68	30	20		
Other	3	3	27	19	-78	-22
Industry						
Manufacturing	28	19	47	30		
Non-manufacturing	72	81	48	32	-102	+2
Unionisation						
Recognition	64	47	72	60		
No recognised union	36	53	5	6	-50	-50

Note: for bases, see appendix to this chapter.

Within-group decline in union membership dwarfs the effect of changes in the composition of the workforce on all but one of the dimensions. The exception is union recognition where half the fall in membership density is accounted for by declining union density in workplaces with recognised unions, while the other half is due to the declining incidence of unionised workplaces. The other compositional changes contributing substantially to declining union density are: the falling share of employment accounted for by the public sector and the fall in the percentage of employees on the 'left' of the left–right scale measuring employees' attitudes to distributive justice. On the other hand, there are two workforce dimensions where compositional change slowed the decline in union density, namely, the ageing of the workforce and growth in high earners.

However, it is not possible to 'read off' the *total* contributions of compositional and within-group changes in union density from the shift-share analysis because the workforce dimensions are interdependent. To do this we need to use multivariate analyses (see the appendix to this chapter for more details).

The next table summarises this analysis. The first column (A) tracks the fall in the actual rate of union density from 48 per cent in 1983–1985 to 32 per cent in 1999–2001. The union density in each time period compared with the 1983–1985 baseline is shown in column B. Column C shows predicted union density in each time period based on our model for that period. Column D shows what would have happened if the changes in workplace composition had happened on their own and there had been no change in within-group union density. Column E shows the contribution to the percentage point change in union density relative to 1983–1985 that is accounted for by the compositional change. And, finally, column F shows the contribution of within-group membership change, holding compositional change constant.

Table 3.2 Contribution of change in composition and within-group change to membership density trend, 1983–2001

	[A]	[B]	[C]	[D]	[E]	[F]	
	Actual density	Density compared with 1983–1985 baseline	Predicted density	Composi-tional change only	Impact of composi-tional change	Impact of within-group change	Base
					[C] - [D]	[B] - [E]	
1983–1985	48						2434
1986–1989	45	-3	45	45	0	-3	4344
1990–1994	41	-7	41	43	-2	-5	4502
1995–1998	35	-13	35	39	-4	-9	4909
1999–2001	32	-16	32	38	-6	-10	4391

Our results thus suggest compositional change had little impact on the decline in density in the second half of the 1980s relative to 1983–1985. This is more in line with Carruth and Disney's (1988) and Freeman and Pelletier's (1990) analyses for the early 1980s, which attribute less of the change to compositional factors than Booth (1989) and Green (1992).[12] But the picture changed in the 1990s. Comparing 1999–2001 with 1983–1985, roughly a third of the fall in membership density is accounted for by compositional change, and two-thirds by within-group changes.[13] The increasing importance of compositional change is a topic for future investigation.

In what segments did union membership decline most rapidly?

Earlier we showed that union density has fallen across all types of worker (except those in non-unionised workplaces), but where has it fallen most? We can get an indication of this from Table 3.1, but the picture is clouded because the different segments are interrelated. To get a clear picture, we must isolate the independent effects for each segment, holding other factors constant, which can only be done by multivariate analysis. For example, we need to control for workplace-level union recognition to get a picture net of the constraints and opportunities for membership associated with the availability of a union on-site. Whereas Table 3.1 showed the propensity for union membership fell across *all* classes of worker, job and workplace, the multivariate analysis shows that, once other factors are held constant, the probability of being a union member fell more quickly in areas of traditional union strength, namely among full-time workers, manual workers, the low paid, those in manufacturing, and workers in unionised workplaces.

Let us consider the results in more detail, beginning with job characteristics.[14] The positive association between membership and full-time working has been in decline since the early 1980s. Although Table 3.1 still shows a ten percentage point gap between full-time and part-time workers' membership rates in 1999–2001, the difference is not statistically significant once we hold other factors constant. Manual workers had higher probabilities of membership than non-manual workers throughout the period, but there has been a gradual convergence in their membership probabilities. Low-paid workers were less likely to be members throughout the period, and the relative probability of low-paid employees being members has diminished even further over time. In the early 1980s, the low-paid had a probability of membership that was eight per cent lower than high paid workers: this had doubled to 15 per cent by 1999–2001. Formal statistical tests indicate that all three trends are statistically significant.[15]

Perhaps most interesting of all is the effect of workplace-level union recognition. Employees in unionised workplaces had a 63 per cent higher probability of membership than similar employees in non-unionised workplaces in 1983–1985. This dropped to 51 per cent by 1999–2001. Again, this trend is statistically significant. The convergence in density in manufacturing relative to other activities was also statistically significant.

On the other hand, changes in the association of gender, ethnicity and age with union membership were not statistically significant.

We also estimated the impact of workplace size, sector, qualifications and attitudes to distributive justice over time for the years that these variables were available. Smaller workplaces (with fewer than 25 employees) were associated with lower density than larger workplaces until the mid-1990s but, since then, the effect has been statistically non-significant. Public sector employees had a much higher probability of union membership than employees in the private and voluntary sectors throughout (ranging between 13 per cent and 20 per cent), but there was no significant trend. Those with mid-level qualifications had lower membership probabilities than those with low or no qualifications during most of the 1990s, but the effect was not significant after 1998.

The *British Social Attitudes* 'left–right' scale (described in detail in Appendix I of this Report) measures employees' attitudes to distributive justice and is a reasonable proxy for individuals' collectivist orientations. Other research has established a strong association between more left-wing attitudes, as measured by the 'left–right' scale, and an increased likelihood of union membership (Bryson and Gomez, 2002b). We found being on the 'right' of this scale (that is, scoring 2.8 or more on a scale of 1 to 5) reduced the probability of union membership by six to twelve per cent relative to being on the 'left' of the scale (scoring less than 2.20) but there was no statistically significant trend. This suggests that individuals' collectivist orientations are strongly linked to whether they are union members but this link has not strengthened significantly over time once we control for other factors.

To summarise thus far, we have shown that union density has declined for virtually every type of worker since the early 1980s. The fall in union density is largely attributable to within-group density decline, as opposed to compositional changes in the workforce, although the latter still accounts for a sizeable part of the decline, particularly in the 1990s. Finally, we have shown that the probability of being a union member declined at a *faster* rate in jobs and workplaces where unions have been traditionally strong, such as among full-time workers, manual workers and the low paid.

The rise of 'never-membership' in Britain

One can think of the rate of union membership at any particular time as a 'stock' of workers. New members are the in-flow to this stock, while the out-flow become ex-members. The 'stock' of members will fall with a rise in the rate of out-flow, or a decline in the in-flow.

In all years except 1994 and 1997 those who were not current members of a union were asked:[16]

Have you ever been a member of a trade union or staff association?

Figure 3.2: The rise of 'never-membership', 1983–2001

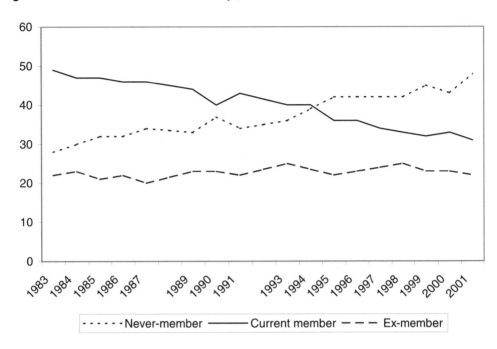

Note: Figures are percentage of employees in the whole economy.

Figure 3.2 shows that the decline in union density in the economy as a whole is almost wholly accounted for by a rise in never-members – in other words, a decline in the rate of in-flow to union membership. The rate of never-membership rose from 28 per cent in 1983 to 48 per cent in 2001. By the mid-1990s, never-members outnumbered members. Ex-membership has remained virtually static between 1983 and 2001, indicating that it is unions' inability to attract new members, rather than a haemorrhaging of existing members, which explains declining membership. Even so, between a fifth and a quarter of members leave membership each year which means that stemming this outflow is another way of achieving higher union density.

Who are these never-members and where have they come from? In the period 1999–2001, never-membership rates were highest among young workers (78 per cent), those in non-unionised workplaces (66 per cent), low-earners (57 per cent), employees in small workplaces with under 25 employees (57 per cent), private sector employees (55 per cent) and those in the South (52 per cent). However, the rate of never-membership rose in every segment of the workforce over the period. Multivariate analysis (Bryson and Gomez, 2002a) reveals compositional change in the workforce accounts for around half the rise in never-membership. The remainder is due to an increase in never-membership rates for all types of worker. More surprising still is the finding that the situation is similar in unionised workplaces, where nine of the twelve percentage point

drop in union density between 1983–1985 and 1999–2001 is due to rising never-membership.

We are, in fact, witnessing the rise of a new cohort of never-members, whose parents were less likely to be members compared to the previous generation (Machin and Blanden, 2001). If workers do not experience any of the potential benefits of unionisation (either directly or by proxy through family or friends), they will be less inclined to become due paying members in workplaces where unions are present and even less likely to organise workplaces lacking in any union presence. What is more, the effect snowballs, since the rise in never-membership in one generation will transmit itself, via a lack of union experience, into growth in non-union membership in the next generation. Unions therefore have a serious problem in convincing potential members that what they offer is of benefit to them.

The benefits of union membership

Employees' evaluation of the work of trade unions

In all years, except 1995 and 1997, all employees in unionised workplaces have been asked:

> On the whole, do you think the union(s)/staff association(s) in your workplace do(es) their job well or not?

Table 3.3 Perceptions of how well unions do their job in unionised workplaces, 1983–1985 to 1999–2001

	Year, grouped				
	1983–1985	1986–1989	1990–1994	1995–1998	1999–2001
% who say unions do their job well	59	60	58	61	62
% who say unions do not do their job well	37	35	36	32	31
Base	*1574*	*2671*	*2880*	*1478*	*2094*

The previous table shows that those saying 'yes' has remained fairly static at around six in ten employees. It seems that, where employees have the opportunity to experience unions first hand, the experience is generally positive. Among members, the figure was 63 per cent in 1983–1985 and 65 per cent in 1999–2001, indicating that close to two-thirds of union membership are satisfied with the service they receive.[17] Over the same period, there was a small

rise in the percentage of non-members saying unions did their job well (from 49 per cent to 58 per cent). The 'satisfaction' gap between members and non-members, as measured by the percentage saying the on-site union did its job well, thus closed from 14 percentage points to 7 percentage points over the series.

There are a number of reasons why non-members remain non-members even if they view the union as doing its job well. Eligibility for the union may be restricted to a sub-group of workers at the workplace, so that the non-member does not have the opportunity to join. Non-members may also be interpreting the question differently to members. Whereas members may be evaluating their value for money from union membership, non-members may be evaluating unions against a less demanding criterion, such as the quality of employee relations in the presence of the union *versus* what it could be like without the union. Another reason, one that is often overlooked, might be that non-members may be content to benefit from the operation of an effective union without paying union dues.

The relevance of this last point is that, even if unions have maintained benefits accruing through membership, many of these benefits are available to workers in the same workplace without joining the union, either because the whole class of workers is covered by collective bargaining – whether they are a member or not – or because, once the union has negotiated improved terms and conditions for its members, the employer offers the benefit (whether it be extra paid paternity, better shift patterns, or whatever) to all workers at the site. If employees are more prepared to 'free-ride' than they were in the past, then this may also contribute to falling union density. Despite its importance in Britain, there is little reliable evidence on the incidence of free-riding over time.

According to Bryson (2002), only 59 per cent of private sector employees in workplaces covered by unions are union members, and only 65 per cent of those in covered occupations are members, indicating that between 41 per cent and 35 per cent of covered workers are free-riders. Using the *Labour Force Survey* Metcalf *et al.* (2001) estimates over 3 million employees were free-riders in Britain in 1999. The 2001 *British Worker Representation and Participation Survey* shows 35 per cent of non-members in workplaces with a union they could join said the fact that they could get the benefits of membership without joining was an important reason for not joining the union. The issue for unions here is how to offer benefits to members that non-members cannot access.

The probability of being a union member was nine to fourteen percentage points higher over the period 1983–2001 if the employee thought that the union was doing its job well, controlling for other factors. There was no trend over time in this association. The fact that the link between membership status and employees' evaluation of the job done by unions did not differ significantly over the period supports the contention that unions' ability to deliver for workers had not deteriorated, and is unlikely to be a source of discontent among employees leading members to quit the union.

The union membership wage premium

Another way to test the value of union membership to employees is to estimate the extent to which members' wages are higher than those of similar non-members. This is often referred to as the 'union wage premium'. It arises because unions bargain on members' behalf for wages that are above the market rate. If the costs of membership have remained constant or, as we suggested earlier, have risen, while the wage benefits of membership have fallen, this might help explain the reticence of employees to join unions. As noted earlier, some studies have suggested a decline in union wage premium, but there have been no studies estimating the union wage premium with consistent time-series data and techniques. We shall now fill this gap in the literature by estimating the union wage premium over the period 1985–2001 using data from the *British Social Attitudes* survey.

Figure 3.3 Trends in the union wage premium, 1985–2001

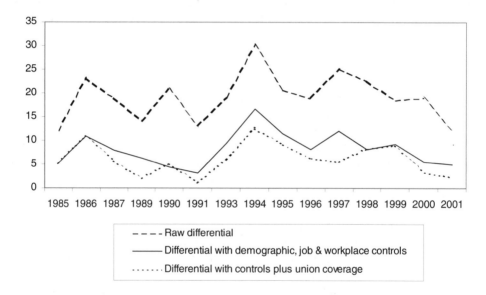

Figure 3.3 presents the percentage difference in log gross hourly wages of union members relative to non-members over time.[18] The dashed line represents the 'raw' differential between members and non-members. In 1985, this premium stood at 12 per cent. It peaked in the mid-1990s at 30 per cent, only to gradually decline to 12 per cent again by the end of the period. However, this 'raw' differential takes no account of differences across members and non-members in terms of demographic, job and workplace characteristics. These controls account for roughly half the raw premium, as indicated by the solid line, but the pattern over time is similar to that for the raw premium. Finally, the dotted line

shows the premium when taking account of whether the employee is covered by collective bargaining (as indicated by whether the employee works in a workplace where there is a recognised union). This control is added to account for the fact that it is only in those workplaces where workers are covered by collective bargaining that we might expect unions to raise wages. Introducing this control reduces the premium still further, so that it ranges between one per cent and 13 per cent over the period. Once again, there is a gradual decline in the premium since the mid-1990s so that, by 2001, the premium is around three per cent. However, looking at the period since the mid-1980s as a whole, there does not seem to have been a secular decline in the union wage premium.

Figure 3.4 The union wage premium and the business cycle, 1985–2001

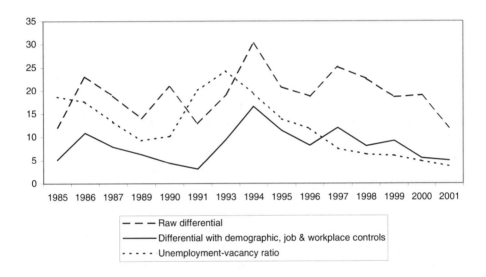

Figure 3.4 superimposes the business cycle (the dotted line), as indicated by the unemployment-vacancy ratio. We can see that the unemployment-vacancy ratio fell in the second half of the 1980s as the economy emerged out of the early 1980s recession and approached the Lawson boom. The economy fell into recession again in the early 1990s, but has been gradually recovering ever since so that, by the end of the period, there were roughly four unemployed people to each vacancy.[19] It is striking that the trend in the union wage premium follows the business cycle, sometimes with a one-year lag, with the bargaining round responding to ambient economic conditions. This indicates that any short-term decline in the union wage premium is not necessarily a secular decline, but induced by favourable labour market conditions. This implies that, when demand for labour is strong, employees are less reliant on unions to bargain for better wages because market wages rise anyway. However, when market conditions are less favourable to workers the premium rises because union bargaining cushions members from market fluctuations. So, although there are

indications that the benefits of membership – as measured by the wage premium – have declined since the mid-1990s, this can be viewed as a cyclical phenomenon. The premium may rise again when economic conditions deteriorate with the next downturn in the business cycle.

The implications of this analysis for the central theme of the chapter are two-fold. First, trends in the wage premium can only help explain falling union density since the mid-1990s, since the premium was fairly stable before that point. Second, although the premium may rise with a deterioration in economic conditions, the decline in the most visible benefit of membership when the economy is doing well places greater emphasis on unions' ability to sell the less visible benefits of membership such as their ability to promote equity and fairness in the workplace.

Conclusions

This review of the reasons for union density decline since the early 1980s and the new analyses presented in the chapter demonstrate that unions have much to do if they wish to recoup lost membership. Compositional change in the workforce is a factor which is beyond union control, but our analysis shows that such change tells only part of the story. It was not a major factor at all in the fall in union density in the 1980s and only accounts for about one third of the fall in the 1990s. Rather, membership declined for all types of worker over the period – particularly in areas of traditional unionisation, such as full-time workers, manual workers and the low paid.

Why should this have happened? There is one possible explanation that we can discount straight away – it is *not* the case that members (or indeed non-members) have become less satisfied with unions. Rather, there seems to have been a shift in the ratio of the benefits of unionisation to the costs of becoming a member. The increase in costs is in part due to the political climate from 1979 onwards and increased employer opposition to unions. The spread of non-union workplaces has certainly increased the cost of union membership for those who must start by organising their workplace before they can join, rather than just sign up to an existing union. The benefits of union membership may also have declined – we find evidence that the union wage premium has weakened since the mid-1990s.

These developments have set up a vicious circle. Unions have been unable to organise new workers, resulting in a big increase in the proportion of all workers who have never been union members (three-quarters of the decline in density in the union sector is due to the rise in never-membership). The rise of never-membership accounts for nearly all the decline in union density in the economy as a whole. At the same time the union sector is shrinking as new non-union workplaces replace older unionised workplaces, and as unionised workplaces continue to grow at a slower rate than their non-union counterparts. This all serves to increase the costs of union membership and possibly also to reduce the benefits.

The biggest challenge facing unions is this: what can they do to entice new 'buyers'? We can point to some hopeful signs for the unions. The political climate has undoubtedly changed since 1997 (albeit not as radically as the unions might wish), which may reduce some of the costs of union membership. And our analysis of the union wage premium (perhaps the most visible benefit of union membership) shows that the recent decline is not part of a long-term secular trend, but rather related to the relatively good economic conditions since the early 1990s. This implies a higher union wage premium next time the economy takes another downturn. To capitalise on this, however, unions must start to reach the growing cohort of never-members and, at the same time, reduce the exit rates from union membership by improving services to existing members. If they can do this, their future could be more secure than some commentators seem to think.

Notes

1. Workplace unionisation and recognition rates are the authors' calculations based on the 1998 *Workplace Employee Relations Survey* which, when appropriately weighted, is representative of all workplaces in Britain with ten or more employees.
2. The *Labour Force Survey* (LFS) question is: "Are you a member of a trade union or staff association?" In *British Social Attitudes* the question is: "Are you now a member of a trade union or staff association?" The LFS estimates are based on all employees, whereas the *British Social Attitudes* question is only asked of employees working at least ten hours per week. Since the relative costs of membership are highest among those working the shortest hours, it is not surprising that the membership rate is lower when calculated using LFS.
3. Workplace-level analyses also reveal an increase in the rate of decline in union density in the 1990s relative to the 1980s (Millward, Bryson and Forth, 2000).
4. The unemployment-vacancy ratio in Figure 3.1 indicates the number of unemployed people per vacancy in the spring of each year, seasonally adjusted. The figures are averaged over the period March–May. However, ONS temporarily discontinued the vacancy series in May 2001 so the 2001 figure is an average over March and April of that year.
5. These figures have been calculated by the authors from the *British Workers Representation and Participation Survey*.
6. If the union wage premium has declined since the early 1980s, this would be unsurprising since it has been a period of sustained real wage growth for most workers, with the market delivering real wage improvements even in the absence of unions. This raises the question: do cyclical trends affect union density? Using union density data for the period 1980–1984, Carruth and Disney (1988) construct a model capable of predicting union density over the period 1971–1984. They find that declining union density over that period is largely accounted for by cyclical factors, notably steady real-wage growth, low inflation, and persistent unemployment.
7. The membership rate for employees with workplace tenure of under five years was 52 per cent of that for employees with five or more years tenure in 1990–1994. This had fallen to 43 per cent by 1995–1998 and 42 per cent by 1999–2001 (authors'

calculations using *British Social Attitudes* data). One-quarter of these low-tenured non-members want union representation (Bryson and Gomez, 2002b).

8. The *British Worker Representation and Participation Survey* was a collaboration between the TUC and the Centre for Economic Performance at the London School of Economics. The survey was conducted in July 2001 by BMRB and involved around 1,500 telephone interviews with British workers.

9. There is some evidence that union militancy can boost union organisation among workers most directly affected. Western (1995) discusses the evidence. However, union militancy reduces the popularity of unions among the general population (Edwards and Bain, 1988).

10. It is difficult to maintain that legislation *causes* rises or falls in union membership since legislative change is often a reflection of an existing social and political climate. Still, one might say that the prospect of legislation may contribute to the perception that future gains to union membership might be higher/lower.

11. The shift-share methodology is used in all the studies discussed earlier which quantify the impact of compositional change. Some authors have questioned the value of this methodology because it is a descriptive device rather than a way of 'explaining' change since it does not address *why* some workers are willing or able to unionise while others are not (Disney, 1990). Disney also questions the value of a focus on compositional effects when explaining the marked cyclical changes in union membership over the course of the 20th century since explanations should be able to predict both upturns and downturns. Compositional change in the workforce is often asymmetrical and thus fails this criterion. We accept the points Disney makes. However, we believe shift-share analysis is one of a number of methodologies which can shed light on trends in unionisation in Britain.

12. In the case of Booth, this is not surprising since her analysis includes the period 1979–1982, a period of very substantial compositional change.

13. *British Social Attitudes* contains a number of variables correlated with membership that are not available in all years. These include public sector, workplace size, qualifications, and the left-right scale. We tested the sensitivity of our results to the inclusion of these variables and the consequential truncation of the time-series. Although the precise contribution of shares in employment and within-group shifts varied with model specification and years included in the analyses, compositional change explained roughly a third of the decline in density, within-group change accounting for the rest.

14. These analyses are based on the models in the appendix to this chapter.

15. Significant differences over time show up as significant changes in coefficients in the models in the appendix. The statistical formula is $\dfrac{\beta_1 - \beta_2}{\sqrt{se_1^2 + se_2^2}}$

where β_1 signifies the coefficient in the first period, β_2 signifies the coefficient in the second period, se_1^2 is the square of the standard error for the coefficient in the first period and se_2^2 is the square of the standard error for the coefficient in the second period.

16. Because the survey did not collect information on never-membership in 1994 and 1997 these years were dropped from the analysis in this section. This accounts for small differences in rates of membership reported compared with the rest of the chapter.

17. However, it is worth recalling evidence from the *British Worker Representation and Participation Survey* 2001 that only 30 per cent of members think membership represents 'good value for money'.
18. The figure depicts the difference in log gross hourly wages between members and non-members, expressed as a percentage of non-members' wages. The figures are derived from the union membership dummy coefficient in single-year interval regression analyses which are explained in detail in the appendix to this chapter. The analyses incorporate the following controls: gender, age, ethnicity, qualifications, manual worker, full-time worker, establishment size, public sector, manufacturing, region. The estimates for 1994 and 1995 exclude the public sector dummy because this was not available in that year, while the 1991 estimates exclude the ethnic minority dummy due to the low number of valid cases with ethnicity in that year. Prior to 1996 the *British Social Attitudes* hours worked question did not explicitly mention overtime hours. The hours denominator used here explicitly includes overtime hours from 1996 onwards. Identical analyses using a post-1995 hours definition excluding overtime hours produces similar patterns. No surveys were conducted in 1988 and 1992.
19. The vacancy data cover only around a third of all vacancies in the economy, making it a poor indicator of the ratio of vacancies to unemployed at any point in time. However, it remains a valuable measure for tracking demand for labour in the economy over time since the data deficiency is likely to be constant over time.

References

Bacon, N. and Storey, J. (1996), 'Individualism and collectivism and the changing role of trade unions', in Ackers, P., Smith, C. and Smith, P. (eds.), *The New Workplace and Trade Unions*, London: Routledge.

Belfield, C. R. and Heywood, J. S. (2002), 'The Desire for Unionization, HRM Practices and Coworkers: UK Evidence', Paper presented at the 23rd Annual Middlebury Economic Conference on Changing Role of Unions.

Booth, A. (1985), 'The Free Rider Problem and a Social Custom Model of Trade Union Membership', *The Quarterly Journal of Economics*, **100(1)**: 253–261.

Booth, A. (1989), '*What Do Unions Do Now?*, Discussion Papers in Economics, No. 8903, Uxbridge: Brunel University.

Booth, A. L. and Bryan, M. L. (2001), *The Union Membership Wage-Premium Puzzle: Is There a Free Rider Problem*, Working Paper, Institute for Social and Economic Research, Colchester: University of Essex.

Bryson, A. (1999), 'Are unions good for industrial relations?' in Jowell, R., Curtice, J., Park, A., and Thomson, K. (eds.), *British Social Attitudes: the 16th Report – Who shares New Labour values?*, Aldershot: Ashgate.

Bryson, A. (2001a), *Union effects on Workplace Governance 1983–1998*, PSI Discussion Paper No. 8, London: Policy Studies Institute.

Bryson, A. (2001b), 'The foundation of "partnership"? Union effects on employee trust in management', *National Institute Economic Review*, **176**: 91–104.

Bryson, A. (2001c), *Union Effects On Managerial and Employee Perceptions of Employee Relations in Britain*, Centre for Economic Performance Discussion Paper No. 494, London: London School of Economics.

Bryson, A. (2001d), *Unions and Performance: What's Going On?*, mimeo, London: London School of Economics.

Bryson, A. (2001e), *Employee voice, workplace closure and employment growth: A Panel Analysis*, PSI Discussion Paper No. 6, London: Policy Studies Institute.

Bryson, A. (2002), *The Union Membership Wage Premium: An Analysis Using Propensity Score Matching*, Centre for Economic Performance Discussion Paper No. 530, London: London School of Economics.

Bryson, A. (2003 forthcoming), 'Unions and Workplace Closure in Britain, 1990–1998', *British Journal of Industrial Relations*.

Bryson, A., Cappellari, L. and Lucifora, C. (2002*), Why So Unhappy? The Effect of Union Membership on Job Satisfaction*, Centre for Economic Performance Working Paper No. 1183, London: London School of Economics.

Bryson, A. and Gomez, R. (2002a), *Why Have People Stopped Joining Unions?*, Centre for Economic Performance Working Paper No. 1184, London: London School of Economics.

Bryson, A. and Gomez, R. (2002b), *You Can't Always Get What You Want: Frustrated Demand for Union Membership and Representation in Britain*, Centre for Economic Performance Working Paper No. 1182, London: London School of Economics.

Bryson, A. and Gomez, R. (2003 forthcoming), 'Buying in to Union Membership: Unionisation as an Experience Good', in Gospel, H. and Wood, S. (eds.) *Representing Workers: Trade Union Recognition and Membership in Britain*, London: Routledge.

Bryson, A. and McKay, S. (1997), 'What about the workers?' in Jowell, R., Curtice, J., Park, A., Brook, L., Thomson, K. and Bryson, C. (eds.), *British Social Attitudes: the 14th Report – The end of Conservative values?*, Aldershot: Ashgate.

Carruth, A. and Disney, R. (1988), 'Where have two million trade union members gone?', *Economica*, **55**: 1–19.

Charlwood, A. (2000), *Prospects for Trade Union Growth in Great Britain: Evidence from the 1998 British Social Attitudes Survey*, Paper for Leverhulme Trust 'Future of Trade Unions in Modern Britain' Workshop, 12 December.

Diamond, W. and Freeman, R. (2001), 'Liking the Workplace You Have: the incumbency effect in preferences toward unions', Working paper 115, Centre for Economic Performance, London: London School of Economics.

Disney, R. (1990), 'Explanations of the Decline in Trade Union Density in Britain: an Appraisal', *British Journal of Industrial Relations*, **28(2)**: 165–177.

Deery, S. and Walsh, J. (1999), 'The Decline of Collectivism? A Comparative Study of White-Collar Employees in Britain and Australia', *British Journal of Industrial Relations*, **37(2)**: 245–269.

Edwards, P. K. and Bain, G. S. (1988), 'Why Are Unions Becoming More Popular? Trade Unions and Public Opinion in Britain', *British Journal of Industrial Relations*, **26**: 311–126.

Farber, H. S. (2001), *Notes on the Economics of Labor Unions*, Working Paper No. 452, Princeton: Princeton University, Industrial Relations Section.

Farber, H. S. and Western, B. (2000), *Round Up the Usual Suspects: The Decline of Unions in the Private Sector, 1973–1998*, Working Paper No. 437, Princeton: Princeton University.

Forth, J. and Millward, N. (2000), 'The Determinants of Pay Levels and Fringe Benefit Provision in Britain', Discussion Paper No. 171, London: National Institute for Economic and Social Research.

Freeman, R. and Pelletier, J. (1990), 'The impact of industrial relations legislation on British union density', *British Journal of Industrial Relations*, **28**: 141–64.

Gomez, R. and Gunderson, M. (2002), *The Experience Good Model of Union Membership*, Paper presented at the 23rd Annual Middlebury Economic Conference on Changing Role of Unions.

Green, F. (1990), 'Trade Union Availability and Trade Union Membership In Britain', *The Manchester School*, **LV111(4)**: 378–394.

Green, F. (1992), 'Recent Trends in British Trade Union Density: How Much of a Compositional Effect?', *British Journal of Industrial Relations*, **30(3)**: 445–458.

Heery, E. (2002), 'Partnership versus organising: alternative futures for British trade unionism', *Industrial Relations Journal*, **33(1)**: 20–35.

Kennedy, P. (1998) *A Guide to Econometrics*, 4th edition, Oxford: Blackwell.

Machin, S. (2000) 'Union Decline in Britain', *British Journal of Industrial Relations*, **38(4)**: 631–645.

Machin, S. (2001), 'Does it still pay to be in or to join a union?', mimeo, London: London School of Economics.

Machin, S. and Blanden, J. (2001), 'Cross-generational Correlations of Union Membership', Centre for Economic Performance Working Paper No. 1181, London: London School of Economics.

Metcalf, D., Hansen, K. and Charlwood, A. (2001), 'Unions and the Sword of Justice: Unions and Pay Systems, Pay Inequality, Pay Discrimination and Low Pay', *National Institute Economic Review,* **176 (April)**: 61–75.

Millward, N., Bryson, A. and Forth, J. (2000), *All Change at Work?*, London: Routledge.

Phelps Brown, H. (1990) 'The counter-revolution of our time', *Industrial Relations*, **29(1)**: 1–14.

Reynolds, L., Masters, S. H. and Moser, C. H. (1999), *Labor Economics and Labor Relations*, 11th edition, Prentice Hall.

Sneade, A. (2001), 'Trade union membership 1999–2000: an analysis of data from the Certification Officer and the Labour Force Survey', *Labour Market Trends*, 433–444

Stewart, M. (1983), 'On Least Squares Estimation when the Dependent Variable is Grouped', *Review of Economic Studies*, **50(4)**: 737–753

Trade Union Congress (TUC) (2001), *Reaching the missing millions: Report of the TUC's Promoting Trade Unionism Task Group*, London: Trades Union Congress.

Western, B. (1995), 'A Comparative Study of Working-Class Disorganization: Union Decline in Eighteen Advanced Capitalist Countries', American Sociological Review, **60**: 179–201.

Wood, S., Moore, S. and Willman, P. (2002 forthcoming) 'Third Time Lucky? Statutory Union Recognition in the UK', *Industrial Relations Journal*.

Acknowledgements

The National Centre for Social Research wishes to thank the Department for Trade and Industry and the Department for Education and Employment for funding towards the modules of questions on industrial relations. The authors would like to thank the Leverhulme Foundation for its financial assistance under its 'Future of Trade Unions in Modern Britain' programme; Funmi Mashigo and Georgia Hay at the Office for National Statistics for providing the seasonally adjusted time-series workforce and vacancies data for Great Britain; and Francis Green for useful comments. Alex Bryson would also like to thank the Economic and Social Research Council (grant R000223958) and the Regent Street Polytechnic Trust for their financial assistance.

Appendix

Description of control variables and their mean values

Mean values for independent variables

Variable	Mean
Female	.49
Non-white	.05
Aged 18–24 years	.14
Full-time employee	.79
Manual occupation	.40
Gross earnings	
High	.38
Medium	.21
Low	.35
Missing	.06
Qualifications	
High	.31
Medium	.37
Low/none	.32
Region	
Scotland/Wales	.13
Midlands/North	.42
South	.44
Manufacturing	.22
Union recognition	.55
Unemployment-vacancy ratio	12.9
Number of employees at workplace	
<10	.16
10–24	.16
25–99	.26
100–499	.24
500+	.17
Sector	
Public	.29
Private	.60
Voluntary/other	.03
Missing	.08
Left–right scale	
High	.36
Medium	.32
Low	.32

Bases:

For those data available since 1983, N = 21,343 employees

Number of employees unavailable in 1983, N = 20,526

Sector unavailable in 1983 and 1995, N = 19,078

Qualifications unavailable in 1983 and 1984, N = 19,511

Left-right scale unavailable before 1986, N = 14,913.

Data derivation

Here we describe the derivation of variables where it is not self-evident what we have done.

Earnings

Respondents are asked to identify which of a number of gross earnings bands covers their own earnings. During the series the number of bands has increased from 11 to 24 with values varying to reflect the rise in earnings over the period. For our analyses of union density and never-membership we recoded the gross earnings bands into an ordinal variable with five categories ranging from 'much below average' to 'much above average'. 'Low' includes 'much below' and 'below average'; 'Medium' is 'average' and 'High' is 'above average' or 'much above average'.

For our analysis of the union wage premium we produce estimates of gross hourly earnings using the banded earnings data and continuous hours data for the period 1983–2001. The estimation technique is described later in the appendix.

Qualifications

These relate to individuals' highest qualification. 'High' means degree or higher education below degree. 'Medium' means 'A level' or 'O level' or equivalent. Low means 'CSE' or equivalent or 'none'.

Unemployment-vacancy ratio

The unemployment-vacancy ratio was constructed by the authors and is a consistent seasonally adjusted time-series for Great Britain derived from series provided by the Office of National Statistics. The unemployment measure is the number of unemployed in the spring of each year using the ILO definition, and the vacancy data are the official figures for the same period.

Left–right scale

The left–right scale is an additive index which is described in more detail in Appendix I to this Report. This well-tried and tested index measures an underlying ('latent') attitudinal dimension relating to employees' perceptions of distributive justice. Those with lower scores on the continuous scale running from 1 to 5 are more likely to favour government economic intervention and the reduction of inequality than are those with higher scores. We distinguish between 'left', 'centre' and 'right' according to scores on the index. Those on the 'left' score below 2.2 on the scale, those in the 'centre' score 2.2–2.75 and those on the 'right' are those with above 2.75. Previous research shows union members are significantly more likely to be 'left-wing' (have a lower score) on the index than non-members (Bryson, 1999).

Analytical Methods

Shift-share analysis
We use shift-share analysis to analyse declining union density and rising never-membership. In what follows, our notation relates to union density, but it can apply similarly to never-membership.

Following Green (1992), the change in union density between the early years in our series (1983–1985) and the later years (1999–2001) can be written as:

$$\Delta M = \sum_g m_g^{9901} p_g^{9901} - \sum_g m_g^{8385} p_g^{8385}$$

where m_g is union density within group g, p_g is the proportion of all employees in group g, superscripts delineate the grouped years, and the sum is over all groups. Shift-share analysis splits the decline in density into three components so the first equation may be rewritten as:

$$\Delta M = \sum (m_g^{9901} - m_g^{8385}) p_g^{8385} + \sum (p_g^{9901} - p_g^{8385}) m_g^{8385} + \sum (m_g^{9901} - m_g^{8385})(p_g^{9901} - p_g^{8385})$$

The first term on the right-hand side of the expression is the fall in membership density that would have occurred if the employee composition had stayed the same in 1999–2001 as in 1983–1985 but within-group densities had fallen. The second term is the fall that would have occurred due to change in employee composition if within-group density had stayed at its 1983–1985 level. The third term is the interaction of the above two effects and is generally small by comparison.

Linear probability estimation of membership and never-membership
Linear probability models are a multivariate extension of the shift-share technique for assessing changing determinants of membership. Let

$$Y_i = \beta X_i + \varepsilon_i$$

where Y_i is a 0/1 dummy variable denoting whether individual i is a member (or a 'never-member' in the case of the never-membership analysis), X_i is a vector of variables representing the groups or workforce dimensions mentioned above, β is a vector of coefficients and ε_i is an error term. The estimated predictions βX_i are interpreted as the probabilities that individual i is a member. There are two drawbacks to the technique. First, the value of βX_i may be outside the range 0–1, so that it can not be interpreted as a predicted probability. In fact, the linear probability model gives results close to the logit model which transforms the probability to avoid this problem. We ran all our models as logits, confirming that results were indeed very similar. Following Green (1992) we chose to use the linear probability model because it is the closest multivariate analogue to the shift-share analysis. The second drawback is that the model is prone to heteroscedasticity (Kennedy, 1998: 243). We employ the Huber-White robust variance estimator that produces consistent standard errors in the presence of heteroscedasticity.

There are two sets of estimates to identify the separate contributions of workforce compositional change and within-group change as described in Table 3.2. The first set of analyses model membership for each group of years, generating a mean predicted rate of membership based on employees' characteristics for that group of years. We call these our 'unrestricted predictions'. The second set of analyses are run for a base group of years (1983–1985): these estimates are used to predict rates of membership in later years, effectively holding within-group changes constant. (In essence, the model coefficients for the 1983–1985 period are applied to the characteristics of the workforce in later years.) The difference between predicted membership rates under the unrestricted models versus the restricted models indicates the contribution of compositional change to falling union density. The contribution of within-group change to declining membership is simply the difference between the actual membership rate for a year, relative to the baseline period, minus the amount of the change arising from employment shares.

Interval regression estimation of the union wage mark up

Our dependent variable is log gross hourly wages. Although *British Social Attitudes* contains continuous hours data for the period 1985–2001, it only contains banded weekly earnings data, so that we only know the lower and upper bounds for each individual's wage. Furthermore, the data are top-coded so that we only have a lower bound for the highest earners. Therefore, we estimate hourly wage for each individual using interval regression, a generalisation of the tobit model for censored data, initially developed by Stewart (1983) for banded earnings data. We use the SVYINTREG procedure in STATA 7, a robust estimation procedure which makes allowance for sample design when calculating point estimates and standard errors. See Forth and Millward (2000, Appendix B) for the log likelihood function and details of the estimation methodology. Analyses are weighted for the individual's probability of sample selection and we employ the Huber-White robust variance estimator that produces consistent standard errors in the presence of heteroscedasticity.

The union wage premium is simply the exponential of the union membership dummy coefficient minus 1, that is exp(coef)-1.

Between 1985 and 1995 the *British Social Attitudes* hours question did not ask respondents to include or exclude overtime hours. Since 1996 hours data including and excluding overtime hours have been available. The results presented here include overtime hours since 1996. Since union members in *British Social Attitudes* work more overtime hours than non-members, the premium is a little lower than in analyses excluding overtime hours. However, the pattern of results is very similar.

The control variables in the analysis are: gender, age, ethnicity, qualifications, manual worker, full-time worker, establishment size, public sector, manufacturing, and region. The size and direction of union effects can be biased by variables omitted from the analysis. However, if we assume that the effects of these omitted variables are fixed over time, our analyses should reasonably represent the movement in the wage premium over time.

Linear probability models estimating membership by grouped year, 1983–2001

	1983–1985	1986–1989	1990–1994	1995–1998	1999–2001
Female	0.046	0.027	0.012	0.014	0.039
	(2.31)*	(1.85)	(0.80)	(1.00)	(2.70)**
Non-white	-0.029	-0.020	0.020	0.047	0.058
	(0.64)	(0.59)	(0.63)	(1.81)	(2.07)*
Aged 18–24	-0.039	-0.041	-0.069	-0.076	-0.079
	(1.85)	(2.52)*	(3.31)**	(3.76)**	(3.88)**
Full-timer	0.149	0.098	0.050	0.041	0.024
	(5.67)**	(5.19)**	(2.72)**	(2.25)*	(1.27)
Manufacturing	-0.116	-0.046	-0.067	-0.049	-0.048
	(6.32)**	(3.34)**	(4.26)**	(3.28)**	(3.06)**
Manual	0.135	0.111	0.098	0.080	0.076
	(7.82)**	(8.45)**	(7.52)**	(6.04)**	(5.68)**
Gross earnings (ref: high)					
Mid-level	0.012	-0.018	-0.023	-0.051	-0.070
	(0.55)	(1.08)	(1.38)	(3.11)**	(3.99)**
Low	-0.082	-0.107	-0.140	-0.142	-0.153
	(3.62)**	(6.11)**	(7.56)**	(7.79)**	(7.53)**
Missing	-0.017	-0.089	-0.071	-0.105	-0.071
	(0.56)	(3.21)**	(2.72)**	(3.80)**	(2.60)**
Region (ref: South)					
Scotland/Wales	0.081	0.122	0.095	0.104	0.100
	(3.25)**	(6.94)**	(4.98)**	(5.45)**	(5.33)**
Midlands/North	0.081	0.077	0.070	0.069	0.074
	(4.79)**	(5.98)**	(5.35)**	(5.38)**	(5.56)**
Union recognition	0.634	0.640	0.606	0.538	0.514
	(41.86)**	(57.13)**	(49.82)**	(43.72)**	(38.69)**
Constant	-0.108	-0.057	0.023	0.045	0.038
	(3.46)**	(2.56)*	(1.00)	(1.99)*	(1.68)
Base	*2434*	*4344*	*4502*	*4909*	*4391*
R-squared	0.45	0.47	0.45	0.38	0.37

Notes:

a. These are linear probability models estimating the (0,1) outcome of being a union member. Results are almost identical when replicated using logistic regression techniques.

b. Coefficients are percentage changes in the probability of membership.

c. T-statistics are in parentheses. * means significant at 95 per cent confidence level. ** means significant at 99 per cent or above.

4 Support for state spending: has New Labour got it right?

Peter Taylor-Gooby and Charlotte Hastie [*]

The 2002 Budget signalled an abrupt change of direction in the government's spending strategy. During its first two years in office, New Labour had followed the highly restrictive spending plans of the 1992–1997 Conservative government, and then permitted cautious increases in highly targeted spending in specific areas, financed through less obtrusive 'stealth taxes' or the rearrangement of existing priorities. The 2002 Budget, however, announced "a significant increase in resources for the NHS" (Treasury, 2002a), to be funded via a one per cent increase in National Insurance contributions. This tax increase (which applies to both employers' and employees' contributions) is expected to raise about £9 billion a year when it is introduced from April 2003 (TUC, 2002:4). It will finance a 7.4 per cent a year increase in NHS spending between 2002–2003 and 2007–2008, in line with the recommendations of the Wanless Review (Treasury, 2002b), and will cost nearly £8 billion in the first year (Treasury, 2002c: 2). The balance of the money raised by the new taxes will go mainly on new Tax Credits for children and increases in the Working Families Tax Credit for low-paid workers.

The new spending plans are a defining moment for New Labour. They mark a shift from spending constraint and 'prudence' to policies which permit tax increases for improvements in highly valued services, more reminiscent of a traditional Labour approach. The Comprehensive Spending Review, published in July, built on this more expansive approach to spending, with an extra six per cent annual increase for education, eight per cent for transport and eight per cent for police and prisons between 2003/2004 and 2005/2006 (Treasury, 2002d: 1). However, these increases are to be financed by savings elsewhere, greater efficiency and general growth, not tax increases.

This chapter considers why the NHS has been singled out for extra tax-financed spending and has been placed at the vanguard of Labour's advance in

---

[*] Peter Taylor-Gooby is Professor of Social Policy at the School of Social Policy, Sociology and Social Research, University of Kent. Charlotte Hastie is a Research Assistant in Social Policy at the School of Social Policy, Sociology and Social Research, University of Kent.

public provision. It discusses how far the new policies will retain their glamour, once the tax increases bite home. It also examines some of the factors that influence willingness to pay more tax, especially the extent to which knowledge – or ignorance – about the cost of different services, and the social context in which they operate, influences support for better welfare.

Public spending priorities

Since the series started in 1983, the *British Social Attitudes* survey has long shown strong and increasing support for higher public spending on the main welfare state services – particularly health, education and pensions. As the next table shows, in 1983 the majority position was that things should stay as they are (54 per cent), with just a third (32 per cent) wanting to see taxes increase and one in ten (9 per cent) wanting them to be cut. However, the position altered in just a few years and, by 1991, as many as 65 per cent saw a need for increased taxation to fund public spending. Over the next decade, the average support for increased taxes was around six in ten, with very few people calling for tax and service cuts. Support for increased taxes fell sharply in 2000, back to levels not seen since 1987, no doubt partly reflecting disillusion with New Labour's performance in office. However, by 2001, it had recovered once again.

Table 4.1 Attitudes to taxation and spending, 1983–2001

Government should:	1983	1987	1991	1995	1996	1998	1999	2000	2001
	%	%	%	%	%	%	%	%	%
Increase taxes and spending on health, education and social benefits	32	50	65	61	59	63	58	50	59
Keep taxes and spending the same as now	54	42	29	31	34	32	35	40	34
Reduce taxes and spending	9	3	3	5	4	3	4	5	3
Base	*1761*	*2847*	*2918*	*1234*	*3620*	*3146*	*3143*	*2292*	*3287*

Of course, this question does not allow people to distinguish between different spending areas. To do this, we can examine responses to two further questions, one of which considers people's first and second priorities for higher spending in the main areas of government spending, while the other focuses specifically on social security spending.

When asked about public spending in general, people consistently prioritise health, followed by education, with both attracting increasing support over time.

In fact, as the following table highlights, by 2001 no other areas of public spending attracted anything close to the levels of support for more spending on health or education, with the next most popular areas of spending (police and prisons, and public transport) just managing to garner 11 per cent each. This increasing enthusiasm for health and education spending appears to have been at the expense of help for industry and housing. This undoubtedly reflects the changing health of the economy since the early 1980s, coupled with the state's retreat from the housing sector. Support for spending on social security and defence has also steadily decreased, while that for public transport has, perhaps unsurprisingly, increased.

Table 4.2 First or second priorities for extra public spending, 1983–2001

	1983	1987	1991	1995	1999	2001	1983–2001 change
	%	%	%	%	%	%	
Health	63	79	74	76	79	83	+20
Education	50	56	62	66	69	67	+17
Public transport	3	1	5	7	10	11	+8
Police and prisons	8	8	6	9	8	11	+3
Housing	21	24	21	14	11	8	-13
Social security	12	12	11	11	7	6	-6
Roads	5	3	5	3	7	5	nc
Help for industry	29	12	10	9	6	4	-25
Defence	8	4	4	3	2	3	-5
Overseas aid	1	1	1	*	1	1	nc
Base	1761	2847	2918	1234	3143	3287	

Note: As the table adds together first and second priorities for extra spending, columns sum to 200 per cent

To what extent do public priorities mirror *actual* spending priorities? The next table shows the proportion of government spending allocated to different spending areas, and how this has changed over time. This shows that there have been increases in health and education spending, and, over the last two decades as a whole, in social security. The NHS and education are, of course, long-standing public priorities and have received support even during the period of rigid spending restraint under the 1979–1997 Conservative governments and the first two years of New Labour. In other areas, spending has either been largely static or has decreased. In fact, echoing what we found when we looked at attitudes towards public spending, defence and help for industry have seen the largest declines in actual spending, followed by housing. It is notable that the high priority given by a minority to increased spending on public transport has

not been mirrored in reality – spending in this area has been generally static and is in fact quite low.

Spending is, of course, influenced by very many factors including demography – particularly relevant to pensions spending, health and education. However, there also appears, at least on the face of it, to be some correspondence between public priorities for public spending and actual spending.

Table 4.3 Spending in the main service areas as a proportion of total government spending, 1982/1983–2000/2001

	1982/ 1983	1986/ 1987	1990/ 1991	1994/ 1995	1998/ 1999	2000/ 2001	1982/1983 – 2000/2001 change
	%	%	%	%	%	%	
Social security	34	37	36	40	41	39	+5
Health	15	15	17	17	19	20	+5
Education	15	15	16	16	16	17	+2
Defence	15	15	13	10	9	9	-6
Police and prisons	3	4	5	5	5	5	+2
Help for industry	8	6	5	4	4	4	-4
Public transport	3	2	2	2	2	2	-1
Roads	2	3	3	3	2	2	0
Housing	4	3	3	2	2	1	-3
Overseas Aid	1	1	1	1	1	1	0

Source: Treasury 1991, 1996, 1998, 2001

Social security spending accounts for a considerable proportion of government spending, and obviously encompasses a wide range of services. The next table shows which of a variety of social security spending areas are people's first and second priorities for extra spending. Clearly, pensions have always been *the* top priority and their popularity has increased over time. Similarly, support for provision for disabled people has always taken second priority, although its level of support has been stable. Endorsement of benefits for unemployed people has fallen sharply from a third (33 per cent) in 1983 to around one in eight (13 per cent) by 2001. Whereas spending on children and lone parents attracted similar levels of public support in 1983, since 1991 children have stood out quite clearly as the public's third most popular area of social security spending, and support for lone parents has declined somewhat.

Table 4.4 First or second priority for extra spending on social security benefits, 1983–2001

	1983	1987	1991	1995	2000	2001	1983–2001 change
	%	%	%	%	%	%	
Pensioners	64	68	63	68	74	76	+12
Disabled people	58	54	58	58	61	57	-1
Children	20	24	35	33	33	35	+15
Lone parents	21	16	19	12	15	15	-6
Unemployed people	33	33	22	25	13	12	-21
Base	1761	2847	2918	1234	3426	3287	

Note: As the table adds together first and second priorities for extra spending, columns sum to 200 per cent.

Social security spending patterns have an equivocal relationship with public opinion. As the next table shows, spending on pensions, which is the public's top priority, remains roughly constant as the highest spending area, accounting for over two-thirds of social security spending. And spending on disabled people (the public's second priority) has risen since 1982/1983, though this in part could reflect changes in the way that unemployed people are classified. Spending on Child Benefit has fallen, although extra resources have been directed to child poverty through the Working Families Tax Credit and related provision. Spending on unemployed people has also fallen, partly because benefits for the unemployed have been held back as part of a make work pay strategy which is well in tune with public opinion (Hills and Lelkes, 2000). Spending specifically directed at the needs of lone parents, not a group prioritised by the public, is so low as to barely register.

Table 4.5 Spending on different areas of social security as a proportion of total social security spending, 1982/1983–2000/2001

	1982/1983	1986/1987	1990/1991	1994/1995	1999/2000	2000/2001	1982/1983–2000/2001 change
	%	%	%	%	%	%	
Pensions	69	69	73	71	67	68	-1
Child Benefit	19	17	15	15	15	15	-4
Disability benefits	4	7	9	10	12	12	+8
Benefits for the unemployed	8	7	3	3	6	6	-2
Lone parent benefits	0.5	0.4	0.6	0.7	0.2	0.2	-0.3

Source: Treasury, 1988, 1992. 2000.

So the spending priorities of both government and the public appear to have broadly similar contours, with notable exceptions in some areas. Pensions is the top public priority for increased social security spending, but policy in this area still implies strict limits on spending, with a substantial emphasis on the state's role being one of social assistance and the bulk of provision being supplied by the private sector. However, the particular priority being given to the NHS corresponds clearly with public opinion, partly explaining why health service spending formed the centrepiece of the Budget at the stage in the electoral cycle when any policies which are to bear fruit before the next general election (probably in 2006) must be put in place.

Why is the NHS people's top spending priority?

Public dissatisfaction with the health service has risen sharply under the current government. Figure 1 shows how the level of public concern about the NHS as a whole rose rapidly in the 1980s, fell in the early 1990s, and then rose sharply in 1996. (Note that the timescale in the graph is compressed in the earlier years.) Dissatisfaction fell immediately after the election of New Labour, but since then has risen to levels similar to those experienced during most of the Conservative years.

Figure 4.1 Dissatisfaction with the NHS, 1983–2001

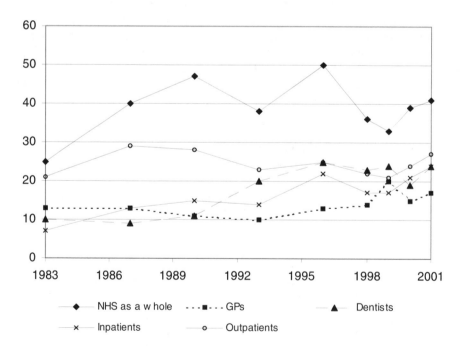

Dissatisfaction with each of the main component services which make up the NHS, especially outpatient and inpatient services, is also increasing. The increased dissatisfaction with outpatient services is particularly disturbing since levels of concern in this area had actually fallen during the Conservatives' term in office. It is particularly striking that dissatisfaction with both outpatients and inpatients services fell between 1996 and 1999, but has risen sharply since. For dentists and GPs the pattern is similar but slightly delayed.

Although the NHS is traditionally seen as an area of Labour strength, public disenchantment with New Labour's performance was clear by the start of the new century. This is reinforced when we consider answers to a question which asked people whether they thought "the general standard of health care on the NHS" had got better or worse over the previous five years. Nearly two-fifths (37 per cent) thought that things had got worse and just over one-fifth (22 per cent) thought they were better. It would appear that, thus far, Labour has failed to satisfy the public in the service area with which it is arguably most closely identified.

Table 4.6 Dissatisfaction with the NHS, by age, income, class, party identification and experience of the NHS, 1987–2001

% "very" or "quite" dissatisfied	1987	Base	1999	Base	2001	Base
Age						
18–36	42	930	36	806	44	586
54+	30	933	28	1234	35	823
Household income[+]						
High	46	672	41	612	48	364
Low	35	627	28	994	34	685
Class						
Professional/managerial	46	456	41	635	44	723
Working class	37	689	30	770	37	711
Party identification						
Labour	50	824	31	1333	37	995
Conservative	29	1095	35	785	46	486
Health service experience						
NHS inpatient in previous 12 months	40	600	33	275	40	616
Has private medical insurance	42	415	41	376	45	416
All	39	2847	33	3143	41	2188

[+]The income levels were defined as follows: 1987 high: £15,000+, low: £4,999 or below; 1999 high: £29,000+, low: £9,999 or below; 2001 high: £38,000+, low £11,999 or below.

We now turn to examine the levels of dissatisfaction expressed by different groups, focusing upon three key time points: 1987, 1999 (two years after New Labour's victory) and 2001. As the previous table shows, in each year, levels of

discontentment with the NHS are highest among higher income, middle-class and younger people and among those with access to private medical insurance (for a more detailed discussion of satisfaction with the NHS see Mulligan and Appleby, 2001). If we look at change over time we find a similar pattern for most groups: dissatisfaction declines somewhat at the end of the 1990s, but by 2001 returns to levels found 14 years before. A slightly different pattern exists when considering Labour and Conservative Party identifiers who, not surprisingly, swapped position on the NHS between 1987 and 2001 (in 1987 it was Labour identifiers who were the most dissatisfied with the NHS; by 2001 this applied to Conservative Party identifiers instead).

This suggests that, as far as their performance with the NHS is concerned, the government is noticeably failing to impress those better-off groups in the electorate who are not traditional Labour supporters and whom the party has been particularly keen to win over. More generally, it is clear that New Labour has not yet succeeded in convincing the public that it is delivering high-class public services in this most traditional Labour-friendly area of the welfare state.

Quite how to improve the quality of the health service has been a contentious issue for many years. For many commentators chronic under-funding is the NHS's main ailment, whereas some argue that money alone cannot make a huge difference unless it is linked to structural reforms. The 2001 survey began to explore these issues by asking whether it was managerial reform or more spending that was most important when it came to improving a range of public services. In the case of the NHS, the question asked:

> *Which of the following statements about the* <u>*NHS*</u> *comes closest to your own view?*
>
> *Changing the way the NHS is run would do a great deal to improve it*
> *Or*
> *Changing the way the NHS is run is not enough, the NHS also needs a lot more money*

Similar questions were asked about three other key areas – schools, police forces and public transport. As the next table shows, most people think that managerial change alone is unlikely to achieve real improvements, irrespective of the area under consideration. That said, for all four areas a significant minority – at least one in four, rising to one in three in the case of the police forces and public transport – felt that managerial reform could improve things a great deal. As we might expect from our earlier discussion, the NHS and education come top of the list in terms of their perceived need for extra resources in order to produce a better service.

So far we have seen that that the quality of NHS service is a matter of public concern across all social groups, but that dissatisfaction is rising most sharply among those groups whose votes the government needs to attract. Moreover, most people see increased spending as essential to solving the NHS's problems. It is thus a prime candidate for extra cash, and the government has clearly responded to this. This then raises questions as to how much people are willing

to pay to improve the NHS, a particularly pressing issue for New Labour in view of the large and visible tax increases to be implemented in 2003. It is to this that we now turn.

Table 4.7 The impact of managerial change versus extra spending

		Needs money to improve	Can be improved by changing the way it is run
NHS	%	69	25
Schools	%	66	26
Police forces	%	52	36
Public transport	%	52	38

Base: 2795

Paying for better public services

We begin by considering how much people would support an increase in income tax if it was set aside and only used to fund additional spending in a specific public service – a measure usually called hypothecation. The six services asked about were: the NHS, unemployment benefits, schools, public transport, pensions, and policing. To test the extent to which people's support for tax increases was dependent on how much the increase would cost, the sample was split randomly into two groups. One group was asked about an increase of 1p in the pound, and was told that on average this would mean about £100 a year for every taxpayer. The other group was asked about a 3p increase (equivalent to £300 annually).

In the next table we show the proportion of people who said that they were "strongly in favour" or just "in favour" of the proposed hypothecated tax increases (and a combined total showing the overall proportion in favour). The first three columns in the table show the levels of support for a 1p tax increase while the next three columns show support for a 3p increase. While the combined totals are a good general indication of their popularity, the extent to which people said they were "*strongly* in favour" is arguably a better indication of how acceptable such a tax increase would in reality be, as it focuses upon the 'hard core' supporters of increased taxation.

The table shows, as we might expect, considerable support for 1p tax increases to help finance the NHS, schools and pensions – all popular areas for additional public spending. Unsurprisingly, tax increases to fund better unemployment benefits were the least popular. When asked about a 3p increase, which would involve substantial payments for most people, the overall pattern of support remains the same, although the strength of feeling declines somewhat. So, for example, four in ten (41 per cent) strongly supported a 1p tax increase for the NHS, falling to one in four (25 per cent) strongly supporting a 3p increase.

However, even when it came to the 3p increase, a majority were still in favour overall of this level of tax increase to fund four of the six areas we considered; only public transport and unemployment benefits attracted limited support.

Table 4.8 Support for hypothecated tax increases

	1p increase			3p increase		
	% in favour	% strongly in favour	% all in favour (1p)	% in favour	% strongly in favour	% all in favour (3p)
	%	%	%	%	%	%
NHS	43	41	84	44	25	79
Schools	54	19	73	49	12	61
Retirement pensions	46	19	65	44	13	57
Policing	49	13	61	41	9	50
Public transport	34	8	43	26	5	31
Unemployment benefits	14	2	16	9	2	11
Base	1657	1657	1657	1630	1630	1630

How does the money that would be generated through our scenarios (an extra 1p and 3p in the pound) compare with the sums likely to result from the 2003 one per cent increase in National Insurance contributions? The employees' half of the £9 billion to be raised by higher National Insurance contributions is £4.5 billion, roughly equivalent in the tax burden that people will experience to an extra 1.6p in the pound on income tax (although the use of National Insurance concentrates the tax on earned incomes and does not spread it across taxable unearned income as an income tax increase would do). So the longer term impact on employees of the National Insurance contribution increase is likely to be somewhere midway between the 1p and 3p in the pound income tax increases referred to in our questions.

Table 4.8 perhaps helps us to understand why it is the Chancellor could be confident about introducing a tax-funded spending injection for the NHS. Of all the services asked about, only the NHS attracted the strong support of more than 40 per cent for a 1p increase, and more than 20 per cent for a 3p increase. For both the 1p and 3p increase, people were twice as likely to say they strongly supported a hypothecated tax for the NHS than they were for the next most popular areas (schools and pensions). The government's judgement in favour of extra taxes to pay for NHS improvements is therefore clearly endorsed in the greater enthusiasm to pay taxes for this particular service. However, only a minority (25 per cent) state very strong support for the policy that has been introduced, and dissent may grow stronger when the tax increases start to affect incomes in 2003/2004.

What will we get for our money?

Having asked people how much they would favour hypothecated taxes for various services, we then asked them how much of a *difference* they thought such tax increases could actually make. Taking the example of the NHS, we asked:

> *Now suppose the government **actually did** increase the basic rate of income tax by 1p/3p in the pound and set it aside just for spending on the **NHS**, how much do you think this would improve the NHS?*

Table 4.9 The perceived impact of tax increases on different public services

	% who think increase would improve the service a great deal/ quite a lot		Total public spending 2001/2002
	1p increase	**3p increase**	**%**
Schools	68	72	12.5
NHS	66	69	14.7
Retirement pensions	62	70	26.4
Policing	57	61	4.0
Public transport	52	54	8.0
Unemployment benefits	47	51	2.3
Base	*1657*	*1630*	

Spending calculated from: Treasury, 2001: 40-42.

Interestingly, the perceived impact of the extra spending did not really vary according to whether people were being asked about a 1p or a 3p tax increase. For example, as the previous table shows, 72 per cent thought that a 3p tax increase to fund extra spending on schools would improve them "a great deal" or "quite a bit", only marginally higher than the 68 per cent who thought a 1p increase would have this effect. However, there was a greater distinction in relation to pensions, where 62 per cent thought a 1p increase would bring about some improvement, and 70 per cent thought this of a 3p increase. The biggest service improvements were expected in schools, the NHS and pensions, broadly matching the pattern of support for each tax increase that we have already seen. This is intriguing because, of course, one would expect a given tax increase to have a greater impact on a service with a *small* budget than on a service with a larger one. These findings indicate that ideas about service improvement as much reflect beliefs about the priority of the service as they do beliefs about the likely impact of a particular sum on a particular budget. Nonetheless, it is clear that the public expects to see real and noticeable improvements in the NHS as a

result of the tax increases introduced in the 2002 Budget. The government has picked out the health service for extra tax-financed spending, and people clearly think it can make some difference; now Labour must deliver.

Public knowledge and public attitudes

The fact that public ideas about what it takes to improve a particular service appear to be influenced as much by attachment to the service area in question (rather than, say, by the relative scale of the increased funding) raises difficult issues for governments seeking to plan public spending in a way that will both meet service goals and obtain an enthusiastic response from the voters. To explore these issues further, we now examine a range of indicators of public knowledge and awareness in order to see how they relate to people's willingness to pay for improved provision. We will focus on two groups of questions; one dealing with people's awareness of the relative size of different government spending areas, and the other with knowledge of specific policy relevant topics.

Table 4.10 Perceptions of the relative size of public spending in different spending areas

	Largest amount of money	Next largest amount of money	Least amount of money	Actual spending on these areas 2001/2002
	%	%	%	%
Social security benefits	33	19	2	39.3
Health	28	26	6	20.1
Education	8	22	3	17.1
Defence	19	14	3	8.8
Police and prisons	3	7	3	4.8
Help for industry	1	2	16	4.2
Roads	2	3	15	2.1
Public transport	0.8	1.5	8	1.4
Housing	1	3	10	1.2
Overseas aid	4	4	31	1.0

Base: 3287

Spending calculated from: Treasury, 2001: 40–42.

Our questions about relative spending levels asked respondents to say which of a range of spending areas they thought had the largest amount of money spent

on it, followed by the next largest, and then the least. As the previous table shows, people judge the relative magnitude of public spending in different areas more or less accurately, although there are some very noticeable exceptions. A third correctly knew that social security has the most money spent on it, and just over a quarter (26 per cent) were accurate in their assessment that health received the next largest amount of money. About a third (31 per cent) correctly knew that, among the areas they were asked to consider, overseas aid is given the smallest amount of money. Leaving aside the assessments of the second largest spending area (probably the hardest of the three estimations to make), the most striking inaccuracy is the one in five people (19 per cent) who think defence represents the largest area of government spending, possibly a hangover from the post-war period and a response to the visibility of military projects (although our survey took place *before* the war in Afghanistan began). There is also some confusion about the smaller spending areas, although when indicating the area they thought got the least money, 83 per cent of people picked one of the spending areas whose overall proportion of public spending was less than five per cent.

Table 4.11 Perceptions of the relative size of social security spending

	Largest amount of money	Next largest amount of money	Least amount of money	Actual spending on these areas 2001–2002
	%	%	%	%
Retirement pensions	28	20	24	67.4
Children	11	22	14	14.7
Benefits for disabled people	4	9	39	11.9
Benefits for unemployed people	44	27	3	5.9
Benefits for single parents	13	22	17	0.2

Base 3287

Spending calculated from: DWP, 2000: 90-92.

There is more public confusion when we focus upon different types of social security spending. As the previous table shows, there is a huge exaggeration of the amount spent on unemployed people and on lone parents (the two groups which attracted the *lowest* support for increased spending), and a concomitant downplaying of spending on disabled people (who were the second most popular nominees for extra spending). So the 'undeserving' groups are clearly seen as consuming very much more of the total social security budget than they do in reality. This may of course influence government enthusiasm for high visibility campaigns to reduce fraud, channelling those without jobs into work

through the New Deal and similar schemes, and ensuring that benefits for the jobless are held down while incomes at the bottom of the labour market are improved through a 'make work pay' strategy (DSS, 1998: 1 and 23). It is likely that spending on these groups bulks larger in popular fantasy than in public budgets partly at least because of the media attention given to such issues.

Clearly, some public confusion exists about spending levels, particularly when it comes to social security spending. But perhaps the knowledge we should be assessing is broader, more to do with the *context* within which British public policy operates than with detailed spending levels. To do this, we asked a series of questions about general 'social issues'. For example, one question asked:

> *Of every 100 children under 16 in Britain today, about how many do you think live in poverty?*

Using the same question format each time, we asked people to give us a number out of 100 for each of the issues shown in the following table. The table also shows current 'reality' for each issue, with the final column presenting an indication of the magnitude of public misconceptions in different areas, by calculating the 'gap' between people's estimations and the current situation.

Table 4.12 Perceptions of social issues compared with reality

Per cent of	Public estimate	Current reality	Gap (estimate – reality)
Crimes involving violence	52	22	+30
People in Britain who are Black or Asian	32	7	+25
Workers paid £40k+ per year	28	8	+20
Secondary pupils in private schools	23	9	+14
Those receiving operations who pay privately	27	13	+14
Children under 16 in poverty	28	21	+7
People who own or have use of a car	77	70	+7
Current workers who will rely mainly on a private pension when they retire	55	57	-2

Base: 3287

Sources for 'current situation', in order: Home Office, 2000: 33-34; ONS, 2001: tables 7.1–7.2; DfEE, 2001: tables 8 and 42; Laing and Buisson, 2000: 87; DWP, 2001: 30 (poverty defined as income below household median after housing costs); ONS, 2000: 197; ONS, 2002: 77; ONS, 2001: 32.

This exercise shows that, in general, people tend to exaggerate reality (the one exception being access to a private pension, which they ever so slightly underestimate). The most extreme example relates to crime, with the public estimate as to the proportion of crimes that involve violence being, at 52 per

cent, wildly in excess of reality, as 'only' 22 per cent of crimes can be classified in this way. (This gap between perception and reality is likely to be related to the fact that violent crime is often featured heavily in the media, is usually *the* key crime indicator of greatest political concern, and as a result therefore seems more common than is actually the case.) The table is presented in ascending order of accuracy, with the most inaccurate at the top and the most accurate at the bottom. It suggests that those areas which are most familiar to people (for instance, car ownership) tend to be judged most accurately, indicated by the fact that, as the numbers in the 'current situation' column increase, those in the 'gap' column fall.

Social knowledge and social groups

Of course, we might expect to find considerable differences between one group and another in their perceptions about levels of government spending, and their levels of knowledge about related areas. After all, certain groups will always have better access to information and a greater ability to evaluate it. So, before considering the relationship between perceptions of spending, and views about increasing taxation to pay for extra spending, we first examine the extent to which groups differ in their understanding of the issues at stake.

Education is a likely candidate – but so too are a range of broader characteristics related to social status. Political ideologies are also important in influencing the way people understand questions which relate to public policy. Accordingly, we examined differences in perceptions and awareness according to a range of measures tapping educational attainment, social class, income and political party support.

We begin by considering people's awareness about basic levels of government spending. The next table shows the views of a range of social groups as to which public service obtains the *biggest* share of the spending cake. For simplicity, we focus only on the four largest areas of public spending, and on the smallest. The results of this exercise are very mixed. On the one hand, the most common response from many groups is indeed the correct one – social security. A third of those without qualifications correctly identify this as attracting the largest share of government spending. Commonly, the next most frequent response is health (chosen by 24 per cent of the non-qualified). However, there are some notable exceptions to this rule – many confined to the 'better off' groups whom we earlier speculated might be among the *most* knowledgeable. Take, for example, people with degrees. This group are most likely to identify the NHS as receiving the most government spending even though, in reality, it lags some way behind social security. One in ten think that education gets the most money – and nearly a quarter think the same of defence! Similarly, professional and managerial workers are more likely to think that the NHS gets the most money, whereas those in working-class occupations are more likely to say – correctly – this applies to social security. The reasons for this are likely to be complex. They may partly reflect the increased exposure of less well-off groups to various elements of the social security system. However,

as we shall see later, less well-off and less well-educated groups tend to wildly overestimate the proportion of the social security budget spent on groups commonly seen as 'undeserving' (such as the unemployed and lone parents). This makes it possible that their correct identification of social security as the recipient of the largest amount of government money is mistaken and actually reflects an overestimate of the amount of money being spent on benefits for these groups.

Table 4.13 Public perceptions of the most expensive public spending area, by education, party identification, income and social class

		Social security (39%)	Health (20%)	Education (17%)	Defence (9%)	Overseas aid (1%)	Base
				Spending area (% of current total expenditure for each area in brackets)			
Education							
Degree	%	28	35	10	23	0	483
No qualifications	%	34	24	8	16	7	831
Party identification							
Labour	%	30	29	8	20	4	1416
Conservative	%	40	29	7	14	3	708
Household income							
£38,000+	%	32	36	7	19	3	545
£11,999 or below	%	35	22	8	18	5	1028
Class							
Professional/ managerial	%	29	35	10	21	2	1031
Working class	%	31	23	8	19	7	1002

When it comes to spending on different aspects of the social security system, as shown in the next table, *everyone*, bar those with degrees, incorrectly thought that benefits for the unemployed accounted for the largest share (whereas it is, of course, only a very small proportion). The scale of some of the misperceptions is striking. Only around one in five (22 per cent) people without qualifications correctly identified pensions as the largest spending area, but six in ten thought benefits for the unemployed and lone parents accounted for the largest share. In reality these two areas account for just six per cent of the total of the five spending areas we considered.

  So, when looking at perceptions of public spending in general, and social security spending in particular, it is remarkably striking that no group have particularly accurate perceptions. Even relatively well-educated and middle-class people share general misunderstandings about basic issues of social

security spending. These findings are of particular importance for the current government since its own supporters are, if anything, more likely than others to *minimise* the proportion spent on education, social security and pensions, and to exaggerate defence spending. They are as likely as other groups to exaggerate unemployment and single parent spending as well. In areas where spending is relatively low, all things being equal, voters should probably expect better results from extra taxes – the tax increases we asked about were of the same magnitude and would therefore result in larger percentage increases when it came to the smaller spending areas.

Table 4.14 Public perceptions of the most expensive social security spending area, by education, party identification, income and social class

		Pensions (67%)	Children (15%)	Disabled people (12%)	Unemploy- ment (6%)	Single parents (0.2%)	Base
		Social security spending area (% of current total expenditure for each area in brackets)					
Education							
Degree	%	48	7	0	38	7	*483*
No qualifications	%	22	13	6	39	20	*831*
Party identification							
Labour	%	27	11	5	44	13	*1416*
Conservative	%	31	10	2	45	12	*708*
Household income							
£38,000+	%	37	9	2	47	7	*545*
£11,999 or below	%	26	13	8	37	17	*1028*
Class							
Professional / managerial	%	39	10	2	43	6	*1031*
Working class	%	19	11	7	45	18	*1002*

Similar results emerge when we look at knowledge about some of the different 'social issues' we considered earlier. In general the answers for each of the different social groups follow a similar pattern – irrespective of education level, political orientation, income or social class, people are still relatively well informed about child poverty and access to cars, and relatively ill-informed about crime and pay differentials. The variations between the different groups follow the pattern we found when looking at perceptions of social security spending – that better off, professional and managerial workers and, particularly, better-educated people tend to be more accurate in their perceptions of social issues than other groups.[1] It is notable, however, that only in their estimation of child poverty were they completely or very nearly correct. Party political differences in knowledge emerge only in relation to child

poverty, with Labour Party identifiers overestimating its prevalence to a much greater extent than their Conservative counterparts. Intriguingly, identifiers with both parties equally misjudged the proportion of workers earning high incomes.

  These findings have two main implications. Firstly, people who have misconceptions about state spending levels may tend to exaggerate the savings to be made, or the money currently wasted, in particular areas – the most notable candidates for confusion being defence, and benefits for unemployed people and single parents. Secondly, inaccurate knowledge may lead to mistaken assumptions about the success (or ineffectiveness) of government policies

Social knowledge and social spending

We conclude by considering the relationship between awareness of public spending and social issues and willingness to pay extra tax. This shows that a person's knowledge (or lack of it) about social spending *is* linked to their views about the acceptability of tax increases. In the next table, each row focuses on a specific area of government spending – the NHS, education, public transport and so on. The key figures in each row relate to two groups of people; those who thought that spending area obtained the *highest* proportion of government spending (the first column of percentages) and those who thought it obtained the *lowest* (the second column). Then, for each group, the proportion who supported a 3p tax increase for the spending area in question is shown. For example, the first row shows that, among those who thought the NHS got the most government funding, two-thirds supported a 3p tax rise. However, among those who thought the NHS got the *least* funding, eight in ten supported a tax increase of this magnitude. The final column shows the overall proportion of people who supported increasing taxes by 3p to pay for this service. The cells in the table based upon numbers which are too small to give a reliable estimate are shown in brackets.

Table 4.15 Perceptions of spending and willingness to pay 3p extra in tax for higher spending

	Perception of spending in the service area				
% who support a 3p tax increase for ...	**Highest**	*Base*	**Lowest**	*Base*	All *(Base 1630)*
... the NHS	66	*410*	80	*106*	79
... schools	53	*127*	(73)	*32*	61
... public transport	(21)	*16*	39	*133*	31
... policing	42	*71*	(76)	*42*	50
... pensions	52	*458*	68	*389*	57
... unemployment benefits	8	*668*	(23)	*59*	11

The table shows that those who believe spending in a particular area is low are, not surprisingly, keener for taxes to be increased in order to fund additional spending than are those who think spending in that area is high. This follows the common-sense view that perceptions of low spending in an area (all things being equal) will enhance support for higher spending, and vice versa. However, the relative enthusiasm for more spending on a particular area (measured by the rank-order of proportions of those willing to pay extra tax) is very similar whether we consider those who think the spending on a particular service is highest or lowest. In both cases, for instance, the NHS clearly emerges as *the* favourite candidate for extra spending, and unemployment benefits as the least. A minor exception is the importance attached to policing among the relatively small group who think this area obtains the lowest levels of funding, indicating the particular importance they attach to this service.

The main implication of this for government is that perceptions of high spending are likely to inhibit support for extra finance in that area. So incorrectly exaggerated assumptions about current NHS spending among a considerable group in the population may reduce their willingness to pay increased sums in tax in order to fund higher spending in this area, and thus reduce support for current government policies. Similarly, commonly held misconceptions about the scale of unemployment benefit spending may make it difficult to increase support for increased spending on those without work. Public education is thus necessary to develop support for welfare policy reforms. However, ideas about spending levels do not appear to exert a major influence on the overall *order* of public priorities for more expenditure; the NHS still remains top of people's wish list, whether they think it gets the most government funding, or the least.

Although perceptions of government spending are related to a person's views about the desirability of increased spending in that area, they are not linked to a person's knowledge about social issues more generally. The one exception relates to unemployment benefits. Those who take the (relatively unusual) stance of supporting tax rises in order to increase spending on benefits for unemployed people tend to have exaggerated misconceptions of the level of both child poverty and high pay.[2] So support for more spending in this area seems, rather plausibly, to be linked to general perceptions about inequality within British society.

Conclusions

The commitment to achieve a step change in NHS spending, financed by substantial increases in National Insurance contributions, marks a substantial shift of direction by New Labour. Our findings clearly show that the government's policies are in tune with public attitudes – whether we consider spending priorities, dissatisfaction with current provision, willingness to pay or the perception that extra money is needed to improve the NHS. Priorities in other service areas are real but are not so pressing. Government awareness of this is reflected in the Comprehensive Spending Review decision to direct

public expenditure towards education, transport and crime. And the public's clear expectations that more tax will result in evident service improvements is reflected in the Review's emphasis on the strict monitoring of the way resources are spent and the 'determination to set demanding targets' so that increased resources are deployed to the greatest effect (Treasury, 2002d: 2–3).

This congruence between the priorities of government and the public follows a pattern revealed in previous surveys. As Hills and Lelkes (2000) showed, New Labour's social security priorities during its first term in office – to direct resources towards low-income working families and to children and to take public concerns about social security fraud seriously – followed the priorities set by public attitudes closely.

The picture is less clear when we consider people's willingness to pay extra tax at levels similar to those being implemented. While most people accept that real improvements in public services require additional spending (rather than managerial reform), enthusiasm to pay substantial tax increases at the levels required is limited. Only a minority express very strong enthusiasm for the changes. So, although the NHS is clearly *the* area in which tax-financed spending increases will be most acceptable to the public, it is uncertain whether support will be eroded once the increase in National Insurance contributions takes effect in 2003. Then their impact will depend on how large they appear to be when considered alongside inflationary pressures, job prospects and people's annual pay awards.

The public have a fairly good level of general understanding about both the rough contours of public spending and the background to various public policy issues. However, there are notable misperceptions. In particular, large numbers exaggerate the scale of spending on benefits for unemployed people and single parents and, to a lesser extent, on defence. These misunderstandings are most marked among less well-off and less educated groups, but are by no means confined to them alone. In general (as one might expect) people are more willing to pay extra taxes for services that they think are less well-funded.

So, overall, we can draw two general conclusions. Firstly, the government *has* correctly judged the public mood. The public are convinced that more spending is necessary to improve public services, and the NHS is the top priority for higher spending. It is also the service for which most people are most willing to pay more in tax. However, the public grossly misunderstands spending on the 'undeserving' poor. Consequently, a responsive government, determined to convince the public that its expenditure policies are prudent, will have considerable scope when it comes to the NHS and other 'popular' spending areas, but will find it difficult to improve benefits for some of the most vulnerable groups in society.

Secondly, willingness to pay tax increases at the levels necessary to have an impact upon the NHS is weaker than general endorsements of the *idea* of extra NHS spending. So the flagship NHS policies are themselves vulnerable to a backlash from public opinion if the extra spending does not produce tangible results and if tax rises coincide with a continuing economic slowdown. The impact of tax increases will depend upon the economic circumstance at that

time – and the future condition of the UK economy is one thing that is not under the direct control of the Chancellor.

Notes

1. For example, when considering the number of crimes that involve violence, the 'gap' between perception and reality (see Table 4.12 for more details as to how this gap is constructed) is lower among people with degrees (a still hefty 17 points) than it is among those with no qualifications whatsoever (39 points).
2. Among those who support increased spending on unemployment benefits, the 'gap' between their perceptions about the prevalence of child poverty and the reality is 16 points, compared with an average of seven points among the sample as a whole.

References

Department for Education and Employment (2001), Statistics of Education: Schools, DfEE/DfES webpages.

Department for Work and Pensions (2000), *Opportunity for All: Second Annual Report*, Cmnd 4865, London: HMSO.

Department for Work and Pensions (2001), *Households Below Average Income 1994/5–1999/00*, London: HMSO.

Department of Social Security (1998), *A New Contract for Welfare*, Cmnd 3805, London: HMSO.

Hills, J. and Lelkes, O. (2000), 'Social security, selectivism and redistribution' in Jowell, R., Curtice, J., Park, A. and Thomson K. (eds.), *British Social Attitudes: the 16th Report – Who shares New Labour values?*, Aldershot: Ashgate.

Home Office (2000), *The 2000 British Crime Survey: England and Wales*, London: HMSO.

Laing and Buisson (2000), *Laing's Healthcare Market Review 2000–2001*.

Office for National Statistics (2000), *Social Trends*, London: The Stationery Office.

Office for National Statistics (2001), *Social Trends*, London: The Stationery Office.

Office for National Statistics (2002), *Social Trends*, London: The Stationery Office.

Mulligan, J. and Appleby, J. (2001), 'The NHS and Labour's battle for public opinion', in Park, A., Curtice, J., Thomson, K., Jarvis, L. and Bromley, C. (eds.), *British Social Attitudes: the 18th Report – Public policy, Social ties*, London: Sage.

Treasury (1988), *The Government's Expenditure plans 1988–89 to 1990–91 Volume II*, Cmnd 288 II, London: HMSO.

Treasury (1991), *Public Expenditure Analyses to 1993–94*, Cmnd 1520, London: HMSO.

Treasury (1992), *Social Security: the Government's Expenditure Plans 1992–93 to 1994–95*, Cmnd 1914, London: HMSO.

Treasury (1996), *Public Expenditure: Statistical Analyses 1996–97*, Cmnd 3201, London: HMSO.

Treasury (1998), *Public Expenditure: Statistical Analyses 1998–99*, Cmnd 3901, London: HMSO.

Treasury (2000), *Social Security Departmental Report: The Governments Expenditure Plans 2000/01–2001/02*, Cmnd 4614, London: HMSO.

Treasury (2001), *Public Expenditure Statistical Analyses 2001–02*, Cmnd 5101, London: HMSO.

Treasury (2002a), *Budget 2002: The Strength to make Long-Term Decisions*, 17 April, Treasury website.

Treasury (2002b), *Securing our Future Health: Taking a Long-Term View* (Wanless Report), Public Enquiry Unit, London: HMSO.

Treasury (2002c), Budget 2002: A Summary leaflet, April.

Treasury (2002d), *2002 Spending Review: Opportunity and security for all*, July.

Trades Union Congress (2002), *TUC Budget Analysis*, TUC Fund Managers, London: TUC.

Acknowledgements

The authors and the *National Centre for Social Research* are grateful to the Economic and Social Research Council for funding this module of questions under grant number R000239188.

5 Education, education, education

Ted Wragg and Katarina Thomson [*]

In education policy terms, the beginning of the 21st century was unique in Britain's history. Not only had the Labour government won a massive three-figure majority for the second general election in succession, but it did so with Prime Minister Tony Blair's assertion still intact that "Education, education, education" would be his three top priorities.

Beneath that general promise lay several more detailed intentions. Primary education, generally agreed to have been neglected since the period of euphoria following the Plowden Report in 1967, was given higher prominence during New Labour's first term in office. There were several aspects to this strategy, including: a daily literacy and numeracy lesson, with detailed prescription of their content; reducing class sizes in infant schools to below 30 pupils; and giving primary schools additional money for teaching resources, such as books and equipment. The strong belief in a link between education and prosperity also affected policy for much older age groups, with universities being given the target of recruiting 50 per cent of under-30 year olds by the year 2010. Universities had already expanded rapidly during the 1990s, from recruiting one in seven young people to one in three. Such expansion was beginning to create financial pressures on students, on universities and on the government itself, thereby opening up a public debate about who should pay for higher education that was much wider than it would have been 40 years earlier when fewer than one in ten went to university.

The issue of selection, which during the 1960s and 1970s had revolved around the abolition of the 11-plus examination in most areas and the establishment of comprehensive schools, had resurrected itself during the last few years of John Major's Conservative government, after he promised that there would be a grammar school in every town. David Blunkett, on his appointment as the first Labour Secretary of State for Education since Shirley Williams in 1979,

[*] Ted Wragg is Professor of Education at Exeter University. Katarina Thomson is a Research Director at the *National Centre for Social Research* and Co-Director of the *British Social Attitudes* survey series.

immediately countered this with an invitation to "read my lips". His message was "no more selection"; yet, by the end of his period of office in 2001, specialist secondary schools were being allowed to select some pupils on the basis of ability in the arts, languages, science, sport (or whatever else they had chosen as their 'specialist school' field). This aspect of policy was criticised as evidence that Labour was veering too far to the right in an attempt to woo middle-class voters who were not their traditional supporters.

The findings of the *British Social Attitudes* series shed fascinating light on these central issues. We begin by examining whether the public shares the government's readiness to pay more for better education. Then we turn to assessing whether the government's priorities for educational reform match the public's, most notably in terms of smaller class sizes and more emphasis on exams. We examine public views about higher education in the light of its expansion in the 1990s. And, finally, we follow up the debate about whether the government is pandering to middle-class voters by looking at whether these policies chime particularly well with the views of the various social classes.

Paying more for better education

First we consider whether the public is prepared to pay more for better education. For this to be the case, we would need to be able to show that the public is both willing to devote resources to public expenditure in general and that it would prioritise education within this expenditure. On the first of these matters, the picture has been pretty clear since the mid-1980s. As we saw in Chapter 4 (Table 4.1), when asked to think about taxation and public expenditure, from 1985 onwards clear majorities have favoured increasing the amount spent on public services, funded through higher taxes (over either the *status quo* or decreasing public expenditure).

On our second big question – whether the public shares the government's desire to keep education at the top of its list of priorities – Figure 5.1 shows that education wins a high level of support. It consistently ranks second behind health as people's top priority for extra public spending, when respondents were asked to choose which, if any, of a range of public services would be their highest priority for extra spending. It has always scored well above the third placed priority and, for most of the period, above all priorities other than health and education put together. Moreover, the gap between health and education has narrowed over the last decade, although it is now broader than it was in the late 1990s. In 1999, for instance, the proportion of people putting education as their first priority was at its highest ever level (34 per cent), leaving it only 13 percentage points behind health (compared with a gap as large as 42 percentage points in 1989). A similar picture emerges when looking at first and second priorities for expenditure combined. Around three-quarters or more mention health as their first or second priority for extra expenditure (83 per cent in 2001), but the proportion mentioning education has grown from around half in the early 1980s to around two-thirds from 1995 onwards (67 per cent in 2001).

Figure 5.1 First priority for extra government spending, 1983–2001

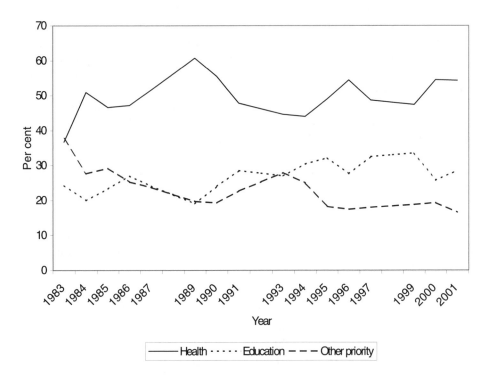

Not surprisingly, people's views vary significantly according to whether or not they have children. In 2001, two-fifths (41 per cent) of those with children under 18 put education as their top priority, compared with a quarter (24 per cent) of those without children of this age. But even this very sympathetic group of parents still favoured health as their top priority, though with the latter at 47 per cent, the gap between health and education was a small six percentage points.

Priorities within education

Political debate about education varied during the 1980s and 1990s, and so too did the public's spending priorities. As seen in the next table, when asked to choose between a range of different education spending areas, special educational needs tended to be the most commonly picked area for extra government spending in the 1980s and early 1990s. In this respect, there was no difference between parents and non-parents. The estimated one in five children with a special need had initially become a major area of focus after the publication of the Warnock Report in 1978, and re-emerged three years later after the 1981 Education Act, which gave parents the right to see statements

written about their child. As a priority, it then recedes somewhat by the mid-1990s, while mainstream primary and secondary education move up in the public mind. Until the 1990s, primary schooling had been a relatively neglected area so its jump from being the main priority of one in six in 1993 to that of a quarter by 2001 marks a notable upward move in the public consciousness. This nevertheless suggests that the public sees special needs and secondary schooling as being more important than primary education, which is the reverse of the actual priorities during the first Blair government.

Nursery and pre-school education experiences a fluctuating profile over time in line with its prominence in public debate. Its low was in 1987 when less than one in ten people chose it as their main priority for extra government spending in this area; at its high, two-fifths opted for it in the mid-1990s when the Conservative government launched nursery vouchers. Meanwhile, increasing spending on students at university has never been a common priority, and hovers consistently at around one in ten throughout the two decades.

Table 5.1 Highest priority for extra government spending within education, 1983–2001

	1983	1985	1987	1990	1993	1994	1995	1996	1998	1999	2000	2001
	%	%	%	%	%	%	%	%	%	%	%	%
Special needs	32	34	29	29	34	28	19	21	21	25	26	22
Secondary school	29	31	37	27	29	28	32	25	24	24	28	29
Primary school	16	13	15	15	16	11	18	21	24	21	22	23
Nursery/pre-school	10	10	8	16	11	21	21	17	17	14	13	10
Students at university	9	9	9	9	7	9	9	11	9	12	9	13
Base	*1761*	*1804*	*2847*	*1400*	*1484*	*1167*	*1227*	*1221*	*1035*	*1052*	*1133*	*1107*

Primary education

One of the major promises made in 1997 by the incoming Labour government was to bring infant school class sizes down to below 30 pupils. This was quite a controversial policy: in addition to being very specific, there were also widespread doubts about whether it was a wise move, either educationally or politically. The real effect of class size on the quality of education is hard to assess because it is not easy to carry out the sort of true experiment that might offer convincing evidence. (Assessing over a significant period of time the learning of groups matched for ability, but varying in size, would no doubt lead to complaints from parents whose children had been placed in very large classes purely for the purposes of research.) Such little research evidence as exists, like the Tennessee 'Star' project, suggests that numbers need to fall below 20 to

ensure significant gains, hence the political sensitivity of such a policy given the increased costs involved (Wood *et al.*, 1990).

Despite the lack of clear research evidence, there is little doubt that class size is widely regarded as important by the public. When asked what measure would most improve primary education, there has been relatively little variation in attitudes over the years, with class size invariably soaring above the other options. After all, one of the common reasons given by parents when opting for private education, is that their child will be in a much smaller class. The next table confirms the public's preoccupation with smaller class sizes, which by 2001 resulted in two-fifths selecting it as the most effective way of improving primary education. Other aspects of primary school improvement to receive support were the development of pupils' skills and interests, and the provision of books. A similar question asked before 1995 confirms that these same areas were also the top priorities in the 1980s. These findings are not surprising, given that large classes and lack of resources had been among the elements of primary schooling most criticised in the press during the 1980s and 1990s, which is why the incoming Labour government promised in the first place to reduce infant school classes to below 30 pupils and soon after election gave each school an additional £4,000 for books.

Table 5.2 Most effective measure to improve primary education, 1995–2001

	1995	1996	1998	1999	2000	2001
	%	%	%	%	%	%
Smaller class sizes	36	35	37	36	39	41
More resources for buildings, books and equipment	19	21	15	19	17	14
Better-quality teachers	16	19	21	16	14	17
More emphasis on developing the child's skills and interests	16	12	12	13	14	13
More links with parents	9	6	8	8	9	8
More information about individual schools	1	1	2	2	1	2
Better leadership within individual schools	n.a.	2	2	2	2	1
More emphasis on exams and tests	1	1	1	1	1	1
Other	1	1	0	1	2	1
Base	*1227*	*1221*	*1035*	*1052*	*1133*	*1107*

n.a. = not asked

However, it is particularly notable that certain policy matters greatly favoured by governments do not chime so closely with the public's preferences. True, 'better-quality teachers' is a common political catchphrase which does strike a chord with respondents, with between one in five and one in six giving it top priority. Nevertheless, surveys tend to show that most parents are satisfied with their children's teachers, so this factor may keep the totals lower than newspaper reports criticising the quality of teaching would suggest. Most striking of all is the lack of priority given to high profile government priorities such as school leadership, information about schools, more exams and tests. These more organisational factors are clearly less closely related to improving school performance in the minds of the public. They barely accumulate five per cent between them, which is surprising, given the massive publicity accorded to 'superheads', parents' charters of one kind or another, public examinations results and school league tables.

It is also interesting that concern over class sizes *rose* rather than fell in 2000 and 2001, despite the fact that infant classes had almost all been reduced to below 30 by the end of that period. Further evidence on this comes from the *British Election Panel Study* 1997–2001. In this study, the same group of people were asked each year how successful they thought Labour had been in meeting each of their key 1997 election pledges. As the next table shows, scepticism as to whether class sizes had been reduced was expressed by over half the respondents as late as 2000, perhaps partly explained by the press publicity given to *junior* school classes increasing in size as infant classes were reduced. Of course, the early years in this table were early days for the policy and it could hardly be expected to transform schools over night. In the end, by 2001, there was recognition by around half the population of its success.

Table 5.3 Success of Labour government in cutting class sizes in schools, 1997–2001

	1997	1998	2000	2001
	%	%	%	%
Very successful	3	2	2	3
Fairly successful	31	24	37	46
Not very successful	30	49	42	35
Not at all successful	11	15	10	11
Too early to tell/Don't know	25	10	9	5
Base	*2989*	*2807*	*2400*	*2312*

Source: *British Election Panel Study 1997–2001.*

Selection

The issue of selection straddles both the primary and the secondary sector, but the question asked as part of the *British Social Attitudes* survey focuses on selection at secondary level:

> *Which of the following statements comes closest to your views about*
> *what kind of secondary school children should go to?*
> *Children should go to a different kind of secondary school, according*
> *to how well they do at primary school*
> *All children should go to the same kind of secondary school, no matter*
> *how well or badly they do at primary school[1]*

This issue became once more a matter of debate when the Labour government committed itself to reforming secondary education during its second period of office. Central to this policy was the dissolution of what the Prime Minister's spokesman controversially called the 'bog standard comprehensive' school. Half of secondary schools were to become specialist schools and to be given permission to select a small proportion of their pupils on ability in their specialist area, like the arts, sport, languages or science.

As seen in the next table, just over a half of people oppose selection at secondary level, and just under a half support it. There appears to have been a slight ebbing away of public support for selection from 1999 onwards, perhaps marking the contrast between the political promises before and after the 1997 election, or the lively debate sparked off by the prominence given to specialist schools and whether or not they marked a defection from Labour's traditional opposition to selection by ability.

Table 5.4   Support for selection in secondary schools, 1984–2001

	1984	1987	1990	1994	1998	2001
	%	%	%	%	%	%
Selective	50	52	48	49	50	45
Non-selective	40	41	44	48	48	52
Base	*1675*	*2847*	*1400*	*1167*	*1035*	*1107*

Secondary education

Labour governments of the 1960s and 1970s made the reorganisation of secondary schools and the ending of selection their top priority for education policy. Very little else was emphasised, as issues such as the curriculum and examinations were traditionally left untouched by politicians at that time. This

situation did not change until the mid-1980s, when governments became more interventionist.

The role of the secondary sector in preparing pupils for adult life and the world of employment had been of some interest, but had not received much detailed attention. However, concern had been expressed about whether or not schools were succeeding in this area. A parliamentary select committee report in 1977 was typical of the criticism of poor-quality careers advice during the late 1970s and 1980s, so a great deal of effort was put into offering young people work experience (Expenditure Committee, 1977). The Technical and Vocational Education Initiative, begun in 1983, was intended to offer a coherent programme for 14–18 year olds.

To assess public confidence about the extent to which secondary schools are fulfilling their different roles we asked:

> *From what you know or have heard, ... how well [do] you think state*
> *secondary schools nowadays ...*
> *... prepare young people for work?*
> *... teach young people basic skills such as reading, writing and maths?*
> *... bring out young people's natural abilities?*

Table 5.5 Success of state secondary schools preparing young people for work, 1987–2001

	1987	1990	1993	1995	1996	1998	1999	2000	2001
	%	%	%	%	%	%	%	%	%
Very well	2	2	5	5	4	6	6	5	5
Quite well	27	35	38	35	34	40	43	50	45
Not very well	54	50	47	49	51	45	41	39	44
Not at all well	15	11	8	7	8	6	7	5	4
Base	1281	1233	1306	1058	1038	847	833	972	941

Table 5.6 Success of state secondary schools bringing out pupils' natural abilities, 1987–2001

	1987	1990	1993	1995	1996	1998	1999	2000	2001
	%	%	%	%	%	%	%	%	%
Very well	3	4	6	5	5	8	7	7	4
Quite well	32	32	40	37	35	43	42	44	44
Not very well	49	50	42	44	46	38	38	41	43
Not at all well	15	12	10	10	11	10	10	6	7
Base	1281	1233	1306	1058	1038	847	833	972	941

Tables 5.5, 5.6 and 5.7 show that public faith in state secondary schools has increased steadily since the late 1980s. About half the population now thinks that secondary schools do "very" or "quite well" in preparing young people for work and in bringing out their natural abilities, up from around a third in 1987.

Around three-quarters think that secondary schools do very or quite well at teaching the three Rs, a notable increase from just over a half in 1987. This seems surprising since it was not until the Labour government's second term that emphasis really extended from the primary to the secondary sector. Nor is this merely a case of partisan attachments (that is, Labour supporters thinking secondary education must be better just because it is run by a Labour government). Supporters of all three main parties think that secondary education has improved under the Labour government on each of the three measures considered here. For example, in 1996, towards the end of the long period of Conservative rule, half of Conservative and Liberal Democrat supporters (49 and 50 per cent respectively) thought that schools were very or quite good at teaching the three Rs, compared with almost two-thirds of Labour supporters (62 per cent). Come 2001, these figures had jumped to around three-quarters for all three groups (76 per cent for Labour and Liberal Democrats, 71 per cent among Conservatives). So the proportion who thought secondary schools were doing well had risen faster among Conservative supporters than among Labour supporters during the 1997–2001 Labour government.

Table 5.7 Success of state secondary schools teaching three Rs, 1987–2001

	1987	1990	1993	1995	1996	1998	1999	2000	2001
	%	%	%	%	%	%	%	%	%
Very well	10	9	12	11	10	12	13	16	12
Quite well	46	48	53	49	46	53	55	59	61
Not very well	31	33	25	30	33	28	24	20	21
Not at all well	11	8	7	6	8	5	7	3	4
Base	*1281*	*1233*	*1306*	*1058*	*1038*	*847*	*833*	*972*	*941*

The finding that the public perceives improving standards in secondary education is open to different possible interpretations. On the one hand, it could mean that the public feels that sufficient steps have been taken to improve the teaching of 'basics' following criticism in this particular area. But, on the other hand, it might be based on a misunderstanding. After all, during 2000 and 2001 a great deal of government publicity was given to reaching national targets in English and mathematics, and to the perceived success of recently introduced literacy and numeracy hours. However, all these developments took place in *primary schools*, so it is possible that secondary schools may have benefited from the surge of publicity.

We also asked what measures respondents thought would be most important in improving secondary schools. As seen in the next table, smaller classes, more competent teachers and more resources are top of their wish-list. These priorities have remained notably steady over time. They are also remarkably similar to the concerns expressed about class sizes and resources in the primary sector (although the proportions indicating smaller class sizes are considerably smaller than the 40 per cent level recorded for younger children). Meanwhile, although it is at secondary level that examinations and tests might perhaps be expected to be seen as more important, only three per cent thought that putting more emphasis on these would be the most effective way to improve secondary education.

Table 5.8 Most effective measure to improve secondary education, 1995–2001

	1995	1996	1998	1999	2000	2001
	%	%	%	%	%	%
Smaller class sizes	21	21	20	22	24	27
Better-quality teachers	19	21	23	20	18	24
More resources for buildings, books and equipment	18	21	17	18	17	15
More training and preparation for jobs	15	13	12	12	11	10
More emphasis on developing the child's skills and interests	13	10	10	11	14	11
More emphasis on exams and tests	6	5	8	4	6	3
More links with parents	4	3	5	5	6	4
Other	1	0	0	1	2	1
More information about individual schools	0	1	1	1	1	1
Better leadership within individual schools	n.a.	2	2	2	2	2
Base	*1227*	*1221*	*1035*	*1052*	*1133*	*1107*

n.a. = not asked

Higher education

Expansion of higher education

Higher education appears, on the surface at any rate, to be a less attractive topic to pragmatic governments. Whereas policies on school education will affect virtually 100 per cent of the population, higher education impacts only on a

successful minority. Furthermore, parents (a significant constituency among voters) are directly involved in their children's schooling in a way that they are not by the time their children enter higher education. However, the importance of this sector has changed dramatically over recent years as higher education has begun to affect the lives of far more families and individuals than before. While 12 to 14 per cent of young people took part in higher education in the 1970s and 1980s, this rose to over a third by 2001. The government then set a target, to be achieved by the year 2010, that 50 per cent of all young people should take part in higher education before they are 30. This significant move from an elite to a mass system of higher education has raised many fundamental questions about the purpose and value of higher education, and about gaining access to it, as well as about financing both the institutions and the individuals within them.

When the *British Social Attitudes* Report series last looked at higher education (Rootes and Heath, 1995), universities had just experienced a period of massive expansion, accompanied by increasing support for further expansion. Despite this, the authors noted several reasons why support for further expansion might wane. First, if more school leavers go on to higher education, then having a degree loses its status as an automatic passport to a well-paid job. This, they speculated, was beginning to be underlined by press reports about graduate unemployment. Parents and young people alike might become more dubious about whether the investment required for a university education was worth the cost. Secondly, those already with degrees – and who expect their children to obtain degrees – may become less keen on a further expansion which could threaten their privileged position in the job market. In other words, they might want to 'pull up the ladder behind themselves'.

In the event, there was an economic boom in the post-1995 period, during which, graduates found that getting a well-paid job was relatively easy. This led to demands that they should shoulder more of the financial burden of higher education themselves, since they would eventually reap the benefits. Unexpectedly, therefore, it was a Labour government which abolished student maintenance grants completely and introduced a £1,000 means-tested tuition fee surcharge on students. Contrast this with the experience of the then Conservative Secretary of State Sir Keith (later Lord) Joseph who, on contemplating a similar charge on students for their tuition during the mid-1980s, was barricaded in his office by anxious MPs from his own party, who feared a backlash from angry parents in their constituency. Then the idea was quietly dropped.

We have already seen that higher education is not – and never has been – a major public priority for additional spending, even when we confine our attentions to priorities *within* the education sector. When asked whether or not "opportunities for young people in Britain to go on to higher education should be increased or reduced, or are they at about the right level now", the majority say that the situation is now about right. What is noticeable, however, is that there may have been some substance in the 1995 predictions made by Rootes

and Heath about waning appetite for expansion. As the next table shows, the proportion opting for expansion in 2000 was, at 44 per cent, almost identical to that found in the early 1980s, compared with 52 and 53 per cent in 1987 and 1990. Of course, the 2000 figure has to be interpreted in the light of the higher education sector now being much larger than in 1983.

Table 5.9 Attitudes towards the expansion of higher education, 1983–2001

Higher education should be ...	1983	1985	1987	1990	1993	1994	1995	1999	2000
	%	%	%	%	%	%	%	%	%
Increased a lot	22	25	29	32	32	32	28	25	27
Increased a little	22	24	24	20	17	17	19	19	17
About right	49	43	42	43	46	46	48	48	49
Reduced a little/ a lot	5	5	3	2	2	2	3	4	5
Base	*1761*	*1804*	*2847*	*1400*	*1484*	*1167*	*1227*	*1052*	*1133*

Further, Rootes and Heath predicted that – if their hypothesis about an impending decline in backing for expansion was correct – support would fall most strongly among those who already had a degree. Again, they found no evidence of this in 1994. Then, a half of all graduates supported expansion, nearly double the rate among those with no qualifications. However, as the next table reveals, between 1994 and 2000[2] there was a substantial fall in support for expansion among those with degrees (from 49 per cent to 29 per cent). As a result, there are no longer any significant differences between the views of people from different educational backgrounds.

Table 5.10 Attitudes towards the expansion of higher education, by level of education, 1994 and 2000

% saying opportunities for higher education should be 'increased a lot'	1994	*Base*	2000	*Base*
Highest qualification				
Higher education: degree level	49	*108*	29	*145*
Higher education: below degree level	35	*139*	30	*134*
A level or equivalent	37	*150*	24	*126*
O level or equivalent	27	*248*	27	*252*
CSE or equivalent or below	28	*515*	27	*474*

Grants, loans and fees

During the 1970s and 1980s about one in seven of the relevant age group went on to higher education. Student loans were introduced in 1990 by a Conservative government when that proportion began to increase substantially, reaching one in three of the age cohort by the end of the 1990s. As universities complained that their funding no longer matched the rapidly increasing student population, it was a Labour government which introduced charges for students' tuition fees to produce more revenue for the expansion.

The *British Social Attitudes* survey has asked about student grants and loans on a number of occasions. Unfortunately, as policy circumstances have changed, so too has the wording of our question. From 1983 to 1990, we asked:

> *When British students go to university or college, they generally get grants from the local authority. Do you think they should get <u>grants</u> as now, or <u>loans</u> which would have to be paid back when they start working?*

From 1995 to 2000, the question concentrated on the issue of loans without reference to grants:

> *Many full-time university students are now taking out government loans to help cover their living costs. They have to start repaying these loans when they begin working. Generally speaking, do you think that ...*
> *... students **should** be expected to take out loans to help cover their living costs,*
> *or, students **should not** be expected to take out loans to help cover living costs?*

Table 5.11 Attitudes towards student grants and loans, 1983–2000

	1983	1985	1987	1990	1995	1999	2000
	%	%	%	%	%	%	%
Grants	57	60	65	71	n.a.	n.a.	n.a.
Not loans	n.a.	n.a.	n.a.	n.a.	64	58	59
Loans	38	34	31	24	26	30	28
Base	*1761*	*1804*	*2847*	*1400*	*1227*	*1052*	*1133*

n.a.= not asked

These changes make it difficult to know whether the apparent slight decline shown in the previous table in support for grants between 1990 and 1995 (back

to the levels of the 1980s) reflects a real change in attitudes, or is the result of a change in question wording. What is clear, however, is that support for loans has *not* increased with their introduction and has remained at less than a third of the population.

However, responses to a different question, asked since 1995, suggest that support for grants might not be as wholehearted as at first appears. This new question produces a more fine-grained analysis of people's attitudes:

> *And, at present, some full-time British university students get grants to help cover their **living** costs. Getting a grant depends upon the student's circumstances and those of their family. Do you think that ... READ OUT ...*
> *... **all** students should get grants to help cover their living costs,*
> ***some** students should get grants to help cover their living costs, as now,*[3]
> *or, that no grants should be given to help cover students' living costs?*

As seen in Table 5.12, the overwhelming support is for a certain degree of discrimination: *some* students being offered grants, not *all* students. Those wanting grants for some students outnumber those supporting grants for all students by more than two to one.

Table 5.12 Attitudes towards student grants, 1995–2000

	1995	1999	2000
	%	%	%
All students should get grants	30	29	27
Some students should get grants	65	64	67
No grants	2	3	2
Base	*1227*	*1052*	*1133*

Further analysis reveals some intriguing variation according to people's educational background.

As Table 5.13 shows, those *without* degrees are more supportive of grants for all students than those with degrees. It is particularly interesting that graduates, who have themselves benefited from a university education and are thus likely to be higher earners, are *less* supportive of universal grants than those who have not been such beneficiaries. This may be related to anticipated income tax consequences for higher earners and to aspirations for their children amongst lower earners.

Table 5.13 Attitudes towards student grants, by level of education, 2000

	Degree	HE below degree	A level	O level	Below
	%	%	%	%	%
All students should get grants	19	28	31	22	30
Some students should get grants	75	67	65	73	61
No grants	1	2	2	1	3
Base	145	134	126	252	474

The quality of university education

As in 1994, we asked about the importance of a number of personal qualities that universities might develop in students. The next table shows that public views about the purpose of higher education are not especially radical and have barely changed since 1994. The qualities most sought are basic utilitarian ones, such as an ability to speak and write clearly, or the skills and knowledge to get a good job. The notion of challenging established ideas does not find much favour. This makes an interesting contrast with millennium aspirations in Japan and Korea, countries now laying more stress on 'individualism' (Cummings *et al.*, 2001).

Table 5.14 Importance of qualities that universities should develop in students, 1994 and 2001

% saying essential to develop	1994	2001
An ability to speak and write clearly	48	48
Knowledge that equips people for life	38	38
Skills and knowledge which help them get a good job	37	38
Self-confidence	31	34
How to live among people from different backgrounds	23	21
A readiness to challenge other people's ideas	14	14
Base	984	941

Rootes and Heath detected a difference in attitudes towards the purpose of universities, with those who had a degree showing the most enthusiasm for the 'civilising' mission of universities. In 1994, for example, a third of graduates thought it essential that the universities should teach students how to live among people from different backgrounds, and over a quarter (27 per cent) thought it essential that they should develop a readiness to challenge other people's ideas.

These figures compared with 22 per cent and 13 per cent respectively for non-graduates. However, by 2001 such differences have largely disappeared. A fifth (21 per cent) of both graduates and non-graduates now think it essential that universities teach students how to live among people from different backgrounds. Nor is there any statistically significant difference between graduates' and non-graduates' views as to whether it is essential that universities develop "a readiness to challenge people's ideas". It may be the case that the move to a mass rather than an elite system of higher education has now brought more people into contact with university students, either directly themselves or indirectly through friends and relatives, reducing the differences in attitudes between graduates and non-graduates.

A more searching question was also put to respondents: what does the public think that universities *actually* achieve? For each of the six areas mentioned above, like "self-confidence", or "an ability to speak and write clearly", we asked whether universities actually develop these "very much", "quite a lot", "not very much" or "hardly at all". As seen in the next table, between half and two-thirds thought that universities achieved these aims in 1994, and the picture is similar in 2001, though the utilitarian category ("skills and knowledge which helps them get a good job") moves up slightly in the public consciousness. Nevertheless, the overall picture is one of stability of attitudes towards the role and performance of higher education despite its considerable expansion.

Table 5.15 Universities' performance in developing qualities in students, 1994 and 2001

% saying developed very much or quite a lot	1994	2001
Self-confidence	65	67
A readiness to challenge other people's ideas	63	59
Skills and knowledge which help them get a good job	63	68
An ability to speak and write clearly	62	64
How to live among people from different backgrounds	56	60
Knowledge that equips people for life	50	51
Base	*984*	*941*

Is Labour reaching the middle class?

One of the criticisms of the Labour government from some of its own supporters is that it tries too hard to appeal to middle-class voters and neglects its traditional working-class constituency. The question arises, therefore, as to whether different social groups react in the same way to educational policy and initiatives. To assess this, we now look in detail at some of our findings to see how some of the policies described earlier, like class size and selection, appeal to the different social classes.

Smaller class sizes in primary schools

In fact, there are hardly any differences between the social classes in their views about how best to improve primary education.[4] Smaller class sizes are singled out by all classes as the most important factor, and this has been the case since the question was first asked in 1995. If we look at how this has developed over time, we can see from the next table that around a third of respondents from both the salariat and the working class mentioned smaller class sizes in the mid-1990s. The priority of this policy rose in the salariat from 1998 onwards, while working-class respondents took until 2000–2001 to follow suit. The figures for the petty bourgeoisie and manual foremen and supervisors need to be treated with caution as the bases are small for these groups.

Table 5.16 Smaller class sizes as most important measure to improve primary education, by social class, 1995–2001

% who gave smaller class sizes as most important improvement for primary schools	1995	1996	1998	1999	2000	2001	Base (smallest)
All	36	35	37	36	39	41	1035
Salariat	36	34	41	38	41	39	291
Routine non-manual	40	39	40	38	43	43	211
Petty bourgeoisie	34	36	35	40	43	45	61
Manual foremen/supervisors	36	33	27	40	34	46	68
Working class	35	34	33	33	36	40	287

Table 5.17 Support for Labour's policy of cutting class sizes, by social class, 1997–2001

% who support cutting class sizes 'a lot'	1997	1998	2000	2001	Base (smallest)
All	77	80	81	80	2312
Salariat	81	85	83	84	759
Routine non-manual	81	83	85	84	483
Petty bourgeoisie	68	75	74	81	192
Manual foremen/supervisors	79	79	78	74	166
Working class	74	76	77	75	640

Source: *British Election Panel Study 1997-2001.*

A slightly different picture emerges from the *British Election Panel Study* 1997–2001, mentioned earlier. Respondents were asked how much they

supported each of Labour's key policy pledges. It is, of course, a very popular policy, but the previous table suggests that the salariat sees smaller class sizes as slightly more important than does the working class. Before 2001, the petty bourgeoisie were the least supportive, but perhaps some are simply too anti-Labour to endorse any of its policies.

Selection

When it comes to the issue of selection there are greater distinctions between socio-economic groups, perhaps reflecting the fact that working-class people have traditionally been disadvantaged by selection practices. After all, when selection at the age of 11 was widely practised, it was working-class children who found it harder to penetrate the grammar schools. The legacy of this is that the salariat is several percentage points above the working class in its favouring of selection as a strategy. Even the salariat, however, seems to be getting slightly less enthusiastic about selection over time, and by 2001 a majority did not support it. So Labour's policies may in fact be appealing to middle-class sentiments that were more marked in the mid-1990s than in the 21st century. Alternatively, there may be some uncertainty in the light of the government's own confusion, between reading David Blunkett's lips ("no more selection") and then witnessing selection possibilities being introduced in the government's flagship specialist schools. In reality, however, it must be said that only seven per cent of specialist schools have actually utilised selection as a tool. The petty bourgeoisie stand out in their support for selection, but this finding should again be treated with caution because of the relatively small sample size.

Table 5.18 Support for selection, by social class, 1994–2001

% who support selection in secondary schools	1994	1995	1996	1998	1999	2000	2001	Base (smallest)
All	49	48	51	50	46	48	45	1035
Salariat	54	56	56	51	48	52	46	291
Routine non-manual	48	46	55	54	44	53	48	211
Petty bourgeoisie	55	53	60	62	55	47	69	61
Manual foremen	56	47	51	48	44	50	43	68
Working class	43	39	41	42	41	43	38	311

Conclusions

The advent of a two-term Labour government, following a four-term Conservative administration, produces some fascinating pictures of public

attitudes in a policy area which is now claimed as central by all political parties. In some respects, the Blair government appears to have identified certain policy issues, such as class size and the quality of teaching, which resonate with public concerns. On other matters, the political agenda seems wide of the mark, notably in its interest in more examinations and tests, and the provision of information about schools, none of which raises more than a tiny flicker of interest from respondents. And, despite the high priority accorded by the government to education, the public continues to rank it in second place to health, a finding that has been consistent over the last two decades, though the gap between the two has narrowed.

As the 21st century unfolds it will be interesting to observe the outcomes of some of these policies. Emphasis on the stratification of schools has already begun to produce greater polarisation, as middle-class professional families gravitate towards higher achieving schools, leaving schools in poorer areas with more pupils in receipt of free school meals (Gibson and Asthana, 1998). Despite this, appetite for overt selection has waned a little in the last few years and is now favoured by fewer than half the population.

The various phases of education will see different changes during the coming years. Nursery and pre-school education are scheduled for expansion, since it is now government policy to offer a nursery place to all three year olds whose parents want to have one. Pre-school education, however, does not achieve highest precedence in the public eye. The 2001 figure of ten per cent citing it as their top priority for extra spending marks a return to the levels of 1983–1985, This may well, of course, be a reflection of the success of the expansion of nursery education for three–four year olds, so that the public see less need for *extra* spending.

Primary education received considerable attention from the first Blair administration and the aim of the second Labour government is to give secondary education a similar treatment. The public appears more satisfied than previously with secondary schools in fields like teaching the three Rs and preparation for employment, with nearly three–quarters approving of schools' performance in the latter of these. But even in secondary schools there is virtually no appetite for more tests and examinations. In 2001, two–thirds mentioned smaller classes, teaching quality and the provision of resources as key factors for improvement, compared with only three per cent wanting more testing. Perhaps recent publicity about British pupils being among the most heavily examined in Europe has contributed to this, though the appetite for tests has never been particularly high.

Higher education is especially interesting. Labour's 2010 target that one in two young people should enter higher education before the age of 30 must, if it is to succeed, not only produce another 100,000 students, but will have to bring them through along different pathways. Alongside those following the traditional route of GCSE, A levels and a three-year degree, there will be others who take vocational GCSEs, introduced from 2002, a modern apprenticeship, and then sign up for a two-year foundation degree. This will produce a variety of challenges for all concerned: universities, politicians and the students themselves. It will certainly stimulate still further the debate about how students

and institutions are to be financed.[5] Certainly, there is no great public appetite for a further massive increase in university education. Whether this will change, given that much of the expansion will be in vocational fields, remains to be seen. After all, the utilitarian job-getting function of higher education is quite high in public esteem. However, our evidence that graduates are more reluctant than non-graduates to foot the bill for all future students will be disappointing for those who would like to see more altruism from beneficiaries.

Finally, there is the question of whether or not the Labour government's attempt to woo more middle-class supporters through its education policies has been successful. In many respects, we found little difference between the views of middle- and working-class respondents. However, on the issue of selection, the middle classes are slightly more in favour than the working class, although they are less keen now than they were in the mid-1990s. Specialist schools, a central plank of Labour's second term post-primary strategy, are permitted to select, even if few do so in practice. Whether or not Labour can still appeal to its traditional supporters through a set of policies that many of them do not support is a political judgement that will no doubt be put to the test in the coming years.

Notes

1. From 1984 to 1990, the question read:
   Some people think it is best for secondary schoolchildren to be separated into grammar and secondary modern schools according to how well they have done when they leave primary school. Others think it is best for secondary schoolchildren not to be separated in this way, and to attend comprehensive schools.
   On balance, which system do you think provides the best all-round education for secondary schoolchildren ... READ OUT ...
   ... a system of grammar and secondary modern schools,
   or – a system of comprehensive schools?
2. Data are from 2000 as this question was not asked in 2001.
3. The words 'as now' were dropped in 2000.
4. The social class classification used in this chapter is the Goldthorpe schema, which is described in more detail in the appendix to this report.
5. This target has, however, already been met in Scotland which has long had a higher university participation rate than the rest of the UK, and where the traditional route is one of Highers, taken a year earlier than A levels, followed by a four-year degree.

References

Cummings, W.K., Tatto, M.T. and Hawkins, J. (eds.) (2001), *Values Education for Dynamic Societies: Individualism or Collectivism*, Hong Kong: Comparative Education Research Centre, University of Hong Kong.

Expenditure Committee (1977), *Tenth Report of the Expenditure Committee*, London: HMSO.

Gibson, A. and Asthana, S. (1998), 'Schools, pupils and examination results: contextualising school "performance"', *British Educational Research Journal*, **24(3)**: 255–268.

Rootes, C. and Heath, A. (1995), 'Differences of degree: attitudes towards universities' in Jowell, R., Curtice, J., Park, A., Brook, L. and Ahrendt, D. (eds.), *British Social Attitudes: the 12th Report*, Aldershot: Dartmouth.

Wood, E., Johnston, J., Bain, H.P., Zaharias, J.B., Lintz, M.N., Achilles, C.M., Fogler, J. and Breda, C. (1990), *Student/Teacher Achievement Ratio (STAR): Tennessee's K-3 Class Size Study, Final Report*, Nashville, Tenn.: Tennessee State Department of Education.

Acknowledgements

The *National Centre for Social Research* are grateful to the Department for Education and Employment, and its successor the Department for Education and Skills, for their financial support which enabled us to ask the questions reported in this chapter.

6 Illegal drugs: highs and lows

Arthur Gould and Nina Stratford [*]

Over the last five years there have been a number of signs that attitudes towards illegal drugs are changing, at least among elite groups such as the media, politicians and senior police officers. In 1997, for instance, the *Independent on Sunday*'s campaign to decriminalise cannabis gained the support of a large number of eminent people from all walks of life. Senior police figures, including the Chief Constable of Cleveland, called for "the legalisation and subsequent regulation of some or all drugs" (Shaw, 1999). However, in the face of the hard line being taken by the incoming Labour government, there seemed little likelihood of a more liberal drugs policy. Three years later, the report of an independent inquiry into the Misuse of Drugs Act called for cannabis to be re-classified as a class C drug (Police Foundation, 2000). That same year, the shadow home secretary, Anne Widdecombe, made a speech at the Conservative Party annual conference calling for on-the-spot fines for cannabis users. Although party members seemed pleased, six of her colleagues let it be known to the press that they had used cannabis themselves when young. Whether or not their main intention was to embarrass Widdecombe, the message that emerged was that they did not consider cannabis to be particularly harmful. More interesting still was the reaction of the press. Widdecombe was dubbed 'Doris the Dope' by the *Daily Mirror*; other newspapers were similarly critical, and even the *Daily Mail* was forced to be even-handed. However, no similar 'confessions' emerged from the existing cabinet, and the government continued to resist any suggestion that a more lenient line might be taken with 'soft' drugs. Nevertheless, a few months after Labour were returned to office in 2001, the Home Secretary, David Blunkett, announced his intention to re-classify cannabis as a class C drug (although in July 2002, he also announced his decision to apply stricter penalties for supply of the drug). As a result, it is likely that by July 2003, possession of cannabis for personal use will no longer

---

[*] Arthur Gould is Reader in Swedish Social Policy in the Department of Social Sciences at Loughborough University and Nina Stratford is a Research Director at the *National Centre for Social Research*.

be an arrestable offence in most cases.[1] However, compared to many other European countries, current legal controls of cannabis in the UK remain relatively restrictive (House of Commons Library, 2000). Some countries have decriminalised possession of cannabis for personal use (most famously the Netherlands, but also Germany and Italy) and possession of all illegal drugs has been decriminalised in Portugal since 2001. Spain, Belgium, Canada, and some states within Australia and the USA also have more liberal regimes. The United Kingdom looks set to follow some of these practices, with, for example, Lambeth Police experimenting with using formal warnings instead of arrest for cannabis possession.

None of this, of course, proves there has been a change in *public* attitudes. However, it is unlikely that senior Conservatives, the press and a cautious Labour government would have been prepared to pursue a more tolerant line on drugs unless they were fairly sure that this was in line with the views of the general public. So our first aim in this chapter is to gauge how far recent policy developments are *actually* in line with public opinion, and the extent to which views about drugs policy have changed over the last five or so years. In doing so, we will focus upon three drugs – cannabis, heroin and ecstasy – and, where possible, will compare our findings with the results obtained in 1995, when we last covered these topics in detail as part of the *British Social Attitudes* survey series (Gould, Shaw and Ahrendt, 1996).

Having established whether attitudes towards legalising drugs have changed, we will then consider *why* such changes might have occurred. An understanding of the forces that might underpin changing views will enable us to better understand what implications this might have for future drugs policy. Among other things, we will focus on change within different age cohorts to determine whether any changes are confined to particular age groups or whether they have taken place among all generations. We will also consider whether there is any evidence to suggest that, as drug use has become more widespread, it has become increasingly 'normalised' (among the young at least) and led to more tolerant attitudes. Evidence for this claim will be examined by looking at the use of cannabis by respondents, their friends and members of their families, and the attitudes of non-users towards those who do take drugs.

Another hypothesis is that changing attitudes are a reflection of increasing knowledge and awareness about the effects of illegal drugs. So we will also examine knowledge about different drugs, their perceived harm, and views about the relationship between crime and illegal drugs. The Misuse of Drugs Act of 1971 classified drugs according to their relative harmfulness[2] and there is considerable debate about reclassifying certain drugs. So finding out how the public view the relative harm of different drugs is of particular importance.

Attitudes towards illegal drugs

Legalisation

Views about the legalisation of cannabis have shifted considerably over the last two decades. Our longest running question on this subject was included on the first *British Social Attitudes* survey back in 1983. Then only 12 per cent wanted to see cannabis legalised. But by 2001 over three times as many (41 per cent) took this view. Now the public is more or less evenly split on the issue, with about the same proportion in favour of and against legalisation.

Table 6.1 Attitudes towards the legalisation of cannabis, 1983–2001

	1983	1993	1995	2001
"Smoking cannabis should be legalised"	%	%	%	%
Agree	12	20	30	41
Neither agree nor disagree	10	17	11	15
Disagree	78	62	57	43
Base	*1650*	*1261*	*1058*	*952*

Increasing liberalism about the legalisation of cannabis is also evident when we look at responses to a question which sets out various options in more detail. This confirms that support for some form of legalisation has grown markedly, particularly over the last six years. However, few wish to see cannabis made legal without any restrictions whatsoever – only six per cent opt for this, a proportion that has not changed markedly since 1993.

Table 6.2 Attitudes towards the legal status of cannabis, 1993, 1995 and 2001

	1993	1995	2001
Taking cannabis …	%	%	%
… should be legal without restrictions	5	6	6
… should be legal but only available from licensed shops	25	28	45
… should remain illegal	67	64	46
Base	*1484*	*1227*	*1077*

These increasingly liberal views about cannabis are by no means replicated when the drug in question is heroin. Attitudes towards this drug remain highly restrictive. In 2001, nearly nine in ten thought it should remain illegal, and only

one per cent wanted to see it legalised without restriction, virtually identical proportions to those obtained in 1993. Nor is there much support for the legalisation of ecstasy. Although the influential Police Foundation report (2000) recommended downgrading ecstasy from class A to class B, the majority of the public clearly sees ecstasy in a similar light to heroin, with nine in ten wishing it to remain illegal. So the view that it is a 'soft' drug similar to cannabis has little public support.

Table 6.3 Attitudes towards the legal status of cannabis, heroin and ecstasy

	Cannabis	Heroin	Ecstasy
Taking cannabis, heroin or ecstasy ...	%	%	%
... should be legal without restrictions	6	1	1
... should be legal but only available from licensed shops	45	10	8
... should remain illegal	46	87	88
Base	*1077*	*1077*	*1077*

Possession and supply

So far we have only considered views about legalising the *use* of various drugs. However, attitudes towards those caught *supplying* cannabis are less lenient than views about those simply caught possessing it for personal use. As the next table shows, one in two people think "people should *not* be prosecuted for possessing small amounts of cannabis for their own use". But, when asked whether people who *sell* cannabis should "always" be prosecuted, 70 per cent agreed. This suggests that there is some measure of public support for the policy shift recently announced by David Blunkett of increasing penalties for supplying cannabis while also effectively removing the more serious legal sanctions for possession.

The proportion who support prosecuting suppliers of cannabis has declined slightly since 1995, down eight points from 78 per cent. But, among this group, the proportion who *strongly* support prosecution has declined very steeply, from 47 per cent in 1995 to only 29 per cent now. So while the majority are still in favour of always prosecuting suppliers, support for this has decreased and views are not as vehement as they were six years ago.

The picture for heroin is quite different. Only 14 per cent agree that possession should not be prosecuted (compared with the 52 per cent who think this about cannabis). And a near unanimous 97 per cent think heroin dealers should always be prosecuted. Unlike cannabis, attitudes have actually hardened on this since 1995. Then, 21 per cent thought that possession of heroin should not be prosecuted, compared with 14 per cent now. There has been little change in

views about heroin suppliers. Views on ecstasy possession and supply are very similar to those about heroin.

Table 6.4 Attitudes towards prosecution for possession and supply of cannabis and heroin, 1995 and 2001

% who agree ...	Cannabis		Heroin	
	1995	**2001**	**1995**	**2001**
... people should **not** be prosecuted for possession	41	52	21	14
... people who sell the drug should **always** be prosecuted	78	70	95	97
Base	*1227*	*1077*	*1227*	*1077*

The medical use of cannabis

Part of the current debate about the legalisation of cannabis relates to its possible therapeutic use. Some people with conditions such as multiple sclerosis use cannabis to relieve their symptoms, and at present risk falling foul of the law for doing so (although juries have sometimes refused to convict such people). Cannabis is a Schedule 1 drug, which means that it can only be supplied or possessed for research or other special purposes licensed by the Home Office (House of Commons Library, 2000). It cannot be used for normal medical purposes and those wishing to use it to treat their symptoms cannot get it prescribed by a doctor. The British Medical Association has recognised that "cannabinoids may have therapeutic potential" and calls for "properly controlled research" to investigate this (BMA, 1997). In 1998, The House of Lords Science and Technology Select Committee recommended that cannabis be reclassified as a Schedule 2 drug, thereby allowing it to be prescribed by doctors, subject to certain regulations (House of Lords Science and Technology Select Committee, 1998). However, the government rejected this recommendation, saying that further clinical trials were needed to prove efficacy and safety.

To assess public opinion about this issue, we asked:

> *Some people with serious illnesses say that cannabis helps to relieve their symptoms. Do you think that doctors should be allowed to prescribe cannabis for these people?*

On this matter there is little congruence between the views of the public and the government's current position; the vast majority of people think doctors should be able to prescribe cannabis for medical reasons. Nearly half (46 per cent) think this should "definitely be allowed", and a further 40 per cent think it

"probably" should be. Those who are more knowledgeable about the effects of drugs, and those who have used cannabis themselves (both issues we shall explore later) are much more likely to support making cannabis available on prescription.

Liberal and restrictive views: who thinks what?

The 2001 survey repeated a set of eight questions about illegal drugs that were first asked in 1995 as part of a 'scale' devised to reflect the liberal attitudes found amongst many drug agency workers in the UK and the more restrictive approach taken by their Swedish counterparts. But they also help shed considerable light upon changing attitudes among the British public. (Details of the origin of the scale and its technical evolution can be found in *The 13th Report* (Gould, Shaw and Ahrendt, 1996)).

The next table shows the broad results of the 1995 and 2001 surveys. Most notable is that six of the statements show a marked swing in a liberal direction, with the largest change relating to the statement "taking illegal drugs can sometimes be beneficial". Over half agreed with this in 2001, double the proportion in 1995. This no doubt partly reflects the increasing prevalence of debates about the medical use of cannabis. Views on the most extreme pro-legalisation statement ("adults should be free to take any drugs they wish") have not changed, with very few people supporting this position in either 1995 or 2001.

There are considerable differences between the views of particular social groups on these issues. To examine these in detail, we calculated scale 'scores' based upon the eight statements shown in the next table. Scores were calculated so that the most liberal position possible is 1.0, while the most restrictive score is 5.0. The mean score in the 2001 survey is 3.27, marking a clear shift in a liberal direction since 1995, when it was 3.53. The youngest age group (those aged between 18 and 24) had the most liberal score (2.92), and scores rise with age, with those above 65 scoring 3.71. There is also a clear correlation with education – those with degrees scored 2.86, while those with no educational qualifications had a score of 3.61. A similar, though narrower, distribution occurs in relation to occupational status, with those in routine jobs having the highest (most restrictive) score of 3.5, compared with scores of 3.11 among higher managers/professionals and 3.06 among lower professionals. Londoners have the lowest (most liberal) score of all the regions (2.94), as do Liberal Democrat identifiers (2.94). With their base of supporters holding such liberal attitudes, it is perhaps not surprising that the Liberal Democrats voted to legalise cannabis at their last spring conference. Finally, those with religious beliefs have higher scores (3.47) and are thus more restrictive in their views than those who are not religious (3.00).

Table 6.5 The liberal/restrictive scale of attitudes towards drugs, 1995 and 2001

% who agree	1995	2001	% change 1995– 2001	Base* 1995	Base* 2001
Liberal statements					
Taking illegal drugs can sometimes be beneficial	27	53	+26	1004	920
Smoking cannabis should be legalised	31	41	+10	1041	923
We need to accept that using illegal drugs is a normal part of some people's lives	32	41	+9	1008	919
Adults should be free to take any drugs they wish	9	8	-1	1005	925
Restrictive statements					
All use of illegal drugs is misuse	60	48	-12	1004	917
Taking drugs is always morally wrong	53	45	-8	1003	925
The use of illegal drugs always leads to addiction	49	43	-6	1008	923
The best way to treat people who are addicted to drugs is to stop them from using drugs altogether	53	52	-1	1009	922

* The base for each statement excludes those who did not answer it

How have the views of these groups changed over time? To assess this we grouped people into three categories: liberal (scoring between 1.0 and 2.5); moderate (between 2.51 and 3.49); or restrictive (3.5–5.0). We then compared the proportion of people in particular groups whose views placed them in the most restrictive category. This demonstrates clear shifts away from restrictive views in every one of the groups we considered; increasing liberalism is *not* simply confined to particular groups. For instance, the next table examines the proportions in different age and educational groups whose views were in the restrictive category, and the change in this between 1995 and 2001. It shows that changing attitudes towards illegal drugs are *not* confined simply to the young, or to those with certain levels of education. In fact, the largest shifts in opinion have occurred amongst those aged 35 and over, and those without degrees. So, while the majority of the 55-plus age group (59 per cent) still have restrictive views, this is down a substantial 18 points on the proportion in this category in 1995.

Table 6.6 Per cent with restrictive scores, by age and education, 1995 and 2001

	1995	2001	% point change 1995–2001	Base* 1995	Base* 2001
	%	%			
All	57	42	-15	995	915
Age					
18–34	39	31	-8	315	223
35–54	57	35	-22	353	338
55+	77	59	-18	326	353
Highest qualification					
Degree	28	25	-3	105	138
Other higher education	57	32	-25	141	131
A level or equivalent	55	40	-15	154	150
O level or equivalent	53	44	-9	203	154
CSE or equivalent	66	43	-23	82	110
None	70	61	-9	300	213

* The base for each statement excludes those who did not answer it

Use of cannabis

Another indicator of how much society's relationship with drugs has changed over the last decade or so is the increase in the proportion of people who have tried cannabis. Our findings confirm several other studies in revealing a steady increase over the years in the proportion who have tried the drug (or, at least, are willing to admit they have). In 1993, 16 per cent said they had used cannabis; in 1995, 21 per cent; and in 2001, 25 per cent. These figures are similar to those obtained by the British Crime Survey (Ramsay and Percy, 1996; Ramsay *et al.*, 2001).

Most sources of information about illegal drug use show that it is mainly the preserve of the young. Consistent with this, Table 6.7 shows that nearly half of all young people aged 18–34 admitted to having tried cannabis compared with only four per cent of those over 55. Other social groups who are more likely to have tried cannabis are graduates, higher occupational groups, Labour or Liberal Democrat supporters, those with no religious beliefs, Londoners and men.

The fact that so many sources of information point to an increase in drug use has lead some to argue that recreational drug use, particularly of cannabis, is becoming an increasingly 'normalised' part of young people's lives. Parker, for instance, claims that it is becoming seen as comparable with activities such as cigarette smoking and excessive drinking. Whereas not all (or even most) young people will actually engage in such behaviours, most will encounter them in

their everyday lives, and will accept others' freedom to choose them. He predicts that the traditional factors associated with drug trying among young people are losing their significance, and that, in urban areas at least, non-drug using adolescents will become a minority, 'deviant' group (Parker *et al.*, 1995; Parker *et al.*, 1998).

Table 6.7 Cannabis use by various social groups, 1993 and 2001

% who have ever used cannabis	1993	2001	% point change 1993–2001	1993 Base	2001 Base
All	16	25	+9	1484	1077
Age					
18–34	29	49	+20	444	288
35–54	16	27	+11	529	411
55+	1	4	+3	507	376
Social class					
Professionals, employers, managers	24	28	+4	65	46
Intermediate non-manual	19	30	+11	324	307
Junior non-manual	12	18	+6	351	260
Skilled manual	17	28	+11	304	215
Semi-skilled manual	17	24	+7	254	172
Unskilled manual	7	10	+3	115	52
Party identification					
Conservative	13	15	+2	470	249
Labour	17	27	+10	560	472
Liberal Democrat	20	26	+6	187	129
Region					
London	27	37	+10	175	115
Other regions	15	23	+8	1309	962
Religion					
Any	10	16	+6	997	626
None	28	38	+10	481	441
Sex					
Male	22	31	+9	611	495
Female	11	20	+9	873	583

Our findings offer mixed evidence as to whether traditional predictors of drug trying, such as gender and social class are becoming less significant. True, the previous table shows that the gap between the proportion of men and women

trying cannabis has closed. In 1993, twice as many men as women had tried it, but by 2001 the ratio had decreased to two women for every three men. However, the association between social class and having tried cannabis has not changed during this period, with those in junior non-manual occupations and unskilled manual workers still being the least likely group to have tried it. (Of course it is possible that we would see the relationship change if our data had covered a longer period.)

On the other hand, we have confirmed that experience of cannabis has indeed been increasing, particularly among the young. Now, a half of 18 to 34 year olds say they have tried cannabis, up 20 percentage points since 1993, but there has been hardly any increase in reported use among those aged 55 or over.

Of course, *ever* having tried cannabis might not be the best test of whether or not illegal drug use is becoming normalised. After all, it tells us little about frequency of use, or attitudes towards it (Shiner and Newburn, 1997). Furthermore, as Shiner and Newburn point out, for a behaviour to move from being considered 'deviant' to being 'normal' it is insufficient that this behaviour simply be widespread. It must also come to be *accepted* as normal by the relevant audience, in this case, young people. So we now turn to examining attitudes to drug use and drug users, focusing particularly on young people.

We asked people whether they agreed or not that "we need to accept that taking drugs is a normal part of some people's lives". In 1995, just under a third agreed with this proposition, increasing to 40 per cent by 2001. The change was greater among 18–34 year olds (an increase from 41 per cent to 55 per cent) than among those aged 55 or over (24 per cent to 28 per cent). This supports the notion that drug use is increasingly normalised among some groups, and suggests that the government has so far not succeeded in its aim to "make the misuse of drugs less culturally acceptable to young people" (Taylor *et al.*, 1998).

Table 6.8 Per cent who agree that "we need to accept that using illegal drugs is a normal part of some people's lives", by age, 1995 and 2001

	1995	2001	% point difference 1995–2001	Base 1995	Base 2001
	%	%			
18–34	41	55	+14	330	226
35–54	28	41	+13	371	348
55+	24	28	+4	355	367
All	31	40	+9	1058	942

If drug-taking is becoming normalised, we would also expect to find that even non-users are encountering drugs in their everyday lives and are accepting of

others freedom to use them. Our findings show that both those who have tried cannabis as well as those who have not have become more tolerant of its use over time. In fact, the shift to greater tolerance is most pronounced among non-users: in 1993, 76 per cent of this group thought cannabis should remain illegal, reducing to just 56 per cent by 2001. However, non-users remain substantially less tolerant than users (only 17 per cent of whom in 2001 thought cannabis should remain illegal).

We also asked people whether, as far as they knew, their friends or family had ever used illegal drugs. Overall, 39 per cent said that they had, reaching nearly two-thirds (63 per cent) among 18–34 year olds. Perhaps unsurprisingly, over eight in ten (83 per cent) of those young people who had tried cannabis themselves said that their friends or family had used illegal drugs. Far fewer of those who had not used the drug had drug-using friends or family, but still one in four did (25 per cent).

So there is some evidence to support the normalisation hypothesis, at least in relation to cannabis. Two-thirds of 18–34 year olds have a friend or family member who has used illegal drugs, half have tried cannabis themselves, and only a third think that cannabis should remain illegal. A majority of young people accepts that drug-taking is a normal part of some people's lives, and although this perception has increased among all age groups, it has increased most among those aged 18–34. And even those who have never used cannabis have become much more liberal about its legalisation.

Why have views changed?

There are a number of plausible reasons as to why attitudes towards cannabis might have become so much more lenient while views about heroin have barely changed. We begin this section by considering the implications of the notable age differences we have already described. We then consider changing perceptions about the dangers of drugs, beliefs about the link between drugs and crime, and knowledge about drugs.

Tolerant generations?

We have already seen that there is a clear relationship between age and views about illegal drugs. There are several quite distinct possible explanations for these differences, the choice of which will have implications for any future changes in attitudes towards drugs (and, it follows, for the acceptability of future drugs policy). One explanation is that the age differences are just a *lifecycle effect*, and that young people will 'mature out' of their more lenient views when, for example, they have children of their own and start to worry about the possibility that they might use drugs. However, this explanation does not fit our evidence as to how attitudes have changed. Table 6.9 shows attitudes towards the legalisation of cannabis for a number of different 'age cohorts' (that is, people born in a particular period). The left-hand column shows when each

of these cohorts was born, and the next two columns show their age in 1983 and 2001. So, for instance, the youngest cohort was born between 1975 and 1983, was aged 0–8 in 1983 and 18–26 in 2001. People belonging to this cohort were obviously too young to be interviewed in 1983, and form the youngest group in the 2001 survey.

If the age differences we have found reflected lifecycle influences, we would expect to see the younger cohorts becoming more restrictive in their attitudes as they get older. However, precisely the opposite has occurred. Take, for example, the youngest cohort interviewed in 1983 (when they were aged 18–26). If we compare their views then with those held by the same cohort in 2001 (when they were aged 36–44), we find a quite considerable increase in the proportion thinking cannabis should be legalised (from 21 per cent in 1983 to 49 per cent in 2001). The next two cohorts (aged 27–44 in 1983) show a similar shift to a more liberal view. The oldest cohorts (aged 45 or over in 1983) show a slightly smaller shift but have still become considerably more liberal on this issue since 1983. This pattern of change among all age cohorts is far more consistent with what is called a *period effect*, that is, where the whole of society has changed due to events which have affected the attitudes of all age groups. In this case, for example, we might point towards the advent of rave culture in the late 1980s/early 1990s and the increase in drug use which accompanied it. Although this increase in drug use occurred mainly among young people, their parents and grandparents may have been affected through the knowledge (direct or indirect) that their children may be taking drugs.

Table 6.9 Per cent who agree that "smoking cannabis should be legalised", by age cohort, 1983 and 2001

Cohort	Age in 1983	Age in 2001	1983 %	Base	2001 %	Base	Difference
1975–1983	0–8	18–26	-	-	55	79	n.a.
1966–1974	9–17	27–35	-	-	51	173	n.a.
1957–1965	18–26	36–44	21	256	49	153	+28
1948–1956	27–35	45–53	14	295	42	152	+28
1939–1947	36–44	54–62	10	274	36	140	+26
1930–1938	45–53	63–71	7	240	25	108	+18
1921–1929	54–62	72+	11	230	19	137	+8
1912–1920	63–71		11	203	-	-	n.a.
Pre 1912	72+		10	152	-	-	n.a.
All			12	1650	40	942	+28

n.a. = not applicable

Another explanation of these age differences in attitudes is that they reflect the prevailing norms of society during people's formative early adult years. Before the 1960s, drug-taking was uncommon in Britain and it is likely that increasing levels of use and familiarity with drugs among subsequent generations has also influenced the pattern shown in Table 6.9. For instance, younger cohorts are consistently more liberal than older ones, with the youngest cohort in 2001 having the most liberal position seen over the last two decades. If anything, the gap between the generations has actually increased; so, although all cohorts have become more liberal since 1983, the youngest cohorts have shown the greatest change, leading to an even steeper age gradient.

So does this mixture of generational and period effects tell us anything about the future shape of attitudes towards illegal drugs? True, it is impossible to tell whether the period effect we have observed will continue to exert a liberalising influence on attitudes over the next few years, or whether it has run its course. However, the involvement of generational influences make it likely that attitudes towards cannabis will continue to become more liberal, with more permissive younger generations gradually replacing more restrictive older ones over time.

Age differences in attitudes to heroin are much less pronounced and there has been virtually no change among any of our age cohorts in their views on legalisation – the vast majority of people of all ages remain opposed to this. So we do not expect to see much change in attitudes towards this drug in the foreseeable future.

Changing perceptions about the dangers of drugs

We now turn to examine a range of possible factors that might have influenced people's views about illegal drug use. In doing so we need to bear two findings in mind. The first is the fact that there has been a sea-change in attitudes towards cannabis throughout society as a whole, but that younger generations remain notably more tolerant of its use than older ones. The second is that views about heroin have barely changed at all, and do not vary markedly from one age group to the next.

We start by looking at public perceptions of the dangers posed by these two drugs to their users. To assess this, we asked people whether they agreed or not with the statement "Cannabis isn't nearly as damaging as some people think". Nearly a half (46 per cent) agreed, and a third disagreed. Not surprisingly, there is a clear link between the perceived dangers of cannabis and its legalisation: people who view it as dangerous are much more likely than those who do not to think it should remain illegal. For instance, among those who *disagreed* with our statement (in other words, the group who *do* think cannabis is damaging), eight in ten want it to remain illegal. By contrast, among those who think cannabis is *not* damaging to users, only two in ten (21 per cent) think it should remain illegal. Precisely the same pattern exists when we consider views about whether or not legalising cannabis will lead to more addiction: those who agree that "if you legalise cannabis, many more people will become addicts" are much

more likely to oppose its legalisation than those who do not (71 and 13 per cent respectively). We asked comparable questions about heroin and found similar, but less pronounced, patterns.

So views about legalisation are indeed linked to perceptions about a drug's danger. And, as the next table shows, there has been considerable change in people's views about the dangers posed by different drugs to their users. Thus, the proportion who think that cannabis "is not nearly as damaging as some people think" has increased from around a third in 1993 to just under a half in 2001. But for heroin the position remains relatively unchanged; only one in ten consider it not to be harmful in 2001, the same proportion as in 1993. This relaxation when it comes to perceptions about the harmfulness of cannabis has occurred in all age groups, which lends support to this factor at least partly underpinning some broad changes in attitudes towards cannabis that we have found (as well as the lack of change in attitudes towards heroin).

Table 6.10 Damage done by cannabis and heroin, 1993 and 2001

	Cannabis		Heroin	
	1993	2001	1993	2001
Cannabis/heroin isn't nearly as damaging as some people think	%	%	%	%
Agree	32	46	10	11
Neither agree nor disagree	11	15	6	5
Disagree	48	34	76	80
Base	*1461*	*1081*	*1461*	*1081*

There has also been a small decline in the belief that legalising cannabis will lead to an increase in addiction – one of the main pillars of the argument against legalisation. In 2001, 51 per cent agreed with the statement "if you legalise cannabis more people will become addicts", down from 60 per cent in 1995. Once again, this change is evenly spread across nearly all age cohorts. A much higher percentage (74 per cent) agree that the legalisation of heroin would lead to more addicts, unchanged since 1995.

Thus far, we have been focusing on why views about cannabis have changed while those about heroin have not – and so have concentrated on comparing our 2001 findings with those from 1995. In 2001 we also asked similar questions about ecstasy, but have no earlier readings with which to compare our findings. The basic message, however, is clear: ecstasy is seen as being on a par with heroin in terms of the damage it is perceived to cause to users, and in its potential to lead to addiction. Only seven per cent agree that it is "not nearly as damaging as some people think" and nearly three-quarters (73 per cent) believe that its legalisation would result in an increase in addiction. This no doubt underpins the lack of support for the legalisation of ecstasy that we have found.

Crime and illegal drugs

Nearly a half of people (45 per cent) believe that "cannabis is a cause of crime and violence", and there is a strong link between this belief and views about legalisation. Three-quarters (74 per cent) of those who see a link between the drug and crime think that the drug should remain illegal, compared with only 14 per cent of those who do not think cannabis causes crime or violence.

There has been a small fall in the proportion who think that cannabis is linked to crime and violence, from 54 per cent in 1993 to 45 per cent in 2001. Once again, this is evident in nearly all age cohorts.

The story for heroin is, however, quite different. Here there has been an *increase* in the proportion who link it with crime and violence – 85 per cent in 1993 and 94 per cent in 2001. This increased perception of heroin as a cause of crime could help explain our earlier finding that attitudes towards those caught in possession of the drug have become less tolerant (Table 6.4).

Table 6.11   Attitudes towards cannabis and heroin as a cause of crime and violence, 1993 and 2001

	Cannabis		Heroin	
	1993	**2001**	**1993**	**2001**
Cannabis/heroin is a cause of crime and violence	%	%	%	%
Agree	54	45	85	94
Neither agree nor disagree	18	19	9	3
Disagree	23	33	4	2
Base	*1461*	*1081*	*1461*	*1081*

Ecstasy is seen as lying somewhere in between heroin and cannabis in its propensity to cause crime and violence, with 61 per cent agreeing that it does so.

Knowledge about drugs

We now turn to examine the relationship between knowledge about drugs and views about their legalisation. Are, for instance, the most knowledgeable also the most liberal, or are people with very restrictive views also knowledgeable about drugs and their effects? Perhaps the changes we have seen in views about the legalisation of cannabis at least partly reflect the fact that the public now has more experience and information about drugs at its fingertips? After all, we

have already seen evidence of increased *use* of illegal drugs, which seems likely to increase knowledge about them. Unfortunately, we cannot test whether or not increasing knowledge explains the changing attitudes we have seen, as the 2001 survey marked the first time that we assessed the public's broad knowledge of drugs and their principal effects. Moreover, even if we did have previous measures of knowledge, it would be very difficult to distinguish cause from effect (after all, knowledge about drugs might just as easily *reflect* liberal views about drugs as *result* in them).

Table 6.12 Knowledge about the effects of different drugs

% who think	Can make people feel relaxed		Can make people feel energetic		Can make people hallucinate	
Cannabis	64	✓	2	X	10	✓
Heroin	15	✓	6	X	28	X
Cocaine	11	X	20	✓	16	X
LSD	13	X	20	X	69	✓
Ecstasy	11	✓	53	✓	28	✓
Amphetamine	7	X	57	✓	12	✓
Don't know	27		23		18	

Base: 1081

Note: respondents could nominate as many drugs as they wished for each question, so totals sum to over 100 per cent.

Measuring knowledge about drugs is likely to be controversial, not only because the area is a complex one but also because the effects of a particular drug can depend as much upon the mental state of the people taking it, and the surroundings within which it is taken, as upon the characteristics of the drugs themselves (Goldberg, 1997). Nonetheless, there are enough rudimentary 'facts' about drugs to make it worth the effort. We asked respondents which drugs, out of a list of six, made people *relaxed*, which made them *energetic*, and which made them *hallucinate*. Table 6.12 shows the percentages who thought that each drug had a particular effect followed by a tick indicating our 'right' answers and a cross against the 'wrong' ones. It shows that majorities seem to be aware of the principal characteristics of the various drugs, with most making clear distinctions between the effects of different drugs. Two-thirds recognised cannabis as a relaxant, and LSD as an hallucinogen. And just over half realised that amphetamine and ecstasy tend to make people energetic. The proportion giving the 'wrong' answers are occasionally above 20 per cent (for example, 28 per cent think that heroin can make people hallucinate), but are often around only the 10 per cent mark. However, with the exception of LSD, the hallucinatory qualities of drugs do not seem to be appreciated – for example,

only 10 per cent believe that cannabis can have this effect. In addition, the effects of heroin and cocaine are less widely known. That heroin is a relaxant is appreciated by only 15 per cent of respondents, and only 20 per cent name cocaine as a stimulant. In addition, significant proportions answered "don't know" to each of the three questions, over a quarter in relation to which drugs could make people relaxed.

We found a strong link between knowledge, behaviour and attitudes. Knowledge scores for each respondent were grouped according to the number of 'right' answers they got. Overall, a quarter of people got 12 or more out of 18 answers correct, 42 per cent got between eight and eleven right, and a third got seven or less right.

The next table demonstrates that knowledge about illegal drugs is clearly linked to attitudes towards them, with the most knowledgeable being twice as likely to favour the legalisation of cannabis as the least knowledgeable. Not surprisingly, there is also a very strong link between knowledge and use of cannabis; half of the most knowledgeable, and over a quarter of those with moderate scores, had used cannabis, while only four per cent of the least knowledgeable had done so.

Table 6.13 Attitudes towards, and use of, cannabis, by drug knowledge score

	High knowledge	Medium knowledge	Low knowledge
Taking cannabis ...	%	%	%
... should be legal without restrictions	10	7	2
... should be legal but only available from licensed shops	60	48	29
... should remain illegal	29	44	63
	%	%	%
Ever tried cannabis	49	26	4
Base	*269*	*448*	*364*

In addition to looking at knowledge about the immediate effects of drugs, we also sought to find out which drugs were considered by the public to be the most harmful to users:

> *This card shows a list of legal and illegal drugs. Please can you read through the whole list and pick the three drugs which you think are the most harmful to* ***frequent*** *users?*

The list of drugs shown on the card, and the proportion nominating them, is shown in the next table. While, predictably perhaps, heroin and crack cocaine head the list (chosen by 64 and 47 per cent respectively), the *legal* drugs alcohol and tobacco were cited much more frequently than all the other illegal drugs on

the list. Even cocaine and ecstasy were cited less often than alcohol and tobacco. This confirms other recent survey evidence (MORI, 2000) and suggests that the public largely agrees with the Police Foundation report that cannabis is less harmful than tobacco and alcohol, and that ecstasy and LSD are less harmful than heroin.

Table 6.14 Per cent who mention particular drugs as being the most harmful to regular users

	All
Heroin	64
Crack cocaine	47
Tobacco	34
Alcohol	32
Cocaine	29
Ecstasy	25
LSD	15
Tranquillisers	12
Amphetamine	7
Cannabis	5
Magic mushrooms	2
Base	*1081*

Whether or not it can be said that the public has got its priorities right, this list does have policy implications. When legal drugs are seen as very harmful and illegal drugs are rated relatively harmless, it is not so easy for governments to argue for blanket prohibition. These results are further evidence of why more and more people are willing to support the legalisation of cannabis. Few regard it as dangerous.

Limits to tolerance

Attitudes towards illegal drugs have become more tolerant over time, but this tolerance has clear limits. In fact, the biggest increase in tolerance relates only to cannabis and does not extend to harder drugs such as heroin. There are some other areas of policy that are also marked by a fairly restrictive outlook and here we consider two – 'harm reduction' and 'drug-driving' (that is, driving while under the influence of illegal drugs).

Harm reduction (or risk minimisation as it is sometimes called) has been the basis for much of the help, advice and treatment offered to drug users in Britain in the last 20 years. In the 1980s, the policy emerged by stealth from a

consensus between the medical profession and drug agency professionals. Its principles were not widely discussed and debated by the general public. To plug this gap, the 2001 survey asked people about three issues of particular relevance to harm reduction – needle exchanges, drug education and the prescribing of drugs to addicts. The proportions who agreed with each of these practices is shown in the final column of the next table. It suggests that aspects of the harm reduction message have yet to be accepted by the general public. True, the idea of giving users clean needles receives endorsement from nearly two-thirds of adults. Only 18 per cent are opposed to the practice. Giving harm reduction information to young people is also accepted by a majority, though opposed by 31 per cent. However, something which has been an established part of medical practice for almost a century – prescribing drugs to addicts – still finds very little support in public opinion. Just over a quarter agree with the statement and nearly half disagree, a reduction on the 33 per cent who agreed with this in 1995.

Are people willing to countenance harm reduction strategies even though they themselves have a restrictive outlook on drugs? There is obviously a tension here between sticking to principles that drug-taking is unacceptable and the pragmatic approach of trying to minimise the risks for those who do. And indeed, fewer of those at the restrictive end of our the liberal-restrictive scale support harm reduction measures (see Table 6.5 for further details about the scale). Support is particularly low for prescribing drugs to addicts, which is agreed with by only 15 per cent of those with a restrictive score.

Table 6.15 Per cent who agree with harm reduction strategies, by score on liberal-restrictive scale

		Liberal	Moderate	Restrictive	All
Drug users should be given clean needles to stop them getting diseases	%	81	72	50	65
Young people should be given information about how to use drugs more safely	%	80	56	41	55
Doctors must be allowed to prescribe drugs for those who are addicted to them	%	51	26	15	26
Base		*182*	*339*	*394*	*915*

One consequence of drug-taking that almost no one is willing to tolerate is driving while under the influence of alcohol or other drugs. 'Drug-driving' is a growing phenomenon in the UK: recent research has found a significant increase in the number of road traffic accident victims who had consumed drugs (Tunbridge *et al.*, 2001). A study by the RAC found that people were more

likely to admit to having been driven by someone under the influence of drugs than by someone breaking the drink-drive laws (RAC, 2000). The government's ten-year plan for tackling drugs makes specific reference to underlining the social unacceptability of driving while influenced by drugs.

It seems that both drink- and drug-driving are already strongly disapproved of by most people. Respondents were asked how much they agreed or disagreed that people should never drive after drinking a small amount of alcohol or taking a small amount of cannabis. Eighty five per cent agreed in both cases.

Conclusions

It is beyond doubt that attitudes towards cannabis in Britain are becoming more liberal, more pragmatic, or both. More people want to see it legalised and fewer wish to see those caught in possession, or selling the drug, dealt with severely. The same cannot be said for heroin, a drug about which the great majority still takes a very tough stance. In fact, views on prosecuting heroin users have become even more intolerant over time. Attitudes to ecstasy are mostly on a par with heroin, although for some items, ecstasy is viewed more liberally than heroin, and is thought to be less harmful.

The factors underpinning such increased liberalism are multi-faceted. It partly reflects generational change, with older, more restrictive, generations dying out and being replaced by younger, more permissive, ones. Our best guess for the future is that this trend will continue and that attitudes towards cannabis will continue to move in a more lenient direction over time. However, there have been other changes which have affected all generations within society. Consequently, even the least tolerant groups have become gradually more accepting of cannabis over time. The reasons for this are likely to include the fact that cannabis is seen as much less dangerous than most other drugs (and, in particular, is considered to be much less harmful than legal drugs like tobacco and alcohol). Perceptions of the dangers associated with it have also changed, with people now being less likely to associate it with crime and violence or addiction. Increased use, of both cannabis and other illegal drugs, may also have led to increased knowledge of their effects, and greater knowledge is associated with more lenient attitudes. However, the causal direction here is very complex and likely to vary from one group to another. Finally, drug use is seen as increasingly normal, especially among young people, a majority of whom know someone who has taken illegal drugs and over half of whom accept that drug-taking is "a normal part of some people's lives".

Our new measure of drug knowledge has shown that people distinguish reasonably accurately between the effects of different drugs. Most are aware of the principal effects of cannabis, LSD, ecstasy and amphetamines, although they are less informed about cocaine and heroin.

While we can speak generally of there being a more liberal climate surrounding cannabis, it is also clear that some sections of the population are much more liberal than others. The young, those who have had higher education, Londoners, higher occupational groups, and the less religious

consistently take a more liberal stance than their respective counterparts. Differences between those who identify with the two main political parties are not that great, but the Liberal Democrats will be pleased to know that it has the backing of many of its supporters in its recent call for the decriminalisation of cannabis.

Governments need to treat these results with caution. While taking a lenient line on cannabis might be more acceptable than in the past, the population is now split down the middle on this subject. This lack of consensus is shown by the debate that has raged in the press in response to every new policy announcement made on the subject. Furthermore, there are drugs and drug issues on which the public remain very restrictive. In particular, heroin is still regarded in an extremely restrictive light by virtually all social groups. Loosening legal controls on heroin would not find favour with the vast majority. Importantly, most still need persuading that prescribing heroin to addicts is an acceptable treatment. If this is to become part of government policy, then it will be necessary to demonstrate to the public why this is a sensible strategy.

Notes

1. There will be a reserve power of arrest linked to possession of cannabis where there is a danger to public order or for the protection of children.
2. The classification of drugs under the Misuse of Drugs Act of 1971 is linked to different penalties, and implies different degrees of harmfulness. Class A covers drugs such as heroin, ecstasy, cocaine and crack, LSD and magic mushrooms; class B includes cannabis and amphetamines; class C covers mild amphetamines, anabolic steroids and minor tranquillisers.

References

British Medical Association (BMA) (1997), *Therapeutic uses of cannabis*, Amsterdam: Harwood Academic Publishers.

Goldberg, T. (1997), *Demystifying drugs*, Basingstoke: Macmillan.

Gould, A. Shaw, A. and Ahrendt, D. (1996), 'Illegal drugs: liberal and restrictive attitudes' in Jowell, R., Curtice, J., Park, A., Brook, L. and Thomson, K. (eds.), *British Social Attitudes: the 13th Report*, Aldershot: Dartmouth.

House of Commons Library (2000), *Research Paper 00/74, Cannabis*, London: House of Commons.

House of Lords Science and Technology Select Committee (1998), *Cannabis: the Scientific and Medical Evidence*, 9th report 1997–98, HL 151.

MORI (2000), *Attitudes towards the law and drugs*, London: The Police Foundation.

Parker, H., Aldridge, J. and Measham, F. (1998), *Illegal Leisure, the Normalisation of Adolescent Recreational Drug Use*, London: Routledge.

Parker, H., Measham, F. and Aldridge, J. (1995), *Drugs Futures: Changing Patterns of Drug Use Amongst English Youth*, London: Institute for the Study of Drug Dependence.

Police Foundation (2000), *Drugs and the law, Report of the Independent Inquiry into the Misuse of Drugs Act 1971*, London: The Police Foundation.

RAC (2000), 'More are driven by drug-drivers than drink-drivers', *The Times*, 26 January.

Ramsay, M and Percy, A. (1996), *Drug misuse declared: results of the 1994 British Crime Survey*, Home Office Research Study 151, London: Home Office.

Ramsay, M., Baker, P., Goulden, C., Sharp, C. and Sondhi, A. (2001) *Drug misuse declared in 2000: results from the British Crime Survey*, Home Office Research Study 224, London: Home Office.

Shaw, B. (1999), *Drugs: Paper to the Cleveland Police Authority*, 10 December, Middlesbrough: Cleveland Police.

Shiner, M. and Newburn, T. (1997), 'Definitely, maybe not? The normalisation of recreational drug use among young people', *Sociology*, **31** (3), 511-529.

Taylor, A., Cook, R., Dewar, D., Prescott, J., Straw, J., Dobson, F., Davies, R., Brown, G., Blunkett, D. and Mowlam, M. (1998), *Tackling Drugs to Build a Better Britain, The Government's Ten-Year Strategy for Tackling Drugs Misuse*, London: The Stationery Office.

Tunbridge, R. J., Keigan, M. and James, F. J. (2001), *The incidence of drugs and alcohol in road accident fatalities*, TRL report 495, London: Transport Research Laboratory.

Acknowledgements

The *National Centre for Social Research* is grateful to the Economic and Social Research Council (Grant number R000 23 9295) for their financial support which enabled us to ask the questions reported in this chapter.

7 Where have all the voters gone?

Catherine Bromley and John Curtice[*]

Just 59.1 per cent of voters went to the polls in the 2001 general election, the lowest figure since 1918, and 12 points lower than the already low figure of 71.4 per cent recorded in 1997. This happened despite the introduction of new regulations, such as allowing people to vote by post on demand, designed to make it easier for voters to exercise their franchise (Electoral Commission, 2001).[1] Nothing could have done more to undermine the claim that Labour's commitment to constitutional reform and a new era of 'clean' politics would help to re-engage citizens with the institutions of democracy (Bromley *et al.*, 2001). Indeed, for perhaps the first time in the study of elections in Britain the most pressing question to be answered is not why people vote for one party rather than another but rather why they do not vote at all.

Explanations of the decline in turnout can be divided into two broad types. The first type focuses on the voters, who might, for example, have become cynical about politics and politicians and so see little reason to turn out and vote. Perhaps they no longer feel an emotional tie to any of the political parties that they wish to express in the ballot box. Or maybe they no longer feel that they have a duty to vote when given the democratic opportunity to do so.

The second type of explanation, in contrast, focuses on the actions of the politicians. It argues that the reason why voters are no longer going to the polls is because they are not being given a good enough reason to do so. The parties may, for example, have come to advocate largely similar policies and as a result offer little real choice to voters. Or one party may be so far ahead of the others in the polls that the outcome of the election may be obvious well before polling day comes around. As a result voters whose personal motivation to go to the polls may not have changed one bit may well still be less likely to do so in practice.

---

[*] Catherine Bromley is a Senior Researcher at the *National Centre for Social Research*, Scotland, and is Co-Director of the *British Social Attitudes* survey series. John Curtice is Head of Research at the *National Centre for Social Research*, Scotland, Deputy Director of the Centre for Research into Elections and Social Trends, and Professor of Politics and Director of the Social Statistics Laboratory at Strathclyde University.

These two types of explanation suggest rather different remedies for reversing the decline in turnout. The second could be said to imply that little need or perhaps even can be done. Eventually politics will become more interesting once more, and voters will then return to the polls. The first, in contrast, suggests that action is required. Programmes of voter education may be necessary – everything from citizenship classes in schools to advertising campaigns at election time – in order to inculcate a sense that voting matters. At the same time government might consider measures such as postal and internet voting to make voting both easier and more attractive (Electoral Commission, 2002). In short, understanding why turnout has fallen is important if a successful strategy for its reversal is to be found.

Our enquiry falls into three sections. In the first we look at whether the motivation and engagement of voters has indeed changed in recent years. In *The 18th Report* we reported that far from seeing a restoration of trust and confidence in politics, the first three years of Labour's first term in office saw a further decline in levels of political trust while political efficacy, that is the degree to which people felt the political system was able to meet their demands, remained at the all-time low it reached in the mid-1990s. So we begin by updating that analysis to see whether trust and confidence in the political system was still low at the time of the 2001 election. We then continue our examination by looking at whether voters have become disengaged from politics, such as whether voters are now less likely to believe that they have a duty to vote, are less likely to feel an emotional tie with a political party, or are simply less likely to have an interest in politics at all. In each case we focus in particular on what might have changed between 1997 and 2001.

Our second section then looks at the other side of the coin and asks how much stimulus voters were given to vote at the 2001 election. Was the election in any way unusual in how much difference there was between the parties? And was the message of the polls about the closeness of the contest in any way unusual? We also consider what kind of changes in the pattern of turnout we would expect to find if indeed the reason why voters did not go to the polls was because they did not think there was a good enough reason to do so. This is followed by our final section which looks at who did and did not vote in 2001, how this compares with 1997, and assesses which of the two types of explanation appears to offer the more plausible account of the decline in turnout between 1997 and 2001.

We are able to pursue our analysis because the 2001 *British Social Attitudes* survey interviewed its respondents in the weeks immediately after the 2001 election, held on 7th June. As a result it was able to ask its respondents whether or not they had voted, before their memories of polling day had faded. But, of course, in order to see what was different about the 2001 election we have to be able to compare the results of our 2001 survey with those of previous surveys, and in particular comparable surveys undertaken immediately after previous elections, and especially so in 1997. This we are able to do because not only were many of the key questions that we asked on our 2001 survey identical to those carried on previous *British Social Attitudes* surveys, but they were also identical to those that have been carried in the *British Election Study* series of

surveys conducted after each general election since 1964. In short, because we asked the same question as in previous surveys, we are able to establish what might have been different about 2001 (Curtice, 2002).

Not that surveys are without their problems when it comes to analysing who does and does not vote. Surveys always find that more people say they have voted than are recorded as having done so by the official results. This does not necessarily mean that our respondents are lying, though a tendency to over-report having voted is part of the explanation (Swaddle and Heath, 1989). It also reflects the fact that those who participate in elections are also more likely to participate in surveys, and the fact that, because of redundancy in the electoral register, the official figures always underestimate the proportion of eligible voters who turn out and vote. Nevertheless, while the proportion of respondents to our survey who said they had voted was, at 68 per cent, 11 points higher than the officially recorded turnout, the 11 point fall that this represents on the turnout recorded by the 1997 *British Election Study* is almost exactly in line with the 12 point drop in the official figures. This clearly lends considerable credence to our approach of comparing the results of the two surveys.[2]

Motivation and disengagement

Political trust

Our chapter in *The 18th Report* revealed a quite dramatic decline in the proportion of people who said they trusted governments of any party to put the needs of the nation above the interests of their own political party "just about always" or "most of the time". In just two years – between 1998 and 2000 – the proportion of people who said this nearly halved, falling from 29 per cent to just 16. However, a first glance at the next table suggests that the 2000 figure was more of an uncharacteristic nadir than an indicator of terminal decline. By 2001 trust was back to its 1998 level. However, a closer look at the table leads to a rather different interpretation.

Remember that our 2001 reading was taken immediately after the general election. And evidence from earlier elections suggests that political trust is always higher in the immediate wake of a general election than it is at other times – contrary to popular wisdom general elections actually bolster people's trust in government (Curtice and Jowell, 1997). We can see this where we have survey readings for both immediately before and immediately after a general election, as is the case for 1987 and 1997. For example, in March and April 1987 the *British Social Attitudes* survey recorded 37 per cent saying they trusted government at least most of the time. Just a few months later, just *after* the general election had been held, the figure as measured by that year's *British Election Study* had risen to 47 per cent. In 1997 the equivalent comparison recorded a rise from 25 per cent to 33 per cent.

So rather than comparing our 2001 reading with the previous year, a more useful approach is to compare it with the other post-election readings we have for 1987 and 1997. This suggests that our conclusion in *The 18th Report* that

political trust had reached a new low was in fact correct. Whereas around half the population had a reasonably high level of political trust after the Conservative's third election victory in a row in 1987, and a third still did in 1997, after the 2001 election only a little over a quarter could muster the same level of enthusiasm. The general election in 2001 may have performed its traditional function of bolstering trust in government, but it still left the electorate in a predominantly cynical mood.

Table 7.1 Trends in trust in government to place the needs of the nation above political party interests, 1986–2001

% who trust government	1986	1987 BSA	1987 BES	1991	1994	1996	1997 BSA	1997 BES	1998	2000	2001
"Just about always" or "most of the time"	38	37	47	33	24	22	25	33	29	16	28
"Only some of the time" or "almost never"	57	60	52	63	73	75	71	65	69	83	70
Base		*1802*	*1410*	*3414*	*1445*	*1137*	*1180*	*1355*	*2906*	*2071*	*2293*	*1099*

Source: 1987 and 1997 BES: *British Election Study*

Feelings about the political system

Public confidence in a political system is not just a question of trust. It is also about whether people believe that the political system can respond to their needs and wishes. This perception is known as 'system efficacy' (Almond and Verba, 1963). In the next table we show the proportion who "strongly agree" with three items that suggest the political system is unresponsive, and who thus have very *low* levels of efficacy. In contrast to political trust it appears that elections do not necessarily increase levels of efficacy. The proportion who strongly agreed that "parties are only interested in people's votes, not in their opinions" was almost exactly the same after the 1987 election as it was beforehand. However, the election of the Labour government in place of the previous Conservative regime does appear to have helped restore efficacy back to the level it was prior to its decline in the mid-1990s (see also Curtice and Jowell, 1997). However, this mood did not last long, and by 2000 the proportion strongly agreeing with the three items in the table was similar to the levels experienced in 1996. And those proportions remained much the same at the time of the 2001 election. As a result, the level of system efficacy was clearly lower than it had been at the previous election four years earlier.

Table 7.2 Trends in system efficacy, 1987–2001

% strongly agree	1987 BSA	1987 BES	1991	1994	1996	1997 BES	1998	2000	2001
Parties are only interested in people's votes, not in their opinions	15	16	16	25	28	16	21	26	27
Generally speaking, those we elect as MPs lose touch with people pretty quickly	16	n.a.	16	25	26	n.a.	20	23	25
It doesn't really matter which party is in power, in the end things go on much the same	n.a.	7	11	16	16	8	17	19	18
Base	*1410*	*3826*	*1445*	*1137*	*1180*	*2906*	*2071*	*2293*	*1099*

Source: 1987 and 1997 BES: *British Election Study*
n.a. = not asked

So, trust and confidence in government appear to have been at an all-time low in 2001. True, it had been low prior to the 1997 election as well, but the prospect of a change of government appears to have helped restore the public's faith in its political system. However, it is now clear that that restoration was but a temporary one.

Who has lost faith?

So who has lost faith in the political system? One group that is often thought to be the most cynical and disengaged from politics is the young. The (all too) often quoted 'statistics' about the enormous number of young people who vote in *Big Brother* or *Pop Idol* style television polls compared with the proportion who vote at elections may on the surface suggest this is so. However, a more thoughtful examination is perhaps needed which acknowledges the difference between the aim of an election and the objectives of light entertainment, and also the crucial difference between elections which only allow each elector one vote and television polls designed specifically to allow as many votes as possible to be registered in the time allotted. For, in practice, as the next table shows, the young are not as cynical as might be expected. Those aged between 18 and 24 are no more or no less trusting of government than are those aged 75 and over and equally no less likely to think that it does not matter who is in power. Meanwhile, they exhibit rather more confidence in MPs and the political parties than do the rest of the adult population.

Table 7.3 Political trust and system efficacy, by age

	18–24	25–39	40–59	60–74	75+	All
% who trust government "always" or "most of the time"	32	27	26	31	33	28
% strongly agree						
It doesn't really matter which party is in power, in the end things go on much the same	19	19	16	19	16	18
Parties are only interested in people's votes, not in their opinions	14	27	27	32	34	27
Generally speaking, those we elect as MPs lose touch with people pretty quickly	12	22	28	32	28	25
Base	*88*	*328*	*354*	*210*	*117*	*1099*

There is, in fact, little new in this (see also Curtice and Jowell, 1995). As the next table shows, in 1997 too, the young were neither particularly distrustful of government nor particularly likely to feel inefficacious. The myth that a new generation of cynical youth is emerging in Britain should evidently be laid to rest.[3]

Table 7.4 Political trust and system efficacy, by age, 1997

	18–24	25–39	40–59	60–74	75+	All
% who trust government "always" or "most of the time"	32	32	33	34	41	33
Base	*316*	*852*	*994*	*529*	*205*	*3615*
% strongly agree						
It doesn't really matter which party is in power, in the end things go on much the same	5	8	8	10	9	8
Parties are only interested in people's votes, not in their opinions	16	12	15	21	25	16
Base	*245*	*729*	*865*	*465*	*158*	*2465*

Source: 1997: *British Election Study*

One of the key social changes to have occurred in recent years is the expansion of higher education coupled with an increase in 'life-long' learning schemes that encourage people to acquire more qualifications. Could it be that an

increasingly well-educated public is also more questioning and perhaps prone to cynicism as well? To address this possibility the next table looks at the relationship between people's educational attainment, and our various measures of trust and efficacy. It does so by comparing the views of people with experience of higher education and those with no qualifications.

We can quickly see that there is little support for our hypothesis. In fact, it is those without qualifications rather than the university educated who are most likely to feel inefficacious, and indeed amongst whom, if anything, confidence in government has fallen most in recent years. The spread of university education should have made the decline in political efficacy less rather than more likely.

Table 7.5 Political trust and system efficacy, by highest educational qualification, 1997 and 2001

	1997		2001	
	Degree/ other HE	None	Degree/ other HE	None
% who trust government "always" or "most of the time"	35	33	28	25
Base	698	908	309	318
% strongly agree				
It doesn't really matter which party is in power, in the end things go on much the same	6	12	14	23
Parties are only interested in people's votes, not in their opinions	13	21	23	36
Generally speaking, those we elect as MPs lose touch with people pretty quickly	n.a.	n.a.	20	34
Base	616	739	309	318

Source: 1997: *British Election Study*
n.a. = not asked

But if age and education tell us little, there is one interesting pattern that does perhaps offer some clue to why trust and efficacy are now so low. As the 1996 figures in the next table illustrate, prior to the 1997 election, identifiers with the then opposition Labour Party were markedly less trustful of government and less likely to report low levels of efficacy than were supporters of the incumbent Conservative government. It appeared that respondents' answers to our questions were influenced by evaluations of the performance of the government in office rather than simply being measures of attitudes towards the political system in general. And indeed, once Labour had been elected to office in 1997

the gap immediately closed. However, it has not, as one might have expected, reappeared (in reverse form) after four years of Labour in office. Instead, cynicism has grown amongst Labour identifiers at about the same rate as it has amongst Conservative identifiers. This could perhaps in part be explained by the fact that in their first term in office Labour suffered allegations of sleaze not dissimilar to those endured by the Conservatives prior to 1997. There was also some suggestion in our data that dissatisfaction with the government's performance in office may be a source of Labour supporters' low levels of trust and efficacy, though this needs further exploration before any strong conclusions can be drawn. So, perhaps the experience of having two governments in a row suffering allegations of sleaze has undermined the confidence of both government and opposition supporters, with the result that neither group is now so inclined to evaluate their political system through partisan eyes.

Table 7.6 Trends in efficacy and trust, by party identification, 1996–2001

	1996			1997			2001		
	Party identification			Party identification			Party identification		
% strongly agree	Lab	Con	None	Lab	Con	None	Lab	Con	None
Parties are only interested in votes	33	18	35	15	16	26	22	25	43
MPs lose touch too quickly	34	15	30	n.a.	n.a.	n.a.	22	22	36
Doesn't matter who is in power	18	7	27	7	7	20	15	11	37
Base	*284*	*1867*	*110*	*1107*	*728*	*152*	*486*	*257*	*128*
% who trust governments always/most of the time to put nation's interests first	19	34	18	40	34	13	34	28	21
Base	*284*	*1867*	*110*	*1308*	*849*	*203*	*486*	*257*	*128*

Source: 1997: *British Election Study*.
n.a. = not asked

A disengaged electorate?

It appears then that voters were more cynical about their political system in 2001 than they were in 1997. But to this we must also add the possibility that they became more disengaged too. To examine this we will look at three key indicators: whether voters still believe that voting is a duty they should perform; whether they have lost interest in politics; and whether they no longer feel any sense of attachment to a political party.

The *British Social Attitudes* survey has asked people on six occasions over the last decade whether they thought voting in elections was a matter of choice or a duty. The question put to them was:

> *Which of these statements comes <u>closest</u> to your view about general elections?*
> *In a general election:*
> *... It's not really worth voting*
> *... People should vote only if they care who wins*
> *... It's everyone's duty to vote*

Almost identical results have been obtained on each occasion, with no less than two-thirds saying that citizens do have a duty to vote. There appears to be no evidence of any significant decline in this sense of civic duty in recent years, and certainly no evidence that any such decline could account for the decline in turnout between 1997 and 2001.[4]

Table 7.7 Trends in civic duty, 1991–2001

% who say	1991	1994	1996	1998	2000	2001	Net change 1991–2001
It's not worth voting	8	9	8	8	11	11	+3
Should vote if you care who wins	24	21	26	26	24	23	-1
Duty to vote	68	68	64	65	64	65	-3
Base	*1224*	*970*	*989*	*1654*	*2008*	*2795*	

The *British Social Attitudes* survey has a long-standing question which asks:

> *How much interest do you generally have in what is going on in politics ...*
> *... a great deal,*
> *quite a lot,*
> *some,*
> *not very much,*
> *or, none at all?*

As the next table shows, the British public is no more disinterested in politics now than they were when Mrs Thatcher was Prime Minister. On each and every occasion that the question has been posed, the proportion saying they have a "great deal" or "quite a lot" of interest in politics has been within three points of 30 per cent. Most importantly for our purposes, the proportion expressing this

view after the 2001 election was within a couple of percentage points of the proportion who did so after the 1997 election.[5]

Table 7.8 Trends in political interest, 1986–2001

	% great deal/quite a lot of interest in politics	Base
1986	29	1548
1989	27	1516
1990	29	1397
1991	32	1445
1994	32	2302
1996	31	3620
1997 BSA	30	1355
1997 BES	33	2906
1998	29	3146
1999	28	3143
2000	33	2293
2001	31	3287

Source: 1997 BES: *British Election Study*

If there is little evidence that civic duty or interest in politics has declined, there is no doubt that there has been a long-term fall in the proportion of people who report a strong 'party identification', that is a strong emotional attachment to a political party (see, for example, Crewe and Thomson, 1999, Bromley *et al.*, 2001). The next table shows the extent of this decline over the last few decades. Whereas in 1987, nearly half (46 per cent) said they felt "very" or "fairly" strongly attached to a party, now only just over a third (37 per cent) feel the same way (and this represents a recovery from 32 per cent in 2000). Perhaps unsurprisingly, this drop has been particularly marked among (but far from confined to) Conservative identifiers. Meanwhile, in the same period, the proportion of people with no party identification increased from eight to 12 per cent.

Still, although there has been a long-term decline in strength of party identification, it has been a slow secular decline rather than a sudden drop. As a result only a very small decline occurred over the relatively short four-year period between 1997 and 2001. In 1997, 37 per cent had a "very" or "fairly" strong attachment, just one point higher than in 2001. And at ten per cent, the proportion saying they had no identification at all was just two points lower.[6] In short, it is far from clear that the electorate was significantly less motivated to vote in 2001 than it had been in 1997.

Table 7.9 Trends in strength of party identification, 1987–2001

Strength of party identification	1987	1989	1991	1993	1995	1997	1998	1999	2000	2001
	%	%	%	%	%	%	%	%	%	%
Very strong	11	11	8	9	10	10	8	7	6	7
Fairly strong	35	33	35	33	28	27	28	27	26	29
Not very strong	40	42	43	44	47	46	48	48	49	49
None	8	7	7	8	9	10	11	13	13	12
Base	*2847*	*3029*	*2918*	*2945*	*3633*	*1355*	*3145*	*3143*	*3426*	*3282*

The demotivated voter?

We have then seen two rather contrasting pictures so far as the motivations of voters are concerned. There is little evidence that voters were any more disengaged from politics in 2001 than they were in 1997. True, there has been a long-term decline in strength of party attachment, but even this only generated a small drop in the period between 1997 and 2001. On the other hand, the electorate was rather more cynical or disillusioned about the political system in 2001 than it had been in 1997. Voters were less likely to feel that they could trust their governments to put the interests of the country first and were more likely to report low levels of political efficacy. So, while it does not appear that we can blame the decline in turnout between 1997 and 2001 on disengagement, we can perhaps lay some of the blame on disillusion.

The political stimulus to vote

But as we noted at the beginning, the motivation that voters have to participate in an election is only one half of the equation that we have to consider. We also have to look at how much encouragement or stimulus there was to vote. If an election lacks excitement or if there does not appear to be much difference between the parties, then voters would seem less likely to turn out and vote than if an election is regarded as exciting or if there appears to be a big difference between the parties, and thus a great deal at stake. After all, analyses of how turnout varies from one constituency to another have long indicated that turnout tends to be higher in marginal seats than in safe ones (see, for example, Denver and Hands, 1997),[7] while international comparative research has found that turnout tends to be lower at elections which are dominated by one party (Bingham Powell, 1980; Lijphart,1999). Moreover, some analyses of why turnout was already relatively low in the 1997 election pointed the finger of blame at the failure of the election to offer much of a stimulus to vote (Heath and Taylor, 1999; Pattie and Johnston, 2001).

Differences between the parties

There is in fact good reason to believe both that the electorate felt that there was little at stake in the 2001 election and that there was little to get excited about. According to a content analysis of the party manifestoes, the Conservative and Labour parties were closer to each other ideologically in 2001 than they had been at any time since the era of 'Butskellism' in the 1950s (Bara and Budge, 2001). Meanwhile, voters' perceptions of how close the parties were can be gauged from the answers to a question that we included on the 2001 *British Social Attitudes* survey that had been asked on the *British Election Studies* after every election since 1964.[8] It ran:

> *Now considering everything that the Conservative and Labour parties*
> *stand for, would you say that ...*
> *... there is a great difference between them,*
> *... some difference,*
> *or, not much difference?*

Table 7.10 Perceived difference between the parties, 1964–2001

	1964	1966	1970	Feb 1974	Oct 1974	1979	1983	1987	1992	1997	2001
	%	%	%	%	%	%	%	%	%	%	%
Great difference	48	44	33	34	40	48	88	85	56	33	17
Some	25	27	28	30	30	30	10	11	32	43	39
Not much	27	29	39	36	30	22	7	5	12	24	44
Base	*1699*	*1804*	*1780*	*2391*	*2332*	*1826*	*3893*	*3776*	*1794*	*2836*	*1076*

Note: respondents who said 'Don't know' or who refused to answer have been excluded.
Source: 1964–1997 *British Election Study*. Figures for 1964–1992 as quoted in Crewe *et al.* (1995).

And as the previous table shows, those perceptions were very different in 2001 compared with any other recent election. Just 17 per cent thought that there was a great difference between the Conservative and Labour parties, just half of the previous all-time low of 33 per cent recorded in both 1970 and 1997.[9] Never before have the electorate felt that there was so little to choose between the two main parties.

The closeness of the race

As in a horse race, the excitement of an election comes from speculation and uncertainty about who will win. But there was no such source of excitement in 2001. Just as in 1997, the opinion polls suggested that Labour were heading for

a large victory. On average the final opinion polls suggested that Labour held a 14 point lead, only two points lower than in the final polls in 1997, and higher than at any other post-war election apart from 1983 (Heath and Taylor, 1999).

Of course, this could simply be taken to mean that 2001 was no different from 1997, and thus does not in itself explain that turnout should have fallen compared with 1997. There are, however, two reasons why 2001 might have been regarded as a less exciting election than was 1997. First, in contrast with 1997, the opinion polls did not suggest that there was even the prospective excitement of the incumbent government tumbling to defeat. Rather, they indicated that the result could well be strikingly similar to 1997, as indeed proved to be the case. Second, this was the first time in post-war British politics that the opinion polls pointed to a large lead for the second election in a row. And this itself was but a reflection of the fact that over the nine years since September 1992 the Labour Party had enjoyed an unparalleled period of opinion poll domination over its main rivals (Curtice, 2001).

Still, when non-voters themselves are asked why they did not vote, few mention that the election was a foregone conclusion (Worcester and Mortimore, 2001; Diplock, 2002), though we cannot necessarily assume that voters are the best judges of what influenced their behaviour. In any event it is difficult to gauge from post-election surveys just how close or exciting people thought the election was on polling day itself, as the survey is undertaken when people actually have knowledge of the real result. Much of our analysis of the impact of the stimulus that voters received at the 2001 election compared with 1997 will therefore focus primarily on the perceived difference between the parties.

However, we should also note one further important point. Not all voters require the same amount of stimulus to be persuaded to go to the polls. Those who do still have a strong party identification, have a high sense of political trust and efficacy, a strong sense of citizen duty and are interested in politics should be sufficiently motivated to go to the polls irrespective of the strength of the encouragement that they receive. On the other hand, those with no party identification, low trust and efficacy, little sense of citizen duty and no interest in politics could be expected to be highly sensitive to the amount of stimulus that they received to go to the polls. In short, if lack of excitement and a lack of a perceived difference between the parties was the reason why turnout fell so heavily between 1997 and 2001 we should find that the difference in the turnout between those with high motivation to vote and those with low motivations should have widened. So this is a pattern that we will be looking for as we turn to our analysis of how best to account for the fall in turnout between 1997 and 2001.

Analysing the fall in turnout, 1997–2001

Political trust

From our analysis so far, it would appear that the best place to start if we are to demonstrate that changing motivations were responsible for the decline in

turnout between 1997 and 2001 is to look at political trust and efficacy. If those who are distrustful or inefficacious are much less likely to vote, then perhaps the falls in trust and efficacy that we saw earlier may be an important part of the story. Whether or not this is the case is, however, the subject of some dispute. While the expectation might seem a reasonable one (Almond and Verba, 1963; Crozier *et al.*, 1975; Wolfinger *et al.*, 1990; Pattie and Johnston, 1998), it has also been argued that such feelings need not dissuade people from participating so long at least as they have not also lost their faith in democracy as a whole. Rather a lack of trust of efficacy can turn people into 'dissatisfied democrats' who have a particularly *strong* motivation to go to the polls in order to express their dissatisfaction (Klingemann, 1999). And indeed, while previous empirical research has sometimes found that those with lower efficacy and/or trust are less likely to vote (Heath and Taylor, 1999; Pattie and Johnston 2001; Bromley *et al.*, 2001), this has not proven to be invariably the case (Curtice and Jowell, 1995, 1997).

Table 7.11 Trust in government and electoral participation, 1997 and 2001

Trust government to place ..needs of the nation above ..those of party ...	% voted 1997	Base	% voted 2001	Base	Change 1997– 2001
... just about always/ most of the time	85	*961*	74	*304*	-11
... only some of the time	78	*1518*	69	*552*	-11
... almost never	67	*356*	51	*220*	-16

Source: 1997: *British Election Study*

In practice, as the previous table reveals, there is a relationship between trust in government and turnout, but only a modest one. Thus, while in 1997 no less than 85 per cent of those who said that they trusted governments to put the interests of the nation above those of party "just about always" or "most of the time" turned out to vote, even amongst those who never trusted governments two-thirds still made it to the polls. In any event, if the fall in political trust is to account fully for the decline in turnout then we should find that those with any given level of trust should have been just as likely to have voted in 2001 as they were in 1997. However, we can see immediately that this requirement is not met. Turnout fell between 1997 and 2001 both amongst those who are trustful of government and those who are not, so other factors must also be at work.

Efficacy

A similar tale applies in respect of efficacy. As the next table shows, those who express doubts about the level of system efficacy were rather less likely to say they voted in 1997, but not dramatically so (see also Heath and Taylor, 1999). Thus the gap in turnout between the most and the least efficacious is no more than 15 points, and it would take a very large fall in political efficacy indeed for such a gap to produce a twelve point fall in turnout. And in practice we can see that, as was the case with trust in government, turnout fell in 2001 amongst those who were still efficacious as well as those who were not.

Table 7.12 Political efficacy and electoral participation, 1997 and 2001

Parties are only interested in people's votes not in their opinions	% voted 1997	Base	% voted 2001	Base	Change 1997– 2001
Strongly agree	77	395	60	294	-17
Agree	79	1141	67	531	-12
Neither agree nor disagree	79	449	73	94	-6
Disagree/strongly disagree	87	428	75	167	-12
It doesn't really matter which party is in power, in the end things go on much the same	**% voted 1997**	*Base*	**% voted 2001**	*Base*	**Change 1997– 2001**
Strongly agree	70	200	52	187	-18
Agree	77	884	65	503	-12
Neither agree nor disagree	78	396	71	90	-7
Disagree/strongly disagree	85	946	77	314	-8

Source: 1997: *British Election Study*.

So it appears that the decline in turnout between 1997 and 2001 cannot be wholly blamed on the continued decline in trust and confidence in the political system. While cynicism may be rife it is not what is corroding citizens' willingness to participate.

Party identification

In contrast to trust and efficacy, strength of party identification has long been recognised as a key influence on turnout (Campbell *et al.*, 1960; Crewe *et al.*, 1977; Wattenberg, 2000). Voters who have a strong emotional attachment to a political party are thought to secure psychic gratification by turning out and expressing their loyalty to their favourite political party. Voters with no such attachments gain no such benefit from voting. The evidence for this can be seen

in the next table. In 1997 nearly nine in ten voters with a very strong identification voted whereas less than half of those without any identification did so.

Trouble is, we have seen that there has only been a small decline in strength of party identification since 1997. So unsurprisingly we do not find the pattern that would be required if a decline in party identification was wholly responsible for the fall in turnout between 1997 and 2001, that is no fall in turnout within each category of party identification. True, turnout was more or less the same at the two elections amongst very and fairly strong identifiers, but in contrast it fell by five points amongst not very strong identifiers and by no less than 30 points amongst those with no party identification at all.

Table 7.13 Strength of party identification and electoral participation, 1997 and 2001

Strength of party identification	% voted 1997	Base	% voted 2001	Base	Change 1997–2001
Very strong	88	450	89	261	+ 1
Fairly strong	86	1219	85	953	-1
Not very strong	72	972	67	1546	-5
None	47	203	17	394	-30

Source: 1997: *British Election Study*

Lack of political stimulus

But if this pattern is not consistent with what we would expect if the decline in turnout was simply the result of a decline in strength of party identification, it *is* consistent with what we suggested earlier we should expect to find if the reason why so many voters did not got to the polls in 2001 was because they did not receive sufficient stimulus to do so – that is that turnout would fall most amongst those with a relatively weak motivation to vote.[10] So while we have so far failed to find much convincing evidence that the decline in participation reflects declining voter motivation, we have now unearthed a first piece of evidence to support the claim that the explanation lies in a lack of stimulus and encouragement from the parties to do so.

And there is indeed further evidence to support the claim. In the next table we show how the fall in turnout varied between those with high and those with low political interest. Turnout fell by only six points amongst those with "a great deal" or "quite a lot" of interest in politics but dropped by nearly five times as much amongst those who profess no interest in politics at all.[11] And indeed further analysis suggests that while turnout was virtually unchanged amongst those who believe it is everyone's duty to vote, it fell by ten points amongst those who did not acknowledge such a duty.[12]

Table 7.14 Political interest and electoral participation, 1997 and 2001

Political interest	% voted 1997	Base	% voted 2001	Base	Change 1997–2001
A great deal	87	278	81	294	-6
Quite a lot	87	662	81	715	-6
Some	81	1066	72	1107	-9
Not very much	74	712	61	806	-13
None at all	59	188	31	365	-28

Source: 1997: *British Election Study*

These findings are supported by a more formal multivariate statistical modelling of the data shown in the appendix to this chapter. This modelling allows us to look at the strength of the association between turnout and each of the indicators we have been examining while controlling for the association that all of the other indicators have with turnout. As expected, it shows that both civic duty and strength of party identification were more strongly associated with turnout in 2001 than they were in 1997, and our model as a whole also accounts for more of the variation in turnout in 2001 than in 1997. In contrast, trust in government appears to have been less important in 2001 than in 1997, while our two indicators of political efficacy do not, in fact, have a significant association with turnout at all in either year.[13]

So we have found that the *principal* reason why turnout fell in 2001 was because the already disengaged stayed at home, rather than because more voters had become disengaged or cynical. But to demonstrate that this was the result of insufficient stimulus to vote, we need to tie our findings more closely to the evidence that we have on the extent of the stimulus that voters received.

Table 7.15 Perceptions of party difference and electoral participation, 1997 and 2001

% who say there is ...	% voted 1997	Base	% vote 2001	Base	Change 1997–2001
A great deal of difference	84	944	77	188	-7
Some	79	1224	72	417	-7
Not much	72	669	60	471	-12

Source: 1997: *British Election Study*

If indeed stimulus makes a difference to turnout, then one thing we should find is that those who do not think that there is much of a difference between the

parties are less likely to vote than are those who do see a difference. The previous table suggests that this indeed is the case. Just three in five of those who did not see much of a difference between the parties turned out in 2001 compared with a little over three-quarters of those who perceived a great difference.

Still, this hardly seems a big difference. However, we should also remember that our expectation is that the extent of the stimulus to vote that voters receive only matters for those who do not have much motivation to vote anyway. And indeed, the next table shows that this is precisely the case. Amongst those with a strong party identification, turnout was just as high in 2001 amongst those who did not see much difference between the parties as it was amongst those who felt there was a great difference. In contrast, amongst those with only a weak party identification, there was a turnout gap between the two groups of no less than 17 points.[14]

Table 7.16 Turnout in the 2001 election, by perceptions of party difference, and strength of party identification

| | Perceptions of the difference between the parties | | | |
| | Great difference | | Not much | |
Strength of party identification	% who voted	Base	% who voted	Base
Very/fairly strong	84	109	84	109
Not very strong/none	68	73	51	340

To this we can add one other important piece of the jigsaw puzzle. For, as the next table shows, it was amongst those with a weak sense of party identification that the perception that there is not much difference between the parties took greatest hold between 1997 and 2001.

Table 7.17 Perceptions of party difference and strength of party ID, 1997 and 2001

| | % who say there is not much difference between the parties | | | |
Strength of Party ID	**1997**	Base	**2001**	Base
Very strong	15	703	20	70
Fairly strong	18	1708	31	299
Not very strong	28	1396	48	566
None	38	303	57	128

Amongst very strong identifiers the proportion who did not see much difference between the parties rose by only five points from 15 to 20 per cent. In contrast it rose by four times as much amongst those with a not very strong identification and those with no identification at all.[15] In short, the perception that there was not much difference between the parties grew most amongst the very group of voters who most needed to hear the opposite message if they were to be persuaded to go to the polls. It should thus perhaps come as little surprise that the already disengaged stayed at home in droves.

What about young voters?

Our analysis so far would appear then to caution against apocalyptic prognoses for the future of electoral participation in Britain. If British electoral politics becomes competitive again, turnout could well return to its previous levels. However, those who take a more pessimistic view of the future point to one potentially important problem – the very low level of turnout amongst young people (Mulgan and Wilkinson, 1997). This pattern, it is suggested, is the shape of things to come as more and more disengaged young people enter the electorate (see Children and Young People's Unit, 2002; Russell *et al.*, 2002).

Of course, just because those who are young today do not vote does not necessarily mean that they will not vote tomorrow when they have reached middle age. Perhaps young voters always fail to see the point of voting, but then start to acquire the habit when they are a little older (Park, 1999). In other words, to show that there is a danger that young voters might have become disengaged, we have to show that the difference between the level of turnout amongst younger voters and that amongst older voters was wider in 2001 than it was in the past.

The next table therefore compares the turnout of each age group in 2001 with the turnout of the same age group in 1997. And indeed there is some suggestion that the gap might have widened somewhat.[16] Turnout appears to have fallen most amongst 18–24 year olds, and least amongst 65 year olds. So perhaps today's youth are more disengaged than were young people before them.

Table 7.18 Age and electoral participation, 1997 and 2001

Age	% voted 1997	Base	% voted 2001	Base	Change 1997–2001
18–24	61	316	43	226	-18
25–34	68	580	55	567	-13
35–44	78	566	65	712	-13
45–54	85	518	78	555	-7
55–64	89	386	74	467	-15
65+	87	532	82	755	-5

However, we should remember that younger voters are always amongst those with the least motivation to vote. They are less likely to have a sense of civic duty, to have a strong party identification or have much interest in politics (Park, 1999). In short, the young have always been disproportionately represented amongst the disengaged, who of course is precisely the kind of voter amongst whom turnout fell most heavily in 2001.

So, a widening of the difference between the turnout amongst younger voters and that amongst older voters is precisely what we would expect to find given that we have found that the already disengaged in all age groups were those amongst whom turnout fell most. A widening of the gap in turnout is not in itself evidence of a widening of the difference in the motivation of younger and older voters to go to the polling station. To demonstrate that, we would have to show that the gap between younger and older voters in terms of their degree of disengagement has widened too. And while we do not demur from Park's suggestion that this gap may have been wider in the late 1990s than it was in the 1980s (Park, 1999), our analysis of the trends in civic duty, strength of party identification and political interest between 1997 and 2001 does not indicate that the widening of the turnout gap was matched by a widening of the motivation gap during that period.

Table 7.19 Age and political interest, 1997 and 2001

Age	% with a "great deal"/"quite a lot" of interest in politics				
	1997	Base	2001	Base	Change 1997–2001
18–24	20	316	20	226	-0
25–34	24	579	22	567	-2
35–44	32	565	27	712	-5
45–54	38	518	37	555	-1
55–64	39	384	39	467	-0
65+	40	532	37	755	-3

Source: 1997: *British Election Study*

An example of this evidence is given in the previous table. It shows how political interest varied amongst the age groups in both 1997 and 2001. We can see that older voters are indeed more likely to express a high level of interest in politics. But at the same time, the pattern in 2001 is almost exactly the same as it was in 1997.[17] In short, we once again see that attempts to explain the fall in turnout between 1997 and 2001 by looking at the characteristics of voters does not take us very far.

Conclusions

The evidence presented in this chapter clearly gives far more credence to the argument that turnout fell in 2001 because the choice that the electorate was being asked to make was not sufficiently interesting, rather than because a wave of apathy and alienation has descended upon the electorate, sapping their motivation to vote. True, the electorate was more cynical about politicians and the political system in 2001 than it was in 1997, constituting a failure to realise Labour's hopes of repairing the apparent damage done to the reputation of the system in the 1990s. But cynical voters are only slightly less likely to vote than trusting ones. True also, the proportion of voters who have a strong attachment to a political party is lower now than it was 20 or 30 years ago. But this did not mean that the electorate was significantly more difficult to motivate in 2001 than it had been just four years earlier.[18] Meanwhile, there is no consistent evidence at all that the belief that voting is a civic duty has eroded or that interest in politics has waned.

Rather than the electorate becoming less motivated to vote, those who were already less motivated to vote stayed at home. They did so because they apparently received inadequate stimulus to persuade them that it was worth making the journey to the polling station this time. Voters felt there was less of a difference between the parties than ever before. And they had experienced an unprecedented near ten-year period of apparent one-party dominance in the polls, rather than two-party competitive elections. Far from heralding a crisis of democracy, the electorate arguably simply gave the 2001 election the scant attention it deserved.

So should we simply sit back and assume that normal service will be resumed in the near future? Should we forget attempts to cajole voters back onto the electoral stage by voter education campaigns or trying to make voting easier and more modern? After all, even the Electoral Commission has suggested that it is what voters are asked to vote for that matters, not how they are asked to vote (Electoral Commission, 2002).

There are perhaps two reasons for not taking quite so complacent a view. First, we should not assume that politics will necessarily become interesting once more. After all, many an analyst has suggested that globalisation has reduced the freedom of policy manoeuvre available to governments, and thus the ability of political parties to offer divergent political programmes. And we can certainly not assume that the Conservative Party is bound to become an effective electoral challenger to the Labour Party once more. There is nothing inevitable about the alternation of political power.

Second, while we have found it useful to draw a distinction between stimulus and motivation, over the longer term the two are bound to be intertwined. A persistent lack of political stimulus is likely in the end to undermine motivation. In particular, while there may so far be nothing very new about the low motivation of young people at present, if all that today's young voters ever experience between youth and middle age is uninteresting politics, then we should not assume that they will become more politically engaged as they get older in the way that their parents and grandparents did.

But even so, these arguments still suggest that the key to persuading Britain's voters to return to the polls is to give them a choice rather than change the electoral process. The real problem is that no one can guarantee that future elections will become more competitive than in 2001.

Notes

1. Just five per cent of our respondents who said they had voted indicated that they did so by post. Given the turnout of just under 60 per cent this is consistent with the Electoral Commission's own estimate that three per cent of all those eligible to vote did so by post.
2. It is possible to replicate some though not all of the analyses in this chapter using the 2001 *British Election Study*. Where this strategy is available the results have been reported in a footnote. The 2001 *British Election Study* recorded an eight point drop in turnout compared with its 1997 counterpart
3. Readers may wonder whether the particularly low levels of 18–24 year olds recording strong agreement with our political efficacy items should be read with caution given the relatively small number of such people upon which our reading is based. However, we obtained exactly the same pattern in 2000 when we have data for nearly three times as many 18–24 year olds.
4. Unfortunately, a rather different version of this question was asked on the 1997 *British Election Study*. It ran: *"Thinking now about voting in general elections, generally speaking, do you think people need not vote unless they really care who wins, or is it everyone's duty to vote?"* No less than 79 per cent said it was people's duty to vote, a product doubtless of being faced with just two alternative answers rather than three. We thus cannot directly compare the level of civic duty in 1997 and 2001, although we do later use the 1997 measure to compare the relationship between civic duty and turnout at the two elections. The 2001 *British Election Study* used a different measure yet again, though Clarke *et al.* (2003 forthcoming) suggest such comparison of the 1997 and 2001 data as can be made does not suggest there has been any erosion of civic duty.
5. Data collected by MORI for the Electoral Commission points to a similar conclusion (Electoral Commission, 2001). Meanwhile, the 2001 *British Election Study*, which administered exactly the same question as that being considered here, reports a very similar level of high political interest (29 per cent) to that found in our survey. The suggestion by Clarke *et al.* (2003 forthcoming) that this *British Election Study* figure indicates that there has been a fall in political interest would appear to be an over-interpretation of a small difference.
6. The *British Election Study* asks the same question to tap strength of identification as does the *British Social Attitudes* survey. However, it is administered after a rather different set of questions about which party the respondent has an attachment to, and this seems to result in rather different figures for strength of party identification in the two survey series. Even so, the trends in the *British Election Study* series are identical to those in the *British Social Attitudes* series – that is a long-term decline (Crewe and Thomson, 1999) but little change between 1997 and 2001. The 2001 *British Election Study* figures (and change since 1997) are: very

strong, 13 per cent (-2); fairly strong, 41 per cent (-1); not very strong, 35 per cent (+2), and none, ten per cent (+3).

7. Though it has also been suggested that the higher level of turnout in marginal seats disappears once differences in the socio-psychological and demographic characteristics have been controlled for (Pattie and Johnston, 1998, 2001), though why those who live in marginal seats should have a higher propensity to vote anyway has not been explained. That marginality may in practice have an independent effect (albeit one that may be too small to be detected when modelling survey data using large numbers of controls) is suggested by the fact that changes in the marginality of a seat are associated with changes in the relative level of turnout (Curtice and Steed, 2001).

8. Between 1964 and October 1974 the question read: *"Considering everything the parties stand for, would you say there is a good deal of difference between them, some difference or not much difference?"*

9. This question was also administered on the 2001 *British Election Study*. That found a rather higher proportion (28 per cent) saying there was a great difference. However, the question was asked on a self-completion questionnaire rather than face-to-face as it had been in previous *British Election Studies*. So comparability with previous years may have been compromised by mode effects. In any event, even this reading is lower than that obtained by any previous *British Election Studies*.

10. The evidence of the 2001 *British Election Study*, where party identification was measured in exactly the same way in 1997 and 2001 (see fn. 7), also supports this contention. The study records a turnout of 88 per cent amongst very strong identifiers, the same as in 1997, 81 per cent amongst fairly strong identifiers (-5), 64 per cent amongst not very strong identifiers (-8), and 33 per cent amongst those without any party identification (-14).

11. This pattern is also replicated if we look at the 2001 *British Election Study*. It finds a one point increase and just a three point drop amongst those with "a great deal" and "quite a lot" of interest respectively, but no less than a twelve point drop amongst those with "not very much interest" and a 23 point fall amongst those with no interest at all.

12. Readers are, however, reminded of the difference between the wording of the civic duty question on the 1997 and 2001 surveys (see fn. 5). Part of the reason why turnout did not appear to fall at all amongst those who did report a civic duty is that the tighter definition of that group in the 2001 survey may have helped mask any fall that occurred. However, it seems unlikely that this accounts for all of the difference reported here.

13. Note that dropping civic duty from the model on the grounds that the wording of the question was very different in the two years does not affect any of the other key findings of the remainder of the model. Party identification is still more strongly related to turnout in 2001 than in 1997, while none of the indicators of trust and efficacy are.

14. The 2001 *British Election Study* tells a similar tale. Turnout was 84 per cent amongst strong identifiers who saw a great difference between the parties and 87 per cent amongst those who did not. The equivalent figures amongst weak identifiers were 73 per cent and 63 per cent respectively.

15. A not dissimilar result is obtained if we compare the results of the 2001 *British Election Study* with those of the 1997 study. Amongst very strong identifiers the proportion saying there was not much difference between the parties actually fell by one point, while it rose by five points amongst those with no party identification at all.

16. However, the evidence is not so strong in the 2001 *British Election Study*. Its figures for turnout in 2001 (and change since 1997) are: 18–24 year olds, 54 per cent (-7); 24–34 year olds, 55 per cent (-13); 35–44 year olds 68 per cent (-10); 45–54 year olds 79 per cent (-6); 55–64 year olds, 78 per cent (-11) and 65 plus, 86 per cent (-1).

17. If we compare the 2001 *British Election Study* figures with the 1997 figures in the table, we again find that the motivation of young voters did not suffer a particularly marked fall. So while this study suggests there was a six point drop in the proportion of 18–24 year olds with a high level of political interest (and no drop amongst 25–34 year olds) it also finds a drop of seven points amongst both 35–44 years olds and 45–54 year olds, a four point fall amongst the over 65s and a two point decrease amongst 55–64 year olds. So as far as party identification is concerned while comparison of the *British Social Attitudes* party identification figures for 1997 and 2001 reveals a three point fall in the proportion of 18–24 year olds who have a "very" or "fairly" strong party identification, there are even larger falls amongst those aged 35–64.

18. What of course could be argued is that if a low stimulus election of the kind that happened in 2001 had occurred 20 years ago, then the higher level of strong party identification in existence at that time would have ensured there was a less precipitate fall in turnout than happened in 2001.

References

Almond, G. and Verba, S. (1963), *The Civic Culture: Political Attitudes and Democracy in Five Nations*, Princeton, NJ: Princeton University Press.

Bara, J. and Budge, I. (2001), 'Party Policy and Ideology: Still New Labour?', in Norris, P. (ed.), *Britain Votes 2001*, Oxford: Oxford University Press.

Bingham Powell, G. (1980), 'Voting turnout in 30 democracies: partisan and socio-economic influences', in Rose, R. (ed.), *Electoral Participation: A Comparative Analysis*, London: Sage.

Bromley, C., Curtice, J. and Seyd, B. (2001), 'Political engagement, trust and constitutional reform', in Park, A., Curtice, J., Thomson, K., Jarvis, L. and Bromley, C. (eds.), *British Social Attitudes: the 18th Report: Public policy, Social ties*, London: Sage.

Campbell, A., Converse, P., Miller, W. and Stokes, D. (1960), *The American Voter*, New York: Wiley.

Children and Young People's Unit (2002), *Young People and Politics*, London: Children and Young People's Unit.

Clarke, H., Sanders, D., Stewart, M. and Whiteley, P. (2003 forthcoming), 'Britain NOT at the Polls', *PS*, **36**.

Crewe, I., Fox, A., and Alt, J. (1977), 'Non-voting in British general elections', in Crouch, C. (ed.), *British Political Sociology Yearbook*, London: Croom Helm.

Crewe, I., Fox, A., and Day, N. (1995), *The British Electorate, 1963–1992*, Cambridge: Cambridge University Press.

Crewe, I. and Thomson, K. (1999), 'Party loyalties: dealignment or realignment?' in Evans, G. and Norris, P. (eds.), *Critical Elections: British Parties and Voters in Long-Term Perspective*, London: Sage.

Crozier, M., Hungton, S., and Watanuki, J. (1975), *The Crisis of Democracy: Report on the Governability of Democracies to the Trilateral Commission*, New York: New York University Press.

Curtice, J. (2001), 'The horserace' in O'Grady, S. (ed.), *The Rough Guide to the Election*, London: Penguin.

Curtice, J. (2002), 'The state of election studies: mid-life crisis or new youth?', *Electoral Studies*, **21**: 161–168.

Curtice, J. and Jowell, R. (1995), 'The sceptical electorate', in Jowell, R., Curtice, J., Park, A., Brook, L. and Ahrendt, D. (eds.), *British Social Attitudes: the 12th Report*, Aldershot: Dartmouth.

Curtice, J., and Jowell, R. (1997), 'Trust in the Political System', in Jowell, R., Curtice, J., Park, A., Brook, L., Thomson, K. and Bryson, C. (eds.), *British Social Attitudes: the 14th Report – The end of Conservative values?*, Aldershot: Ashgate.

Curtice, J., and Steed, M. (2001), 'Appendix 2: The Results Analysed', in Butler, D. and Kavanagh, D. (eds.), *The British General Election of 2001*, Basingstoke: Palgrave.

Denver, D. and Hands, G. (1997), 'Turnout' in *Parliamentary Affairs*, **50**: 720-732.

Diplock, S. (2002), *None of the Above: Non-voters and the 2001 election*, London: Hansard Society for Parliamentary Government.

Electoral Commission (2001), *Election 2001: The Official Results*, London: Politicos.

Electoral Commission (2002), *Modernising Local Elections: A strategic evaluation of the 2002 electoral pilot schemes*, London: Electoral Commission.

Heath, A. and Taylor, B. (1999), 'New Sources of Abstention?', in Evans, G. and Norris, P. (eds.), *Critical Elections: British Parties and Voters in Long-Term Perspective*, London: Sage.

Klingemann, H. (1999), 'Mapping Political Support in the 1990s: A Global Analysis', in Norris, P. (ed.), *Critical Citizens: Global Support for Democratic Governance*, Oxford: Oxford University Press.

Lijphart, A. (1999), *Patterns of Democracy*, New Haven, Conn.: Yale University Press.

Mulgan, G. and Wilkinson, H. (1997), 'Freedom's children and the rise of generational politics', in Mulgan, G. (ed.), *Life after Politics: New Thinking for the Twenty-First Century*, London: Fontana.

Park, A. (1999), 'Young People and Political Apathy', in Jowell, R., Curtice, J., Park, A. and Thomson, K. (eds.), *British Social Attitudes: the 16th Report – Who shares New Labour values?*, Aldershot: Ashgate.

Pattie, C. and Johnston, R. (1998), 'Voter turnout at the British general election of 1992: rational choice, social standing or political efficacy?', *European Journal of Political Research*, **33**: 263–283.

Pattie, C. and Johnston, R. (2001), 'A Low Turnout Landslide: Abstention at the British General Election of 1997', *Political Studies*, **49**: 286–305.

Russell, A. Fieldhouse, E., Purdam, K. and Kalra, V. (2002), *Voter Engagement and Young People*, London: Electoral Commission.

Swaddle, K. and Heath, A. (1989), 'Official and Reported Turnout in the British General Election of 1987', *British Journal of Political Science*, **19**: 537–570.

Wattenberg, M. (2000), 'The Decline of Party Mobilization', in Dalton, R. and Wattenberg, M. (eds.), *Parties Without Partisans: Political Change in Advanced Industrial Democracies*, Oxford: Oxford University Press.

Wolfinger, R., Glass, D. and Squire, P. (1990), 'Predictors of electoral turnout: An international comparison', *Policy Studies Review*, **9**: 551–574.

Worcester, R. and Mortimore, R. (2001), *Explaining Labour's Second Landslide*, London: Politicos.

Acknowledgements

The *National Centre for Social Research* would like to thank the Economic and Social Research Council, which financed many of the questions reported in this chapter through grants as part of its Democracy and Participation Programme (grant no. L215252032) and Devolution and Constitutional Change Programme (grant no. L219 25 2018).

Appendix: Modelling turnout in 1997 and 2001

The following table shows the results of logistic modelling of turnout in 1997 and 2001. The independent variables are coded as follows:

Civic duty
1 = have a duty to vote
0 = all other answers

Strength of party ID
Interval level variable ranging from 3 (very strong) to 0 (no identification)

Political interest
Interval level variable ranging from 5 (a great deal) to 0 (none at all)

Trust government
Interval level variable ranging from 3 (trust government to put the nation's interests just about always) to 0 (almost never)

Parties interested in votes
Interval level variable ranging from 4 (strongly disagree that parties are only interested in people's votes) to 0 (strongly agree)

Doesn't matter who is in power
Interval level variable ranging from 4 (strongly disagree that it doesn't matter who is in power) to 0 (strongly agree)

Logistic modelling of turnout in 1997 and 2001

	1997		2001	
	Coefficient	**Standard error**	**Coefficient**	**Standard error**
Civic duty	1.44	.12	1.93	(.18)
Strength of party ID	.43	.08	.95	(.15)
Political interest	.19	.06	.12	(.09)
Trust government	.27	.09	.07	(.13)
Parties interested in votes	.00	.07	-.16	(.11)
Doesn't matter who is in power	-.04	.06	.11	(.09)
Cox & Snell R2	12%		27%	
Base	*2876*		*854*	

Source: 1997: *British Election Study*

8 English to the core?

Anthony Heath, Catherine Rothon and Lindsey Jarvis *

For many years Britain was seen as "essentially a homogeneous nation" (Blondel, 1963). But with the rise of Scottish and Welsh nationalism in the 1970s, and the subsequent debates over devolution, it has become more common to think of Britain (strictly the UK) as a multinational state. This has led to a great deal of research focusing on differences between England, Wales and Scotland (see, for example, Taylor and Thomson, 1999). However, not everyone would agree that this is the right approach to take. As Steed (1986: S92) has cogently argued:

> There is much evidence that this trichotomous organization of the data and of research has simplified reality in a misleading way. Take voting behaviour ...

Steed suggests that treating England as homogeneous is no more sensible than was the earlier tendency to treat Britain as homogeneous and to ignore the differences between England, Wales and Scotland. In place of this trichotomous view, he has suggested an analysis based on the notions of core and periphery, with a more graduated set of distinctions within both core and periphery. In other words, he distinguishes an inner core of London and the South East, an outer core of the Midlands, East Anglia and Wessex, an inner periphery of the North of England, Wales and the South West peninsula (or Dumnonia as he terms it), and an outer periphery of Scotland. These boundaries "correspond reasonably well with arcs drawn around London at 80, 200 and 300 miles" (Steed, 1986: S99). He suggests that there is a gradation in political attitudes

* Anthony Heath is Professor of Sociology at the University of Oxford and Co-director of the ESRC *Centre for Research into Elections and Social Trends (CREST)*. Catherine Rothon is a Research Officer for *CREST* at the University of Oxford. Lindsey Jarvis is a Research Director at the *National Centre for Social Research* and Co-Director of the *British Social Attitudes* survey series.

and behaviour as we move from the inner core to the outer periphery rather than a sharp contrast between England on the one hand and Scotland and Wales on the other.

The theoretical ideas lying behind the core/periphery dimension are not always clearly articulated (for a good overview see Wellhofer, 1989). We can distinguish several different versions but common to them all is the claim that cores are advantaged and peripheries economically disadvantaged. The periphery is thought of as being less developed, involving primary economies, with low technology and labour-intensive activities (Rokkan and Urwin, 1982, 1983).

Unequal political power is a second key element (which is often, as in Hechter's 1975 work, used to explain the economic inequalities). The core is seen to be the locus of political power with the implication that the interests of the periphery will therefore receive less recognition than those of the core. An extreme case of this would be one where the core has expanded its power from its original territorial base and colonised the peripheral regions, and this is the essence of Hechter's concept of 'internal colonialism'.

Thirdly, there are expected to be cultural differences between core and periphery. The core is seen to be the cultural centre and to be culturally dominant. Although the peripheral regions are seen to have their own local cultures, these are fragmented from each other and linked through the core rather than directly to each other. This can be developed into the notion of a network with the core at the hub of the network (Borgatti and Everett, 2000). Furthermore, the core will also be the centre of the communications system which will therefore tend to make it easier for the culture of the core to be disseminated.

These three aspects of core/periphery inequalities imply that members of the periphery are likely to accord the core lower support and legitimacy and to be less satisfied with existing economic and political arrangements. It is suggested that they may show less support for national symbols since these will tend to be identified with the core. This kind of reasoning has been used to explain support for separatist movements in peripheral territories such as Scotland and Wales, although most theories would emphasise the importance of having a distinct ethnic or national group in the peripheral region to form the focus of the separatist movement. In the case of peripheral regions within England, therefore, we would not expect to find anything like the pressures for political change or devolution that have been seen in Scotland or Wales. However, where there are distinct regional cultural identities we may find some pressure for political reform.

Based on these accounts of centre/periphery relations, our expectations of our analysis of the *British Social Attitudes* data would be that:

- The peripheral regions in England will tend to be economically disadvantaged.
- They will show lower levels of support for central, core political institutions.

- Where there are distinct regional cultures, they will also show higher levels of support for regional devolution.

Of course, these analytical concerns now have added interest given the context of current debates about regional government for England. The proposal for regional assemblies appears to be based on an analogy with the new Scottish and Welsh institutions, and the idea that there are distinct interests and/or identities in the English regions comparable to the distinct claims made by Welsh and Scots. The arguments in favour of regional assemblies seem to involve both economic and political aspects. Economically, it is implied that regions may have distinct local interests (perhaps for inward investment or for economic regeneration) that diverge to some degree from those of the country as a whole. Politically, it is suggested that regional assemblies would provide greater local accountability for current regional institutions that are presently answerable only to Westminster. The new White Paper (Office of the Deputy Prime Minister, 2002) emphasises the way in which the proposed assemblies can cater for regional diversity. If England is indeed homogeneous, both economically and culturally, it is less clear what useful role there is for regional assemblies and one suspects there will be less demand for them.

In this chapter we therefore propose to examine these issues by exploring regional differences in:

- Economic situation
- Culture and identity
- Perceived political legitimacy
- Demand for regional devolution.

The regional classification we use on the *British Social Attitudes* survey and throughout this chapter is based on the Government Office Regions (GOR) classification. This corresponds exactly with the areas covered by the main current institutions, Regional Development Agencies (RDAs) and Regional Chambers, which are likely to be the basis of any future regional assemblies. The GOR classification does not correspond directly with all the areas discussed by Steed as he uses smaller area breakdowns but it does provide a good overall basis for comparison.

Economic situation

We start by looking at objective economic measures of regional differences. The following table shows gross domestic product and disposable household income for the nations within the UK and for the English regions, grouped under Steed's core and periphery headings. Looking at the 'per head indexes', we see that the regions broadly fit into Steed's model but with clear exceptions. London and the South East certainly belong to the inner core with *per capita* indexes well above the UK average. However, the East region would appear better placed in the inner core rather than in the outer core where Steed located

it alongside the Midlands. This may be because the data shown in the table is for the Eastern GOR which covers not only the more peripheral areas of East Anglia but also the London-oriented southern parts, such as Hertfordshire, Bedfordshire and Essex, which Steed would have included in the South East.

Nor is there a very clear distinction between the outer core and the inner periphery. The Midlands (supposedly outer core) appear to be rather similar to the South West (inner periphery), and indeed to the North West and Yorkshire and Humber. Furthermore, within the outer periphery, Scotland completely breaks the pattern, with economic indicators that exceed those of most of Steed's outer core. This leaves Northern Ireland (from the outer periphery) and the North East (from the inner periphery) as the most economically disadvantaged areas.

Table 8.1 Objective economic measures by region, 1999

	Gross domestic product *per capita* £	Per head index	Gross disposable household income *per capita* £	Per head index
Inner core				
London	16,900	130.0	12,036	119.4
South East	15,100	116.4	11,249	111.6
Outer core				
East	15,100	116.4	11,255	111.7
East Midlands	12,100	93.6	9,346	92.7
West Midlands	11,900	91.7	9,195	91.2
Inner periphery				
North East	10,000	77.3	8,353	82.9
North West	11.300	86.9	9,375	93.0
Yorkshire & Humber	11,400	87.9	9,305	92.3
South West	11,800	90.8	9,825	97.5
Wales	10,400	80.5	9,113	90.4
England	**13,300**	**102.4**	**10,237**	**101.6**
Outer periphery				
Scotland	12,500	96.5	9,558	94.8
N. Ireland	10,100	77.5	8,659	85.9
UK	**13,000**	**100.0**	**10,088**	**100.0**

Source: National Statistics 2001a, 2001b.

There are, then, quite a number of anomalies that do not fit well into Steed's overall categorization, loosely based on distance from London. To be sure, London and its environs stand out as a core, but the distinctions between outer

core, inner periphery and outer periphery do not look quite so convincing. On the other hand Steed is right to reject a simple trichotomous model of England, Wales and Scotland. There are clearly major regional variations *within* England that are greater than the overall variations between England, Wales and Scotland. And although there is some division between the North and the South with the South generally more economically advantaged, the notion of a North/South divide is also too simplistic as it hides regional differences within it.

We can check to see whether these *objective* economic measures are reflected by more subjective experience from answers to a series of *British Social Attitudes* questions. First, we asked respondents whether they would place themselves in a "high-", "middle-" or "low-income" group. They were also asked to select their gross household income from a set of banded options. Finally, they were asked to choose a phrase to describe how they were currently managing on their household's income. The next table shows the regional differences in the proportion belonging to the most disadvantaged groups – they placed themselves in the low-income category, they had a household income below £8,000 and they were "finding it difficult/very difficult on their present income".

Table 8.2 Perceptions of own economic situation

	% in low-income group	% with income <£8,000	% who find it difficult on income	Base
Inner core				
London	41	12	21	345
South East	32	10	10	448
Outer core				
East	35	14	11	318
East Midlands	42	13	13	256
West Midlands	40	14	17	293
Inner periphery				
North East	47	21	10	185
North West	48	16	14	342
Yorkshire & Humber	48	18	13	305
South West	47	14	15	269
England	**41**	**15**	**14**	2761

There does seem to be some regional variation in the first two measures shown in the previous table. Overall, we see a gradual increase in those who consider themselves to be in the low-income group as we move from the core to the

periphery (but with the exception of London). The East again seems to fit better within the inner core as it has a similar proportion to the South East who place themselves in the low-income bracket with around a third doing so. Slightly more label themselves as low-income households in the outer core of the Midlands. And there is a further increase in the inner periphery, almost a half of whom think of themselves in this way (although the figures for the North East are not statistically significantly different from those for the Midlands).

When we look at those who say they have household incomes of less than £8,000, we find that people's perceptions of being on low income are generally matched by the level of their reported income apart from those in the South West. Although few of these differences are significant, the pattern again seems to be that people become more economically disadvantaged the further they are from the inner core.

However, on the last measure – those who "find it difficult or very difficult on their present income", there is no clear-cut regional variation. London has the highest proportion – one in five – who report that they find it difficult to manage on their current income. This is completely at odds with the centre/periphery concept. This may well be because of the high cost of living, especially housing, in London, and draws our attention to the huge variation in experience within a region. While London has the highest average household income, it will also have greater variation around that average.

Culture and identity

So, there does seem to be evidence of objective economic differences between the regions of England, although this does not appear to extend to subjective experience of economic difficulty. Does it extend to cultural differences? The next section looks at this in terms of regional pride and identification with the national flag.

We asked respondents how much pride they had in being someone who lives in their region (with the name of their Government Office Region inserted into the question text) or did they not think of themselves in that way at all. Here we see a very clear pattern with much higher levels of local pride in the three northern regions than elsewhere, while lower levels are generally found in the inner and outer core areas. Strikingly, the proportion of those in the three northern regions who feel "very proud" of being from that area is greater than the proportion who feel both "very proud" *and* "somewhat proud" in being from the South East, East and East Midlands. Unlike the economic pattern, then, there does seem to be a clear North/South divide on this particular measure of cultural identity, with a clear break between the three northern regions and all the others, rather than a gradual pattern of increasing pride as distance increases from the centre.

However, London once more spoils the core/periphery pattern with rather higher levels than expected of regional pride. Yet, it may be a mistake to think of the Londoner's pride as a specifically regional pride. It may instead be based on an identification with the metropolis and it is possible that the inhabitants of

other great cities such as Birmingham may feel a pride in their city that does not extend to the broader geographical region. Something similar may be happening in the South West. The South West has a lower sense of regional pride than the other three regions of the inner periphery. Perhaps those in the South West feel a strong regional identity with being "Cornish" for example, but do not respond to the Government Office Region descriptions used in the question, that is "the South West of England". Part of the problem seems to be that the regions set up by government for administrative reasons do not always correspond with the main focus of local pride.

Table 8.3 Regional pride

		Very proud	Somewhat proud	Not very/ not at all proud	Don't think in that way	Base
Inner core						
London	%	19	31	7	43	345
South East	%	8	17	3	72	448
Outer core						
East	%	11	13	3	73	318
East Midlands	%	12	21	4	62	256
West Midlands	%	17	20	6	58	293
Inner periphery						
North East	%	44	26	3	27	185
North West	%	34	29	3	34	342
Yorkshire & Humber	%	46	24	3	27	305
South West	%	21	21	2	56	269
England	%	**22**	**22**	**4**	**52**	2761

We also gauged opinions about national symbols by showing English respondents, firstly, the Union flag and, secondly, the Cross of St George and asking whether the flags made them "feel proud, hostile or not feel much either way". Following Steed, we would expect more attachment to national symbols in the core regions as these symbols are typically identified with the core. We might also have expected higher levels of regional pride (as we have just found in the three northern regions) to be associated with reduced levels of pride in national symbols. However, in the three northern regions levels of pride in the national flag are virtually the same as or higher than the national average for the whole of England. So there is little evidence that regional loyalties conflict with British loyalties. This, of course, contrasts strongly with the very clear pattern found in the outer periphery of Wales and Scotland where those who feel proud

of the Union flag are in a minority, 38 per cent in Wales and 31 per cent in Scotland.

London also spoils any straightforward core/periphery model with rather lower levels of attachment to national symbols than might have been expected from its position in the inner core. It is logically possible that, in London, there is an inverse relation between local and national pride. However, more detailed analysis suggests that the low levels of attachment to the Union flag in London are to be attributed to the relatively large numbers of residents in London who are not actually British, rather than to the rival attractions of local pride.

Table 8.4 Attachment to the Union flag

		Proud	Does not feel much either way	A bit/very hostile	Base
Inner core					
London	%	51	42	4	345
South East	%	66	31	2	448
Outer core					
East	%	57	39	2	318
East Midlands	%	57	36	3	256
West Midlands	%	61	37	2	293
Inner periphery					
North East	%	61	38	1	185
North West	%	58	40	1	342
Yorkshire & Humber	%	65	34	0	305
South West	%	52	44	3	269
England	%	**59**	**37**	**2**	2761

When we look at English loyalty through levels of pride in the Cross of St George, we obtain very similar results to those found for the Union flag.

Perceived political legitimacy

Turning now to regional differences in political response, we asked respondents for their opinion on the "present system of governing Britain". We would again expect from Steed's viewpoint that the inner core would show more support for the existing political system as they would feel more closely aligned with the present system as they live nearer central government in London. Although there is remarkably little variation, the slight differences found would indicate the opposite of this to be true. Those in the peripheral region of Yorkshire and

Humber were slightly *less* likely to criticise the present system of governing Britain than those in all other areas apart from the North East and North West. Other areas showed similar levels of support for change as each other, with the highest level of discontent found in the East Midlands (although this was not significantly different to levels in the West Midlands and London). It is perhaps not surprising that there is little variation given that even in the outer periphery areas of Wales and Scotland with their rather different constitutional experience, dissatisfaction with the British political system is not much higher than in England (56 per cent in Wales and 59 per cent in Scotland express the desire for a great deal or quite a lot of improvement in the government of Britain).

Table 8.5 Opinions about present system of governing Britain

		Needs a great deal/quite a lot of improvement	Could be improved in small ways	Works extremely well	*Base*
Inner core					
London	%	56	40	2	*345*
South East	%	52	45	2	*448*
Outer core					
East	%	52	45	2	*318*
East Midlands	%	61	38	0	*256*
West Midlands	%	56	41	2	*293*
Inner periphery					
North East	%	50	45	5	*185*
North West	%	49	47	2	*342*
Yorkshire & Humber	%	44	52	2	*305*
South West	%	54	42	2	*269*
England	%	**52**	**44**	**2**	*2761*

A further question on perceived political legitimacy was asked:

> *Some people say that it makes no difference which party wins in elections, things go on much the same. Using this card, please say how much of a difference **you** think it makes who wins in general elections to the House of Commons?*

However, this question also elicited little regional difference. Around four in ten in all regions gave the positive view that it made "a great deal" or "quite a lot" of difference who won. So we have not found any evidence of a politically marginalised periphery in terms of the national government. However, perhaps

it is in opinions about regional government that the core and periphery areas differ and it is to this question that we now turn.

Demand for regional devolution

To investigate views on how England should be governed, we asked the following question:

> *With all the changes going on in the way the different parts of Great Britain are run, which of the following do you think would be best for England?*
> *For England to be governed as it is now, with laws made by the UK parliament*
> *For each region of England to have its own assembly that runs services like health*
> *Or for England as a whole to have its own new parliament with law-making powers?*

Table 8.6 Demands for regional government in England

		England to be governed as it is now	Each region of England to have its own assembly	England as a whole to have its own new parliament	None/ Don't know	*Base*
Inner core						
London	%	59	21	13	7	*345*
South East	%	58	19	20	3	*448*
Outer core						
East	%	60	18	19	3	*318*
East Midlands	%	49	22	20	8	*256*
West Midlands	%	60	22	13	5	*293*
Inner periphery						
North East	%	58	29	10	4	*185*
North West	%	54	28	13	5	*342*
Yorkshire & Humber	%	58	25	12	5	*305*
South West	%	54	25	19	2	*269*
England	%	**57**	**23**	**16**	**5**	*2761*

In the previous table, we see some indication that those regions with stronger regional identities have greater support for regional government, although the differences are not statistically significant. Those who live in the periphery have

slightly greater demand for regional assemblies. In all four of the inner periphery regions we find that support for regional assemblies is higher than the national average for the whole of England. For example, almost three in ten of those in the North East and North West take this view compared with about two in ten in the core regions.

But why do those in the inner periphery feel more enthusiasm for regional government? Do they expect it to provide more benefits for their area, which the distant London-run government does not? We assessed this through two questions about the possible benefits of regional assemblies. Firstly, we asked respondents whether they thought their local regional chamber or assembly would give ordinary people more of a say in how their region is governed, less say or make no difference. Secondly, we asked whether they thought a regional chamber or assembly would make the region's economy better, worse or make no difference. Responses shown in the following table suggest that the three northern regions are slightly more optimistic about the potential benefits of having regional government. This would lend support to the idea that the periphery does feel somewhat alienated and poorly served by a distant central government. However, London again contradicts this theory by showing some of the strongest support for regional assemblies despite also being the location of central government. This may perhaps reflect enthusiasm for the new London Assembly, which Londoners elected only one month before fieldwork began.

Table 8.7 Reasons for preferring regional government

	% who say regional assemblies will give ordinary people more of a say	% who say regional assemblies will make the region's economy better	Base
Inner core			
London	38	34	345
South East	25	20	448
Outer core			
East	29	28	318
East Midlands	35	25	256
West Midlands	22	25	293
Inner periphery			
North East	35	42	185
North West	39	31	342
Yorkshire & Humber	36	31	305
South West	32	27	269
England	**32**	**29**	2761

So, the main conclusions we have identified so far in examining regional differences are that:

- Objective economic indicators are reasonably close to Steed's core/periphery model although there are some anomalies.
- Our measure of subjective economic dissatisfaction does not fit at all well with the core/periphery model, London in particular being a major anomaly.
- Regional pride is much stronger in the three northern regions than elsewhere but the fourth region of the inner periphery, the South West, does not exhibit as much regional pride as might have been expected while London again proves to be a deviant case too.
- There is no systematic core/periphery variation in a sense of attachment to national symbols.
- There is little difference between the regions in support for the present system of British democracy and, if anything, the northern regions were more positive than others.
- There is slightly more support for regional assemblies in the three northern regions and in the South West than in the inner and outer core.
- Those in the north and in London had a tendency to express more enthusiasm for the benefits of regional assemblies than elsewhere in England.

Who supports regional devolution?

The pattern that we have found so far, therefore, gives only limited support to Steed's core/periphery model. This model works only partially when we look at objective economic indicators and it does not translate particularly well into subjective economic dissatisfaction. In any case, regional patterns of economic disadvantage do not seem to translate in any straightforward way into views on the present system of government or demands for regional assemblies. There is, however, a clear pattern with the three northern regions having both higher levels of regional pride and higher levels of support for assemblies (while the other member of the inner periphery – the South West – supports regional assemblies but has low regional pride). This suggests, therefore, that the key factor in explaining support for political change may not be the inequalities in economic and political power suggested by the centre/periphery theorists but the presence (or absence) of local cultures (analogous perhaps to the ethnic cleavages that play such a key role in understanding separatist nationalist movements).

One way to pursue this question further is to carry out a multivariate analysis in which we attempt to explain why individuals support the proposals for regional assemblies. Does this support depend on the kinds of factor suggested by the centre/periphery theorists, such as economic or political disadvantage, or does it depend more on regional pride and attachment?

To explore this question we employ a logistic regression model (for full details, see the appendix to this chapter). We look at whether respondents agreed with the statement that it would be best "for each region of England to have its own assembly that runs services like health". Our explanatory variables are our various measures of economic position (measured by the respondents' reported income), economic dissatisfaction (measured by the question on how respondents felt about current income), political dissatisfaction (measured by the item on respondents' opinions about the current system of governing Britain), and regional pride (measured by the question asking how much pride the respondent has in being someone who lives in the region). We also include, as control variables, the region of the respondent in order to see how far the variables manage to explain the regional differences observed in Table 8.6.

We find that political dissatisfaction has a statistically significant relationship with support for regional assemblies. So, people who thought that the present system of governing Britain needed only small changes were less inclined to support regional assemblies than were people who were more dissatisfied with the system of governing Britain.

Surprisingly, regional pride, was *not* associated with demand for regional devolution and nor was economic dissatisfaction. Instead, even after taking account of other variables, we still find that significant regional differences persist. The North East, North West and South West show significantly higher levels of support for regional assemblies than does the reference category of the South East. This means that we have not fully explained the regional differences that we observed in Table 8.6. One possibility is that there are additional factors that we ought to include in our analysis. The likeliest omission here is some measure of our respondents' perceptions of regional economic interests. The measure of economic dissatisfaction included in our analysis refers simply to the individual and his or her family. There may be many reasons why an individual is facing difficulty living on their current income – such as a recent divorce or the cost of school fees – which have nothing to do with the region in which he or she lives. Other factors, such as the cost of housing, may be ones that are more specific to the region but that will only be one among many other possible ingredients of our measure. In addition, we do not have any historical or cultural measures, which are likely to influence the views in each region about local democracy.

There is, therefore, something of a paradox in the results of our multivariate analysis. On the one hand the patterns that we have found do lend some support to one of the key ideas underlying the theories of core and periphery, that political dissatisfaction with the central government may lead to demands for greater power to be given to the periphery. But on the other hand, economic measures and regional pride have no association with support for regional devolution once other variables have been taken into account. And these other factors seem unable to explain the regional variations in support for devolved assemblies. The resolution of this paradox is actually provided by some of our earlier tables, notably Tables 8.2 and 8.5. These tables showed very little regional variation in levels of economic and political dissatisfaction. Even if at the individual level (as in our multiple regression) economic dissatisfaction has

a strong relationship with support for regional assemblies, it cannot explain regional differences if the regions are all much of a muchness in their levels of economic dissatisfaction.

Conclusions

While the theory of core/periphery relations clearly has some merit, it has not been a great success in explaining regional variations in support for political change in general or for regional assemblies in particular. To be sure, we have on the whole seen rather small differences between regions in levels of political satisfaction and in demands for assemblies. In almost every region a majority of respondents favoured a continuation of the present constitutional arrangements for governing England. It is important to remember, therefore, that there is not a great deal of regional variation to explain. This is not to say that there is contentment with British democracy in general. Indeed, the proportions who felt that British democracy worked extremely well was very low in every single region. However, this dissatisfaction with the workings of our system of government in general does not appear to lead to any great demand for either an English parliament or for regional assemblies in particular. Perhaps these two constitutional changes are not believed to be the appropriate remedies for Britain's current ills. (Of course, there may be no consensus on any other possible remedy to the perceived ills either.)

However, there are some clear differences between the regions that we have identified. The North East, the North West and the South West clearly show higher levels of support for regional assemblies than is found elsewhere, and the other region in Steed's inner periphery, Yorkshire and Humber, is also above average in its support. The three northern regions also showed levels of pride in their region greater than generally found across the country as a whole.

Another factor that we believe might be important, although we cannot demonstrate it from our data, is whether the Government Office Region corresponds at all closely to local cultural identities. As we noted earlier, there may be strong pride in a Cornish identity and strong support for Cornish political institutions, but it does not follow that the Cornish would support an assembly for the South West region as a whole.

Finally, we should address the London anomaly. More than any other region London failed to fit in with the theory of core and periphery. London, despite its clear position as the economic core (and shown by the objective economic indicators in Table 8.1), nevertheless had higher than expected proportions who found it difficult economically, who expressed pride in London, and who voiced political dissatisfaction, while also having lower than expected support for the Union flag. This is not what core/periphery theory expects to find in the capital city.

The explanation may be that London (perhaps like capital cities in general) is a very diverse and unequal social environment. It may contain on the one hand a cosmopolitan elite with considerable economic and political power. But at the same time there are also substantial numbers of people who do not share in

these benefits. They may place more value on their local roots, and these 'locals' may be the ones who have greater attachment to London and favour local institutions, while the cosmopolitan elite may be more oriented towards national or international institutions. It may be the former who exhibit pride in London while it is the latter who fail to support the Union flag. This clearly merits further research.

References

Blondel, J (1963), *Voters, Parties and Leaders*. London: Penguin.

Borgatti, S. and Everett, M. (2000), 'Models of core/periphery structures', *Social Networks*, **21**: 375–395.

Hechter, M. (1975), *Internal Colonialism*, London: Routledge and Kegan Paul.

National Statistics (2001a), *Regional Gross Domestic Product*, www.statistics.gov.uk/themes/economy/articles/regionalaccounts.asp.

National Statistics (2001b), *Regional Household Sector Income and Consumption Expenditure*, www.statistics.gov.uk/themes/economy/articles/regionalaccounts.asp.

Office of the Deputy Prime Minister (2002), *Your Region, Your Choice: Revitalising the English Regions*, www.regions.odpm.gov.uk/governance/whitepaper.

Rokkan, S. and Urwin, D. (1982), *The Politics of Territorial Identity: Studies in European Regionalism*, Beverly Hills: Sage.

Rokkan, S. and Urwin, D. (1983), *Economy, Territory, Identity: Politics of European Peripheries*, Beverly Hills: Sage.

Steed, M. (1986), 'The core-periphery dimension of British politics', *Political Geography Quarterly*, supplement to **5**: S91–S103.

Taylor, B. and Thomson, K. (eds.) (1999), *Scotland and Wales: Nations Again?*, Cardiff: University of Wales Press.

Wellhofer, E. (1989), 'Core and periphery: territorial dimensions in politics', *Urban Studies*, **26**: 340–355.

Acknowledgements

The *National Centre for Social Research* is grateful to the Economic and Social Research Council for their financial support via the Devolution and Constitutional Change Programme (grant number L219252018) which enabled us to ask the questions reported in this chapter.

Appendix

The logistic regression on support for regional devolution described in the chapter is shown below. Logistic regression is explained in more detail in Appendix I to this Report.

The model reports the parameter estimates for each of the characteristics specified on the left side of the table. Strictly speaking, these parameter estimates tell us about the natural logarithm of the odds of someone in a particular category favouring a regional assembly compared with the odds of someone from the reference category (shown in brackets) favouring an assembly. Informally, we can say that, the bigger the estimate (either negative or positive), the bigger the difference between people in that category and those in the reference category in their support for an assembly. We should also note that, because this is a multivariate analysis, the parameter estimates tell us about the net effects of a particular variable, controlling for the other variables in the model. For example, the parameters for regional pride estimate the effect of regional pride among people who share similar levels of economic and political dissatisfaction.

Logistic regression model of demand for regional devolution

Variable (comparison group in brackets)	Parameter estimate
Region (South East)	
North East	0.55**
North West	0.51***
Yorkshire and Humber	0.27
East Midlands	0.10
West Midlands	0.16
South West	0.35*
Eastern	-0.09
London	0.18
Income	-0.01
Economic dissatisfaction (Living comfortably)	
Coping	0.09
Finding it difficult/very difficult	0.23
Political dissatisfaction (System could be improved quite a lot/needs a great deal of improvement)	
System could not be improved	-0.32
System could be improved in small ways	-0.51***
Pride in region (Doesn't think of oneself in that way)	
Very proud	0.24
Somewhat proud	0.20
Not proud	0.02
Constant	-1.33
Base	*2413*

* = significant at 10% level; ** = significant at 5% level; *** = significant at 1% level

9 The ties that bind

Alison Park and Ceridwen Roberts [*]

This chapter examines the many social networks that connect individuals to one another and to society as a whole, whether these are ties with family members, with friends, or with more formal organisations within wider society.

First we consider family ties. During much of the 1990s, popular discussion about family life has assumed that the growth of individualism was challenging the more traditional concepts of family ties and values. More people were living alone and households were generally becoming less stable. This trend continues as people live longer and experience more periods of living alone, either before relationship formation or after relationships are ended by death, separation or divorce. So we begin by examining patterns of family contact. In doing so, we examine a number of key questions. Who lives with whom, for example? How frequent is contact with non-resident family members? How supportive is family in times of trouble? Is there any evidence that family is being replaced by friends? And is there any suggestion that these patterns are changing over time?

One particularly common view of the family is that it has become more 'nuclear' in structure (that is, that it comprises a two-generation household), and that the wider 'extended' family is less relevant to people's lives than was the case in the 1950s and 1960s. But this popular view is now challenged by researchers, policy makers and practitioners alike. In particular, research about kinship patterns over the last few years has shown the importance of three-generation links across households, even if the generations in question do not actually live together (Willmott, 1986; McGlone *et al.*, 1998; Grundy *et.al.*, 1999).

A clear understanding of current living arrangements and contact patterns among different family generations is important for the public policy debate in several areas. One of these is the care of the elderly, an issue which has become

---

[*] Alison Park is a Research Director at the *National Centre for Social Research* and a Co-director of the *British Social Attitudes* surveys series. Ceridwen Roberts is Senior Research Fellow at the Department of Social Policy and Social Work at the University of Oxford.

particularly prominent given Britain's ageing population. Another is the recent unprecedented espousal by the government of the valuable role that grandparents can play as key sources of support for parents of young children (Home Office, 1998). We have also seen the rise of campaigning and self-help groups for grandparents, and other family members, with examples including the Family Rights Group and Grandparents Federation. Such bodies have been particularly concerned with ensuring that links with wider family members are maintained and recognised in the difficult circumstances of family breakdown and that the role of the extended family is more publicly valued. To address these issues, the chapter considers the links that do (and do not) exist between different family generations, and specifically focuses on the role that grandparents play as sources of help and support. It also considers whether or not the provision of help might be a burden for some of those concerned, as well as a blessing.

We also examine friendship patterns. We consider the number of 'close' or 'best' friends that people feel they have and the levels of contact they have with them. Of course, friendships and friendliness may have very different meaning for different groups. Traditionally, middle-class people are more likely to report interaction with, and greater numbers of, friends (Allen, 1979) and we examine whether or not our evidence corresponds to this view. More recently, it has been suggested that friends are becoming 'families of choice' and supplanting kin among certain groups (Weeks *et al.*, 1999). We examine how far our data bears this out.

Recent debates about 'social capital' have brought interest in organisational membership to the fore (Putnam, 2000). Belonging to organisations (whether these be neighbourhood or resident associations, voluntary groups or political parties) is seen to provide individuals with the potential for fellowship as well as the chance to construct reciprocal relationships and networks, relationships that Putnam sees as a form of 'capital'. So we also consider patterns of 'belonging' to these forms of network and, crucially, how such organisational membership interacts with less formal family and friendship networks. Are, for example, the most 'family centred' more likely also to be part of strong organisational networks, or is there any evidence of an 'inward looking' tendency among those with particularly strong family ties?

To address these issues we make use of a series of questions about kinship and friendship designed as part of the *International Social Survey Programme*. Where possible, we will look at whether there has been any change over time, by comparing our findings with those we obtained when we last covered this subject in 1986 and 1995.[1]

Family ties

We begin by looking at family networks and levels of contact with different members of the family. What sort of contact do people have with their family? Who lives with whom? Is there any evidence that contact over the telephone (or

by e-mail, or letter) is replacing face-to-face contact, especially in this increasingly geographically mobile age?

Face-to-face contact with close relatives

Our first task is to establish what proportions of people actually *have* the various family members in which we are interested. As the following table shows, although six in ten have mothers who are still alive, only just under half have a living father. Clear majorities, nearly nine in ten, have a brother or sister, and nearly half have an adult child. Understandably, there is marked variation between different age groups, with the proportions who have a living parent falling as we move up the age range. Despite this, it is notable that over a half of people aged between 45 and 54 still have a mother who is alive, as do nearly a third of those aged 55 to 65, and one in 20 of those aged 65 or more.

Table 9.1 Existence of particular family members, by age

% with relative	Mother	Father	Adult sibling	Adult child	Base
All	60	47	86	47	*912*
18–24	99	90	81	3	*70*
25–34	93	86	94	5	*156*
35–44	83	65	93	26	*204*
45–54	54	30	87	73	*147*
55–64	31	11	83	85	*130*
65+	5	6	72	88	*204*

Having established which family members people actually have, we then asked how often they met up with them. (In cases where a person had more than one adult child or sibling, we asked about their contact with the one they saw most often.) The next table shows that, among those who have the particular relative in question, regular contact with parents and adult children is widespread. In fact, of those whose mother is still alive, around one in seven (14 per cent) lives with her (mainly young people), while one in five of those with an adult child share a home with him or her. Regular contact with non-resident family members is also common; among those with a non-resident mother, half see her *at least* once a week, the same proportion as see a non-resident adult child this often. Contact with non-resident fathers is slightly less frequent; in fact, around one in nine people *never* see their non-resident father, compared with the one in 33 who never see a non-resident mother.

These findings confirm the centrality of the parent-child bond. Certainly, contact with adult siblings occurs less regularly than contact with parents or

adult children. That said, nearly a third of those with a non-resident adult sibling see him or her at least once a week, and a further 16 per cent see him or her at least once a month.

Table 9.2 Face-to-face contact with particular family members

	Mother	Father	Adult sibling	Adult child
	%	%	%	%
Lives in same household	14	13	4	21
Base (those with relative)	*551*	*433*	*762*	*442*
Contact with non-resident family member	%	%	%	%
Weekly	52	42	31	54
Monthly	16	16	16	13
Several times a year	19	18	24	9
Less frequent contact	8	11	15	2
No contact at all	3	9	6	2
Base (those with non-resident relative)	*458*	*365*	*733*	*374*

Note: in cases where a respondent had more than one sibling or adult children, they were asked to think about the one with whom they have the most contact.

These findings are based only upon those who have the particular relative in question, and only about the child or sibling they have most contact with (if they have several). Moreover, they tell us only about contact with one family member at a time. However, if we combine responses to *all* the different questions we have considered so far, we find that, overall, nearly two-thirds (64 per cent) of people had some form of weekly face-to-face contact with at least one close family member. (For this calculation we included people who live with a relative as being in weekly contact.)

Other ways of staying in touch

Of course, meeting up face to face is not the only way of staying in touch with family members and, for those who do not live nearby, will often not be practical. So we also asked how often respondents were in contact with family members by telephone, letter, fax or e-mail. Not surprisingly, these forms of staying in touch took place more frequently than face-to-face visits. For example, among those with a non-resident mother, three-quarters reported having weekly contact with her, compared with half who actually met up with her. And around six in ten said they had weekly contact with a non-resident

father, compared with four in ten who met with him. The same pattern was evident for non-resident siblings, although at a lower level (just over two-fifths were in contact this often, and just under a third actually met up with him or her).

Table 9.3 Frequency of contact by phone, letter, fax or e-mail with non-resident family members

	Mother	Father	Sibling	Adult child
	%	%	%	%
Weekly	76	58	43	64
Monthly	10	16	18	8
Several times a year	4	7	14	3
Less frequent contact	3	4	6	1
No contact at all	4	12	8	3
Base: those with non-resident relative	*458*	*365*	*733*	*374*

Note: in cases where a respondent had more than one sibling or adult children, they were asked to think about the one with whom they have the most contact.

It is often assumed that contact by telephone, e-mail and so on might become a substitute for direct face-to-face contact, especially as many people do not live near enough their relatives to see them as often as they might like. Our findings do not support this assumption. Although our questions do not allow us to assess the extent to which this has changed over time, it is clear that those who meet their relatives are also more frequently in contact with them in other ways. For example, among those who see their mother each week, a near unanimous 93 per cent are also in touch with her by telephone, e-mail, etc. on a weekly basis, compared with only 62 per cent of those who see their mother less than once a week. Exactly the same pattern exists when looking at contact with other family members. So, rather than being a substitute for seeing each other, regular contact over the telephone seems more to coexist or even reinforce face-to-face meetings.

The extended family

So far we have concentrated on people's immediate family – their parents, siblings and own children. What about contact with wider family? To assess this, we asked respondents how often, if at all, they had been in touch with various other relations over the previous four weeks. This shows that, once again, it is parent-child relationships that tend to dominate family relations, even when it is a spouse's parent rather than one's own wider family. Thus,

while over two-thirds of those with parents-in-law had seen them over the previous month, only around a third had seen one of their own uncles or aunts (35 per cent).

The declining family?

So far we have seen what appear to be fairly healthy levels of contact between different family members, with parent-child contact tending to be more frequent than contact with siblings or more distant relations. But how does this compare to levels of contact in the past? As we reported in *The 13th Report*, considerable concern has been expressed about the state of the 'modern' family and an alleged weakening of traditional family ties over time (McGlone *et al.*, 1996). So we now compare our findings with those from the two earlier rounds of these questions on the *British Social Attitudes* survey, in 1986 and 1995. The next table shows an apparent decline in face-to-face meetings with mother and father between 1986 and 1995, but stability between 1995 and 2001.[2] Similar patterns exist in relation to the proportions of people living with particular family members.

Table 9.4 Frequency of face-to-face contact with non-resident family member, 1986, 1995 and 2001

% who see/visit non-resident family member at least once a week	1986	Base	1995	Base	2001	Base
Mother	59	643	49	1026	52	458
Father	51	477	40	822	42	365

Note: the base for each figure in this table is the number of people with the particular relative (non-resident) in question.

The reasons for this trend are unclear. Certainly, the decline between 1986 and 1995 is less steep if we also take into account the increased life expectancy over the same period. This means that those respondents whose parents were alive in 1995 were slightly older than their counterparts in 1986 (Grundy and Shelton, 2001) and so our findings may slightly overstate any 'real' decline in contact between 1986 and 1995. Changes in geographical proximity also, no doubt, play a part in the story (McGlone *et al.*, 1996). Neither, however, entirely explains the decline in contact we found between the mid-1980s and mid-1990s, and the levelling off since then. Of course, our two most recent readings (1995 and 2001) are relatively close to one another and it may well be that we shall have to wait a little longer before a definitive pattern emerges.

Who are the most 'family focused'?

Patterns of family contact vary markedly from one group to another. To illustrate this, we consider two measures: first, the proportion of people who *live* with an adult relative and, second, rates of *weekly face-to-face contact* with non-resident relatives. The most pronounced differences relate to age. Not surprisingly, the group to live with a parent are the young. Over half (55 per cent) of 18–24 year olds live with their mother, and 44 per cent with their father (obviously many of this group will live with both parents). Moreover, although most young people have left home by the age of 25, one in eight (12 per cent) 25–34 year olds still lives with his or her mother (some because they have moved out of the parental home and then returned, and some who have never moved out in the first place). Intriguingly, sons are twice as likely as daughters to live with their mother (19 and 11 per cent respectively), despite – as we shall see later – being markedly less likely to have regular contact with her once they have left the parental home. This pattern is not confined to Britain alone; although British young people tend to leave home at a slightly younger age than their counterparts elsewhere in Europe, all European Union countries show a similar difference between young men and young women (Iacovou, 2001).

Table 9.5 Co-residence with family members, by age

% co-residing with family members	18–24	25–34	35–44	45–54	55–64	65+
Mother	56	12	2	3	*	*
Father	48	9	1	4	*	*
Adult child	*	*	*	33	14	5
Base: those with relative (range)	62–68	132–145	128–165	48–100	106	174

Note: in cases where a respondent had more than one adult child, they were asked to answer in relation to the one with whom they have the most contact.
* indicates that the number of cases where the respondent had the relative in question was too small for meaningful analysis.

Britain's ageing population has led to an upsurge in policy interest in, and debate about, the provision and funding of care for the increasing numbers of frail, elderly and infirm people within society. Throughout, a key question is whether it should be individuals and their families or the state who should broadly take responsibility for this. Overwhelmingly, the majority of care is currently provided within the family, with varying degrees of more formal support. Consequently, there is considerable interest in knowing more about the living arrangements, and contact patterns, of the different generations within a family. Traditional notions of the nuclear family assume that, despite the centrality of the parent-child bond, children will rarely live with their parents

after a certain age. The previous table confirms the truth of this stereotype; inter-generational households of this sort are now very rare, and once people have reached their mid-30s, only a very small proportion will share a home with a parent. Thus, when we focused only on those whose mothers were still alive, only three per cent of 45–54 year olds shared a home with her, and the same similar proportion with their father (some would, of course, be living with both parents at the same time). And, although 14 per cent of 55–64 year olds with adult children were living with at least one of them, a significant proportion of this group will be people still living with a young adult child who will shortly be leaving home. More telling, perhaps, is the fact that only five per cent of the 65-plus age group live with an adult child.

Contact with non-resident family members also varied markedly by age, with 25–34 year olds being the most likely to see a non-resident mother or father at least once a week. This partly reflects the fact that this age group will be the most likely to have young children of their own, something that we might expect to increase contact between the generations (whether for emotional or practical reasons, or both). The next table bears this out. It shows that, among respondents with a child of their own aged 16 or under, nearly six in ten saw their mother every week, compared with under half of non-parents. This difference is more marked still in relation to contact with fathers; whereas a half of parents with young children see their father every week, this applies to only a third of those without children. These findings clearly hint at the important role played by the addition of a third generation to a family in terms of increasing family closeness and regularity of contact.

Table 9.6 Frequency of face-to-face contact with non-resident family member, by parenthood

% who see/visit non-resident family member at least once a week	Parent living with child aged 0–16	Base	Not parent living with child aged 0–16	Base
Mother	58	188	46	270
Father	50	149	35	216

Note: in cases where a respondent had more than one adult child, they were asked to answer in relation to the one with whom they have the most contact.

This link between frequent contact and the arrival of a third generation is demonstrated even more clearly when we look at contact between older respondents and their adult children. This shows that grandparents are much more likely than non-grandparents to be in regular contact with an adult child. Over six in ten (61 per cent) grandparents see an adult child at least once a week, almost exactly double the rate among those who have adult children but no grandchildren (30 per cent). However, as we shall see later, this is not necessarily a recipe for a trouble-free life.

Women have long been seen as the main 'kin keepers', taking primary responsibility for maintaining family ties across the generations (Firth, 1956; Young and Willmott, 1957; Willmott and Young, 1960). Our data confirm that little has changed in this respect. Among women with non-resident mothers, one in ten (11 per cent) saw her *every* day (compared with five per cent of men), while a further 45 per cent saw her less often than this, but at least once a week (compared with 40 per cent of men).

Table 9.7 Frequency of face-to-face contact with non-resident family members, by sex

% who see/visit non-resident family members at least once a week	Men	Women
Mother	44	56
Father	37	44
Adult child	48	54
Adult sibling	26	33
Base: those with non-resident relative (range)	*146–316*	*212–417*

This higher level of contact between mothers and daughters is also apparent when we consider other forms of contact (whether by telephone, letter or e-mail). In fact, women are three times more likely than men to be in touch with their mother once a day through these means (18 and six per cent respectively). All in all, a resounding 84 per cent of women with non-resident mothers were in touch with her one way or another at least once a week, compared with only two-thirds of men. Similar, but less marked, gender gaps exist in contact patterns with fathers, siblings and adult children.

Research has long found a link between family contact and a range of related socio-economic indicators such as income, class and educational background (Willmott, 1986; Grundy and Shelton, 2001). Our findings confirm this. In particular, we found a notable difference between those who had left school relatively young and those who remained in full-time education until 19 or above. Six in ten (62 per cent) of those who left at 16 were in weekly contact with a non-resident mother, compared with only four in ten (41 per cent) of the latter. Similar patterns were found in relation to household income, with poorer groups being in more frequent contact with non-resident parents than richer ones. And, although there were no consistent class differences in parental contact, respondents in working-class occupations who had non-resident adult children were significantly more likely to see them at least once a week than were those in middle-class occupations.

Of course, one explanation for some of these differences is geographical proximity. Put simply; those who live near their relatives are more likely to see them each week than those who live further away. For example, nine in ten (88

per cent) of those who live within 30 minutes journey time of a non-resident mother see her at least once a week – nearly seven times the rate found among those whose mother lives further away (13 per cent). And proximity is very closely linked to many of the other characteristics we have examined. In particular, there are notable socio-economic differences, with those in higher paid, middle-class occupations which require high levels of educational attainment tending to be more geographically mobile than average (Shelton and Grundy, 2000). In addition, women are more likely than men to live close to their mother. Of course, in making these observations we must remember that living near one's mother may well reflect a positive choice to remain in (or move to) an area, precisely because of its family connections. So the fact that proximity is strongly related to contact does not disprove that the other factors we have discussed are unrelated to regular contact with kin.

Because of the close relationship between many of the characteristics in which we are interested, we used multivariate analysis techniques to tease out their relative importance. In the appendix to this chapter, we present two models to predict the likelihood of a person being in weekly contact with a non-resident mother. Both models took account of the following: sex, marital status, whether or not the respondent was in paid employment (full-time or part-time), whether they had children aged 16 or under living with them, household income, class, and the age at which they finished full-time education. The first model (Model 1) shows that, if we do *not* take account of variations in geographical proximity, a person's age, educational background and sex are all significantly linked to frequent contact with a non-resident mother. Women, 18 to 34 year olds, and those who finished full-time education at 16 or younger, were more likely to see their mothers at least once a week. However, when we take into account variations in geographical proximity (Model 2), the importance of sex and educational background vanish – confirming our earlier assertion that women and those who left education early are more likely to live near their mothers. However, age remains a key predictor of maternal contact even when geographical proximity is taken into account; irrespective of how near or far a person lives from their mother, younger groups (aged 18 to 34) will tend to have more frequent contact than older ones.

We carried out similar analyses to look at contact with non-resident adult children (Model 3). Once again, we took account of age, sex, marital status, whether or not the respondent was in paid employment and household income. We also specified whether or not the respondent was a grandparent. This exercise confirmed the close relationship between being a grandparent and weekly contact with an adult child. In fact, none of our other characteristics proved to be significantly related to contact once this was taken into account. Unfortunately, we do not have information about the geographical proximity of the respondent to their adult child, so could not include this in our analyses.

Friends

Clearly, people's social networks include a far wider group than family members alone. Moreover, friends are 'chosen' in a way that family members are not. So we turn now to examine friendship patterns and the relationship between these and family contact. We shall consider the number of close friends that people have, and the levels of contact that they have with them. We shall also examine the extent to which there is any suggestion that friends might be supplanting family among some groups.

We began by asking people to "think about your best friend, the friend you feel closest too (but not your partner)". Eight in ten identified someone who fitted that description. Nearly one in six – 14 per cent – said they had no best friend at all. However, this group is likely to include those who see their spouse or partner as their "best friend", as well as those who do not have any friends they would describe in this way.

Earlier we saw that one in two people see their mother or an adult child at least once a week, excluding those who live with him or her. Weekly face-to-face contact with "best" friends, again excluding the small number who share a home with them, is slightly higher, at 57 per cent. And two-thirds are in touch with this person in some other way on a weekly basis, again higher than any family member bar mothers.

Because the meaning of a term like "best friend" will no doubt vary from one group to another, we also asked people to think about three categories of what we called "close" friends – those at work, those who live in the same local area, and any other friends they might describe as close. Not surprisingly, there was a huge range in the number of close friends that people reported having. The median number was ten (with a mean of 14). Roughly a quarter of people reported having no or few (three or less) close friends, a quarter between four and nine, a quarter between 10 and 18 and a quarter even more than that.

Earlier we saw that different groups varied considerably in the levels of contact they have with different members of their family. The same is true of contact with friends, in relation to both the number of close friends that a person has and whether a person has a "best friend" or not.

We start with age. The first column in the next table shows the percentage of people in each age group who describe themselves as having a large number of close friends (defined here as ten or more). And the second column shows the percentage who do *not* have what they would call a "best friend". The table shows that, as we move from younger to older age groups, the proportion with a large number of close friends falls, and the proportion saying they have no best friend rises. For instance, well over a half of 18–45 year olds have ten or more close friends, compared with 43 per cent of 55–64 year olds, and only 39 per cent of the 65-plus age group. Conversely, the number of people with no best friend increases with age – from three per cent among 18–24 year olds, to 17 per cent among 44–54 year olds, to a quarter of those aged 65 or more.

What accounts for these age differences? To some extent they will reflect the different life circumstances and competing pressures on people's time as they get older. This is confirmed when we look at contact patterns among different age groups. Seven in ten 18–24 year olds see their best friend at least once a week, double the rate found among any other age group. It is also likely that

different age groups will have different conceptions as to what constitutes a "close" or a "best" friend, as well as different social needs. The particularly high rate of elderly people with no best friend will, of course, also reflect the increasing death rate among their cohort of friends. This suggests that there may be a danger of some elderly people being socially rather isolated. True, around nine in ten have adult children – but, as we saw earlier, only around half of this group see their adult children at least once a week.

Table 9.8 Friends, by age

Age	% with ten or more close friends	% with no best friend	Base
18–24	56	3	70
25–34	56	5	148
34–45	58	13	198
44–54	46	17	145
55–64	43	14	123
65+	39	26	176

A range of other characteristics were linked to friendship patterns, including sex, marital status and parenthood. Although women report having fewer close friends than men (45 per cent have ten or more close friends, compared with 56 per cent of men), men are more likely than women to have no best friend at all (17 and 11 per cent respectively). This might be interpreted as implying that quantity does not necessarily guarantee 'quality'; it might also of course reflect differences between the sexes as to what exactly comprises a close or a best friend. Married people were less likely than single ones to have a best friend, and tended to have fewer close friends (47 per cent had ten or more, compared with 61 per cent of single people). Similar differences were found between those with and without children in the home. These differences go some way to back up our suggestion that the reasons for friendship rates declining with age are either increasing competition from other priorities and/or a decreasing need for an extensive social circle. But they will also no doubt reflect the fact that we asked people to exclude their spouse or partner when thinking of their "best friend", even though this is precisely how some think of them.

We also found marked socio-economic differences in friendship patterns. Two, in particular, stand out. Firstly, as the next table shows, friendship patterns appear to vary by class, with the self-employed and those in routine manual occupations being the most likely groups to feel they have no close friends. And, secondly, people living in poorer households have fewer friends than richer groups, and are much more likely to say that they have no best friend. Nearly a quarter of those in the poorest households say they have no best friend, three times as many as is found among those with an annual household income

of £35,000 or more. There are two possible interpretations of these findings. On the one hand, they might suggest that some of the most economically disadvantaged groups are also at risk of being socially excluded as well. On the other hand, they may merely indicate that the concept of a "close" or "best" friend is in itself a class-ridden term, something with which the middle classes can particularly identify. Indeed, research into 'neighbourliness' and the community-based links that can be particularly common among some older people suggests that some people who report having few 'friends' do, in fact, have long-standing and supportive links with close neighbours. These relationships may be as practically sustaining on a day-to-day basis as some of the relationships that other people have with family members and with friends (Allen, 1979).

Table 9.9 Friends, by class and household income

	% with ten or more close friends	% with no close friends	Base
NS-SEC			
Managerial or professional	54	14	296
Intermediate occupations	48	4	120
Small employer or own account workers	47	24	70
Lower supervisory or technical staff	61	17	102
Semi-routine occupations	45	9	140
Routine manual occupations	41	26	116
Household income per annum			
Less than £12,000	43	24	243
£12,000, less than £23,000	50	16	192
£23,000, less than £35,000	53	6	138
£35,000 or more	54	8	195

Because many of these characteristics are linked to one another, multivariate analysis is necessary to tease out those with the strongest association with friendship patterns. This confirms that, when examining those with no "best friend" at all (Model 4 in the appendix), household income has a particularly strong association (with poorer groups being the most likely to have no best friend). This is followed by marital status (those who are married or living as married are more likely to say they have no best friend), class (routine non-manual workers), sex (men) and age (the 65-plus group). Age and sex both also emerge as significantly related to having a large number of close friends (Model 5 in the appendix), as does whether or not a person has children (those who have children are less likely to have a large number of close friends).

Wider social networks

We turn now to examine the wider social networks that people might be involved with, focusing on a range of possible groups – from churches and trade unions to neighbourhood associations and sports clubs. We asked people whether they belonged to any of the groups described in the next table and, if they did, how often they had participated in its activities over the previous 12 months. Nearly two-thirds belonged to at least one, the most popular being a sports group, hobby or leisure club (40 per cent) and religious groups (25 per cent). 'Passive' membership (that is, belonging to a group but not having taken part in its activities over the last year) was most evident among those who belonged to trade unions or professional associations, or to a church or other religious organisation.

Table 9.10 Organisational membership and participation over last 12 months

		Member, has taken part	Member, has not taken part	Not member
Sports, hobby, leisure club	%	38	2	51
Church or other religious organisation	%	19	6	64
Charitable organisation or group	%	14	3	71
Association or group not listed	%	14	2	71
Neighbourhood association or group	%	8	3	75
Trade union or professional association	%	6	15	67
Political party, club, association	%	4	1	81

Base: 912

As our primary interest is in social networks, rather than formal organisational membership, we focus now only on those who had *taken part* within at least one activity over the past 12 months. In common with many other studies, we find that men are more likely than women to have participated, and older age groups more likely than the young (Johnston and Jowell, 2001), despite the inclusion of sports groups in our list! However, the most notable differences related to educational background, with those who had remained in education the longest being much more likely to belong to one or more groups than those who had left very early. The next table illustrates this quite clearly, showing, for instance, that among those who finished their education at 17 or older, seven in ten had participated in the activities of at least one of the groups we asked about over the last 12 months, compared with only four in ten among those who left at 15.

Table 9.11 Organisational participation, by age of leaving full-time education

Age at which completed full-time education		Taken part in two or more groups	Taken part in one group	Not taken part/ not member	Base
15	%	19	24	58	287
16	%	25	27	48	274
17/18	%	38	32	31	166
19 or older	%	40	30	31	183

Other socio-economic differences were also apparent. Four in ten (41 per cent) of those whose annual household income was less than £12,000 had participated in the activities of one or more organisations, rising to 55 per cent among those whose household income was between £12,000 and £22,999, and 66 per cent among those whose household income was £35,000 or more. Finally, people who were married were less likely than average to have participated in one or more groups' activities. All these differences remained when we carried out multivariate analysis which also took into account other factors such as class, whether or not a person was in paid work, and parenthood (Model 6 in the appendix to this chapter).

Partly, no doubt, these findings will reflect competing pressures on a person's time, this perhaps being particularly relevant when considering the low participation rates among the married. However, in interpreting the patterns we have found, we must also be aware that our focus has been very much upon formal organisations, rather than the many more fluid and informal social networks to which many people also belong. Moreover, these forms of network and relationship (for example, with neighbours or colleagues) might be particularly important for some of the groups who show relatively low levels of participation in the more formal networks covered in Table 9.10 – including, for example, those in working-class occupations, or poorer social groups. That said, the patterns we have found do reflect a well-known tendency for groups in more 'difficult' social and economic circumstances to participate less than those whose situation is more advantageous (Johnson and Jowell, 2001). And, as Johnson and Jowell remark, the relatively low participation levels among these groups can reinforce their disadvantaged situation by depriving them of the 'social capital' that can flow from such extended networks.

Network rich, network poor?

So far we have seen considerable variation in the social networks that different groups inhabit. So we turn now to consider whether there is any connection between the different forms of ties that we have considered so far – family,

friendship and organisational. Is it the case, for instance, that those with strong family or friendship ties are more likely than others to participate in formal social networks? Is there any evidence that those without family ties have strong friendship ones instead? We also consider whether our findings throw any light on the distinction made by Robert Putnam between 'bridging' and 'bonding' social capital (Putnam, 2000).

To examine this, we make a distinction between the two-thirds (65 per cent) of people who have weekly contact with at least one of the adult family members we have considered (a parent, an adult child, or a sibling) and those who do not, either because they do not have the relative in question or because they do not see them that often. (For the purposes of this analysis, if someone lives with an adult family member, we shall include that as contact.) We then examine these two groups' friendship patterns, paying particular attention to whether those without frequent family contact are more or less likely to have alternative networks of friends.

The next table suggests that, rather than friends being a *replacement* for family, the two types of network tend to *reinforce* one another. Thus, among those who do *not* have weekly contact with at least one adult family member, a quarter (27 per cent) have three or fewer close friends, and nearly one in five (19 per cent) have no best friend at all. This compares with 22 and 12 per cent respectively among those who are in regular weekly contact with an adult member of their family. So, those without strong family ties – who, after all, are perhaps those in the most need of close friends – are actually less likely to have them (for whatever reason) than those who see their family fairly regularly.

Table 9.12 Family contact and friendship networks

	No weekly family contact	Weekly family contact
% with no "best" friend	19	12
% with 0 to 3 close friends	27	22
% with 10 or more close friends	46	52
Base	*343*	*569*

When it comes to friendship patterns and organisational membership we find that the two appear to reinforce one another – the more friends a person has, the more likely he or she is to belong to an organisation and the more likely he or she is to participate in its activities. So it certainly does not seem that 'joiners' do so at a cost to their other social commitments; in fact, they may well pick up friends along the way! For example, among those with a large number of close friends (19 or more), over a third (35 per cent) belong to two or more organisations – more than double the rate found among those with fewer than four friends. This is mirrored in organisational participation rates, as seen in the

next table: among those with a large number of close friends, over four in ten have participated in two or more activities, which is double the rate among those with three or fewer friends.

Table 9.13 Organisational participation, and friendship patterns

Participation in organisational activities over past 12 months	0–3 friends	4–9 friends	10–18 friends	19+ friends
	%	%	%	%
Has not participated in any activities	57	35	25	25
Participated in one activity	22	28	24	31
Participated in two or more activities	22	38	52	44
Base	*203*	*232*	*218*	*181*

However, the same pattern does not hold when we look at family contact. Although there is no difference between those who are and are not frequently in touch with their family in terms of whether they belong to *any* organisations, those who are *not* in weekly contact are the most likely to belong to two or more (36 per cent doing so, compared with only a quarter of those who are in weekly contact). And, as the next table shows, the same holds true for organisational participation rates. So, while strong friendship networks do not get in the way of organisational membership, the same does not appear to be true of strong family ties.

Table 9.14 Organisational participation, and family contact patterns

Participation in organisational activities over past 12 months	No weekly family contact	Weekly family contact
	%	%
Has not participated in any activities	42	45
Participated in one activity	22	31
Participated in two or more activities	36	25
Base	*243*	*569*

How might we interpret these findings? Earlier we speculated that the friendship patterns of those who are married might reflect pressures on the time they have available to spend outside their immediate family and their different social needs. So too might the lower than average rates of organisational membership among those with frequent family contact. But these findings may

also point towards an 'inward looking' tendency of those with strong family ties – a tendency to focus on family, perhaps to the exclusion of participation in wider and more formal social networks ties. Read in this way, close family connections might actually be seen as an example of what Putnam terms 'bonding' social capital – that is, connections and behaviour which can create or reinforce boundaries between 'them' and 'us'. Although some organisational memberships will also provide primarily 'bonding' social capital, others will fall into the category of 'bridging' capital – that is, connections that can cross social divides and help bring people together.

The role of different social networks

Social networks can be seen as having a number of functions, both for the individuals within them and society as a whole. For individuals, they can be critical sources of support and help, both in everyday life and in specific circumstances. This partly explains some of the variations we have already identified – for example, the strong family ties that can be evident among young parents who need help with childcare. But, given the variation we have seen in the sorts of social networks that people have available to them, to whom do people turn in terms of crisis? What would people do if, for example, they needed help while they were ill, or felt a bit depressed? In this section, we explore the extent to which family is the main port of call for people in times of trouble – or whether friends (or indeed other more formal sources of support) can also play a similar role?

To find out more about whom people might rely upon we asked:

> Now we would like to ask you how you would get help in situations that anyone could find herself or himself in. First, suppose you had the 'flu and had to stay in bed for a few days and needed help around the house, with shopping and so on. Who would you turn to first for help? And who would you turn to second?

> Suppose you needed to borrow a large sum of money. Who would you turn to first for help ...?

> Suppose you felt just a bit down or depressed and you wanted to talk about it. Who would you turn to first for help ...?

Our findings show, quite clearly, that the family overwhelmingly remains the main source of help for the majority of people in times of trouble. For instance, when asked who they would call upon if they were unwell in bed, nearly nine in ten said they would first approach either their spouse/partner or another family member. Two-thirds would do the same if they felt "a bit down or depressed". And, although three in ten would first approach a bank if they needed a loan, six in ten would approach a member of their family first. Friends only emerged as

important when it came to thinking about who you would turn to when depressed – but still only one in five would go to friends first.

Table 9.15 Sources of support in times of need

	Flu	Money	Depressed
	%	%	%
Spouse or partner	64	23	51
Other relation	23	31	17
Friend, neighbour, colleague	6	1	21
Someone else	1	2	3
Bank	n.a.	30	n.a.
No-one	1	9	3
Base: 912			

n.a. = not applicable

Clearly, not everyone has access to some of the people commonly mentioned as potential suppliers of help and support. In particular, we have seen a clear indication of the key role often played by a person's spouse or partner. So what do people who are *not* living with someone think they would do in these sorts of circumstances? The answer is that they would rely more on their wider family and friends – and which it would be depends on what problem they have. So, in the case of being ill in bed with flu, the proportion turning to other relatives rises from the 23 per cent we saw in the previous table to 57 per cent among those who are single. Only a fifth (19 per cent) would involve their friends in the first instance. However, if they were feeling a bit down and depressed, the proportion of single people turning to friends in the first instance jumps to 46 per cent. This is clearly an area where it is seen as appropriate to call on one's friends for support if you are not married or cohabiting.

Family clearly remains most people's first source of support when things go wrong. Although friends *do* play an important role, particularly for those who are not married, even most of this group would turn to family first in many serious situations. Little evidence here, then, that friends are replacing family.

The downside to strong social ties?

Of course, strong social networks may not always be a good thing for everyone involved. Perhaps for some there is a downside to strong family or friendship links, a sense in which these can be a source of strain or excessive demand as well as (or instead of) support. To assess this, we asked:

> *Do you feel that your family, relatives and/or friends make too many demands on you?*

Nearly half (48 per cent) said that this was never the case, and a further 18 per cent said it was seldom true. However, just over a quarter (26 per cent) said that family or friends sometimes made too many demands, and six per cent said this was "often" the case.

There was a notable difference between men and women. Over a third of women (36 per cent) said that they felt their friends and relations made too many demands on them "often" or "sometimes", compared with 28 per cent of men. The most likely age group to feel over-burdened, at least occasionally, were 45–54 year olds, nearly a half of whom (47 per cent) did so. The fact that this particular age group emerges as the most 'stressed' by their family obligations is very telling as they are at precisely the age at which their children (as well as their parents) might be making particularly heavy demands for help and support. By contrast, the over 65 age group were far less likely to say they felt that too many demands were made of them, only one in five (20 per cent) doing so.

Our speculation that the distinct views of the 45–54 age group might, at least partially, be to do with demands made by their children is confirmed when we focus on the views of grandparents. This shows that they are significantly more likely than non-grandparents to feel over-burdened at least some of the time. Four in ten (39 per cent) grandparents said they felt this, compared with three in ten non-grandparents. There was also a socio-economic dimension to feelings of being over-burdened, although it is not clear-cut. The two groups who stand out are those in lower supervisory and technical manual occupations (the most likely to say they *did* feel over-burdened at times), and those in routine manual occupations (the least likely to express this view). In fact, these four factors – age, sex, whether or not one is a grandparent, and class all proved significantly linked to a feeling of being over-burdened by family at times, even when multivariate analysis was used to take account of variations in education, income, paid employment rates, parenthood, marital status, and family and friendship patterns (see Model 7 in the appendix to this chapter).

Although over a half of grandparents say they seldom or never feel too over-burdened, these findings show clearly that a very substantial minority feel overwhelmed at times. Moreover, these feelings are particularly apparent among a very specific group; those who are 'young' grand*mothers* (that is, women aged under 54). This also confirms some of the findings from an earlier *British Social Attitudes* study of grandparents, reported in *The 16th Report* (Dench *et al.*, 1999).

Conclusions

This picture of family ties painted by this chapter is one of seemingly robust good health. Although obviously not everyone has close family, the majority of people are in touch (either in person or over the telephone) with at least one member of their immediate family on a weekly basis. Among those whose mothers are still alive or who have adult children, levels of contact are very high indeed. This is particularly so among women who continue to live up to their

reputation as the 'keepers' of kinship networks. The arrival of a third generation within a family has a critical bearing on levels of contact, with grandparents being substantially more likely than non-grandparents to be in regular contact with their adult children.

Family members remain very important sources of help, and clear majorities would turn first to their spouse or another family member if they were feeling unwell, depressed, or needed to borrow some money. Friends are mentioned far less as a first port of call, even among the young and single. However, for some, the family can impose demands that at times seem excessive. In this respect, grandmothers, particularly those who are relatively young (aged 45 to 55), are most at risk. So care clearly needs to be taken when promoting the role that grandparents can play in the upbringing of their grandchildren.

Our findings show that friendship patterns vary markedly from one group to another, reflecting both choice and constraint. Although some of these differences reflect the simple fact that people have different needs for friends at different stages of their lives, we also find possibly worrying signs that some socio-economically disadvantaged groups are less likely than others to feel that they have close friends. Similar patterns exist when we consider more formal social networks, with rates of organisational belonging being lowest among the poor and less well-educated. In both cases, then, potential exists for lower than average rates of social connectedness among these already disadvantaged groups.

Finally, we found some intriguing relationships between family, friendship and organisational membership. Two stand out. The first is the fact that those who participate in organisations do not do so at a cost to their friendship networks. In fact, the more friends a person has, the more likely they are to be a 'joiner'. And, secondly, we find hints of a less desirable side to high levels of family contact – a possible inward looking tendency that precludes 'joining in' with more formal networks outside the immediate family.

Notes

1. Our ability to compare our findings with those obtained in 1986 and 1995 is limited by a number of discontinuities between the 2001 questions and their predecessors. Because the *International Social Survey Programme* is an international survey, with the same questions being administered in a wide range of countries, we were not able to modify the questions to suit specifically British needs. Further details about the ISSP can be found in Appendix I of this Report. Note also that, in common with other chapters in this Report, percentages in tables do not necessarily sum to 100 per cent, partly because cases where the respondent did not answer the question are not shown in the tables. However, the proportion of these "not answereds" is rather higher in the group of questions considered in this chapter (which were administered using a self-completion questionnaire) than elsewhere in the survey. Full frequencies for the questions, including "not answereds" can be seen in the annotated

questionnaires in Appendix III to the Report (see questions 1–24 of self-completion version C).

2. A similar pattern is in part evident for adult children, with a fall from 66 per cent to 58 per cent between 1986 and 1995. However, the figure of 51 per cent for 2001 is not really comparable with the earlier years because of a rise in the proportion who skipped and did not answer the question, which is at least in part attributable to a redesign of the questionnaire. The equivalent figure for 2001 excluding the "not answereds" is 65 per cent.

References

Allen, G. (1979), *A Sociology of Friendship and Kinship*, London: George Allen and Unwin.

Dench, G., Ogg, J. and Thomson, K. (1999), 'The role of grandparents' in Jowell, R., Curtice, J., Park, A. and Thomson, K. (eds.) *British Social Attitudes: the 16th Report – Who shares New Labour values?* Aldershot: Ashgate.

Firth, R. (1956), *Two Studies of Kinship in Britain*, London: Athlone Press.

Grundy, E., Murphy, M. and Shelton, N. (1999), 'Looking beyond the household intergenerational perspectives on living with kin and contacts with kin in Great Britain', *Population Trends* **97**: 19–27.

Grundy, E. and Shelton, N. (2001), 'Contact between adult children and their parents in Great Britain 1986 to 1999', *Environment and Planning*, **33**.

Home Office (1998), *Supporting Families – A consultation document*, London: The Stationery Office.

Iacovou, M. (2001), 'Leaving home in the European Union', Working Paper 18, Colchester: University of Essex Institute for Social and Economic Research (ISER).

Johnston, M. and Jowell, R. (2001), 'How robust is British civil society', in Park, A., Curtice, J., Thomson, K., Jarvis, L. and Bromley, C. (eds.), *British Social Attitudes: the 18th Report – Public policy, Social ties*, London: Sage.

McGlone, F., Park, A. and Roberts, C. (1996), 'Relative values: family and kinship', in Jowell, R., Curtice, J., Park, A., Brook, L. and Thomson, K. (eds.), *British Social Attitudes: the 13th Report*, Aldershot: Dartmouth.

McGlone, F., Park, A. and Smith, K. (1998), *Families and Kinship*, London: Family Policies Study Centre.

Putnam, R. (2000), *Bowling Alone – the Collapse and Revival of American Community*, New York: Simon and Schuster.

Shelton, N. and Grundy, E. (2000), 'Proximity of adult children to their parents in Great Britain', *International Journal of Population Geography*, **6**.

Weeks, J., Donovan, C. and Heaphy, B. (1999), 'Families of choice: autonomy and mutuality in non-heterosexual relationships', in McRae, S. (ed.), *Changing Britain: Families and Households in the 1990s*, Oxford: Oxford University Press.

Willmott, P. (1986), *Social Networks, Informal Care and Public Policy*, London: Policy Studies Institute.

Willmott, P. and Young, M. (1960), *Family and Class in a London Suburb*, London: Routledge and Kegan Paul.

Young, M. and Willmott, P. (1957), *Family and Kinship in East London*, London: Routledge and Kegan Paul.

Acknowledgements

The questions discussed in this chapter are part of a module designed for the *International Social Survey Programme* (*ISSP*). The *National Centre for Social Research* would like to thank the ESRC for funding its participation in the *ISSP*, through its funding of the *Centre for Research into Elections and Social Trends* (grant reference M543285002).

Appendix

Model 1 and 2 Face-to-face contact with mother

Dependent variable: face-to-face contact with mother at least once a week (among those who have a non-resident mother)

Model 1: Not including geographic proximity

	B	Exp(B)	Sig.
Gender			
Male	-0.270	0.763	**
Female	0.270	1.310	**
Age			
18–34	0.517	1.677	**
35–44	-0.186	0.831	
45 plus	-0.331	0.718	*
Age of leaving full-time education			
Less than 16	0.337	1.400	
At 16	0.422	1.526	*
17–18	-0.210	0.811	
19 plus	-0.550	0.577	**
Constant	0.041	1.042	

Other variables included in the model, but which did not reach statistical significance:

- Household income
- Child(ren) aged under 16 in the household
- Whether in work (full-time or part-time)
- Marital status
- Class

Model 2: Including geographic proximity

	B	Exp(B)	Sig.
Age			
18–34	0.654	1.923	**
35–44	-0.661	0.516	**
45 plus	0.007	1.007	
Distance from mother			
Less than 30 minutes journey time	2.007	7.440	**
More than 30 minutes journey time	-2.007	0.134	**
Constant	0.018	1.018	

Other variables included in the model, but which did not reach statistical significance:

- Sex
- Age of leaving full-time education
- Household income
- Child(ren) aged under 16 in the household
- Whether in work (full-time or part-time)
- Marital status
- Class

Model 3 Face-to-face contact with adult child

Dependent variable: face-to-face contact with adult child at least once a week (among those who have a non-resident adult child)

	B	Exp(B)	Sig.
Grandchild			
Does not have grandchild	-0.690	0.501	**
Has grandchild	0.690	1.994	**
Constant	0.499	1.646	**

Other variables included in the model, but which did not reach statistical significance:
- Age
- Sex
- Household income
- Whether in work (full-time or part-time)
- Marital status
- Class

Model 4 Having no best friend

Dependent variable: having no best friend

	B	Exp(B)	Sig.
Gender			
Male	0.321	1.379	*
Female	-0.321	0.725	*
Marital status			
Married	0.415	1.514	**
Not married	-0.415	0.660	**
Class			
Higher managerial or professional	-0.061	0.941	
Lower managerial or professional	0.192	1.211	
Intermediate occupations	-0.857	0.424	
Small employer or own account worker	0.621	1.862	*
Lower supervisory or technical staff	-0.199	0.820	
Semi-routine occupations	-0.561	0.571	
Routine manual occupations	0.864	2.373	**
Age			
18–34	-0.787	0.455	**
35–44	0.036	1.037	
45–54	0.567	1.763	*
55–64	-0.069	0.934	
65 plus	0.253	1.287	**
Household income			
Lowest quartile	1.054	2.870	**
Second quartile	0.422	1.525	*
Third quartile	-0.919	0.399	**
Highest quartile	-0.557	0.573	*
Constant	-2.297	0.101	**

Other variables included in the model, but which did not reach statistical significance:
- Age of leaving full-time education
- Child(ren) aged under 16 in the household
- Whether in work (full-time or part-time)

Model 5 Number of close friends
Dependent variable: having ten or more close friends

	B	Exp(B)	Sig.
Gender			
Male	0.217	1.242	**
Female	-0.217	0.805	**
Children under 16 in household			
No children under 16	0.293	1.341	**
Children under 16	-0.293	0.746	**
Age			
18–34	0.281	1.324	*
35–44	0.683	1.980	**
45–54	-0.036	0.965	
55–64	-0.559	0.572	**
65 plus	-0.369	0.691	*
Constant	-0.214	0.807	*

Other variables included in the model, but which did not reach statistical significance:
- Age of leaving full-time education
- Whether in work (full-time or part-time)
- Class
- Marital status
- Household income

Model 6 Participation in organisational activity
Dependent variable: taken part in at least one organisational activity in last 12 months

	B	Exp(B)	Sig.
Gender			
Male	-0.199	0.819	*
Female	0.199	1.221	*
Marital status			
Married	0.221	1.247	*
Not married	-0.221	0.802	*
Age			
18–34	0.339	1.404	*
35–44	0.517	1.677	**
45–54	0.029	1.029	
55–64	-0.442	0.643	*
65 plus	-0.443	0.642	*
Household income			
Lowest quartile	0.741	2.097	**
Second quartile	0.015	1.015	
Third quartile	-0.351	0.704	*
Highest quartile	-0.405	0.642	*
Age of leaving full-time education			
Less than 16	0.690	1.994	**
At 16	0.130	1.138	
17–18	-0.485	0.616	**
19 plus	-0.335	0.716	*
Constant	-0.566	0.568	**

Other variables included in the model, but which did not reach statistical significance:
- Child(ren) aged under 16 in the household
- Whether in work (full-time or part-time)
- Class

Model 7 Whether too many demands from relatives and friends

Dependent variable: agreement that "your family, relatives and/or friends make too many demands on you"

	B	Exp(B)	Sig.
Gender			
Male	-0.269	0.764	**
Female	0.269	1.309	**
Class			
Higher managerial or professional	0.008	1.008	
Lower managerial or professional	-0.294	0.745	
Intermediate occupations	0.002	1.002	
Small employer or own account worker	0.067	1.070	
Lower supervisory or technical staff	0.555	1.742	**
Semi-routine occupations	0.104	1.110	
Routine manual occupations	-0.442	0.643	*
Age			
18–34	-0.129	0.879	
35–44	0.509	1.663	**
45–54	0.776	2.173	**
55–64	-0.120	0.887	
65 plus	-1.037	0.355	**
Grandchild			
Does not have grandchild/ren	-0.447	0.640	**
Has grandchild/ren	0.447	1.564	**
Constant	-0.559	0.549	**

Other variables included in the model, but which did not reach statistical significance:
- Child(ren) aged under 16 in the household
- Household income
- Marital status
- Whether in work (full-time or part-time)

10 In search of tolerance

Geoffrey Evans [*]

What does it mean to be tolerant? Tolerance can take many forms: tolerance of speech, of opinions, of actions, of differences in appearance. These various types of tolerance can be manifest through acceptance of different lifestyle choices, of differences in ascribed characteristics, of differences in political beliefs. Often, it is the absence of tolerance that is most visible and it tends to concern us most when it is translated into action. But the possession of intolerant beliefs provides the ever-present possibility of their expression through action, and is thus a source of latent concern – at least for those who believe in the value of tolerance. And, indeed, it is commonly supposed that one of the pre-requisites of a healthy democracy is a commitment to liberal principles by its citizenry – a commitment expressed through the presence of a widespread toleration of 'difference', whether that difference refers to the very presence of minorities, of minority practices, or of minority viewpoints.

So, how tolerant are the British? Certainly, there is widespread concern about the state of democratic culture in Britain: falling electoral turnout, falling interest in politics, and a lack of trust in politicians and other sources of authority (see chapters in *The 18th Report* and in this volume – Bromley *et al.*, 2001; Bromley and Curtice, 2002). There is also very public concern about the presence of ingrained, supposedly 'institutional', racism or homophobia, especially since the murder of Stephen Lawrence and the subsequent Macpherson Report surrounding its investigation (Macpherson, 1999). And, particularly since 11th September 2001, there has been widespread evidence of intolerance of groups such as Muslims, immigrants and asylum seekers. So there is at least a vague sense that the cherished principles of inclusiveness and liberal democracy might not be as widespread as may be desired. Against such pessimism, however, there are at least some grounds for believing that tolerance has increased in recent years. It is generally assumed that tolerance is linked to higher levels of education (Hyman and Wright, 1979; Bobo and Licari, 1989; Nie *et al.*, 1996). The last 20 or so years have seen a great leap in the proportion

[*] Geoffrey Evans is Official Fellow in Politics, Nuffield College, Oxford and Professor of the Sociology of Politics.

of young people going on to higher education, as well as in pressure from the Commission for Racial Equality, Parliament and many other institutions in society to protect and extend the rights of minorities. It is not clear therefore which set of influences will have held most sway.

In this chapter, we pursue this set of questions in two quite different ways: firstly, by examining what has happened to British attitudes towards two key minority groups in our society – racial minorities and homosexuals – over the period of the *British Social Attitudes* surveys since the 1980s. We look at how changes in such attitudes can be accounted for and what they suggest for the future. We then move on to focus in more detail on the nature of tolerance of minorities by extending this to include those who espouse unpopular political viewpoints, particularly viewpoints that are at odds with the liberal consensus on inclusiveness and equality with respect to ethnic minorities.

Our aim in this part of the chapter is to assess whether tolerance is *generalised*, in the sense that it not only endorses the rights of those of whom liberals are typically supportive – particularly racial minorities – but also the rights of those on the other end of the social and political spectrum: racists. We do this because it can be argued that a required feature of tolerance is that it should apply to groups or views that are *disliked*. Thus tolerance of left-liberal views, or groups to which left-liberal politics is sympathetic, such as ethnic minorities and gays, by people who are already sympathetic to those views ('*Guardian* readers', 'the higher educated') is a rather low hurdle in the expression of tolerance. In contrast, tolerance of right-wing views or groups by such individuals is a more demanding and revealing test.[1] In a similar vein, tolerance of gay rights by gays, of ethnic minorities by ethnic minorities, of hunting by members of the Countryside Alliance, and so on, are effectively tautological. To tolerate that of which one approves, or identifies with, is no great achievement. True tolerance is generalised. Clearly, this is a far more demanding test of tolerance than is usually examined using data from the *British Social Attitudes* surveys, but it is one that we need at least to explore if we are to give a rounded consideration to issues of tolerance in Britain today.

A growing tolerance of minorities?

First though we look at evidence on the way tolerance of racial minorities has changed in Britain during the span of the *British Social Attitudes* surveys since the mid-1980s. The best time-series question available is one that might raise eyebrows:

> *How would you describe yourself: ... as very prejudiced against people of other races, a little prejudiced, or, not prejudiced at all?*

Can people really be relied upon to have such insight, not to mention blatant honesty in expressing a potentially negative self-definition? One way of checking the validity of the responses is to see what other responses they are associated with – do they discriminate racially prejudiced people from others on

questions that are less blunt and less demanding of explicit self-definition? In some years, we have asked respondents a set of questions on whether they would mind if a suitably qualified person from an ethnic minority was appointed as their boss and whether they would mind if such a person married a close relative of theirs. As seen in the following table, the self-rated prejudice question is closely associated with people's answers to these other questions. For example, among the small number who described themselves as "very" prejudiced, over nine in ten would "mind a lot" if a close relative married someone of Asian origin. Among those who described themselves as "a little" prejudiced, this fell to under a third, and among those who described themselves as "not at all" prejudiced to one in 15.[2] For survey responses these relationships are as close to a perfect association as is ever likely to be found. People do seem to be serious when they describe themselves as prejudiced, or not.

Table 10.1 Self-reported racial prejudice and related racial attitudes, 1994

	Extent of self-reported racial prejudice		
	Very	**A little**	**Not at all**
% "mind a lot" having an Asian as a boss	62	13	1
% "mind a lot" an Asian marrying close relative	91	30	6
Base	*25*	*388*	*671*
% "mind a lot" having a black person as a boss	68	8	*
% "mind a lot" a black person marrying close relative	78	31	8
Base	*24*	*351*	*699*

Having established that it is worthwhile using the self-rated racial prejudice question as an indicator, we then turn to look at it over time. In the next table, we can see evidence of a moderate decline in prejudice over time. The proportion who were prepared to describe themselves as "very" or "a little" prejudiced, has fallen from a high point of two-fifths in 1987 to a quarter by 2001. By their own definition, Britons have become less prejudiced.

Table 10.2 Racial prejudice, 1985–2001

	1985	1986	1987	1989	1990	1991	1994	1996	1998	2000	2001
Very prejudiced	5	4	5	4	4	2	2	2	2	2	2
A little prejudiced	29	32	34	32	32	29	34	27	24	24	23
Not at all prejudiced	65	64	60	63	64	68	64	71	74	74	75
Base:		*1752*	*3034*	*2729*	*2908*	*1383*	*1452*	*2272*	*2378*	*1017*	*2265*	*2154*

What has been happening over the past two decades to explain these changes? There are two main processes which we expect would help to explain the changes that have occurred: generational replacement, and increased access to higher education.[3]

Education

As mentioned earlier, education is typically seen as strongly linked to tolerance. In the next table, we see that degree-level educated respondents were indeed noticeably less prejudiced than others in the 1980s but that the gap has since declined as other groups have 'caught up'.

Table 10.3 Self-reported racial prejudice, by education, 1985–2001

% reporting any racial prejudice	1985	1986	1987	1989	1990	1991	1994	1996	1998	2000	2001	Base (smallest)
No qualific.	31	35	37	32	35	30	33	31	27	26	29	320
GCSE to A levels	38	39	42	42	35	35	40	30	26	27	26	376
Higher educ below degree	43	37	44	39	45	35	39	31	27	22	26	199
Degree	23	29	27	29	31	28	31	24	22	22	19	102

The biggest changes have taken place among those with A or O levels, CSE, GCSE and similar, and among those with non-degree level further or higher education. It is only recently that people with these levels of qualifications began to be slightly less prejudiced than those with no qualifications. Prior to the mid-1990s, levels of prejudice were most marked in these mid-levels of education. So, overall, during the period we are examining, the views of those with some education changed at a greater rate than those without any educational qualifications or those with degrees. One way of interpreting this is as part of a diffusion process by which the already tolerant degree-level group were followed by mid-range groups, but not by those with no qualifications – or not yet at any rate. The significance of this follow-the-leader pattern is heightened by the fact that the proportion of the population with higher levels of education has been continuously increasing. In 1985 only about one in 14 (seven per cent) of our sample had degrees whereas by 2001 it was more or less twice that proportion (14 per cent). Substantial increases have also occurred in the size of the mid-range qualification groups, while the size of the group with no qualifications has declined. In short, the most educated have caught on first

to tolerance and there are increasingly more and more such people in the population.

Age

The effects of education have some connection with age-related changes in tolerance. As we can see in the next table, the early *British Social Attitudes* surveys found that young people, and those in latish middle age actually used to describe themselves as *more* prejudiced than the oldest group. However, the views of younger people and those in middle age have become less prejudiced over time, while the views of the older age group have stayed more or less the same. By 2001 we find that those aged over 60 were more prejudiced than those in younger age groups.

Table 10.4 Racial prejudice, by age, 1985–2001

% reporting any racial prejudice	1985	1986	1987	1989	1990	1991	1994	1996	1998	2000	2001	Base (small-est)
Under 30	37	35	37	34	33	35	35	26	21	21	22	160
30–39	36	36	38	38	35	27	34	29	25	22	23	226
40–49	32	38	45	40	41	29	40	27	31	24	21	161
50–59	41	41	38	36	40	41	38	33	22	27	24	168
60+	28	33	38	36	33	31	35	32	30	30	32	302

A growing tolerance of homosexuality?

The picture of changes in tolerance of homosexual behaviour is even more pronounced than that for tolerance of ethnic minorities. The best time-series question available has reasonable face validity: after being asked about sex before marriage and extramarital affairs, respondents were asked:

> *What about sexual relations between two adults of the same sex?*
> *Always wrong*
> *Mostly wrong*
> *Sometimes wrong*
> *Rarely wrong*
> *Not wrong at all*

In the mid-1980s little more than one in ten of respondents thought that homosexual behaviour was "not wrong at all", as seen in the next table.[4] Only 15 years or so later the figure was around a third. Similarly dramatic declines

occurred at the other end of the scale. We have seen a real sea-change in tolerance of homosexuality.

Table 10.5 Attitudes towards homosexuality, 1985–2000

Homosexual sex is ...	1985	1987	1989	1990	1993	1995	1998	1999	2000
	%	%	%	%	%	%	%	%	%
Always/mostly wrong	70	75	69	69	64	57	52	49	47
Not wrong at all	13	11	14	14	19	21	23	28	33
Base	1745	1385	1459	1478	1248	1166	1063	1036	3418

Again, education plays an important part in this change. Among those with no qualifications there was a drop of around 20 percentage points in the proportion who thought that homosexual sex was always wrong – from around three-quarters to just over half. A similar trend is found among degree-educated respondents. In particular, the proportion of graduates who thought that homosexual sex was "not at all wrong" increased markedly from around a quarter to about a half. Because both educational groups have changed, differences by education remain: only a fifth of those with no qualifications see nothing wrong with homosexuality.

Table 10.6 Attitudes towards homosexuality, by education, 1985–2000

Homosexual sex is ...	1985	1987	1989	1990	1993	1995	1998	1999	2000	Base (smallest)
No qualific.	%	%	%	%	%	%	%	%	%	324
Always wrong	72	76	70	74	63	61	60	57	54	
Not wrong at all	8	6	8	8	9	12	12	15	19	
Degree	%	%	%	%	%	%	%	%	%	96
Always wrong	27	39	24	23	39	20	20	21	17	
Not wrong at all	24	26	28	28	32	43	45	47	52	

As the next table shows, sweeping changes in attitudes towards homosexuality have occurred in most age groups, with the exception of the oldest. Although they did become more positive, the change was far less marked than among, for example, those in the 18–29 age group. Over time, therefore, the age gap has grown.

Table 10.7 Attitudes towards homosexuality, by age, 1985–2000

Homosexual sex is ...	1985	1987	1989	1990	1993	1995	1998	1999	2000	Base (smallest)
Under 30	%	%	%	%	%	%	%	%	%	*155*
Always wrong	50	48	42	49	36	27	19	20	23	
Not wrong at all	18	18	22	19	29	33	38	47	48	
30–39	%	%	%	%	%	%	%	%	%	*216*
Always wrong	46	51	42	42	44	34	30	24	25	
Not wrong at all	18	17	22	19	23	33	33	35	47	
40–49	%	%	%	%	%	%	%	%	%	*171*
Always wrong	58	60	52	58	45	37	33	25	28	
Not wrong at all	16	10	13	17	21	26	23	35	40	
50–59	%	%	%	%	%	%	%	%	%	*135*
Always wrong	67	75	69	62	62	55	43	40	35	
Not wrong at all	5	7	7	14	11	16	23	22	32	
60+	%	%	%	%	%	%	%	%	%	*319*
Always wrong	79	84	75	77	72	67	62	66	60	
Not wrong at all	4	2	5	6	5	7	8	11	14	

New fashions or new commitments?

On both race and homosexuality we have seen evidence of progressive change. But what does this suggest for the future? The young are more tolerant, but will they always be more tolerant, or will they grow out of it as they age? Is tolerance a lasting characteristic, or simply a result of being younger at the point of asking? In other words, the longer-term implications of age differences will be influenced by whether or not they reflect generational changes or lifecycle changes (see, for example, Heath and McMahon, 1991). To address this issue we can compare the views of different birth cohorts by dividing the samples across several waves of the *British Social Attitudes* surveys into bands based on the year in which they were born.

From the next table, we can see that younger birth cohorts became markedly more tolerant as the years went on – and they were already far more tolerant of homosexuality than older birth cohorts to start off with.

Table 10.8 Attitudes towards homosexuality – birth cohort analysis

% saying "not wrong at all"	Age in 1985	Age in 2000	1985	1990	1994	1998	2000	Change 1985–2000
Born 1970–79	n.a.	21–30	n.a.	19	47	37	48	n.a.
Born 1960–69	18*–25	31–40	17	20	30	34	47	+30
Born 1950–59	26–35	41–50	21	18	27	24	38	+17
Born 1940–49	36–45	51–60	17	17	21	26	30	+13
Born 1930–39	46–55	61–70	7	13	12	8	21	+14
Born 1920–29	56–65	71–80	5	7	8	7	7	+2
Born pre-1920	66+	81+	3	4	2	5	7	+4

n.a. = not applicable
* respondents younger than 18 were not interviewed.

For racial prejudice we see a similar tendency, though again less marked, in which there is more pro-tolerance change among newer birth cohorts than their immediate elders (although the very oldest age cohort stand out as being remarkably tolerant). Younger people do not lose their liberalism as they age – nowadays they actually get more liberal. This eventually washes out the originally less intolerant character of older age groups.

Table 10.9 Self-reported racial prejudice – birth cohort analysis

% reporting any racial prejudice	Age in 1985	Age in 2000	1985	1990	1994	1998	2000	Change 1985–2000
Born 1970–79	n.a.	21–30	n.a.	33	36	19	20	n.a.
Born 1960–69	18*–25	31–40	38	33	35	25	23	-15
Born 1950–59	26–35	41–50	35	36	35	29	24	-11
Born 1940–49	36–45	51–60	34	40	40	22	30	-4
Born 1930–39	46–55	61–70	38	39	37	27	29	-9
Born 1920–29	56–65	71–80	38	35	37	36	32	-6
Born pre-1920	66+	81+	23	31	33	24	17	-6

n.a. = not applicable
* respondents younger than 18 were not interviewed.

We should keep in mind, of course, that we are not examining the same individuals through time, and that there are also some fluctuations in the patterns observable. These provisos notwithstanding, the general picture to be

taken from this brief examination of birth cohort changes, is that not only are more recent birth cohorts more tolerant to begin with, but they have moved far more towards greater tolerance between 1985 and 2001 than have older birth cohorts. And, as these more recent birth cohorts make up more and more of our population and the older ones die off, we can more than likely look forward to a more and more tolerant British society in the coming decades.

Generalised tolerance?

So far, so good. As time goes by the population is getting more tolerant and looks likely to continue to do so. But can we be confident that what we are witnessing is tolerance? Or is it instead simply the spread of a more benign attitude to two groups who have become, for one reason or another, more acceptable? Has tolerance, *per se*, increased?[5] To throw some light on this conundrum, we now turn to examine whether there is actually such a thing as *generalised* tolerance; that is, tolerance that stretches across rather different areas of beliefs, lifestyles and ascriptive features – tolerance of diverse viewpoints and behaviour, some of which are likely to be disliked. Sniderman *et al.* (1991: 135) argue that this form of tolerance is not only present in the United States, but also that its presence is an important element of a liberal democracy: "The person who does not honour and protect the rights of those whose point of view clashes with his own is ... a bad bet to protect the rights even of those whose points of view supports his own ...". Even more explicitly, they state (1991: 135) that: "It is the racial bigot, not the person committed to racial tolerance, who is the more likely to oppose free speech for racists." Using the *British Social Attitudes* surveys we can see if this generalised tolerance exists in Britain today.

If this form of tolerance does exist, it is important to identify what sorts of people are likely to demonstrate it. If there are sectors of the population who can be seen as possessing this broader conception of tolerance and who might provide a social core of generalised tolerance around which the penumbra of more minimally, or perhaps more accurately partially (in both senses of the word), tolerant groups engage in limited tolerance, then they might truly be called 'the guardians of tolerance'. If not, then we can at least see what sorts of people demonstrate which types of tolerance and consider the implications of this diversity of 'focused' tolerance as a source of a form of 'self-interested pluralism' which serves to defend multiple viewpoints from exclusion or prohibition.

The idea of generalised tolerance, involving as it does the tolerance of disliked viewpoints, is quite difficult to measure. We need to know that a particular idea or behaviour runs counter to other beliefs held by a respondent yet at the same time that the respondent upholds the right to express such views or engage in such behaviour. We can find some instances where these two pieces of information are available in a *British Social Attitudes* data set, but they are not easy to come by. In 1994, however, the *British Social Attitudes* survey ran a series of questions not only about attitudes towards ethnic minorities (see those

used above, for example), but also about attitudes towards the freedom of speech of people who believe that whites are superior to other races:

> *... consider people who believe that whites are racially superior to all other races. Do you think such people should be allowed to ...*
> *... teach 15 year olds in schools?*
> *... give interviews on television to put their case?*
> *... stand as candidates in elections?*

Table 10.10 Support for racial supremacists' civil rights, 1994

Should white supremacists be allowed to ...		Definitely	Probably	Probably not	Definitely not
Teach 15 year olds	%	3	5	18	70
Give interviews on TV	%	7	21	21	45
Stand in elections	%	8	15	16	55
Base: 970					

As can be seen in the previous table, there is considerable opposition to the rights of white supremacists, particularly to them teaching 15 year olds, which seven out of ten respondents oppose outright. However, we do have fairly sizeable minorities who think that the civil rights of racialist groups should be defended. There are 28 per cent who think they should "definitely" or "probably" be allowed to give interviews on television, 23 per cent who think they should "definitely" or "probably" be allowed to stand in elections.

So we can now explore whether those who are tolerant of minorities are also tolerant of the civil rights of racialist groups. In other words, is their tolerance generalised? Alternatively, are those who support racial supremacists simply the prejudiced? These two potential sources of support for racialists' rights need to be disentangled.

First, we conducted a principal components analysis of responses to the civil rights and prejudice questions, which allows us to see if there is a uni-dimensional general attitude structure. We find that this is not the case. There is a clear-cut two-dimensional structure to the items. One dimension contains self-rated prejudice and attitudes towards the prospect of black and Asian bosses and spouses, while the other contains the three questions on civil rights for racial supremacists.

This general analysis is also confirmed by a more detailed examination: as we can see in the next table, there is little evidence of any link between any of the measures of prejudice and support for civil rights for racialist groups. Specifically, there is no difference in attitudes between those who claim to be "a little" prejudiced and those who say they are not prejudiced at all. Only the

small handful of "very prejudiced" people are more likely to support racialists' civil rights. Similarly, weak or no relationships are found when looking at attitudes towards inter-racial marriage or bosses. Hence it is not the case that those who support civil rights for white supremacists are in the main simply racially prejudiced themselves.

Table 10.11 Tolerance of racial supremacists' civil rights, by measures of own prejudice, 1994

| | Self-reported racial prejudice | | |
	Very	A little	Not at all
Allow white supremacist to teach	%	%	%
Definitely/Probably	35	8	7
Probably not/Definitely not	60	89	90
Allow white supremacist to give TV interview	%	%	%
Definitely/Probably	60	36	25
Probably not/Definitely not	35	63	72
Allow white supremacist to stand in election	%	%	%
Definitely/Probably	55	26	21
Probably not/Definitely not	40	72	76
Base (smallest)	*20*	*310*	*599*

We would expect to see most generalised tolerance among the most 'enlightened' sections of the population – groups who could provide the vanguard for a more tolerant attitude towards all sorts of minorities, both those who suffer from prejudice and those who are prejudiced against them. Thus we might expect the higher educated to have a more principled and therefore more generalised tolerance. That is indeed exactly what we see. As the next table shows, over half of people with degrees endorse the right of racial supremacists to run for political office and over half also support their right to be interviewed on television. Only one in nine and a fifth, respectively, of those with no qualifications support this right.

That this liberalism among the educated reflects a commitment to political tolerance, and not merely an expression of prejudice, is supported by the difference in answers to the question about the right of racial supremacists to teach in schools. Here we are perhaps going beyond a basic civil right to an opportunity to proselytise among the young. And, in contrast to the questions about being interviewed on television and standing in elections, there is no clear relationship between education and support for the right of supremacists to teach 15 year olds – most educational groups are similarly opposed, with less

than one in ten supporting this proposition. Only those with no qualifications are a little less likely to oppose this.

As we already know from Tables 10.3 and 10.6, educated groups display no more racism than those without qualifications – quite the opposite, in fact. This is even more so when measures of prejudice that make concrete reference to inter-racial marriage or having a black or Asian boss are used instead of the self-report question, which suggests that educated groups have more demanding conceptions of what it means to not be prejudiced. The true education-related differences in levels of prejudice may therefore be even greater than those shown in the tables.

Table 10.12 Support for racial supremacists' civil rights, by education, 1994

	Educational qualification			
	Degree	Higher education below degree	GCSE to A levels	None
Allow white supremacist to teach	%	%	%	%
Definitely/Probably	8	5	7	10
Probably not/Definitely not	92	93	91	84
Allow white supremacist to give TV interview	%	%	%	%
Definitely/Probably	59	34	27	19
Probably not/Definitely not	41	65	71	77
Allow white supremacist to stand in election	%	%	%	%
Definitely/Probably	56	29	23	11
Probably not/Definitely not	43	69	76	84
Base	*101*	*121*	*362*	*338*

That support for the civil rights of racial supremacists arises from a principled commitment to tolerance and not from prejudice is also supported by the strong relationship between, on the one hand, liberal values (as measured by the libertarian–authoritarian scale – see the Appendix to this report) and, on the other, the same discriminating support for racial supremacists (that is, support for their basic civil rights but not for their right to teach 15 year olds). As seen in the next table, those holding liberal values in general are more likely to support the basic civil rights of white supremacists, but less likely to support their right to teach. There is a similar link between interest in politics (which we take as a useful proxy for political involvement – see Evans *et al.*, 1996) and views on white supremacists. However, the association between liberal values and political involvement, on the one hand, and basic civil rights for white

supremacists, on the other, holds only for those with education to A level or above.

Table 10.13   Liberal values, political involvement and tolerance of white supremacists' civil rights, 1994 (Pearson correlations)

	Liberals	Politically involved
All		
Have white supremacists teach 15 year olds	-0.08 *	-0.11 *
Have white supremacists give TV interviews	0.13 *	0.11 *
Have white supremacists stand in election	0.16 *	0.17 *
Base (smallest): 913		
Those with A levels or above		
Have white supremacists teach 15 year olds	0.01	0.00
Have white supremacists give TV interviews	0.17 *	0.24 *
Have white supremacists stand in election	0.22 *	0.33 *
Base (smallest): 345		
Education below A level		
Have white supremacists teach 15 year olds	-0.11 *	-0.16 *
Have white supremacists give TV interviews	0.01	-0.07
Have white supremacists stand in election	0.00	-0.04
Base (smallest): 541		

* = significant at 5 per cent level

All of these findings show that it is not in the main prejudiced respondents who support racial supremacists' democratic rights. On the contrary, it is those who fit the profile of 'political sophisticates' (Luskin, 1987). This is consistent with North American research that demonstrates that the well-educated and politically-informed link their general political principles to quite diverse applications of those principles, whereas many others do not (Converse, 1964; Feldman, 1988). Therefore, not only are people with higher levels of education more likely to support racial supremacists' civil rights, but they have rather more principled reasons for doing so than have the less well-educated.

By comparison, age has far less noticeable effects than education, although younger people are slightly more tolerant of racialists' rights, again with the exception of teaching young people. Gender also has effects: men support racialists' civil rights more than do women. But of course, we should always take care not to confuse the impact of correlated characteristics on tolerance: education, liberal values and age, in particular, are quite closely correlated. As

are, for example, political interest and gender. We need to control for their inter-relationship using a multivariate statistical model.

Who are the guardians of tolerance?

The literature leads us to expect that the main factors linked to tolerance (or intolerance) should be education, age, religiosity, gender, commitment to democratic principles, feelings of being threatened, and social class (Sullivan *et al.*, 1982; Bobo and Licari, 1989; Sniderman *et al.*, 1991; Gibson, 1992; Sullivan and Transue, 1999). In the models shown in the appendix to this chapter, we have included measures of age, sex, education, social class and commitment to liberal values, but we cannot operationalise feelings of threat, as ethnic minorities were not asked their views on racial supremacists (it might well be expected that ethnic minorities feel more threatened by racialists).

The most exacting requirement for classifying respondents as displaying generalised tolerance is to require them to give full support to racial supremacists' rights to political representation even when they themselves are not at all racially prejudiced. According to our estimates this group composes between one in eight and one in five (13 to 20 per cent) of the sample. The former figure is arrived at if self-rated prejudice is used in the calculation, and the latter if acceptance of a black or Asian boss is used (the figure is 14 per cent if inter-marriage is used). Between them these different approaches give a robust estimate of the size of the group who display generalised tolerance. In the logistic regression models shown in the appendix, we use all three measures so as to obtain a reliable picture of the types of people displaying such tolerance.

Across the models shown, we find that generalised tolerance is predicted by having higher education, being male,[6] and having a commitment to liberal values. High levels of political involvement are positively associated with tolerance in two of three models – those concerning inter-marriage and having minorities as bosses. Age predicts tolerance, but only when inter-marriage is used to calculate it. This is presumably because, as we have noted above, younger people are noticeably more tolerant of inter-marriage. There are no social class effects at all; nor any for church attendance (perhaps because religious involvements in Britain are less value-laden than those in the United States where most research on such matters is undertaken).

Conclusions

In this chapter we have set out in search of tolerance. We have seen that as time goes by the population is getting more tolerant and looks likely to continue to do so. The reasons for this cannot easily be pinned down, but we have seen the contribution made by the entry of new cohorts of tolerant people into adulthood, the gradual diffusion of tolerance through educational groups, and the growth of more highly educated groups as a proportion of the population. All of these at

least help to explain why we are now more tolerant of racial and sexual minorities than we were less than 20 years ago.

Also, however, we have sought to examine the nature of tolerance in Britain; and who most clearly corresponds to the 'ideal' of tolerance where liberal democratic principles are applied even to groups whose opinions are likely to be distasteful. We have found that tolerance of the civil rights of racial supremacists is not just a case of supporting political groups that people agree with. The higher educated, liberals, the politically involved, and men all tend to be more supportive of racial supremacists' civil rights without being prejudiced themselves. Except for a very small minority of respondents, there is only a weak link between prejudice against racial minorities and tolerance of the expression of racialist ideas or allowing racialist political candidates. These findings are, in general, contrary to those proposed in the 'conservative model' of democratic processes which stresses the role of an illiberal self-interested pluralism in ensuring the defence of multiple viewpoints from exclusion or prohibition (Sullivan *et al.*, 1982), and which assumes that there is in fact little evidence of generalised tolerance among citizens. Our findings suggest that to a large degree this model does not hold in contemporary Britain.

"Education, education, education"? Possibly our most prominent finding with respect to both over time change and the sources of generalised tolerance concerns the importance of education. Mr Blair's famous mantra seems far less consequential now than when first announced in 1997, as Britain struggles with an over-burdened health service and the reality that as more and more people get degrees, degrees buy less and less. However, our findings at least point towards the possibility that a more educated populace might well provide the key to the maintenance of liberal democratic practices through its impact on levels of tolerance. It is also associated with the growth of liberal values more generally (de Graaf and Evans, 1996, Evans *et al.*, 1996), and more highly educated respondents link their liberal values more closely to their attitudes towards freedom of speech and political practice for racial supremacists.

A possible counter to our emphasis on the positive contribution of education to the spread of tolerance is the argument that the more highly educated are particularly aware that homophobia and racism are frowned upon 'in polite company' and in consequence, as Jackman and Muha (1984), for example, assert, just 'play the politically correct game' better than others. Thus the highly educated are less likely to demonstrate 'politically incorrect' views to an interviewer even if they hold them. But this argument does not stand up to close examination. In the first case, many questions examined on these topics are in the self-completion part of the *British Social Attitudes* questionnaire – these views do not need to be expressed face-to-face. Secondly, these same supposedly politically correct respondents are far more willing to endorse rights for racists than are others. And, thirdly, even the presence of such enhanced awareness of and compliance with what is politically correct with respect to race or sexual preference helps to de-legitimate the expression of such views in social encounters. It is 'real in its consequences'. Also, of course, we should bear in mind that to the extent that policy makers and the strategists of parties competing for political office take note of monitoring procedures such as public

opinion polls and focus groups, even 'insincere' answers are, again, real in their consequences.

Even so, the reasons for education's effects remain open to debate: studies have demonstrated the effects of enhanced cognitive skills and learned capacity to empathise with alternative viewpoints of others, the absorption of liberal values, or the internalization of democratic principles (Hyman and Wright, 1979; Bobo and Licari, 1989; Sniderman *et al.*, 1991). But despite this uncertainty about *why* education has its effect, it undoubtedly is there. So as long as the higher educated are able to endorse freedom of expression they do not like and have tolerant attitudes towards minorities, and link general liberal principles of tolerance to specific applications more effectively than do other sections of the population – thus implying their acceptance of agreement on the procedural rules of the democratic process regardless of the political position adopted – so the growth of higher education can provide a bulwark against the undermining of liberal democracy through intolerance.

Notes

1. The major work on this approach to tolerance is that of Sullivan and his colleagues (Sullivan *et al.*, 1982).
2. Throughout this chapter, refusals and "not answereds" have been excluded from the calculation of percentages.
3. Analyses that exclude self-identified black and Asian respondents find little substantive difference from those reported here.
4. Compared with the early 1980s, tolerance of homosexual behaviour hardened a little during the mid-1980s, probably in response to the AIDS crisis that was particularly pronounced at that time, as it increased again afterwards (Wellings and Wadsworth, 1990).
5. This issue echoes the controversy (Sullivan *et al.*, 1982) that followed after it was shown that Americans were more tolerant of communists and atheists in the 1970s than they had been in Samuel Stouffer's (1955) study of American intolerance in the McCarthy era. Was it changing tolerance, or changing acceptance of left-wing and secular viewpoints?
6. Women's lesser tolerance of racial supremacists' civil rights might be because they tend to be less informed about politics (see, for example, Andersen *et al.*, 2002).

References

Andersen, R, Heath, A. and Sinnott, R (2002), 'Political knowledge and electoral choices', *British Elections & Parties Review*, **12**: 11–27.

Bobo, L. and Licari, F.C. (1989), 'Education and political tolerance', *Public Opinion Quarterly*, **53**: 285–308.

Bromley, C., Curtice, J. and Seyd, B. (2001), 'Political engagement, trust and constitutional reform', in Park, A., Curtice, J., Thomson, K., Jarvis, L. and Bromley,

C. (eds.), *British Social Attitudes: the 18ᵗʰ Report – Public policy, Social ties*, London: Sage.

Bromley, C. and Curtice, J. (2002), 'Where have all the voters gone?' in Park, A., Curtice, J., Thomson, K., Jarvis, L. and Bromley, C. (eds.), *British Social Attitudes: the 19ᵗʰ Report*, London: Sage.

Converse, P.E. (1964), 'The nature of belief systems in mass publics' in Apter, D.E. (ed.), *Ideology and Discontent*, Glencoe: Free Press.

De Graaf, N.D. and Evans, G. (1996), 'Why are the young more postmaterialist? A cross-national analysis of individual and contextual influences on postmaterial values', *Comparative Political Studies*, **28**: 608–635.

Evans, G., Heath, A.F. and Lalljee, M.G. (1996), 'Measuring left–right and libertarian–authoritarian values in the British electorate', *British Journal of Sociology*, **47**: 93–112.

Feldman, S. (1988), 'Structure and consistency in public opinion: the role of core beliefs and values', *American Journal of Political Science,* **32**: 416–440.

Gibson, J.L. (1992), 'The political consequences of intolerance: cultural conformity and political freedom', *American Political Science Review*, **86**: 338–356.

Heath, A.F. and McMahon, D. (1991), 'Consensus and dissensus', in Jowell, R., Brook, L. and Taylor, B. (eds.), *British Social Attitudes: the 8th Report,*: Aldershot: Dartmouth.

Hyman, H.H. and Wright, C.R. (1979), *Education's Lasting Influence on Values*, Chicago: University of Chicago Press.

Jackman, M. and Muha, M. (1984), 'Education and intergroup attitudes: Moral enlightenment, superficial democratic commitment, or ideological refinement?', *American Sociological Review*, **49**: 751–769.

Luskin, R. (1987), 'Measuring political sophistication', *American Journal of Political Science*, **31(4)**: 856–899.

Macpherson, W. (1999), *The Stephen Lawrence Inquiry: Report of an inquiry by Sir William Macpherson of Cluny*, Cmnd 4262-I, London: The Stationery Office.

Nie, N.H., Junn J. and Stehlik-Barry K. (1996), *Education and Democratic Citizenship in America*, Chicago: University of Chicago Press.

Sniderman, P.M., Brody, R.A. and Tetlock, P.E. (1991), *Reasoning and Choice: Explorations in Political Psychology*, Cambridge: Cambridge University Press.

Stouffer, S.A. (1955), *Communism, Conformity, and Civil Liberties*, New York: Doubleday.

Sullivan, J.L., Piereson, J. and Marcus, G.E. (1982), *Political Tolerance and American Democracy,* Chicago: University of Chicago Press.

Sullivan, J.L. and Transue, J.E. (1999), 'The psychological underpinnings of democracy: A Selective Review of Research on Political Tolerance, Interpersonal Trust, and Social Capital', *Annual Review of Psychology*, **50**: 625–650.

Wellings, K. and Wadsworth, J. (1990), 'AIDS and the moral climate' in Jowell, R., Witherspoon, S and Brook, L. (eds.), *British Social Attitudes: the 7ᵗʰ Report*, Aldershot: Gower.

Appendix

Logistic models of generalised tolerance

Generalised tolerance is measured as a dichotomous variable coded zero or one. We therefore use logistic regression to model these responses. Respondents score one when they both support racial supremacists' rights to political representation and at same time are not at all prejudiced on one of the three measures of prejudice used in this chapter. This produces three measures of generalised tolerance. The model shown in the first column in the table measures generalised tolerance using self-rated prejudice in the calculation, the second model uses acceptance of inter-marriage, and the third, acceptance of a black or Asian boss.

Education is measured using a scale running from no qualifications through to degree level qualifications. Social class is measured by comparing the effects of being in the salariat, the petty bourgeoisie, being a routine non-manual worker, or having no class position, with being in the working class (the 'reference category'). Church attendance is measured on a scale running from never, through to once a week or more often. Age is measured as a scale running from 18-29 through to 65 and over. Liberal values are measured using the liberal-authoritarian scale referred to in the appendix to the book; a high score equals a liberal position. Political involvement is a scale measuring 'interest in politics'.

Generalised tolerance measured using:	Self-rated prejudice		Attitudes to inter-marriage		Attitudes to black/Asian as boss	
	B	S.E.	B	S.E.	B	S.E.
Education	0.3933	(0.1238) **	0.3723	(0.1312) **	0.5033	(0.1123) **
Social class (ref: working class)						
Salariat	0.0107	(0.3036)	-0.1874	(0.3168)	0.1428	(0.2717)
Routine non-manual	0.1017	(0.3214)	0.2602	(0.3262)	0.1922	(0.2942)
Petty bourgeoisie	-0.1910	(0.4550)	-0.3413	(0.4853)	0.0277	(0.3895)
No class	0.5122	(0.7182)	0.5422	(0.7244)	0.3989	(0.7108)
Church attendance	-0.3544	(0.2648)	0.3547	(0.3265)	0.2582	(0.2673)
Male	0.5670	(0.2298) *	0.7407	(0.2432) **	0.7471	(0.2078) **
Age	0.0499	(0.1129)	-0.3328	(0.1243) **	-0.0567	(0.1028)
Liberal values	0.0875	(0.0272) **	0.0858	(0.0275) **	0.0653	(0.0249) **
Political involvement	0.1577	(0.1106)	0.2971	(0.1171) *	0.2790	(0.1005) **
Constant	1.0510	(0.8493)	-0.4663	(0.8673)	-0.8228	(0.7641)
Model Chi^2	66.54**		90.091**		116.199**	

* Significant at 5% level
** Significant at 1% level

Appendix I
Technical details of the survey

In 2001, three versions of the *British Social Attitudes* questionnaire were fielded. Each 'module' of questions is asked either of the full sample (3,287 respondents) or of a random two-thirds or one-third of the sample. The structure of the questionnaire (versions A, B and C) is shown at the beginning of Appendix III.

Sample design

The *British Social Attitudes* survey is designed to yield a representative sample of adults aged 18 or over. Since 1993, the sampling frame for the survey has been the Postcode Address File (PAF), a list of addresses (or postal delivery points) compiled by the Post Office.[1]

For practical reasons, the sample is confined to those living in private households. People living in institutions (though not in private households at such institutions) are excluded, as are households whose addresses were not on the PAF.

The sampling method involved a multi-stage design, with three separate stages of selection.

Selection of sectors

At the first stage, postcode sectors were selected systematically from a list of all postal sectors in Great Britain. Before selection, any sectors with fewer than 1,000 addresses were identified and grouped together with an adjacent sector; in Scotland all sectors north of the Caledonian Canal were excluded (because of the prohibitive costs of interviewing there). Sectors were then stratified on the basis of:

- 37 sub-regions
- population density with variable banding used, in order to create three equal-sized strata per sub-region
- ranking by percentage of homes that were owner-occupied in England and Wales and percentage of homes where the head of household was non-manual in Scotland.

Two hundred postcode sectors were selected, with probability proportional to the number of addresses in each sector.

Selection of addresses

Thirty-one addresses were selected in each of the 200 sectors. The sample was therefore 200 x 31 = 6,200 addresses, selected by starting from a random point on the list of addresses for each sector, and choosing each address at a fixed interval. The fixed interval was calculated for each sector in order to generate the correct number of addresses.

The Multiple-Output Indicator (MOI) available through PAF was used when selecting addresses in Scotland. The MOI shows the number of accommodation spaces sharing one address. Thus, if the MOI indicates more than one accommodation space at a given address, the chances of the given address being selected from the list of addresses would increase so that it matched the total number of accommodation spaces. The MOI is largely irrelevant in England and Wales as separate dwelling units generally appear as separate entries on PAF. In Scotland, tenements with many flats tend to appear as one entry on PAF. However, even in Scotland, the vast majority of MOIs had a value of one. The remainder, which ranged between three and 16, were incorporated into the weighting procedures (described below).

Selection of individuals

Interviewers called at each address selected from PAF and listed all those eligible for inclusion in the sample – that is, all persons currently aged 18 or over and resident at the selected address. The interviewer then selected one respondent using a computer-generated random selection procedure. Where there were two or more households or 'dwelling units' at the selected address, interviewers first had to select one household or dwelling unit using the same random procedure. They then followed the same procedure to select a person for interview.

Weighting

Data were weighted to take account of the fact that not all the units covered in the survey had the same probability of selection. The weighting reflected the relative selection probabilities of the individual at the three main stages of selection: address, household and individual.

First, because addresses in Scotland were selected using the MOI, weights had to be applied to compensate for the greater probability of an address with an MOI of more than one being selected, compared to an address with an MOI of one. (This stage was omitted for the English and Welsh data.) Secondly, data were weighted to compensate for the fact that dwelling units at an address which contained a large number of dwelling units were less likely to be selected for inclusion in the survey than ones which did not share an address. (We use this procedure because in most cases of MOIs greater than one, the two stages will cancel each other out, resulting in more efficient weights.) Thirdly, data were weighted to compensate for the lower selection probabilities of adults living in large households compared with those living in small households. The weights were capped at 8.0 (causing five cases to have their weights reduced). The resulting weight is called 'WtFactor' and the distribution of weights is shown in the next table.

Table A.1 Distribution of unscaled and scaled weights

Unscaled weight	Number	%	Scaled weight
0.0625	6	0.2	0.0347
0.1667	1	0.0	0.0926
0.5000	1	0.0	0.2779
0.6667	2	0.1	0.3706
0.7500	1	0.0	0.4169
1.0000	1158	35.2	0.5559
2.0000	1763	53.6	1.1118
3.0000	249	7.6	1.6676
4.0000	77	2.3	2.2235
5.0000	15	0.5	2.7794
6.0000	8	0.2	3.3353
8.0000	6	0.2	4.4471

Base: 3287

The mean weight was 1.80. The weights were then scaled down to make the number of weighted productive cases exactly equal to the number of unweighted productive cases (n = 3,287).

All the percentages presented in this Report are based on weighted data.

Questionnaire versions

Each address in each sector (sampling point) was allocated to either the A, B or C third of the sample. If one serial number was version A, the next was version B and the next after that version C. Thus each interviewer was allocated ten or 11 cases from each version and each version was assigned to 2,066 or 2,067 addresses.

Fieldwork

Interviewing was mainly carried out between June and September 2001, with a small number of interviews taking place in October and November.

Fieldwork was conducted by interviewers drawn from the *National Centre for Social Research*'s regular panel and conducted using face-to-face computer-assisted interviewing.[2] Interviewers attended a one-day briefing conference to familiarise them with the selection procedures and questionnaires.

The mean interview length was 65 minutes for version A of the questionnaire, 68 minutes for version B and 62 minutes for version C.[3] Interviewers achieved an overall response rate of 59 per cent. Details are shown in the next table.

Table A.2 Response rate on *British Social Attitudes* 2001

	Number	%
Addresses issued	6,200	
Vacant, derelict and other out of scope	623	
In scope	5,577	100.0
Interview achieved	3,287	58.9
Interview not achieved	2,290	41.1
Refused[1]	1,719	30.8
Non-contacted[2]	332	6.0
Other non-response	239	4.3

1 'Refused' comprises refusals before selection of an individual at the address, refusals to the office, refusal by the selected person, 'proxy' refusals (on behalf of the selected respondent) and broken appointments after which the selected person could not be recontacted.

2 'Non-contacted' comprises households where no one was contacted and those where the selected person could not be contacted.

As in earlier rounds of the series, the respondent was asked to fill in a self-completion questionnaire which, whenever possible, was collected by the interviewer. Otherwise, the respondent was asked to post it to the *National*

Centre for Social Research. If necessary, up to three postal reminders were sent to obtain the self-completion supplement.

A total of 492 respondents (15 per cent of those interviewed) did not return their self-completion questionnaire. Version A of the self-completion questionnaire was returned by 85 per cent of respondents to the face-to-face interview, version B by 87 per cent and version C by 83 per cent. As in previous rounds, we judged that it was not necessary to apply additional weights to correct for non-response.

Advance letter

Interviewers were supplied with letters describing the purpose of the survey and the coverage of the questionnaire, which they posted to sampled addresses before making any calls.[4]

Analysis variables

A number of standard analyses have been used in the tables that appear in this report. The analysis groups requiring further definition are set out below. For further details see Thomson *et al.* (2001).

Region

The ten Standard Statistical Regions (with Greater London distinguished from the rest of the South East) or twelve Government Office Regions have been used. Sometimes these have been grouped into what we have termed 'compressed region': 'Northern' includes the North, North West, Yorkshire and Humberside. East Anglia is included in the 'South', as is the South West.

Standard Occupational Classification

Respondents are classified according to their own occupation, not that of the 'head of household'. Each respondent was asked about their current or last job, so that all respondents except those who had never worked were coded. Additionally, if the respondent was not working but their spouse or partner *was* working, their spouse or partner is similarly classified.

With the 2001 survey, we began coding occupation to the new Standard Occupational Classification 2000 (SOC 2000) instead of the Standard Occupational Classification 1990 (SOC 90). The main socio-economic grouping based on SOC 2000 is the National Statistics Socio-Economic Classification (NS-SEC). However, to maintain time series, some analysis has continued to use the older schemes based on SOC 90 – Registrar General's Social Class, Socio-Economic Group and the Goldthorpe schema.

National Statistics Socio-Economic Classification (NS-SEC)

The combination of SOC 2000 an employment status for current or last job generates the following NS-SEC analytic classes:

- Employers in large organisations, higher managerial and professional
- Lower professional and managerial; higher technical and supervisory
- Intermediate occupations
- Small employers and own account workers
- Lower supervisory and technical occupations
- Semi-routine occupations
- Routine occupations

The remaining respondents are grouped as "never had a job" or "not classifiable". For some analyses, it may be more appropriate to classify respondents according to their current socio-economic status, which takes into account only their present economic position. In this case, in addition to the seven classes listed above, the remaining respondents not currently in paid work fall into one of the following categories: "not classifiable", "retired", "looking after the home", "unemployed" or "others not in paid occupations".

Registrar General's Social Class

As with NS-SEC , each respondent's Social Class is based on his or her current or last occupation. The combination of SOC 90 with employment status for current or last job generates the following six Social Classes:

I	Professional etc. occupations	
II	Managerial and technical occupations	'Non-manual'
III (Non-manual)	Skilled occupations	
III (Manual)	Skilled occupations	
IV	Partly skilled occupations	'Manual'
V	Unskilled occupations	

They are usually collapsed into four groups: I & II, III Non-manual, III Manual, and IV & V.

Socio-Economic Group

As with NS-SEC, each respondent's Socio-economic Group (SEG) is based on his or her current or last occupation. SEG aims to bring together people with jobs of similar social and economic status, and is derived from a combination of employment status and occupation. The full SEG classification identifies 18 categories, but these are usually condensed into six groups:

- Professionals, employers and managers
- Intermediate non-manual workers
- Junior non-manual workers
- Skilled manual workers
- Semi-skilled manual workers
- Unskilled manual workers

As with NS-SEC, the remaining respondents are grouped as "never had a job" or "not classifiable".

Goldthorpe schema

The Goldthorpe schema classifies occupations by their 'general comparability', considering such factors as sources and levels of income, economic security, promotion prospects, and level of job autonomy and authority. The Goldthorpe schema was derived from the SOC 90 codes combined with employment status. Two versions of the schema are coded: the full schema has 11 categories; the 'compressed schema' combines these into the five classes shown below.

- Salariat (professional and managerial)
- Routine non-manual workers (office and sales)
- Petty bourgeoisie (the self-employed, including farmers, with and without employees)
- Manual foremen and supervisors
- Working class (skilled, semi-skilled and unskilled manual workers, personal service and agricultural workers)

There is a residual category comprising those who have never had a job or who gave insufficient information for classification purposes.

Industry

All respondents whose occupation could be coded were allocated a Standard Industrial Classification 1992 (SIC 92). Two-digit class codes are used. As with Social Class, SIC may be generated on the basis of the respondent's current occupation only, or on his or her most recently classifiable occupation.

Party identification

Respondents can be classified as identifying with a particular political party on one of three counts: if they consider themselves supporters of that party, as closer to it than to others, or as more likely to support it in the event of a general election (responses are derived from Qs.151–153). The three groups are

generally described respectively as *partisans, sympathisers* and *residual identifiers*. In combination, the three groups are referred to as 'identifiers'.

Attitude scales

Since 1986, the *British Social Attitudes* surveys have included two attitude scales which aim to measure where respondents stand on certain underlying value dimensions – left–right and libertarian–authoritarian. Since 1987 (except 1990), a similar scale on 'welfarism' has been asked.[5]

A useful way of summarising the information from a number of questions of this sort is to construct an additive index (DeVellis, 1991; Spector, 1992). This approach rests on the assumption that there is an underlying – 'latent' – attitudinal dimension which characterises the answers to all the questions within each scale. If so, scores on the index are likely to be a more reliable indication of the underlying attitude than the answers to any one question.

Each of these scales consists of a number of statements to which the respondent is invited to "agree strongly", "agree", "neither agree nor disagree", "disagree", or "disagree strongly".

The items are:

Left–right scale

Government should redistribute income from the better-off to those who are less well off. *[Redistrb]*

Big business benefits owners at the expense of workers. *[BigBusnN]*

Ordinary working people do not get their fair share of the nation's wealth. *[Wealth]*[6]

There is one law for the rich and one for the poor. *[RichLaw]*

Management will always try to get the better of employees if it gets the chance. *[Indust4]*

Libertarian–authoritarian scale

Young people today don't have enough respect for traditional British values. *[TradVals]*

People who break the law should be given stiffer sentences. *[StifSent]*

For some crimes, the death penalty is the most appropriate sentence. *[DeathApp]*

Schools should teach children to obey authority. *[Obey]*

The law should always be obeyed, even if a particular law is wrong. *[WrongLaw]*

Censorship of films and magazines is necessary to uphold moral standards. *[Censor]*

Welfarism scale

> The welfare state encourages people to stop helping each other. *[WelfHelp]*

> The government should spend more money on welfare benefits for the poor, even if it leads to higher taxes. *[MoreWelf]*

> Around here, most unemployed people could find a job if they really wanted one. *[UnempJob]*

> Many people who get social security don't really deserve any help. *[SocHelp]*

> Most people on the dole are fiddling in one way or another. *[DoleFidl]*

> If welfare benefits weren't so generous, people would learn to stand on their own two feet. *[WelfFeet]*

> Cutting welfare benefits would damage too many people's lives. *[DamLives]*

> The creation of the welfare state is one of Britain's proudest achievements. *[ProudWlf]*

The indices for the three scales are formed by scoring the leftmost, most libertarian or most pro-welfare position, as 1 and the rightmost, most authoritarian or most anti-welfarist position, as 5. The "neither agree nor disagree" option is scored as 3. The scores to all the questions in each scale are added and then divided by the number of items in the scale giving indices ranging from 1 (leftmost, most libertarian, most pro-welfare) to 5 (rightmost, most authoritarian, most anti-welfare). The scores on the three indices have been placed on the dataset.[7]

The scales have been tested for reliability (as measured by Cronbach's alpha). The Cronbach's alpha (unstandardized items) for the scales in 2000 are 0.81 for the left–right scale, 0.80 for the 'welfarism' scale and 0.73 for the libertarian–authoritarian scale. This level of reliability can be considered "very good" for the left–right scale and welfarism scales and "acceptable" for the libertarian–authoritarian scale (DeVellis, 1991: 85).

Other analysis variables

These are taken directly from the questionnaire and to that extent are self-explanatory. The principal ones are:

Sex (Q.35)
Age (Q.36)
Household income (Q.1001)
Economic position (Q.307)
Religion (Q.753)

Highest educational qualification
  obtained (Qs.803–860)
Marital status (Q.127)
Benefits received (Qs.951–993)

Sampling errors

No sample precisely reflects the characteristics of the population it represents because of both sampling and non-sampling errors. If a sample were designed as a random sample (if every adult had an equal and independent chance of inclusion in the sample) then we could calculate the sampling error of any percentage, p, using the formula:

$$s.e.\ (p) = \sqrt{\frac{p(100-p)}{n}}$$

where n is the number of respondents on which the percentage is based. Once the sampling error had been calculated, it would be a straightforward exercise to calculate a confidence interval for the true population percentage. For example, a 95 per cent confidence interval would be given by the formula:

$$p \pm 1.96 \times s.e.(p)$$

Clearly, for a simple random sample (srs), the sampling error depends only on the values of p and n. However, simple random sampling is almost never used in practice because of its inefficiency in terms of time and cost.

As noted above, the *British Social Attitudes* sample, like that drawn for most large-scale surveys, was clustered according to a stratified multi-stage design into 200 postcode sectors (or combinations of sectors). With a complex design like this, the sampling error of a percentage giving a particular response is not simply a function of the number of respondents in the sample and the size of the percentage; it also depends on how that percentage response is spread within and between sample points.

The complex design may be assessed relative to simple random sampling by calculating a range of design factors (DEFTs) associated with it, where

$$DEFT = \sqrt{\frac{\text{Variance of estimator with complex design, sample size } n}{\text{Variance of estimator with srs design, sample size } n}}$$

and represents the multiplying factor to be applied to the simple random sampling error to produce its complex equivalent. A design factor of one means that the complex sample has achieved the same precision as a simple random sample of the same size. A design factor greater than one means the complex sample is less precise than its simple random sample equivalent. If the DEFT for a particular characteristic is known, a 95 per cent confidence interval for a percentage may be calculated using the formula:

$$p \pm 1.96 \times complex\ sampling\ error\ (p)$$

$$= p \pm 1.96 \times DEFT \times \sqrt{\frac{p(100-p)}{n}}$$

Calculations of sampling errors and design effects were made using the statistical analysis package STATA.

The following table gives examples of the confidence intervals and DEFTs calculated for a range of different questions: some fielded on all three versions of the questionnaire and some on one only; some asked on the interview questionnaire and some on the self-completion supplement. It shows that most of the questions asked of all sample members have a confidence interval of around plus or minus two to three per cent of the survey proportion. This means that we can be 95 per cent certain that the true population proportion is within two to three per cent (in either direction) of the proportion we report.

It should be noted that the design effects for certain variables (notably those most associated with the area a person lives in) are greater than those for other variables. For example, the question about benefit levels for the unemployed has high design effects, which may reflect differing rates of unemployment across the country. Another case in point is housing tenure, as different kinds of tenures (such as council housing, or owner-occupied properties) tend to be concentrated in certain areas; consequently the design effects calculated for these variables in a clustered sample are greater than the design effects calculated for variables less strongly associated with area, such as attitudinal variables.

These calculations are based on the 3,287 respondents to the main questionnaire and 2,795 returning self-completion questionnaires; on the A version respondents (1,107 for the main questionnaire and 941 for the self-completion); on the B version respondents (1,081 and 942 respectively); or on the C version respondents (1,099 and 912 respectively). As the examples above show, sampling errors for proportions based only on respondents to just one of the three versions of the questionnaire, or on subgroups within the sample, are somewhat larger than they would have been had the questions been asked of everyone.

Table A.3 Complex standard errors and confidence intervals of selected variables

		% (p)	Complex standard error of p	95% confidence interval	DEFT	Base
	Classification variables					
Q154	**Party identification**					3287
	Conservative	23.0	1.2	20.7 – 25.4	1.63	
	Labour	44.7	1.3	42.2 – 47.2	1.47	
	Liberal Democrat	12.9	0.7	11.7 – 14.2	1.11	
	Housing tenure					3287
	Owns	71.3	1.2	68.9 – 73.8	1.57	
	Rents from local authority	12.9	1.0	10.9 – 15.0	1.78	
	Rents privately/ HA	14.0	1.0	12.0 – 16.0	1.67	
Q746	**Religion**					3287
	No religion	41.2	1.0	39.2 – 43.2	1.17	
	Church of England	29.4	1.4	26.5 – 32.2	1.81	
	Roman Catholic	10.7	0.7	9.3 – 12.2	1.37	
Q800	**Age of completing continuous full-time education**					3287
	16 or under	60.1	1.5	57.2 – 63.1	1.76	
	17 or 18	17.8	0.9	16.1 – 19.5	1.31	
	19 or over	21.0	1.2	18.7 – 23.3	1.67	
Q861	**Home internet access**					3287
	Yes	44.2	1.2	41.8 – 46.6	1.41	
	intern	55.2	1.2	52.8 – 57.6	1.43	
Q749	**Urban or rural residence**					3287
	A big city	34.2	3.5	27.4 – 41.0	4.18	
	A small city/town	44.0	3.0	38.0 – 49.9	3.50	
	Village/countryside	20.7	2.5	15.9 – 25.5	3.47	
	Attitudinal variables (face-to-face interview)					
Q168	**Benefits for the unemployed are ... (3 versions)**					3287
	... too low	36.8	1.3	34.2 – 39.3	1.54	
	... too high	37.5	1.3	35.0 – 40.0	1.53	
Q208	**NHS should be available to those with lower incomes (2 versions)**					2188
	Support a lot	9.8	0.7	8.6 – 11.1	1.04	
	Support a little	17.0	1.0	15.1 – 18.9	1.22	
	Oppose a little	17.4	0.9	15.6 – 19.1	1.09	
	Oppose a lot	53.4	1.4	50.6 – 56.1	1.32	
Q684	**Cannabis should be ... (1 version)**					1081
	...legalised	6.2	0.9	4.6 – 7.9	1.17	
	...available only from licensed shops	45.2	1.8	41.7 – 48.7	1.17	
	...remain illegal	46.1	1.8	42.6 – 49.7	1.19	

Attitudinal variables (self-completion)

A2.20a B2.20a C2.47a	Those with high incomes should ... (3 versions)					2795
	...pay a much larger share in tax	11.2	0.7	9.9 – 12.5	1.12	
	...pay a larger share in tax	54.8	1.0	52.8 – 56.7	1.05	
	...pay the same share in tax	28.8	0.9	27.0 – 30.6	1.07	
	...pay a smaller/ much smaller share in tax	1.1	0.2	0.6 – 1.5	1.13	
A2.14b B2.14b	Right or wrong to refuse a job to a black/Asian applicant (2 versions)					1883
	Always/usually right	3.1	0.4	2.3 – 3.9	1.02	
	Neither	13.5	0.9	11.8 – 15.2	1.11	
	Usually wrong	32.1	1.1	29.9 – 34.2	1.00	
	Always wrong	44.5	1.2	42.2 – 46.7	1.01	
C2.55a	How important to cut the number of cars (1 version)					912
	Very important	25.0	1.6	21.9 – 28.1	1.11	
	Fairly important	48.3	1.8	44.7 – 51.9	1.12	
	Not very/ not at all important	20.2	1.5	17.2 – 23.2	1.16	

Analysis techniques

Regression

Regression analysis aims to summarise the relationship between a 'dependent' variable and one or more 'independent' variables. It shows how well we can estimate a respondent's score on the dependent variable from knowledge of their scores on the independent variables. It is often undertaken to support a claim that the phenomena measured by the independent variables cause the phenomenon measured by the dependent variable. However, the causal ordering, if any, between the variables cannot be verified or falsified by the technique. Causality can only be inferred through special experimental designs or through assumptions made by the analyst.

All regression analysis assumes that the relationship between the dependent and each of the independent variables takes a particular form. In *linear regression*, the most common form of regression analysis, it is assumed that the relationship can be adequately summarised by a straight line. This means that a one point increase in the value of an independent variable is assumed to have the same impact on the value of the dependent variable on average irrespective of the previous values of those variables.

Strictly speaking the technique assumes that both the dependent and the independent variables are measured on an interval level scale, although it may sometimes still be applied even where this is not the case. For example, one can

use an ordinal variable (e.g. a Likert scale) as a *dependent* variable if one is willing to assume that there is an underlying interval level scale and the difference between the observed ordinal scale and the underlying interval scale is due to random measurement error. Categorical or nominal data can be used as *independent* variables by converting them into dummy or binary variables; these are variables where the only valid scores are 0 and 1, with 1 signifying membership of a particular category and 0 otherwise.

The assumptions of linear regression can cause particular difficulties where the *dependent* variable is binary. The assumption that the relationship between the dependent and the independent variables is a straight line means that it can produce estimated values for the dependent variable of less than 0 or greater than 1. In this case it may be more appropriate to assume that the relationship between the dependent and the independent variables takes the form of an S-curve, where the impact on the dependent variable of a one-point increase in an independent variable becomes progressively less the closer the value of the dependent variable approaches 0 or 1. *Logistic regression* is an alternative form of regression which fits such an S-curve rather than a straight line. The technique can also be adapted to analyse multinomial non-interval level dependent variables, that is, variables which classify respondents into more than two categories.

The two statistical scores most commonly reported from the results of regression analyses are:

A measure of variance explained: This summarises how well all the independent variables combined can account for the variation in respondent's scores in the dependent variable. The higher the measure, the more accurately we are able in general to estimate the correct value of each respondent's score on the dependent variable from knowledge of their scores on the independent variables.

A parameter estimate: This shows how much the dependent variable will change on average, given a one unit change in the independent variable (while holding all other independent variables in the model constant). The parameter estimate has a positive sign if an increase in the value of the independent variable results in an increase in the value of the dependent variable. It has a negative sign if an increase in the value of the independent variable results in a decrease in the value of the dependent variable. If the parameter estimates are standardised, it is possible to compare the relative impact of different independent variables; those variables with the largest standardised estimates can be said to have the biggest impact on the value of the dependent variable.

Regression also tests for the statistical significance of parameter estimates. A parameter estimate is said to be significant at the five per cent level, if the range of the values encompassed by its 95 per cent confidence interval (see also section on sampling errors) are either all positive or all negative. This means that there is less than a five per cent chance that the association we have found between the dependent variable and the independent variable is simply the result of sampling error and does not reflect a relationship that actually exists in the general population.

Factor analysis

Factor analysis is a statistical technique which aims to identify whether there are one or more apparent sources of commonality to the answers given by respondents to a set of questions. It ascertains the smallest number of *factors* (or dimensions) which can most economically summarise all of the variation found in the set of questions being analysed. Factors are established where respondents who give a particular answer to one question in the set, tend to give the same answer as each other to one or more of the other questions in the set. The technique is most useful when a relatively small number of factors is able to account for a relatively large proportion of the variance in all of the questions in the set.

The technique produces a *factor loading* for each question (or variable) on each factor. Where questions have a high loading on the same factor then it will be the case that respondents who give a particular answer to one of these questions tend to give a similar answer to the other questions. The technique is most commonly used in attitudinal research to try to identify the underlying ideological dimensions which apparently structure attitudes towards the subject in question.

International Social Survey Programme

The *International Social Survey Programme* (*ISSP*) is run by a group of research organisations, each of which undertakes to field annually an agreed module of questions on a chosen topic area. Since 1985, an *International Social Survey Programme* module has been included in one of the *British Social Attitudes* self-completion questionnaires. Each module is chosen for repetition at intervals to allow comparisons both between countries (membership is currently standing at 38) and over time. In 2001, the chosen subject was Social Networks, and the module was carried on the C version of the self-completion questionnaire (Qs.1–33).

Notes

1. Until 1991 all *British Social Attitudes* samples were drawn from the Electoral Register (ER). However, following concern that this sampling frame might be deficient in its coverage of certain population subgroups, a 'splicing' experiment was conducted in 1991. We are grateful to the Market Research Development Fund for contributing towards the costs of this experiment. Its purpose was to investigate whether a switch to PAF would disrupt the time-series – for instance, by lowering response rates or affecting the distribution of responses to particular questions. In the event, it was concluded that the change from ER to PAF was unlikely to affect time trends in any noticeable ways, and that no adjustment factors were necessary. Since significant differences in efficiency exist between PAF and ER, and because

we considered it untenable to continue to use a frame that is known to be biased, we decided to adopt PAF as the sampling frame for future *British Social Attitudes* surveys. For details of the PAF/ER 'splicing' experiment, see Lynn and Taylor (1995).

2. In 1993 it was decided to mount a split-sample experiment designed to test the applicability of Computer-Assisted Personal Interviewing (CAPI) to the *British Social Attitudes* survey series. CAPI has been used increasingly over the past decade as an alternative to traditional interviewing techniques. As the name implies, CAPI involves the use of lap-top computers during the interview, with interviewers entering responses directly into the computer. One of the advantages of CAPI is that it significantly reduces both the amount of time spent on data processing and the number of coding and editing errors. Over a longer period, there could also be significant cost savings. There was, however, concern that a different interviewing technique might alter the distribution of responses and so affect the year-on-year consistency of *British Social Attitudes* data.

    Following the experiment, it was decided to change over to CAPI completely in 1994 (the self-completion questionnaire still being administered in the conventional way). The results of the experiment are discussed in *The 11th Report* (Lynn and Purdon, 1994).

3. Interview times of less than 20 and more than 150 minutes were excluded as these were likely to be errors.

4. An experiment was conducted on the 1991 *British Social Attitudes* survey (Jowell *et al.*,1992), which showed that sending advance letters to sampled addresses before fieldwork begins has very little impact on response rates. However, interviewers do find that an advance letter helps them to introduce the survey on the doorstep, and a majority of respondents have said that they preferred some advance notice. For these reasons, advance letters have been used on the *British Social Attitudes* surveys since 1991.

5. Because of methodological experiments on scale development, the exact items detailed in this section have not been asked on all versions of the questionnaire each year.

6. In 1994 only, this item was replaced by: Ordinary people get their fair share of the nation's wealth. *[Wealth1]*

7. In constructing the scale, a decision had to be taken on how to treat missing values ('Don't knows' and 'Refused'/not answered). Respondents who had more than two missing values on the left–right scale and more than three missing values on the libertarian–authoritarian and welfare scale were excluded from that scale. For respondents with just a few missing values, 'Don't knows' were recoded to the midpoint of the scale and not answered or 'Refused' were recoded to the scale mean for that respondent on their valid items.

References

DeVellis, R. F. (1991), 'Scale development: theory and applications', *Applied Social Research Methods Series*, **26**, Newbury Park: Sage.

Jowell, R., Brook, L., Prior, G. and Taylor, B. (1992), *British Social Attitudes: the 9th Report*, Aldershot: Dartmouth.

Lynn, P. and Purdon, S. (1994), 'Time-series and lap-tops: the change to computer-assisted interviewing' in Jowell, R., Curtice, J., Brook, L. and Ahrendt, D. (eds.), *British Social Attitudes: the 11th Report*, Aldershot: Dartmouth.

Lynn, P. and Taylor, B. (1995), 'On the bias and variance of samples of individuals: a comparison of the Electoral Registers and Postcode Address File as sampling frames', *The Statistician*, **44**: 173–194.

Spector, P. E. (1992), 'Summated rating scale construction: an introduction', *Quantitative Applications in the Social Sciences*, **82**, Newbury Park: Sage.

Thomson, K., Park, A., Jarvis, L., Bromley, C. and Stratford, N. (2001), *British Social Attitudes 1999 survey: Technical Report*, London: National Centre for Social Research.

Appendix II
Notes on the tabulations

1. Figures in the tables are from the 2001 *British Social Attitudes* survey unless otherwise indicated.
2. Tables are percentaged as indicated.
3. In tables, '*' indicates less than 0.5 per cent but greater than zero, and '-' indicates zero.
4. When findings based on the responses of fewer than 100 respondents are reported in the text, reference is generally made to the small base size.
5. Percentages equal to or greater than 0.5 have been rounded up in all tables (e.g. 0.5 per cent = one per cent, 36.5 per cent = 37 per cent).
6. In many tables the proportions of respondents answering "Don't know" or not giving an answer are omitted. This, together with the effects of rounding and weighting, means that percentages will not always add to 100 per cent.
7. The self-completion questionnaire was not completed by all respondents to the main questionnaire (see Appendix I). Percentage responses to the self-completion questionnaire are based on all those who completed it.
8. The bases shown in the tables (the number of respondents who answered the question) are printed in small italics. The bases are unweighted, unless otherwise stated.

Appendix III
The questionnaires

As explained in Appendix I, three different versions of the questionnaire (A, B and C) were administered, each with its own self-completion supplement. The diagram that follows shows the structure of the questionnaires and the topics covered (not all of which are reported on in this volume).

The three interview questionnaires reproduced on the following pages are derived from the Blaise program in which they were written. For ease of reference, each item has been allocated a question number. Gaps in the numbering system indicate items that are essential components of the Blaise program but which are not themselves questions, and so have been omitted. In addition, we have removed the keying codes and inserted instead the percentage distribution of answers to each question. We have also included the SPSS variable name, in square brackets, beside each question. Above the questions we have included filter instructions. A filter instruction should be considered as staying in force until the next filter instruction. Percentages for the core questions are based on the total weighted sample, while those for questions in versions A, B or C are based on the appropriate weighted sub-samples. We reproduce first version A of the interview questionnaire in full; then those parts of version B and version C that differ. The three versions of the self-completion questionnaire follow, with those parts fielded in more than one version reproduced in one version only.

The percentage distributions do not necessarily add up to 100 because of weighting and rounding, or for one or more of the following reasons:

(i)   Some sub-questions are filtered – that is, they are asked of only a proportion of respondents. In these cases the percentages add up (approximately) to the proportions who were asked them. Where, however, a series of questions is filtered, we have indicated the weighted base at the beginning of that series (for example, all employees), and throughout have derived percentages from that base.

(ii) At a few questions, respondents were invited to give more than one answer and so percentages may add to well over 100 per cent. These are clearly marked by interviewer instructions on the questionnaires.

As reported in Appendix I, the 2001 *British Social Attitudes* self-completion questionnaire was not completed by 15 per cent of respondents who were successfully interviewed. The answers in the supplement have been percentaged on the base of those respondents who returned it. This means that the distribution of responses to questions asked in earlier years are comparable with those given in Appendix III of all earlier reports in this series except in *The 1984 Report*, where the percentages for the self-completion questionnaire need to be recalculated if comparisons are to be made.

BRITISH SOCIAL ATTITUDES: 2001 SURVEY
Main questionnaire plan

Version A	Version B	Version C

Household grid		
Newspaper readership		
Party identification		
Public spending and social welfare		
Health care		Politics
National identity (England only)		
Employment		
Health and safety in the workplace		
Understanding of public policy		
Education	Drugs	Transport
Classification		

Self-completion questionnaire plan

–	–	ISSP (Family and friends)
Public spending and social welfare		
Health care		–
Politics		
Discrimination		–
Health and safety in the workplace		
Understanding of public policy		
Education	Drugs	Transport
Attitude scales		

BRITISH SOCIAL ATTITUDES 2001: FACE TO FACE QUESTIONNAIRE

Contents page

VERSION A

Introduction

ASK ALL

Q1 *[SerialNo]* **(NOT ON SCREEN)**
Serial Number
Range: 130001 ... 139999

Q8 *[StRegion]*
%   Standard region
9.3 Scotland
6.6 Northern
9.7 North West
9.5 Yorkshire and Humberside
8.7 West Midlands
7.9 East Midlands
3.6 East Anglia
8.3 South West
19.6 South East (excluding Greater London)
10.8 Greater London
6.0 Wales

Q25 *[ABCVer]*
%   A, B or C?
33.5 A
32.8 B
33.7 C
–   (Don't know)
–   (Refusal/Not answered)

N = 3287

Household grid

N = 3287

ASK ALL

Q33 *[Household]*
(You have just been telling me about the adults that live in
this household. Thinking now of **everyone** living in the
household, **including children**:)
Including yourself, how many people live here regularly as
members of this household?
CHECK INTERVIEWER MANUAL FOR DEFINITION OF HOUSEHOLD IF
NECESSARY.
IF YOU DISCOVER THAT YOU WERE GIVEN THE WRONG INFORMATION FOR
THE RESPONDENT SELECTION ON THE ARF:
* **DO NOT** REDO THE ARF SELECTION PRODECURE
* **DO** ENTER THE CORRECT INFORMATION HERE
* **DO** USE <CTRL + M> TO MAKE A NOTE OF WHAT HAPPENED.
%   **Median: 2 people**
–   (Don't know)
–   (Refusal/Not answered)

FOR EACH PERSON AT [Househld]

[Name] **(NOT ON DATA FILE)**
FOR RESPONDENT: (Can I just check what is your first name?)
PLEASE TYPE IN THE FIRST NAME (OR INITIALS) OF RESPONDENT
FOR OTHER HOUSEHOLD MEMBERS: PLEASE TYPE IN THE FIRST NAME (OR
INITIALS) OF PERSON NUMBER *(number)*

[RSex], [P2Sex]-[P11Sex] (Figures refer to respondent)
PLEASE CODE SEX OF *(name)*
%   Male
45.8 Male
54.2 Female
–   (Don't know)
–   (Refusal/Not answered)

[RAge], [P2Age]-[P22Age] (Figures refer to respondent)
FOR RESPONDENT IF ONLY ONE PERSON IN HOUSEHOLD: I would like
to ask you a few details about yourself. What was your **age**
last birthday?
FOR RESPONDENT IF SEVERAL PERSONS IN HOUSEHOLD: I would like
to ask you a few details about each person in your household.
Starting with yourself, what was your **age** last birthday?
FOR OTHER PERSONS IN HOUSEHOLD: What was *(name)*'s age last
birthday?
FOR 97+, CODE 97.
%   **Median: 45 years**
–   (Don't know)
0.1 (Refusal/Not answered)

FOR PEOPLE IN HOUSEHOLD OTHER THAN RESPONDENT   N = 3287

[P2Rel3]-[P11Rel3] (Figures refer to second person in household)

PLEASE ENTER RELATIONSHIP OF (name) TO RESPONDENT
%
63.7 Partner/ spouse/ cohabitee
8.1 Son/ daughter (inc step/adopted)
0.1 Grandson/ daughter (inc step/adopted)
7.1 Parent/ parent-in-law
0.1 Grand-parent
0.8 Brother/ sister (inc. in-law)
0.3 Other relative
2.0 Other non-relative
- (Don't know)
- (Refusal/Not answered)

ASK ALL
Q127 [MarStat2]
CARD A1
Can I just check, which of these applies to you at present?
CODE FIRST TO APPLY
%
55.7 Married
8.8 Living as married
2.1 Separated (after being married)
6.6 Divorced
7.7 Widowed
19.1 Single (never married)
- (Don't know)
0.1 (Refusal/Not answered)

Q132-CARD A2
Q138 Can I just check which, if any, of these types of relatives do you yourself have alive at the moment. Please include adoptive and step-relatives.
PROBE: Which others?
DO NOT INCLUDE FOSTER RELATIVES
CODE ALL THAT APPLY
%
61.3 Brother   [RelBroth]
62.3 Sister   [RelSist]
53.3 Son   [RelSon]
51.4 Daughter   [RelDaugh]
21.2 Grandchild (daughter's child)   [RelGrChD]
18.1 Grandchild (son's child)   [RelGrChS]
3.9 None of these   [RelNone2]
- (Don't know)
- (Refusal/Not answered)

Newspaper readership

ASK ALL
Q146 [ReadPap]
Do you normally read any daily **morning** newspaper at least 3 times a week?
%
52.9 Yes
47.1 No
- (Don't know)
- (Refusal/Not answered)

IF 'yes' AT [ReadPap]
Q147 [WhPaper]
Which one do you normally read?
IF MORE THAN ONE: Which one do you read **most** frequently?
%
3.3 (Scottish) Daily Express
11.0 (Scottish) Daily Mail
10.3 (Daily Mirror/ Record)
1.2 Daily Star
11.8 The Sun
4.8 Daily Telegraph
0.7 Financial Times
2.3 The Guardian
0.9 The Independent
3.3 The Times
3.1 Morning Star
0.1 Other Irish/Northern Irish/Scottish regional or local **daily morning** paper (WRITE IN)
0.1 Other (WRITE IN)
0.0 (Don't know)
- (Refusal/Not answered)

IN ENGLAND: ASK ALL   N = 2786
Q150 [TVRgNwsE]
Do you normally watch a **regional** television news program on either BBC or ITV at least three times a week?
FOR RESPONDENTS WHO WATCH ONLY SHORT BULLETINS, CODE YES
%
80.7 Yes
19.2 No
0.0 (Don't know)
- (Refusal/Not answered)

N = 3287

Party identification

ASK ALL

Q151 *[SupParty]*
Generally speaking, do you think of yourself as a supporter of
any one political party?
%
42.8 Yes
57.1 No
0.2 (Don't know)
– (Refusal/Not answered)

IF 'no' OR DON'T KNOW AT [SupParty]

Q152 *[ClosePty]*
Do you think of yourself as a little closer to one political
party than to the others?
%
25.8 Yes
31.3 No
0.1 (Don't know)
– (Refusal/Not answered)

IF 'yes' AT [SupParty] OR 'yes'/'no'/DON'T KNOW AT [ClosePty]
[PartyID1]
IF 'yes' AT [SupParty] OR AT [ClosePty]: Which one?
IF 'no'/DON'T KNOW AT [ClosePty]: If there were a general
election tomorrow, which political party do you think you
would be most likely to support?
DO NOT PROMPT
%
23.0 Conservative
44.7 Labour
12.9 Liberal Democrat
1.7 Scottish National Party
0.6 Plaid Cymru
1.0 Other party
0.7 Other answer
11.5 None
0.9 Green Party
1.6 (Don't know)
1.4 (Refusal/Not answered)

IF PARTY GIVEN AT [PartyID1]

Q159 *[Idstrng]*
Would you call yourself very strong *(party)*, fairly strong, or
not very strong?
%
7.4 Very strong (party)
28.6 Fairly strong
48.6 Not very strong
0.1 (Don't know)
3.9 (Refusal/Not answered)

N = 3287

ASK ALL

Q160 *[Politics]*
How much interest do you generally have in what is going on in
politics
% ... READ OUT ...
8.7 ... a great deal,
22.3 quite a lot,
34.5 some,
23.9 not very much,
10.6 or, none at all?

Public spending and social welfare

N = 3287

ASK ALL
Q162 [Spend1]
CARD B1
Here are some items of government spending. Which of them, if any, would be your highest priority for **extra** spending?
Please read through the whole list before deciding.
ENTER ONE CODE ONLY FOR HIGHEST PRIORITY

```
%
28.5   Education
1.2    Defence
54.3   Health
2.6    Housing
3.7    Public transport
1.8    Roads
3.3    Police and prisons
2.3    Social security benefits
1.1    Help for industry
0.5    Overseas aid
0.4    (None of these)
0.3    (Don't know)
-      (Refusal/Not answered)
```

IF NOT NONE/DK/REFUSAL AT [Spend1]
Q163 [Spend2]
CARD B1 AGAIN
And which next?
ENTER ONE CODE ONLY FOR NEXT HIGHEST

	[Spend1]	[Spend2]
	%	%
Education	28.5	38.9
Defence	1.2	1.7
Health	54.3	28.5
Housing	2.6	5.0
Public transport	3.7	7.3
Roads	1.8	3.1
Police and prisons	3.3	7.5
Social security benefits	2.3	3.7
Help for industry	1.1	2.7
Overseas aid	0.5	0.5
(None of these)	0.4	0.4
(Don't know)	0.3	-
(Refusal/Not answered)	-	-

N = 3287

ASK ALL
Q164 [SocBen1]
CARD B2
Thinking now only of the government's spending on **social benefits** like those on the card.
Which, if any, of these would be your highest priority for **extra** spending?
ENTER ONE CODE ONLY FOR HIGHEST PRIORITY

IF NOT NONE/DK/REFUSAL AT [SocBen1]
Q165 [SocBen2]
CARD B2 AGAIN
And which next?
ENTER ONE CODE ONLY FOR NEXT HIGHEST

	[SocBen1]	[SocBen2]
	%	%
Retirement pensions	54.1	21.5
Child benefits	14.7	20.4
Benefits for the unemployed	3.6	8.6
Benefits for disabled people	19.5	37.6
Benefits for single parents	6.5	7.9
(None of these)	1.1	2.0
(Don't know)	0.5	0.3
(Refusal/Not answered)	-	-

ASK ALL
Q166 [FalseClm]
I will read two statements. For each one please say whether you agree or disagree. Firstly...
Large numbers of people these days **falsely** claim benefits.
IF AGREE OR DISAGREE: Strongly or slightly?

Q167 [FailClm]
(And do you agree or disagree that...)
Large numbers of people who are eligible for benefits these days **fail** to claim them.
IF AGREE OR DISAGREE: Strongly or slightly?

	[FalseClm]	[FailClm]
	%	%
Agree strongly	53.0	40.8
Agree slightly	26.1	38.9
Disagree slightly	9.6	10.9
Disagree strongly	6.7	3.5
(Don't know)	4.6	6.0
(Refusal/Not answered)	-	-

N = 3287

N = 3287

Q168 [Dole]
Opinions differ about the level of benefits for unemployed people.
Which of these two statements comes closest to your own view

%   ...READ OUT...
36.8   ...benefits for unemployed people are **too low** and cause hardship,
37.5   or, benefits for unemployed people are **too high** and discourage them from finding jobs?
16.4   (Neither)
0.2   **EDIT ONLY:** BOTH: UNEMPLOYMENT BENEFIT CAUSES HARDSHIP BUT CAN'T BE HIGHER OR THERE WOULD BE NO INCENTIVE TO WORK
0.8   **EDIT ONLY:** BOTH: UNEMPLOYMENT BENEFIT CAUSES HARDSHIP TO SOME, WHILE OTHERS DO WELL OUT OF IT
0.5   **EDIT ONLY:** ABOUT RIGHT/IN BETWEEN
3.1   Other answer (WRITE IN)
4.8   (Don't know)
-      (Refusal/Not answered)

ASK ALL
Q170 [TaxSpend]
CARD B3
Suppose the government had to choose between the three options on this card. Which do you think it should choose?

%
2.7   Reduce taxes and spend **less** on health, education and social benefits
34.3   Keep taxes and spending on these services at the **same** level as now
59.3   Increase taxes and spend **more** on health, education and social benefits
2.9   (None)
0.8   (Don't know)
-      (Refusal/Not answered)

Q171 [MstUnemp]
Suppose two people working for a large firm each became unemployed through no fault of their own. One had a very high income, one had a very low income. Do you think the very high earner should be entitled to ...READ OUT...

%   ... more unemployment benefit than the very low earner,
10.2
76.2   the same amount,
9.7   less benefit,
1.8   or, no unemployment benefit at all?
0.6   **EDIT ONLY:** IT DEPENDS
0.3   Other answer (WRITE IN)
1.1   (Don't know)
.   (Refusal/Not answered)

Q173 [MstRetir]
Now suppose a very high earner and a very low earner in a large firm retired. Do you think the very high earner should be entitled to ...READ OUT...

%
12.9   ... a bigger **state** retirement pension than the very low earner,
73.6   the same amount,
9.2   a lower **state** pension,
2.6   or, no **state** pension at all?
0.9   **EDIT ONLY:** IT DEPENDS
0.2   Other answer (WRITE IN)
0.6   (Don't know)
-      (Refusal/Not answered)

Q175 [MstChild]
Now what about child benefit. Should very high earners be entitled to ...READ OUT...

%
1.1   ... more child benefit than very low earners,
55.4   the same amount,
23.3   less,
18.4   or, no child benefit at all?
0.0   **EDIT ONLY:** IT DEPENDS
1.0   Other answer (WRITE IN)
0.7   (Don't know)
-      (Refusal/Not answered)

Q177 [MstDisab]
Now what about disability benefits. Should disabled people with very high incomes be entitled to ...READ OUT...

%
4.3   ... more disability benefits than those with very low incomes,
66.8   the same amount,
20.9   less disability benefits,
5.4   or, no disability benefits at all?
0.7   **EDIT ONLY:** IT DEPENDS
0.8   Other answer (WRITE IN)
0.9   (Don't know)
0.0   (Refusal/Not answered)

N = 3287

Q179 [MstWork]

Suppose two people go to claim unemployment benefit. One
person has just become unemployed through no fault of their
own after working for a long time and the other person has not
worked for a long time.
Do you think that the person who has recently worked should be
entitled to ..READ OUT...

%
27.3 ... more unemployment benefit than the person who has not
worked for a long time,
64.5 the same amount,
4.4 less benefit,
0.2 or, no unemployment benefit at all?
1.6 **EDIT ONLY:** IT DEPENDS
0.6 Other answer (WRITE IN)
1.3 (Don't know)
0.1 (Refusal/Not answered)

Q181 [HealResp]
CARD B4
Please say from this card who you think should **mainly** be
responsible for paying for the cost of health care when
someone is ill?

Q182 [RetResp]
CARD B4 AGAIN
Still looking at this card, who you think should **mainly** be
responsible for ensuring that people have enough money to live
on in retirement?

Q183 [SickResp]
CARD B4 AGAIN
And who do you think should **mainly** be responsible for ensuring
that people have enough to live on if they become sick for a
long time or disabled?

Q184 [UnemResp]
CARD B4 AGAIN
And who do you think should **mainly** be responsible for ensuring
that people have enough to live on if they become unemployed?

	[HealResp]	[RetResp]	[SickResp]	[UnemResp]
	%	%	%	%
Mainly the government	87.2	62.2	84.0	87.7
Mainly a person's employer	7.3	7.2	7.6	2.1
Mainly a person themselves and their family	4.2	28.7	7.2	8.7
(Don't Know)	1.3	1.9	1.1	1.4
(Refusal/Not answered)	0.0	-	0.0	-

N = 3287

Q185 [CareResp]
CARD B5
And who do you think should **mainly** be responsible for paying
for the care needs of elderly people living in residential and
nursing homes?
%
86.2 Mainly the government
10.9 Mainly a person themselves and their family
2.9 (Don't know)
- (Refusal/Not answered)

Q186 [LonePaWk]

Suppose a lone parent on benefits was asked to visit the job
centre every year or so to talk about ways in which they might
find work. Which of the following comes closest to what you
think should happen to their benefits if they did not go?
READ OUT ...
%
17.3 ... their benefits should not be affected,
43.4 their benefits should be reduced a little,
12.1 their benefits should be reduced a lot,
23.2 or, their benefits should be stopped?
3.0 (Other (PLEASE WRITE IN))
1.0 (Don't know)
- (Refusal/Not answered)

Q188 [SickWk]
Now think about someone on long-term sickness or disability
benefits. Which of the following comes closest to what you
think should happen to their benefits if they did not go to
the job centre to talk about ways in which they might find
work?
READ OUT ...
%
33.6 ... their benefits should not be affected,
37.9 their benefits should be reduced a little,
8.0 their benefits should be reduced a lot,
14.0 or, their benefits should be stopped?
5.0 (Other (PLEASE WRITE IN))
1.4 (Don't know)
0.0 (Refusal/Not answered)

N = 3287

Q190 [CarerWk]
And suppose a carer on benefits was asked to visit the job centre every year or so to talk about ways in which they might find work. Which of the following comes closest to what you think should happen to their benefits if they did not go?
READ OUT ...
%
47.5 ... their benefits should not be affected,
30.2 their benefits should be reduced a little,
5.2 their benefits should be reduced a lot,
12.6 or, their benefits should be stopped?
2.8 (Other (PLEASE WRITE IN))
1.7 (Don't know)
0.0 (Refusal/Not answered)

Q192 [PayHols]
Suppose a person wants to go on holiday but hasn't got the money to pay for it. In your view ... **READ OUT** ...

Q193 [PaySofa]
Now think about someone else who wants to replace their sofa but hasn't got the money to pay for it. In your view ... **READ OUT** ...

Q194 [PayOven]
And now think about someone who wants to replace their broken cooker but hasn't got the money to pay for it. In your view ... **READ OUT** ...

	[PayHols]	[PaySofa]	[PayOven]
	%	%	%
... should they save up the money beforehand?	90.1	75.6	21.0
or, should they borrow the money and pay it back later?	7.3	21.5	76.8
(Don't know)	2.6	2.9	2.2
(Refusal/Not answered)	0.0	0.0	0.0

Q195 [IncomGap]
Thinking of income levels generally in Britain today, would you say that the **gap** between those with high incomes and those with low incomes is
... READ OUT ...
%
80.1 ... too large,
14.3 about right,
1.1 or, too small?
4.5 (Don't know)
0.0 (Refusal/Not answered)

N = 3287

Q196 [SRInc]
%   Among which group would you place yourself ... READ OUT ...
4.1 ... high income,
52.7 middle income,
42.4 or, low income?
0.6 (Don't know)
0.2 (Refusal/Not answered)

Q197 [HIncDiff]
CARD B6
Which of the phrases on this card would you say comes closest to your feelings about your household's income these days?
%
38.5 Living comfortably on present income
46.9 Coping on present income
11.0 Finding it difficult on present income
3.2 Finding it very difficult on present income
0.1 (Other answer (WRITE IN))
0.1 (Don't know)
0.0 (Refusal/Not answered)

Health

N = 2179

VERSIONS A AND B: ASK ALL

Q200 [NHSSat]
CARD C1
All in all, how satisfied or dissatisfied would you say you are with the way in which the National Health Service runs nowadays?
Choose a phrase from this card.

Q201 [GPSat]
CARD C1 AGAIN
From your own experience, or from what you have heard, please say how satisfied or dissatisfied you are with the way in which each of these parts of the National Health Service runs nowadays:
First, local doctors or GPs?

Q202 [DentSat]
CARD C1 AGAIN
(And how satisfied or dissatisfied are you with the NHS as regards...)
... National Health Service dentists?

Q203 [InpatSat]
CARD C1 AGAIN
(And how satisfied or dissatisfied are you with the NHS as regards...)
... Being in hospital as an **in**-patient?

Q204 [OutpaSat]
CARD C1 AGAIN
(And how satisfied or dissatisfied are you with the NHS as regards...)
... Attending hospital as an **out**-patient?

Q205 [AESat]
CARD C1 AGAIN
(And how satisfied or dissatisfied are you with the NHS as regards...)
... Accident and emergency departments?

	[NHSSat]	[GPSat]	[DentSat]
	%	%	%
Very satisfied	6.9	25.3	13.9
Quite satisfied	31.6	45.9	38.9
Neither satisfied nor dissatisfied	20.4	11.4	16.9
Quite dissatisfied	26.8	13.1	14.1
Very dissatisfied	13.8	3.7	10.3
(Don't know)	0.5	0.6	5.8
(Refusal/Not answered)	-	-	-

N = 2179

	[InPatSat]	[OutPaSat]	[AESat]
	%	%	%
Very satisfied	13.9	10.5	13.0
Quite satisfied	37.1	39.6	30.3
Neither satisfied nor dissatisfied	18.8	18.9	17.6
Quite dissatisfied	17.9	19.4	19.4
Very dissatisfied	6.0	7.5	12.6
(Don't know)	6.6	4.1	7.0
(Refusal/Not answered)	-	-	-

Q206 [PrivMed]
Are **you yourself** covered by a private health insurance scheme, that is an insurance scheme that allows you to get private medical **treatment**?
ADD IF NECESSARY: 'For example, BUPA or PPP.'
IF INSURANCE COVERS DENTISTRY **ONLY**, CODE No.

%
19.8 Yes
79.9 No
0.3 (Don't know)
- (Refusal/Not answered)

Q207 [PrivPaid]
IF 'yes' AT [PrivMed]
Does your employer (or your partner's employer) pay the majority of the cost of membership of this scheme?

%
10.7 Yes
9.0 No
0.1 (Don't know)
0.3 (Refusal/Not answered)

VERSIONS A AND B: ASK ALL

Q208 [NHSLimit]
It has been suggested that the National Health Service should be available **only to those with lower incomes**. This would mean that contributions and taxes could be lower and most people would then take out medical insurance or pay for health care.
Do you support or oppose this idea?
IF 'SUPPORT' OR 'OPPOSE': A lot or a little?

Q209 [DentLimt]
Many dentists now provide NHS treatment only to those with lower incomes. This means that other people have to pay the full amount for their dental treatment, or take out private insurance to cover their treatment.
Do you support or oppose this happening?
IF 'SUPPORT' OR 'OPPOSE': 'A lot or a little?'

N = 2179

	[NSHLimit]	[DentLimit]
	%	%
Support a lot	9.8	9.0
Supprt a little	17.0	19.5
Oppose a little	17.4	21.5
Oppose a lot	53.4	47.6
(Don't know)	2.4	2.4
(Refusal/Not answered)	-	-

Q210 [InPat1]
CARD C2
Now, suppose you had to go into a local NHS hospital for observation and maybe an operation. From what you know or have heard, please say whether you think the hospital doctors would tell you all you feel you need to know?

Q211 [InPat2]
CARD C2 AGAIN
(And please say whether you think ...)
...the hospital doctors would take seriously any views you may have on the sorts of treatment available?

Q212 [InPat3]
CARD C2 AGAIN
(And please say whether you think ...)
...the operation would take place on the day it was booked for?

Q213 [InPat4]
CARD C2 AGAIN
(And please say whether you think ...)
...you would be allowed home only when you were really well enough to leave?

Q214 [InPat5]
CARD C2 AGAIN
(And please say whether you think ...)
...the nurses would take seriously any complaints you may have?

Q215 [InPat6]
CARD C2 AGAIN
(And please say whether you think ...)
...the hospital doctors would take seriously any complaints you may have?

N = 2179

Q216 [InPat7]
CARD C2 AGAIN
(And please say whether you think ...)
...there would be a particular nurse responsible for dealing with any problems you may have?

Q217 [OutPat1]
CARD C2 AGAIN
Now suppose you had a back problem and your GP referred you to a hospital out-patients' department. From what you know or have heard, please say whether you think...
...you would get an appointment within three months?

Q218 [OutPat2]
CARD C2 AGAIN
(And please say whether you think ...)
...when you arrived, the doctor would see you within half an hour of your appointment time?

Q219 [OutPat3]
CARD C2 AGAIN
(And please say whether you think ...)
...if you wanted to complain about the treatment you received, you would be able to without any fuss or bother?

	[InPat1]	[InPat2]	[InPat3]
	%	%	%
Definitely would	19.3	12.7	6.1
Probably would	51.2	48.6	38.6
Probably would not	22.0	29.7	41.9
Definitely would not	6.2	5.7	10.8
(Don't know)	1.2	3.3	2.6
(Refusal/Not answered)	-	-	-

	[InPat4]	[InPat5]	[InPat6]
	%	%	%
Definitely would	11.5	17.5	14.6
Probably would	38.7	59.5	59.0
Probably would not	35.9	17.6	20.1
Definitely would not	11.7	3.2	3.9
(Don't know)	2.2	2.1	2.4
(Refusal/Not answered)	-	-	-

	[InPat7]	[OutPat1]	[OutPat2]
	%	%	%
Definitely would	13.4	6.5	5.5
Probably would	39.8	29.2	27.0
Probably would not	33.2	41.4	42.8
Definitely would not	6.4	18.4	22.9
(Don't know)	7.1	4.4	1.7
(Refusal/Not answered)	-	-	-

[OutPat3]

	%
Definitely would	9.4
Probably would	43.2
Probably would not	33.1
Definitely would not	9.5
(Don't know)	4.8
(Refusal/Not answered)	-

Q220 [SRHealth]
How is your health in general for someone of your age? Would you say that it is ... READ OUT ...

%	
39.0	... very good,
41.2	fairly good,
13.8	fair,
4.5	bad,
1.6	or, very bad?
0.0	(Don't know)
-	(Refusal/Not answered)

Q221 [NHS5Yrs]
CARD C3
Please say how much better or worse you think each of these things has been getting **over the last five years**)
... the general standard of health care on the **NHS**?

Q222 [WtOp5Yrs]
CARD C3 AGAIN
(Please say how much better or worse you think each of these things has been getting **over the last five years**)
... the time most people wait to get **operations** in NHS hospitals?

Q223 [WtAp5Yrs]
CARD C3 AGAIN
(Please say how much better or worse you think each of these things has been getting **over the last five years**)
... the time most people wait to get outpatients' **appointments** in NHS hospitals?

Q224 [WtCo5Yrs]
CARD C3 AGAIN
(Please say how much better or worse you think each of these things has been getting **over the last five years**)
... the time most people wait in **outpatients'** departments in NHS hospitals?

Q225 [WtGP5Yrs]
CARD C3 AGAIN
(Please say how much better or worse you think each of these things has been getting **over the last five years**)
... the time most people wait at their **GP's surgery** before a doctor sees them?

	[NHS5YRS]	[WtOp5Yrs]	[WtAp5Yrs]
	%	%	%
Much better	2.1	0.4	0.8
Better	19.5	11.0	11.1
About the same	36.5	29.0	38.7
Worse	33.4	41.2	34.8
Much worse	6.1	13.7	10.1
(Don't know)	2.3	4.7	4.6
(Refusal/Not answered)	-	-	-

	[WtCo5Yrs]	[WtGP5Yrs]
	%	%
Much better	0.9	3.5
Better	10.1	19.6
About the same	41.7	50.8
Worse	32.9	19.1
Much worse	9.4	5.0
(Don't know)	4.9	2.0
(Refusal/Not answered)	-	-

Devolution and constitutional change

ASK ALL

Q227 *[Voted]*

Talking to people about the general election on the 7th of June, we have found that a lot of people didn't manage to vote. How about you - did you manage to vote in the general election?

IF NOT ELIGIBLE / TOO YOUNG TO VOTE: CODE 'NO'.

%
67.9 Yes, voted
32.1 No
0.0 (Don't know)
0.0 (Refusal/Not answered)

IF VOTED

Q228 *[Vote]*

Which party did you vote for in the general election?
DO NOT PROMPT

%
17.9 Conservative
31.7 Labour
12.2 Liberal Democrat
1.6 Scottish National party
0.4 Plaid Cymru
0.7 Green Party
1.0 Other party (WRITE IN)
2.4 Refused to disclose voting
0.1 (Don't know)
0.1 (Refusal/Notanswered)

ASK ALL WHO VOTED

Q230 *[VotePost]*

%   Did you vote ...READ OUT...
94.6 ...in person at a polling station,
4.8 by post,
0.5 or, did someone vote on your behalf?
-       (Don't know)
0.1 (Refusal/Notanswered)

IN ENGLAND: ASK ALL

Q231 *[DifWnGEE]*

CARD D1
Some people say that it makes no difference which party wins in elections, things go on much the same. Using this card, please say how much of a difference **you** think it makes who ins in general elections to the House of Commons?

%
17.9 A great deal
25.7 Quite a lot
21.9 Some
26.5 Not very much
7.5 None at all
0.6 (Don't know)
0.0 (Refusal/Not answered)

VERSION C: ASK ALL

Q232 *[VoteSyst]*

Some people say we should change the voting system for general elections to the (UK) House of Commons to allow smaller political parties to get a fairer share of MPs. Others say that we should keep the voting system for the House of Commons as it is to produce effective government. Which view comes **closer** to your own ... READ OUT...

IF ASKED: THIS REFERS TO 'PROPORTIONAL REPRESENTATION'

%
38.6 ... that we should change the voting system for the House of Commons,
56.6 or, keep it as it is?
4.9 (Don't know)
-       (Refusal/Not answered)

Q233 *[ConLabDf]*

Now considering everything the Conservative and Labour parties stand for, would you say that ... READ OUT ...

%
16.3 ... there is a great difference between them,
38.4 some difference,
43.1 or, not much difference?
2.2 (Don't know)
-       (Refusal/Not answered)

IN ENGLAND: ASK ALL

Q234 *[SNHSIESW]*
CARD D2
Thinking back to the general election in 1997 – the one where
Tony Blair won against John Major. Would you say that since
that election **the standard of the health service** in England
has increased or fallen? Please choose an answer from this
card.

%
2.1 Increased a lot
24.6 Increased a little
31.9 Stayed the same
24.2 Fallen a little
12.6 Fallen a lot
4.6 (Don't know)
- (Refusal/Not answered)

IF NOT DK/REFUSAL AT [SNHSIESW]

Q235 *[StNHSWhE]*
%   Do you think this has been ... READ OUT ...
62.2 ... mainly the result of the government's policies,
28.0 or, for some other reason?
5.3 (Don't know)
4.6 (Refusal/Not answered)

IN ENGLAND: ASK ALL

Q236 *[EdStIESW]*
CARD D2 AGAIN
And what about the quality of education in England? Has it
increased or fallen (since that election)? (Again, please
choose an answer from the card.)

%
4.3 Increased a lot
29.5 Increased a little
25.7 Stayed the same
19.9 Fallen a little
9.0 Fallen a lot
11.7 (Don't know)
- (Refusal/Not answered)

IF NOT DK/REFUSAL AT [EdStIESW]

Q237 *[EdStWhyE]*
%   Do you think this has been ... READ OUT ...
63.5 ... mainly the result of the government's policies,
21.7 or, for some other reason?
3.1 (Don't know)
11.7 (Refusal/Not answered)

IN ENGLAND: ASK ALL

Q238 *[SLivIESW]*
CARD D2 AGAIN
And what about the general standard of living in England? Has
it increased or fallen (since that election)? (Again, please
choose an answer from the card).

%
4.8 Increased a lot
35.9 Increased a little
36.2 Stayed the same
13.6 Fallen a little
5.3 Fallen a lot
4.2 (Don't know)
- (Refusal/Not answered)

IF NOT DK/REFUSAL AT [SLivIESW]

Q239 *[SLivWhyE]*
%   Do you think this has been ... READ OUT ...
58.3 ... mainly the result of the government's policies,
33.8 or, for some other reason?
3.8 (Don't know)
4.2 (Refusal/Not answered)

IN ENGLAND: ASK ALL

Q240 *[BPrioF1E]*
CARD D3
Looking at the things on this card, which one do you think
should be Britain's highest priority, the most important thing
it should do?

%
41.1 Maintain order in the nation
32.7 Give people more say in government decisions
13.0 Fight rising prices
11.1 Protect freedom of speech
1.1 (Don't know)
0.1 (Refusal/Not answered)

IF NOT DK/REFUSAL AT [BPrioF1E]

Q241 *[BPrioF2E]*
CARD D3 AGAIN
And which one do you think should be Britain's next highest
priority, the second most important thing it should do?

%
24.4 Maintain order in the nation
25.9 Give people more say in government decisions
26.1 Fight rising prices
21.4 Protect freedom of speech
0.9 (Don't know)
1.3 (Refusal/Not answered)

N = 1108

VERSION C: ASK ALL

Q242 *[ECPolicy]*
CARD D4
Do you think Britain's long-term policy should be... READ OUT

% ...
14.4 ... to leave the European Union,
37.7 to stay in the EU and try to reduce the EU's powers,
21.4 to leave things as they are,
10.5 to stay in the EU and try to increase the EU's powers,
6.6 or, to work for the formation of a single European government?
9.4 (Don't know)
\- (Refusal/Not answered)

Q243 *[EuroRef]*
If there were a referendum on whether Britain should join the single European currency, the Euro, how do you think you would vote? Would you vote to join the Euro, or not to join the Euro?
IF WOULD NOT VOTE, PROBE: If you did vote, how would you vote?
% IF RESPONDENT INSISTS THEY WOULD NOT VOTE, CODE DON'T KNOW
29.9 To join the Euro
58.8 Not to join the Euro
11.2 (Don't know)
\- (Refusal/Not answered)

Q244 *[EURfLike]*
(Can I just check,) How likely do you think that you would be
% to vote in such a referendum? Would you be . . . READ OUT . .
66.0 . . . very likely,
20.8 fairly likely,
6.3 not very likely,
5.2 or, not at all likely?
1.7 (Don't know)
\- (Refusal/Not answered)

Q245 *[EuroLkly]*
And how likely do you think it is that Britain **will** join the
% single European currency in the next ten years ... READ OUT
41.6 . . . very likely,
38.8 fairly likely,
10.6 not very likely,
2.8 or, not at all likely?
6.3 (Don't know)
\- (Refusal/Not answered)

N = 1108

VERSION C: ASK ALL
IN ENGLAND: ASK ALL

Q246 *[GovtWork]* **(Figures refer to British respondents on Version C)**
CARD D5
Which of these statements best describes your opinion on the
% present system of governing Britain?
1.8 Works extremely well and could not be improved
40.7 Could be improved in small ways but mainly works well
43.5 Could be improved quite a lot
12.6 Needs a great deal of improvement
1.5 (Don't know)
\- (Refusal/Not answered)

VERSION C: ASK ALL

Q248 *[GovNoSay]*
CARD D6
Using this card, please say how much you agree or disagree with the following statements:
People like me have no say in what the government does.

VERSION C: ASK ALL
IN ENGLAND: ASK ALL

Q249 [LoseTch] **(Figures refer to British respondents on Version C)**
CARD D6 *(AGAIN)*
(Using this card, please say how much you agree or disagree with *(this statement:/these statements)*
Generally speaking those we elect as MPs lose touch with people pretty quickly.

Q251 *[VoteIntr]* **(Figures refer to British respondents on Version C)**
CARD D6 AGAIN
(Using this card, please say how much you agree or disagree with this statement:)
Parties are only interested in people's votes, not in their opinions.

	[GovNoSay]	*[LoseTch]*	*[VoteIntr]*
	%	%	%
Agree strongly	21.6	25.3	27.1
Agree	43.8	47.0	48.5
Neither agree nor disagree	10.7	12.0	7.8
Disagree	22.2	14.1	14.9
Disagree strongly	1.2	0.8	0.6
(Don't know)	0.5	0.9	1.1
(Refusal/Not answered)	-	0.2	-

VERSION C: ASK ALL

N = 1108

Q253 [PtyNMat2]
CARD D6 AGAIN
(Using this card, please say how much you agree or disagree with this statement:)
It doesn't really matter which party is in power, in the end things go on much the same.

%
17.6 Agree strongly
45.4 Agree
8.0 Neither agree nor disagree
24.9 Disagree
3.7 Disagree strongly
0.2 (It depends on the level of government)
0.3 (Don't know)
- (Refusal/Not answered)

Q254 [GovTrust]
CARD D7
How much do you trust British governments of any party to place the needs of the nation above the interests of their own political party?
Please choose a phrase from this card.

%
1.7 Just about always
26.6 Most of the time
50.4 Only some of the time
19.6 Almost never
1.7 (Don't know)
- (Refusal/Not answered)

IN ENGLAND: ASK ALL

N = 2786

Q255 [QuizSVoE] (False)
Here is a quick quiz. For each thing I say, please tell me whether you think it is true or false. If you don't know, just say so and we'll skip to the next one. Remember - true, false or don't know.
Scottish MPs in the UK House of Commons cannot vote on laws that only apply in England.
FOR DON'T KNOW, CODE CTRL+K

Q256 [QuizSMPE] (True)
It has been decided to cut the number of Scottish MPs in the UK House of Commons.
(True, false or don't know?)
FOR DON'T KNOW, CODE CTRL+K

Q257 [QuizBenE] (False)
The Scottish parliament can increase the level of social security benefits in Scotland.
(True, false or don't know?)
FOR DON'T KNOW, CODE CTRL+K

N = 2786

Q258 [QuizLond] (True)
London is the only region in England with its own elected regional assembly.
(True, false or don't know?)
FOR DON'T KNOW, CODE CTRL+K

	[QuizVOE]	[QuizSMPE]	[QuizBenE]	[QuizLond]
	%	%	%	%
True	25.5	17.7	56.0	32.8
False	37.7	33.2	12.1	24.7
(Don't know	36.8	49.0	31.9	42.5
(Refusal/Not answered)	-	-	-	-

Q259 [ImpGScPE]
CARD D8
Do you think that so far creating the Scottish Parliament has improved the way Britain is governed, made it worse, or has it made no difference?

Q260 [ImpGWAsE]
CARD D8 AGAIN
(And has this improved the way Britain as a whole is governed, made it worse, or made no difference...)
Creating the Welsh Assembly

Q261 [ImpGNAsE]
CARD D8 AGAIN
(And has this improved the way Britain as a whole is governed, made it worse, or made no difference...)
Creating the Northern Ireland Assembly

	[ImpGScPE]	[ImpGWASE]	[ImpGNASE]
	%	%	%
Improved it a lot	2.0	1.1	2.5
Improved it a little	13.4	10.0	15.8
Made no difference	62.1	65.4	52.2
Made it a little worse	6.5	5.2	8.2
Made it a lot worse	2.3	1.9	3.6
(It is too erly to tell)	1.8	2.0	2.5
(Don't know)	12.0	14.4	14.9
(Refusal/Not answered)	-	-	0.0

Q262 *[UKInNatE]*
CARD D9
The United Kingdom government at Westminster has
responsibility for England, Scotland, Wales and Northern
Ireland. How much do you trust the UK government at
Westminster to work in the best long-term interests of
England? Please take your answer from this card.
```
%
 8.5 Just about always
48.4 Most of the time
32.7 Only some of the time
 6.4 Almost never
 4.0 (Don't know)
   - (Refusal/Not answered)
```

Q263 *[ScotPayE]*
CARD D10
Taking your answers from this card, please say how much you
agree or disagree with this statement:
Now that Scotland has its own parliament, it should pay for
its services out of taxes collected in Scotland.
```
%
19.8 Agree strongly
53.0 Agree
11.8 Neither agree nor disagree
10.9 Disagree
 0.7 Disagree strongly
 3.9 (Don't know)
   - (Refusal/Not answered)
```

Q264 *[SRSocC1E]*
Do you ever think of yourself as belonging to any particular
class?
```
%
     IF YES: Which class is that?
18.5 Yes, middle class
21.4 Yes, working class
 1.7 Yes, other (WRITE IN)
58.0 No
 0.3 (Don't know)
 0.1 (Refusal/Not answered_
```

IF **'other'**/**'no'**/**'DON'T KNOW AT [SRSocC1E]**

Q266 *[SRSocC2E]*
Most people say they belong either to the middle class or the
working class. If you **had** to make a choice, would you call
yourself ... READ OUT ...
```
%
18.3 ... middle class
37.7 or, working class?
 3.1 (Don't know)
 0.9 (Refusal/Not answered)
```

IN ENGLAND: ASK ALL
Q268 *[NatID]*
CARD D11
Which, if any, of the following best describes how you see
yourself?
```
%
17.1 English not British
12.6 More English than British
41.9 Equally English and British
 9.3 More British than English
10.8 British not English
 6.5 Other description (WRITE IN)
 1.6 (None of these)
 0.2 (Don't know)
   - (Refusal/Not answered)
```

Q270 *[Ident1E]*
CARD D12
Some people say that whether they feel British or `EnScish is
not as important as other things about them. Other people say
their national identity is the key to who they are.
If you had to pick just one thing from this list to describe
yourself – something that is very important to you when you
think of yourself, what would it be?

IF NOT **'none of these'**/**DK/REFUSAL AT [Ident1E]**
Q272 *[Ident2E]*
CARD D12 AGAIN
And what would the second most important thing be?

IF NOT **'none of these/no further answer'**/**DK/REFUSAL AT
[Ident2E]**
Q274 *[Ident3E]*
CARD D12 AGAIN
And what would the third most important thing be?

	[Ident1E]	[Ident2E]	[Ident3E]
	%	%	%
Working class	7.8	5.3	5.4
British	10.7	9.2	7.4
Elderly	2.0	2.6	1.6
A woman/A man	11.9	10.0	8.3
Not religious	0.9	1.3	3.4
A wife/A husband	5.0	13.0	9.1
A Catholic	1.4	1.4	1.2
A country person	2.7	3.3	4.2
A city person	0.7	1.4	2.0
A Protestant	0.5	1.4	1.0
A mother/A father	21.8	14.4	12.2
Middle class	0.9	2.0	2.5
Black	1.2	0.3	0.2
Retired	2.8	3.4	3.7
Religious	1.3	1.7	2.5
A working person	10.1	11.5	10.7
Young	3.5	3.3	3.8
White	1.4	2.8	4.0
English	8.1	6.2	6.0
Asian	1.0	0.7	0.3
Unemployed	0.7	0.6	0.4
Other (WRITE IN)	2.6	1.6	2.7
(None of these/No further answer)	1.1	1.7	4.0
(Don't know)	0.2	0.2	0.2
(Refusal/Not answered)	0.0	-	-

IN ENGLAND: ASK ALL

Q276 [FlagUJE]
CARD D13
I am going to show you two flags. First of all, here is the Union Jack. When you see the Union Jack, does it make you feel proud, hostile or do you not feel much either way?
IF PROUD/HOSTILE: Is that very proud/hostile or just a bit proud/hostile?

Q277 [FlagNatE]
CARD D14
And here is the cross of St. George. When you see this, does it make you feel proud, hostile or do you not feel much either way?
IF PROUD/HOSTILE: Is that very proud/hostile or just a bit proud/hostile?

	[FlagUJE]	[FlagNatE]
	%	%
Very proud	33.0	21.1
A bit proud	25.9	19.4
Does not feel much either way	37.4	55.7
A bit hostile	1.6	1.9
Very hostile	0.5	0.6
(It depends)	1.5	0.9
(Don't know)	0.2	0.3
(Refusal/Not answered)	-	-

Q278 [ScoPar2E]
CARD D15

%   Which of these statements comes closest to your view?
6.7   Scotland should become independent, separate from the UK and the European Union
12.3   Scotland should become independent, separate from the UK but part of the European Union
52.6   Scotland should remain part of the UK, with its own elected parliament which has **some** taxation powers
6.8   Scotland should remain part of the UK, with its own elected parliament which has **no** taxation powers
11.3   Scotland should remain part of the UK **without** an elected parliament
10.3   (Don't kow)
0.0   (Refusal/Not answered)

Q279 [WelshAsE]
CARD D16

%   Which of these statements comes closest to your view?
5.8   Wales should become independent, separate from the UK and the European Union
11.4   Wales should become independent, separate from the UK but part of the European Union
39.1   Wales should remain part of the UK, with its own elected parliament which has law-making and taxation powers
19.4   Wales should remain part of the UK, with its own elected assembly which has limited law-making powers only
13.7   Wales should remain part of the UK without an elected assembly
10.6   (Don't know)
0.0   (Refusal/Not answered)

N = 2786

N = 2786

Q280 *[SEBenGBE]*

On the whole, do you think that England's economy benefits more from having Scotland in the UK, or that Scotland's economy benefits more from being part of the UK, or is it about equal?

%
7.2 England benefits more
42.3 Scotland benefits more
38.1 Equal
1.6 (Neither/both lose)
11.0 (Don't know)
- (Refusal/Not answered)

Q281 *[UKSpnGBE]*
CARD D17

Would you say that compared with other parts of the United Kingdom, Scotland gets **pretty much** its fair share of government spending, **more** than its fair share, or **less** than its fair share of government spending?

Please choose your answer from this card.

%
8.8 Much more than its fair share of government spending
14.7 A little more than its fair share of government spending
44.1 Pretty much its fair share of government spending
7.7 A little less than its fair share of government spending
1.3 Much less than its fair share of government spending
23.3 (Don't know)
- (Refusal/Not answered)

Q282 *[NIrelanE]*

Do you think the long-term policy for Northern Ireland should be for it ... READ OUT ...

%
25.3 ...to remain part of the United Kingdom
56.0 or, to unify with the rest of Ireland?
0.7 **EDIT ONLY:** NORTHERN IRELAND SHOULD BE AN INDEPENDENT STATE
0.0 **EDIT ONLY:** NORTHERN IRELAND SHOULD BE SPLIT UP INTO TWO
3.5 **EDIT ONLY:** IT SHOULD BE UP TO THE IRISH TO DECIDE
2.7 Other answer (WRITE IN)
11.6 (Don't know)
0.2 (Refusal/Not answered)

Q284 *[RegPridE]*
CARD D18

How much pride do you have in being someone who lives in *(government office region)* or do you not think of yourself in that way at all?

%
22.2 Very proud
22.4 Somewhat proud
2.4 Not very proud
1.2 Not at all proud
51.6 Don't think of themselves in that way
0.2 (Don't know)
- (Refusal/Not answered)

Q285 *[EngParl]*
CARD D19

With all the changes going on in the way the different parts of Great Britain are run, which of the following do you think would be best for England ..READ OUT...

%
56.7 ..for England to be governed as it is now, with laws made by the UK parliament,
22.9 for each region of England to have its own assembly that runs services like health,
15.8 or, for England as a whole to have its own new parliament with law-making powers?
1.3 (None of these)
3.3 (Don't know)
- (Refusal/Not answered)

Q286 *[HearRAss]*

In recent years, the government has set up chambers or assemblies in each of the regions of England. How much have you heard about the work of the *(government office region chamber or assembly)* ... READ OUT ...

%
1.0 ..a great deal,
4.5 quite a lot,
32.0 not very much,
61.2 or nothing at all?
1.3 (Don't know)
- (Refusal/Not answered)

Q287 *[SayInRgE]*

From what you have seen or heard so far, do you think that having the *(regional chamber or assembly)* for *(government office region)* will give ordinary people ... READ OUT ...

%
32.1 ..more of a say in how *(government office region)* is governed,
1.9 less say,
55.2 or, will it make no difference?
10.8 (Don't know)
0.0 (Refusal/Not answered)

N = 2786

N = 2786

Q288 [ERegEcon]
And as a result of having the (regional chamber or assembly)
for (government office region) will the region's economy
become better, worse or will it make no difference?
IF BETTER/WORSE: Is that a lot better/worse or a little
better/worse?

%
4.5 A lot better
23.9 A little better
55.1 No difference
2.0 A little worse
0.7 A lot worse
13.8 (Don't know)
- (Refusal/Not answered)

Q289 [DoesInfE]
CARD D20
Taking your answers from this card, which of the following do
you think currently **has** most influence over the way England is
run?

%
1.7 English regional chambers or assemblies
75.1 The UK government at Westminster
7.8 Local councils in England
11.2 The European Union
4.1 (Don't know)
0.0 (Refusal/Not answered)

Q290 [OughInfE]
CARD D21
Taking your answers from this card, which do you think **ought**
to have most influence over the way England is run?

Q291 [OuDeFooE]
CARD D21 AGAIN
Important decisions for England about some issues could be
made by different institutions.
Still thinking of the institutions on this card, which do you
think **ought** to make most of the important decisions for
England about ...:
... setting standards for food safety?

Q292 [OuDeBuGE]
CARD D21 AGAIN
(And which do you think **ought** to make most of the important
decisions for England about ...)
... whether new businesses get start-up grants?

Q293 [OuDeBenE]
CARD D21 AGAIN
(And which do you think **ought** to make most of the important
decisions for England about ...)
... levels of welfare benefits?

	[OughInfE]	[OuDeFooE]
	%	%
English regional chambers or assemblies	10.5	5.2
A new English parliament	10.2	6.7
The UK government at Westminster	53.9	60.0
Local councils in England	19.6	14.4
The European Union	1.2	9.5
(Don't know)	4.6	4.3
(Refusal/Not answered)	-	-

	[OuDeBuGE]	[OuDeBenE]
	%	%
English regional chambers or assemblies	18.3	6.9
A new English parliament	4.5	6.9
The UK government at Westminster	34.8	64.6
Local councils in England	34.7	16.2
The European Union	2.0	1.7
(Don't know)	5.6	3.8
(Refusal/Not answered)	-	-

Economic activity

N = 3287

ASK ALL

Q307 [REconAct] (Percentages refer to **highest answer on the list**)
CARD E1
Which of these descriptions applied to what you were doing last week, that is the seven days ending last Sunday?
PROBE: Which others? CODE ALL THAT APPLY
Multicoded (Maximum of 11 codes)

%
2.1 In full-time education (not paid for by employer, including on vacation)
0.3 On government training/ employment programme
57.0 In paid work (or away temporarily) for at least 10 hours in week
0.5 Waiting to take up paid work already accepted
2.2 Unemployed and registered at a benefit office
1.0 Unemployed, **not** registered, but actively looking for a job (of at least 10 hrs a week)
0.4 Unemployed, wanting a job (of at least 10 hrs a week) but **not** actively looking for a job
5.2 Permanently sick or disabled
20.9 Wholly retired from work
9.7 Looking after the home
0.5 (Doing something else) (WRITE IN)
– (Don't know)
0.0 (Refusal/Not answered)

ASK ALL NOT WORKING OR WAITING TO TAKE UP WORK   N = 1397

Q308 [RLastJob]
How long ago did you last have a paid job of at least 10 hours a week?
GOVERNMENT PROGRAMS/SCHEMES DO NOT COUNT AS `PAID JOBS'.

%
14.9 Within past 12 months
21.1 Over 1, up to 5 years ago
18.3 Over 5, up to 10 years ago
25.0 Over 10, up to 20 years ago
15.0 Over 20 years ago
5.5 Never had a paid job of 10+ hours a week
0.1 (Don't know)
0.1 (Refusal/Not answered)

N = 3211

ASK ALL WHO HAVE EVER WORKED

Q309 [Title] (NOT ON DATAFILE)
IF 'in paid work' AT [ReconAct]: Now I want to ask you about your present job. What is your job?
PROBE IF NECESSARY: What is the name or title of the job?
IF 'waiting to take up work' AT [ReconAct]: Now I want to ask you about your future job. What will your job be?
PROBE IF NECESSARY: What is the name or title of the job?
IF EVER HAD A JOB AT [RlastJob]: Now I want to ask you about your last job. What was your job?
PROBE IF NECESSARY: What is the name or title of the job
Open Question

Q310 [Typewk] (NOT ON DATAFILE)
What kind of work (do/did/will) you do most of the time?
IF RELEVANT: What materials/machinery (do/did/will) you use?
Open Question

Q311 [Train] (NOT ON DATAFILE)
What training or qualifications (are/were) needed for that job?
Open Question

Q312 [RSuper2]
(Do/Did/Will) you directly supervise or (are/were/will) you
% (be) directly responsible for the work of any other people?
35.5 Yes
64.4 No
0.0 (Don't know)
0.1 (Refusal/Not answered)

IF 'yes' AT [Super2]
Q313 [RMany]
How many?
% **Median: 5** (of those supervising any)
0.1 (Don't know)
0.1 (Refusal/Not answered)

Q315 [REmplyee]
% In your (main) job (are/were/will) you (be) ...READ OUT...
89.9 ... an employee,
9.9 or self-employed?
0.0 (Don't know)
0.1 (Refusal/Not answered)

ASK ALL EMPLOYEES IN CURRENT OR LAST JOB   `N = 2891`

Q317 [RSupman2]
%   Can I just check, (are/were/will) you (be) ...READ OUT...
18.6   ...a manager,
13.8   a foreman or supervisor,
67.5   or not?
-      (Don't know)
0.1   (Refusal/Not answered)

Q318 [ROcSect2]
     CARD E2
     Which of the types of organisation on this card (do you
     work/did you work/will you be working) for?
%
66.9   PRIVATE SECTOR FIRM OR COMPANY Including, for example, limited
       companies and PLCs
2.7   NATIONALISED INDUSTRY OR PUBLIC CORPORATION Including, for
       example, the Post Office and the BBC
27.0   OTHER PUBLIC SECTOR EMPLOYER
       Incl eg: - Central govt/ Civil Service/ Govt Agency
            - Local authority/ Local Educ Auth (incl `opted out' schools)
            - Universities
            - Health Authority / NHS hospitals / NHS Trusts/ GP surgeries
            - Police / Armed forces
2.8   CHARITY/ VOLUNTARY SECTOR Including, for example, charitable
       companies, churches, trade unions
0.4   Other answer (WRITE IN)
0.1   (Don't know)
0.1   (Refusal/Not answered)

ASK ALL WHO HAVE EVER WORKED (NOT ON DATAFILE)   `N = 3211`

Q320 [EmpMake] What (does/did) your employer make or do at the
     IF EMPLOYEE: What (does/did) your employer make or do at the
     place where you (usually work/usually worked/will usually
     work) (from)?
     IF SELF-EMPLOYED: What (do/did/will) you make or do at the
     place where you (usually work/usually worked/will usually
     work) (from)?
     Open Question

ASK ALL CURRENTLY SELF-EMPLOYED   `N = 224`

Q321 [SPartnrs]
     In your work or business, do you have any partners or other
     self-employed colleagues?
%   NOTE: DOES NOT INCLUDE EMPLOYEES
36.2   Yes, has partner(s)
62.3   No
0.5   (Don't know)
1.0   (Refusal/Not answered)

ASK ALL SELF-EMPLOYED IN CURRENT OR LAST JOB   `N = 323`

Q323 [SEmpNum]
     In your work or business, (do/did/will) you have any
     employees, or not?
     IF YES: How many?
     IF NO EMPLOYEES', CODE 0.
     FOR 500+ EMPLOYEES, CODE 500.
     NOTE: FAMILY MEMBERS MAY BE EMPLOYEES ONLY IF THEY RECEIVE A
     REGULAR WAGE OR SALARY.
     Median: 0 employees
-      (Don't know)
1.2   (Refusal/Not answered)

ASK ALL WHO HAVE EVER WORKED   `N = 3211`

Q324 [REmpWork] **(For self-employed, derived from [SempNurse])**
     Including yourself, how many people (are/were) employed at the
     place where you usually (work/worked/will work) (from)?
     PROBE FOR CORRECT PRECODE.
%   R dv
6.1   None
18.4   Under 10
14.1   10-24
22.4   25-99
23.6   100-499
13.9   500 or more
1.4   (Don't know)
0.1   (Refusal/Not answered)

ASK ALL IN PAID WORK   `N = 1876`

Q328 [WkJbTim]
     In your present job, are you working ... READ OUT ...
     RESPONDENT'S OWN DEFINITION
%   ... full-time,
75.6
24.2   or, part-time?
0.1   (Don't know)
0.1   (Refusal/Not answered)

ASK ALL IN PAID WORK

Q331 [WkJbHrsI]
     How many hours do you normally work a week in your main job -
     including any paid or unpaid overtime?
     ROUND TO NEAREST HOUR.
     IF RESPONDENT CANNOT ANSWER, ASK ABOUT LAST WEEK.
     IF RESPONDENT DOES NOT KNOW EXACTLY, ACCEPT AN ESTIMATE.
     FOR 95+ HOURS, CODE 95.
     FOR `VARIES TOO MUCH TO SAY', CODE 96.
     Median: 40 hours
%
0.4   (Varies too much to say)
0.1   (Don't know)
0.2   (Refusal/Not answered)

ASK ALL CURRENT EMPLOYEES   N = 1654

Q332 [EJbHrsX]
What are your **basic or contractual hours** each week in your main job - **excluding** any paid and unpaid overtime?
ROUND TO NEAREST HOUR.
IF RESPONDENT CANNOT ANSWER, ASK ABOUT LAST WEEK.
IF RESPONDENT DOES NOT KNOW EXACTLY, ACCEPT AN ESTIMATE.
FOR 95+ HOURS, CODE 95.
FOR 'VARIES TOO MUCH TO SAY', CODE 96.
Median: 37 hours
%
2.6 (Varies too much to say)
0.8 (Don't know)
0.3 (Refusal/Not answered)

ASK ALL NOT CURRENTLY AT WORK BUT HAVE WORKED IN THE PAST   N = 1335

Q333 [ExPrtFul]
(Is/Was/Will) the job *(be)* ...READ OUT...
%
69.5 ... full-time - that is, 30 or more hours per week,
30.4 or, part-time?
-    (Don't know)
0.1 (Refusal/Not answered)

ASK ALL WHO HAVE EVER WORKED

Q365 [UnionSA]
(May I just check) are you **now** a member of a trade union or staff association?
CODE FIRST TO APPLY
%
17.1 Yes, trade union
3.2 Yes, staff association
79.4 No
0.2 (Don't know)
0.1 (Refusal/Not answered)

IF 'no'/DK AT [UnionSA]

Q366 [TUSAEver]
Have you **ever** been a member of a trade union or staff association?
CODE FIRST TO APPLY
%
27.4 Yes, trade union
2.6 Yes, staff association
49.5 No
0.1 (Don't know)
0.1 (Refusal/Not answered)

ASK ALL CURRENT EMPLOYEES   N = 1654

Q381 [Employd1]
For how long have you been continuously employed by your present employer?
ENTER NUMBER. THEN SPECIFY MONTHS OR YEARS
Median: 48 months
0.1 (Don't know)
0.2 (Refusal/Not answered)

ASK ALL NOT IN PAID WORK   N = 1412

Q382 [NPWork10]
In the seven days ending last Sunday, did you have any paid work of less than 10 hours a week?
%
3.8 Yes
96.1 No
-    (Don't know)
0.1 (Refusal/Not answered)

ASK ALL CURRENT EMPLOYEES   N = 1654

Q383 [WageNow]
How would you describe the wages or salary you are paid for the job you do - on the low side, reasonable, or on the high side?
IF LOW: Very low or a bit low?
%
13.1 Very low
27.9 A bit low
53.7 Reasonable
4.9 On the high side
-    Other answer (WRITE IN)
0.1 (Don't know)
0.3 (Refusal/Not answered)

Q385 [PayGap]
CARD E3
Thinking of the **highest** and the **lowest** paid people at your place of work, how would you describe the **gap** between their pay, as far as you know?
Please choose a phrase from this card.
%
16.5 Much too big a gap
28.9 Too big
43.7 About right
2.5 Too small
0.4 Much too small a gap
EDIT ONLY: OTHER ANSWERS
7.7 (Don't know)
0.3 (Refusal/Not answered)

Q386 [WageXpct]
If you stay in this job, would you expect your wages or salary over the coming year to ... READ OUT ...
%
25.9 ... rise by **more** than the cost of living,
46.3 ... rise by the **same** as the cost of living,
16.5 rise by **less** than the cost of living,
7.8 or, not to rise at all?
1.4 (Will **not** stay in job)
1.7 (Don't know)
0.3 (Refusal/Not answered)

IF 'not rise at all' AT [WageXpct]
Q387 [WageDrop]
Would you expect your wages or salary to stay the same, or in fact to go down?
%
7.2 Stay the same
0.6 Go down
- (Don't know)
2.0 (Refusal/Not answered)

ASK ALL CURRENT EMPLOYEES ('employee'/DK AT [EmployB])
Q388 [NumEmp]
Over the coming year do you expect your workplace to be ...READ OUT...
%
31.3 ... increasing its number of employees,
14.3 reducing its number of employees,
50.9 or, will the number of employees stay about the same?
0.8 Other answer (WRITE IN)
2.5 (Don't know)
0.3 (Refusal/Not answered)

Q390 [LeaveJob]
Thinking now about your own job.
How likely or unlikely is it that you will leave this employer over the next year for any reason?
Is it ...READ OUT...
%
13.0 ... very likely,
14.2 quite likely,
29.3 not very likely,
42.1 or, not at all likely?
1.1 (Don't know)
0.3 (Refusal/Not answered)

IF 'very likely' OR 'quite likely' AT [LeaveJob]
Q400-CARD E4
Q410 Why do you think you will leave? Please choose a phrase from this card or tell me what other reason there is.
CODE ALL THAT APPLY
% Multicoded (Maximum of 9 codes)
1.1 Firm will close down [WhyGo1]
1.7 I will be declared redundant [WhyGo2]
1.1 I will reach normal retirement age [WhyGo3]
1.6 My contract of employment will expire [WhyGo4]
1.1 I will take early retirement [WhyGo5]
15.4 I will decide to leave and work for another employer [WhyGo6]
1.8 I will decide to leave and work for myself, as self-employed [WhyGo7]
1.1 I will leave to look after home/children/relative [WhyGo10] [WhyGo11]
1.1 **EDIT ONLY:** RETURN TO EDUCATION
3.1 Other answer (WRITE IN) [WhyGo8]
1.2 (Don't know)
0.3 (Refusal/Not answered)

ASK ALL CURRENT EMPLOYEES
Q412 [ELookJob]
Suppose you lost your job for one reason or another - would you start looking for another job, would you wait for several months or longer before you started looking, or would you decide **not** to look for another job?
%
89.9 Start looking
4.2 Wait several months or longer
5.4 Decide not to look
0.3 (Don't know)
0.3 (Refusal/Not answered)

IF 'start looking' AT [ELookJob]
Q415 [EFindJob]
How long do you think it would take you to find an acceptable replacement job?
IF LESS THAN ONE MONTH, CODE AS ONE MONTH
IF 'NEVER' PLEASE CODE 996
ENTER NUMBER. THEN SPECIFY MONTHS OR YEARS
Median: 1 month
%
0.1 (Never)
6.1 (Don't know)
0.6 (Refusal/Not answered)

Q416 [ERetrain]   N = 1654
IF 3 MONTHS OR MORE/NEVER/DK AT [EFindJob]
How willing do you think you would be in these circumstances to retrain for a different job ... READ OUT ...
%
15.6 ...very willing,
8.3 quite willing,
5.6 or - not very willing?
0.1 (Don't know)
0.6 (Refusal/Not answered)

ASK ALL CURRENT EMPLOYEES
Q417 [ESelfEm]
For any period during the last five years, have you worked as a **self-employed** person as your main job?
%
5.9 Yes
93.8 No
- (Don't know)
0.3 (Refusal/Not answered)

ASK ALL NOT UNEMPLOYED, PERMANENTLY SICK OR RETIRED   N = 2305
Q419 [NwUnemp]
During the last **five years** – that is since May 1996 – have you been unemployed and seeking work for any period?
%
16.8 Yes
83.0 No
0.1 (Don't know)
0.1 (Refusal/Not answered)

ASK ALL WHO ARE CURRENTLY UNEMPLOYED OR HAVE BEEN UNEMPOYED IN LAST FIVE YEARS   N = 391
Q420 [NwUnempT]
For how many **months** in total during the last five years that is, since May 1996, have you been unemployed and seeking work?
INTERVIEWER: IF LESS THAN ONE MONTH, CODE AS 1.
Median: 4 months
0.1 (Don't know)
1.1 (Refusal/Not answered)

ASK ALL CURRENTLY UNEMPLOYED   N = 123
Q423 [CurUnemp]
How long has this **present** period of unemployment and seeking work lasted so far?
ENTER NUMBER. THEN SPECIFY MONTHS OR YEARS
Median: 6 months
2.7 (Don't know)
0.9 (Refusal/Not answered)

Q424 [JobQual]   N = 123
How confident are you that you will find a job to match your qualifications ... READ OUT ...
%
... very confident,
quite confident.
not very confident,
or, not at all confident?

Q427 [UFindJob]
Although it may be difficult to judge, how long **from now** do you think it will be before you find an acceptable job?
ENTER NUMBER. THEN SPECIFY MONTHS OR YEARS
CODE 996 FOR NEVER
Median: 2 months
%
9.0 (Never)
18.6 (Don't know)
0.9 (Refusal/Not answered)

IF MORE THAN 3 MONTHS/NEVER/DON'T KNOW AT [UFindJob]
Q428 [URetrain]
How willing do you think you would be in these circumstances to retrain for a different job ... READ OUT ...
%
29.4 ... very willing,
16.3 quite willing,
16.7 or, not very willing?
- (Don't know)
0.9 (Refusal/Not answered)

Q429 [UJobMove]
How willing would you be to move to a different area to find an acceptable job ... READ OUT ...
%
13.6 ... very willing,
9.5 quite willing,
38.9 or, not very willing?
0.5 (Don't know)
0.9 (Refusal/Not answered)

Q430 [UBadJob]
And how willing do you think you would be in these circumstances to take what you now consider to be an **unacceptable** job ... READ OUT ...
%
2.7 ... very willing,
14.9 quite willing,
43.9 or, not very willing?
0.9 (Don't know)
0.9 (Refusal/Not answered)

ASK ALL CURRENTLY UNEMPLOYED `N = 123`

Q431 [ConMove]
Have you ever **actually** considered moving to a different area - an area other than the one you live in now - to try to find work?

%
38.9 Yes
60.2 No
- (Don't know)
0.9 (Refusal;Not answered)

Q432 [UJobChnc]
Do you think that there is a real chance nowadays that you will get a job in this area, or is there **no** real chance nowadays?

%
63.8 Real chance
34.8 No real chance
0.5 (Don't know)
0.9 (Refusal/Not answered)

Q433 [FPtWork]
Would you prefer full- or part-time work, if you had the choice?

%
67.9 Full-time
27.6 Part-time
3.6 Not looking for work
- (Don't know)
0.9 (Refusal/Not answered)

IF 'part-time' AT [FPtWork]
Q434 [Parttime]
About how many hours per week would you like to work?
PROBE FOR BEST ESTIMATE
Median: 20 hours
1.8 (Don't know)
0.9 (Refusal/Not answered)

ASK ALL LOOKING AFTER THE HOME `N = 321`

Q435 [EverJob]
Have you, during **the last five years**, ever had a full- or part-time job of 10 hours or more a week?

%
33.9 Yes
65.7 No
- (Don't know)
0.3 (Refusal/Not answered)

IF 'no' AT [EverJob]
Q436 [FtJobSer]
How seriously in the past five years have you considered getting a **full-time job**...
PROMPT, IF NECESSARY: Full-time is 30 or more hours a week ... READ OUT ...

%
2.3 ... very seriously,
5.7 quite seriously,
9.7 not very seriously,
48.1 or, not at all seriously?
- (Don't know)
0.3 (Refusal/Not answered)

IF 'not very seriously', 'not at all seriously' OR DON'T KNOW AT [FtJobSer]
Q437 [PtJobSer]
How seriously, in the past five years, have you considered getting a **part-time** job ... READ OUT ...

%
3.3 ... very seriously,
7.8 quite seriously,
7.3 not very seriously,
39.4 or, not at all seriously?
- (Don't know)
0.3 (Refusal/Not answered)

ASK ALL CURRENTLY SELF-EMPLOYED `N = 224`

Q438 [SEmplee]
Have you, for any period in the last five years, worked as an **employee** as your main job rather than as self-employed?

%
28.1 Yes
70.4 No
0.5 (Don't know)
1.0 (Refusal/Not answered)

IF 'yes' AT [SEmplee]
Q439 [SEmpleeT]
In total for how many months during the last five years have you been an employee?
ENTER NUMBER OF MONTHS
Median: 24 months
- (Don't know)
1.0 (Refusal/Not answered)

IF 'no'/DK AT [SEmplee] [N = 224]

Q440 [SEmplSer]
How seriously in the last five years have you considered getting a job as an **employee** ... READ OUT ...
%
4.6 ... very seriously,
6.5 quite seriously,
12.7 not very seriously,
46.2 or, not at all seriously?
1.0 (Don't know)
1.0 (Refusal/Not answered)

ASK ALL CURRENTLY SELF-EMPLOYED

Q441 [BusiOK]
Compared with **a year ago**, would you say your business is doing ... READ OUT ...
%
21.6 ... very well,
18.6 quite well,
42.9 about the same,
7.2 not very well,
2.7 or, not at all well?
5.5 (Business not in existence then)
0.5 (Don't know)
1.0 (Refusal/Not answered)

Q442 [BusiFut]
And over **the coming year**, do you think your business will do ... READ OUT ...
%
33.0 ... better,
48.2 about the same,
11.4 or, worse than this year?
4.4 Other answer (WRITE IN)
2.0 (Don't know)
1.0 (Refusal/Not answered)

ASK ALL CURRENT EMPLOYEES [N = 1654]

Q444 [WpUnions]
At your place of work are there unions, staff associations, or groups of unions recognised by the management for negotiating pay and conditions of employment?
IF YES, PROBE FOR UNION OR STAFF ASSOCIATION
IF 'BOTH', CODE '1'.
%
42.4 Yes : trade union(s)
4.5 Yes : staff association
47.8 No, none
5.0 (Don't know)
0.3 (Refusal/Not answered)

IF 'yes, trade unions' OR 'yes, staff associations' AT [WpUnions] [N = 1654]

Q445 [WpUnsure]
Can I just check: does management **recognise** these unions or staff associations for the purposes of negotiating **pay** and **conditions of employment**?

Q446 [WpUnionW]
On the whole, do you think (these unions do their/this staff association does its) job well or not?

	[WpUnsure]	[WpUnionW]
	%	%
Yes	43.7	29.6
No	2.0	13.6
(Don't know)	1.1	3.7
(Refusal/Not answered)	5.3	5.3

Q447 [TUShould]
CARD E5
Listed on the card are a number of things trade unions or staff associations can do. Which, if any, do you think is the **most important** thing they should try to do **at your workplace**?
UNIONS OR STAFF ASSOCIATIONS SHOULD TRY TO:
%
14.8 Improve working conditions
9.2 Improve pay
12.9 Protect existing jobs
1.7 Have more say over how work is done day-to-day
4.4 Have more say over management's long-term plans
0.5 Work for equal opportunities for women
0.3 Work for equal opportunities for ethnic minorities
1.7 Reduce pay differences at the workplace
0.9 (None of these)
0.4 (Don't know)
5.3 (Refusal/Not answered)

ASK ALL CURRENT EMPLOYEES

Q448 [IndRel]
In general how would you describe relations between management and other employees at your workplace ... READ OUT ...
%
32.5 ... very good,
46.5 quite good,
16.1 not very good,
3.8 or, not at all good?
0.8 (Don't know)
0.3 (Refusal/Not answered)

Q449 [WorkRun]
And in general, would you say your workplace was ... READ OUT

N = 1654

%
25.4 ... very well managed,
53.1 quite well managed,
20.8 or, not well managed?
0.5 (Don't know)
0.3 (Refusal/Not answered)

ASK ALL EXCEPT THOSE WHOLLY RETIRED OR PERMANENTLY SICK OR DISABLED

Q450 [NwEmpErn]
IF IN PAID WORK: Now for some more general questions about your work. For some people their job is simply something they do in order to earn a living. For others it means much more than that. On balance, is your present job ... READ OUT ...
IF NOT IN PAID WORK: For some people work is simply something they do in order to earn a living. For others it means much more than that. In general, do you think of work as ... READ OUT ...

N = 2427

%
33.5 ...just a means of earning a living,
65.7 or, does it mean much more to you than that?
0.7 (Don't know)
0.1 (Refusal/Not answered)

IF 'just a means of earning a living' AT [NwEmpErn]

Q451 [NwEmpLiv]
% Is that because ... READ OUT ...
7.4 ...there are no (better/good) jobs around here,
8.4 you don't have the right skills to get a (better/good) job
15.3 or, because you would feel the same about any job you had?
2.3 (Don't know)
1.0 (Refusal/Not answered)

ASK ALL IN PAID WORK

Q452-CARD E6
Q460 Now I'd like you to look at the statements on the card and tell me which ones best describe **your own** reasons for working at present.
PROBE: Which others? CODE ALL THAT APPLY

N = 1987

% Multicoded (Maximum of 9 codes)
37.1 Working is the normal thing to do   [WkWork1]
69.4 Need money for basic essentials such as food, rent or mortgage [WkWork2]
42.0 To earn money to buy extras   [WkWork3]
29.3 To earn money of my own   [WkWork4]
24.8 For the company of other people   [WkWork5]
53.4 I enjoy working   [WkWork6]
27.7 To follow my career   [WkWork7]
6.9 For a change from my children or housework   [WkWork8]
4.8 Other answer (WRITE IN)   [WkWork9]
0.2 (Don't know)
0.2 (Refusal/Not answered)

IF MORE THAN ONE ANSWER GIVEN AT [WkWork]

Q472 [WkWkMain]
CARD E6 AGAIN
And which one of these would you say is your **main** reason for working?
%
5.1 Working is the normal thing to do
46.6 Need money for basic essentials such as food, rent or mortgage
6.6 To earn money to buy extras
5.5 To earn money of my own
0.4 For the company of other people
10.4 I enjoy working
4.2 To follow my career
0.5 For a change from my children or housework
1.5 Other answer (WRITE IN)
- (Don't know)
0.4 (Refusal/Not answered)

ASK ALL CURRENT EMPLOYEES

Q473 [SayJob]
Suppose there was going to be some decision made at your place of work that changed the way you do your job. Do you think that **you personally** would have any say in the decision about the change, or not?
IF 'DEPENDS': Code as 'Don't know' <CTRL+K>

N = 1654

%
55.9 Yes
41.7 No
2.1 (Don't know)
0.3 (Refusal/Not answered)

IF 'yes' AT [SayJob]   N = 1654

Q474 [MuchSay]
How much say or chance to influence the decision do you think you would have ... READ OUT ...
%
14.5 ...a great deal,
23.8 quite a lot,
17.4 or, just a little?
0.2 (Don't know)
2.4 (Refusal/Not answered)

ASK ALL CURRENT EMPLOYEES

Q475 [MoreSay]
Do you think you should have **more** say in decisions affecting your work, or are you satisfied with the way things are?
%
48.9 Should have more say
50.3 Satisfied with way things are
0.5 (Don't know)
0.3 (Refusal/Not answered)

ASK ALL IN PAID WORK   N = 1876

Q476 [WkPrefJb]
If without having to work, you had what you would regard as a reasonable living income, do you think you would still prefer to (have a paid job/do paid work) or wouldn't you bother?
%
69.3 Still prefer paid (job/work)
27.4 Wouldn't bother
2.5 Other answer (WRITE IN)
0.5 (Don't know)
0.2 (Refusal/Not answered)

ASK ALL CURRENT EMPLOYEES   N = 1654

Q478 [PrefHour]
Thinking about the number of hours you work each week including regular overtime, would you prefer a job where you worked ... READ OUT ...
%
3.6 ...more hours per week,
41.7 fewer hours per week,
54.3 or, are you happy with the number of hours you work at present?
0.1 (Don't know)
0.3 (Refusal/Not answered)

IF 'more hours per week' AT [PrefHour]   N = 1654

Q479 [MoreHour]
Is the reason why you don't work more hours because ... READ OUT ...
%
2.5 ..your employer can't offer you more hours,
0.7 or, your personal circumstances don't allow it?
0.0 (Both)
0.2 Other answer (WRITE IN)
0.1 (Don't know)
0.4 (Refusal/Not answered)

IF 'fewer hours per week' AT [PrefHour]

Q481 [FewHour]
In which of these ways would you like your working hours to be shortened ... READ OUT ...
%
12.5 ... shorter hours each day,
27.9 or, fewer days each week?
1.2 Other answer (WRITE IN)
0.0 (Don't know)
0.4 (Refusal/Not answered)

Q483 [EarnHour]
Would you still like to work fewer hours, if it meant earning less money as a result?
%
12.0 Yes
27.4 No
2.2 It depends
0.2 (Don't know)
0.4 (Refusal/Not answered)

ASK ALL IN PAID WORK   N = 1876

Q484 [WkWorkHd]
CARD E7
Which of these statements best describes your feelings about your job?
In my job :
%
8.2 I only work as hard as I have to
41.7 I work hard, but not so that it interferes with the rest of my life
49.6 I make a point of doing the best I can, even if it sometimes does interfere with the rest of my life
0.3 (Don't know)
0.3 (Refusal/Not answered)

VERSIONS A AND C: ASK ALL ALL CURRENT EMPLOYEES

N = 1112

Q485 *[ECourse]*
In the last **two** years, have you been on any courses or had other formal training, which was part of your work or helpful to your to your work?
ANY TRAINING WHICH IS RELATED TO RESPONDENT'S PAST, PRESENT OR FUTURE WORK MAY BE COUNTED, BUT DO NOT INCLUDE LEISURE COURSES OR HOBBIES WHICH ARE NOT JOB-RELATED.

%
59.8 Yes, had training related to work
39.9 No, had none
- (Don't know)
0.3 (Refusal/Not answered)

IF 'yes' AT [ECourse]

Q486 *[ECourseT]*
In all, about how many full days have you spent in this kind of training over the last two years?
PROBE FOR TOTAL TIME SPENT IN JOB-RELATED TRAINING IN PAST OR PRESENT JOB.
IF LESS THAN HALF A DAY, CODE 0.
Median: 7 days
%
0.9 (Don't know)
0.3 (Refusal/Not answered)

Q487 *[ECrsWhen]*
And did you do this training **entirely** in your own time, **entirely** in work time, or partly one and partly the other?
Please include any 'homework' you might have done in your own time.
%
6.3 Entirely in own time
36.8 Entirely in work time
16.7 Partly one / party other
- (Don't know)
0.3 (Refusal/Not answered)

Q495-CARD E8
Q500 From this card, please say who paid the **fees** for this training.
PROBE: Who else?
CODE ALL THAT APPLY
Multicoded (Maximum of 6 codes)
%
5.2 No fees   *[ECPNoFee]*
3.8 Self / family / relative   *[ECPSelf]*
49.9 Employer / potential employer   *[ECPEmplo]*
2.8 Government-sponsored training programme
(e.g. New Deal)   *[ECPGovt]*
0.5 Other (WRITE IN)   *[ECPOth]*
0.1 Don't know who paid   *[ECPDKnow]*
0.3 (Refusal/Not answered)

ASK ALL WHOLLY RETIRED FROM WORK

N = 689

Q501 *[REmplPen]*
Do you receive a pension from any past employer?
%
56.3 Yes
43.5 No
- (Don't know)
0.2 (Refusal/Not answered)

ASK ALL WHOLLY RETIRED FROM WORK: IF MARRIED

Q502 *[SEmplPen]*
Does your **(husband/wife)** receive a pension from any past employer?
%
26.1 Yes
33.2 No
- (Don't know)
0.9 (Refusal/Not answered)

ASK ALL WHOLLY RETIRED FROM WORK

Q503 *[PrPenGet]*
And do you receive a pension from any **private** arrangements you have made in the past, that is **apart** from the state pension or one arranged through an employer?
%
14.8 Yes
84.8 No
- (Don't know)
0.4 (Refusal/Not answered)

ASK ALL WHOLLY RETIRED FROM WORK: IF MARRIED

Q504 *[SPrPnGet]*
And does your *(husband/wife)* receive a pension from any **private** arrangements *(he/she)* has made in the past, that is **apart** from the state pension or one arranged through an employer?
%
6.3 Yes
53.1 No
- (Don't know)
0.7 (Refusal/Not answered)

ASK ALL WHOLLY RETIRED AND MALE AGED 66 OR OVER OR FEMALE AGED 61 OR OVER

N = 575

Q506 *[RPension]*
On the whole would you say the present **state** pension is on the low side, reasonable, or on the high side?
IF 'ON THE LOW SIDE': Very low or a bit low?
%
42.0 Very low
31.2 A bit low
24.7 Reasonable
0.6 On the high side
0.7 (Don't know)
0.9 (Refusal/Not answered)

Q507 [RPenInYr]
Do you expect your state pension in a year's time to purchase **more** than it does now, **less**, or about the **same**?

N = 575

%
10.0 More
48.1 Less
38.5 About the same
2.5 (Don't know)
0.9 (Refusal/Not answered)

ASK ALL WHOLLY RETIRED FROM WORK
Q508 [RetirAg2]
At what age did you retire from work?
NEVER WORKED, CODE: 00

N = 689

%   **Median: 60 years**
0.3 (Don't know)
0.4 (Refusal/Not answered)

Health and safety

N = 3287

ASK ALL
Q510 [AttnRisk]
Some people work in jobs where there is risk of injury or damage to their health. Do you think that the attention paid in this country to protecting such workers is ... READ OUT ...
%
3.5 ..too much,
42.1 about right,
49.3 or, not enough?
5.1 (Don't know)
- (Refusal/Not answered)

ASK ALL IN PAID WORK, WAITING TO TAKE UP WORK OR WHO HAVE WORKED IN LAST 10 YEARS

N = 2652

Q511 [HSQuiz1] **(False)**
For each of these statements, please tell me whether you think it is true or false. If you don't know, please just say so and we'll go on to the next one. So - true, false or don't know. Employers only have to consult their employees about health and safety at work if the issue is considered life threatening
FOR 'DON'T KNOW', CODE CTRL+K

Q512 [HSQuiz2] **(True)**
(Please tell me whether you think this statement is true or false or whether you don't know:)
Employers are legally responsible for the health and safety of their employees at work
FOR 'DON'T KNOW', CODE CTRL+K

Q513 [HSQuiz3] **(True)**
(Please tell me whether you think this statement is true or false or whether you don't know:)
Workers who 'blow the whistle' on dangerous working conditions are protected by law from being penalised afterwards.
FOR 'DON'T KNOW', CODE CTRL+K

Q514 [HSQuiz4] **(True)**
(Please tell me whether you think this statement is true or false or whether you don't know:)
Employers have to record details of all accidents at work.
FOR 'DON'T KNOW', CODE CTRL+K

	[HSQuiz1]	[HSQuiz2]	[HSQuiz3]	[HSQuiz4]
	%	%	%	%
True	19.3	96.8	56.1	97.6
False	70.7	1.8	20.2	0.8
(Don't know)	9.9	1.3	23.6	1.5
(Refusal/Not answered)	0.1	0.1	0.1	0.1

N = 892

ASK ALL WHO HAVE HAD ACCIDENT
Q529 CARD F1
Q539 Did you report this to any of the people on this card?
(If you have had several accidents, please think about the most recent one.)
PROBE: Which others?
CODE ALL THAT APPLY
% Multicoded (Maximum of 10 codes)
10.0 No one [AcRpNone]
46.2 Any doctor or hospital [AcRpDoct]
25.8 Employer's health and safety officer at my workplace [AcRpHSOf]
59.4 Directly to my employer [AcRpEmpl]
9.2 Trade union representative [AcRpTU]
1.2 Local authority [AcRpLocA]
3.9 Health and Safety Executive [AcRpHSE]
3.7 Police [AcRpPoli]
5.3 Solicitor [AcRpSoli]
0.2 Newspaper, radio or television [AcRpMedi]
1.6 Other (WRITE IN) [AcRpOth]
0.3 (Don't know)
0.4 (Refusal/Not answered)

N = 2100

ASK ALL IN PAID WORK, WAITING TO TAKE UP WORK OR WHO HAVE WORKED IN LAST YEAR
Q540 [IllLstYr]
In the last 12 months, have you suffered from any illness or other physical problem that was caused or made worse by your work?
%
15.2 Yes
84.4 No
0.2 (Don't know)
0.2 (Refusal/Not answered)

N = 2333

ASK ALL SAID 'no'/DON'T KNOW AT [IllLstYr] OR HAVE WORKED ONLY IN LAST 2-10 YEARS
Q541 [IllEver]
Have you ever suffered from any illness or other physical problem that was caused or made worse by your work?
%
14.5 Yes
85.2 No
0.2 (Don't know)
0.1 (Refusal/Not answered)

N = 2100

ASK ALL IN PAID WORK, WAITING TO TAKE UP WORK OR WHO HAVE WORKED IN LAST YEAR
Q515 [AccLstYr]
Thinking of the last 12 months, have you had any accident resulting in injury at work or in the course of your work?
%
11.3 Yes
88.5 No
0.0 (Don't know)
0.2 (Refusal/Not answered)

N = 2414

ASK ALL SAID 'no'/DON'T KNOW AT [AccLstYr] OR HAVE WORKED ONLY IN LAST 2-10 YEARS
Q516 [AccEver]
Have you ever had any accident resulting in injury at work or in the course of your work?
%
27.0 Yes
72.9 No
-    (Don't know)
0.1 (Refusal/Not answered)

N = 1760

ASK ALL WHO HAVE HAD ACCIDENT (AT [AccLstYr] OR AT [AccEver]): IF NOT WAITING TO TAKE UP WORK
Q517 [AccWhJob]
Was that accident in your (present/last) job? If you have had several accidents, please think about the most recent one.
%
58.4 Yes
41.2 No
-    (Don't know)
0.4 (Refusal/Not answered)

ASK ALL WHO HAVE HAD ILLNES/PHYSICAL PROBLEM
(AT [IllLstYr] OR AT [IllEver]): IF NOT WAITING TO
TAKE UP WORK   N = 664

Q542 [IllWhJob]
Was that illness or physical problem caused by your
(present/last) job? If you have had several illnesses or
physical problems, please think about the most recent one.
%
60.2 Yes
37.5 No
0.7 (Don't know)
1.6 (Refusal/Not answered)

ASK ALL WHO HAVE HAD ILLNES/PHYSICAL
PROBLEM [AT [IllLstYr] OR AT [IllEver])   N = 665

Q554 CARD F1 (AGAIN)
Q564 Did you report this to any of the people on this card?
(If you have had several illnesses or physical problems,
please think about the most recent one.)
PROBE: Which others?
CODE ALL THAT APPLY
% Multicoded (Maximum of 10 codes)
23.8 No one   [IllNone]
53.9 Any doctor or hospital   [IllDoct]
12.0 Employer's health and safety officer at my workplace   [IllHSof]
39.5 Directly to my employer   [IllEmpl]
4.3 Trade union representative   [IllTU]
1.1 Local authority   [IllLocA]
1.2 Health and Safety Executive   [IllHSE]
0.8 Police   [IllPoli]
2.3 Solicitor   [IllSoli]
1.3 Newspaper, radio or television   [IllMedi]
1.3 Other (WRITE IN)   [IllOth]
-    (Don't know)
1.3 (Refusal/Not answered)

ASK ALL IN PAID WORK OR WHO HAVE WORKED IN LAST
10 YEARS   N = 2637

Q575-CARD F2
Q584 Which, if any, of the things on this card (are/were) the **most**
common causes of accidents or health damage where you
(work/worked) or (are/were) there never any?
PROBE: Which others?
CODE ALL THAT APPLY
% Multicoded (Maximum of 9 codes)
31.6 Never any accidents/health damage   [AccNever]
9.9 Lack of adequate health and safety
    precautions   [AccHSPre]
15.6 Lack of training   [AccTrain]
4.6 Lack of consultation with employees   [AccConsu]
12.0 Corner cutting by management   [AccCornM]
15.9 Corner cutting by employees   [AccCornE]
43.6 Human error or carelessness   [AccHErro]
14.0 Tiredness   [AccTired]
2.1 Drink or drugs   [AccDrink]
0.9 **EDIT ONLY:** Stress   [AccStres]
0.5 **EDIT ONLY:** Attacks by clients/customers/patients/
    pupils   [AccAttac]
2.2 Other (WRITE IN)   [AccOth]
1.8 (Don't know)
0.0 (Refusal/Not answered)

ASK ALL IN PAID WORK OR WHO HAVE WORKED IN LAST YEAR   N = 3085

Q585 [AccAtWrk]
As far as you know, have there, in fact, been any accidents or
damage to health at your (present/last) work in the last 12
months?
%
34.1 Yes
62.3 No
3.4 (Don't know)
0.2 (Refusal/Not answered)

ASK ALL IN PAID WORK OR WHO HAVE WORKED
IN LAST 10 YEARS   N = 2637

Q586 [ReduRisk]
Could the level of risk in your (last) job realistically
(be/have been) reduced . . . READ OUT . . .
%
7.1 . . . a great deal,
13.2 a fair amount,
28.4 a little bit,
49.7 or, not at all?
1.5 (Don't know)
0.1 (Refusal/Not answered)

ASK ALL CURRENT EMPLOYEES OR WHO HAVE WORKED AS AN EMPLOYEE IN LAST 10 YEARS   N = 2349

Q587 [HSSerio]

How seriously do you think your employer (takes/took) health and safety in the workplace . . READ OUT . . .

%
53.5 . . . very seriously,
33.4 fairly seriously,
9.3 not very seriously,
2.6 or, not at all seriously?
1.1 (Don't know)
0.1 (Refusal/Not answered)

ASK ALL IN PAID WORK OR WHO HAVE WORKED IN LAST 10 YEARS   N = 2637

Q588 [EachLook]
CARD F3
For each of these statements, please say how much you agree or disagree with it:
It is up to each person at work to look after themselves, not to rely on the employer to keep them safe

Q589 [WorkSafe]
CARD F3 AGAIN
(Please say how much you agree or disagree with this statement:)
My (last) workplace (is/was) safe and healthy.

ASK ALL CURRENT EMPLOYEES OR WHO HAVE WORKED AS AN EMPLOYEE IN LAST 10 YEARS   N = 2349

Q590 [EmplSort]
CARD F3 AGAIN
(Please say how much you agree or disagree with this statement:)
If there (is/was) a problem with health and safety at work, my employer would (sort/have sorted) it out.

Q591 [TroubleM]
CARD F3 AGAIN
(Please say how much you agree or disagree with this statement:)
If I reported a health and safety problem to my employer, they would (see/have seen) me as a trouble-maker.

	[EachLook]	[WorkSafe]	[EmplSort]	[TroubleM]
	%	%	%	%
Agree strongly	18.6	16.3	19.2	1.8
Agree	42.4	60.1	63.7	10.7
Neither agree nor disagree	12.4	9.4	7.6	7.8
Disagree	22.4	12.4	7.7	61.5
Disagree strongly	4.0	1.5	0.9	16.9
(Don't know)	0.1	0.1	0.6	1.1
(Refusal/Not answered)	0.1	0.2	0.2	0.2

Q592 [SafetyOf]
At your (present/last) place of work, (do/did) you have a Safety Officer **appointed by your employer**, or are you not sure?
IF NOT SURE, CODE DON'T KNOW (Ctrl + K)

Q593 [TUSafRep]
(Do/Did) you have a Safety Representative appointed by a trade union or anyone else other than your employer, or are you not sure?
IF NOT SURE, CODE DON'T KNOW (Ctrl + K)

	[SafetyOf]	[TUSafRep]
	%	%
Yes	60.9	27.4
No	23.3	48.3
(Don't know)	15.6	24.0
(Refusal/Not answered)	0.2	0.2

ASK ALL IN PAID WORK OR WHO HAVE WORKED IN LAST 10 YEARS   N = 2637

Q594 [ProtClth]
As far as you know, (are/were) you supposed to wear any type of special protective clothing in your (last) job?

%
40.3 Yes
59.1 No
0.4 (Don't know)
0.2 (Refusal/Not answered)

IF 'yes' AT [ProtClth]
Q595 [WearPrC1]
When you (are/were) meant to wear this protective clothing, how often (do/did) you actually wear it . . READ OUT . . .

%
28.9 . . . always,
6.4 mostly,
3.7 sometimes,
1.2 or, never?
0.1 (Don't know)
0.5 (Refusal/Not answered)

ASK ALL IN PAID WORK OR WHO HAVE WORKED IN LAST 10 YEARS   [N = 2637]

Q596 [HSRules]
As far as you know, (are/were) there any rules or advice about what you should or shouldn't do in your (last) workplace to protect your health and safety?
%
70.6 Yes
27.7 No
1.5 (Don't know)
0.2 (Refusal/Not answered)

IF 'yes' AT [HSRules]
Q597 [DoHSRule]
When you (are/were) meant to follow these rules or advice, how often (do/did) you follow them **strictly**. . . READ OUT . .
%
35.3 . . . always,
28.5 mostly,
6.0 sometimes,
0.8 or, never?
0.0 (Don't know)
1.7 (Refusal/Not answered)

ASK ALL CURRENT EMPLOYEES OR WHO HAVE WORKED AS AN EMPLOYEE IN LAST 10 YEARS   [N = 2349]

Q598 [HSPoster]
(Has/Did) your (present/last) employer displayed a health and safety poster or (handed/hand) out a health and safety leaflet at your work?
IF YES: Which?
%
19.5 No poster or leaflet
30.1 Health and safety poster only
6.8 Health and safety leaflet only
41.5 Both poster and leaflet
1.9 (Don't know)
0.2 (Refusal/Not answered)

Q599 [HSTrain]
(Have/Did) you (had/have) any training in health and safety provided or paid for by your (present/last) employer?
%
45.5 Yes
54.2 No
0.1 (Don't know)
0.2 (Refusal/Not answered)

[N = 2349]

Q600 [HSConsul]
(Does/Did) your employer consult you about health and safety issues . . . .READ OUT . .
%
30.2 . . . most of the time,
27.6 sometimes,
17.1 hardly ever,
24.1 or, never?
0.8 (Don't Know)
0.2 (Refusal/Not answered)

Q601 [HSMorSay]
Do you think you should have (had) more say over health and safety issues at your work or (are/were) you satisfied with the way things (are/were)
%
77.5 Satisfied with the way things (are/were)
21.8 Should have (had) more say
0.4 (Don't know)
0.2 (Refusal/Not answered)

Q602 [LiftLoa1]
CARD F4
Suppose the following happened at your (last) place of work:
You (notice/noticed) someone trying to lift a very heavy load on their own.
Which if any of the things on this card would you (do/have done) first?
%
6.8 Leave it to my employer to notice and deal with
65.1 Deal with it myself
8.6 Speak to my employer's health and safety officer
15.1 Speak to my employer directly
0.9 Speak to a trade union representative
0.1 Speak to the local authority
0.9 Speak to the Health and Safety Executive
- Speak to the police
0.1 Speak to a solicitor
- Speak to a newspaper, radio or television
1.0 Other (WRITE IN)
1.3 (Don't know)
0.1 (Refusal/Not answered)

IF NOT 'deal with it myself'/
DON'T KNOW/REFUSAL AT [LiftLoa1]

Q604 *[LiftLoa2]*
CARD F4 AGAIN
And if nobody did anything about it, which would you *(do/have done)* next?
%
3.1 Leave it to my employer to notice and deal with
5.6 Deal with it myself
6.2 Speak to my employer's health and safety officer
6.8 Speak to my employer directly
3.8 Speak to a trade union representative
0.8 Speak to the local authority
5.0 Speak to the Health and Safety Executive
0.0 Speak to the police
0.2 Speak to a solicitor
– Speak to a newspaper, radio or television
1.1 Other (WRITE IN)
0.9 (Don't know)
1.4 (Refusal/Not answered)

ASK ALL CURRENT EMPLOYEES OR WHO HAVE WORKED AS AN EMPLOYEE IN LAST 10 YEARS

Q606 *[HighResp]*
CARD F5
If there was a health and safety problem at your *(last)* place of work and your employer didn't deal with it properly, which of the people on this card do you think *(is/was)* **mainly** responsible for making sure that your employer *(meets/met)* his or her legal responsibility?
%
4.2 No one
14.7 The trade union
10.2 The local authority
64.7 The Health and Safety Executive
0.7 The police
1.8 Other (WRITE IN)
3.3 (Don't know)
0.3 (Refusal/Not answered)

ASK ALL IN PAID WORK   N = 1876

Q608 *[AccNxtYr]*
How likely do you think it is that you will **have an accident** as a result of your job in the next 12 months? Do you think it is ... READ OUT ...
%
2.6 ...very likely,
9.6 fairly likely,
40.0 not very likely,
45.5 or, not at all likely?
1.8 (Don't know)
0.4 (Refusal/Not answered)

N = 2349

Q609 *[PrevAcc]*
How much do you feel you yourself can do to prevent having an accident at work ... READ OUT ...
%
42.7 ... a great deal,
30.9 a fair amount,
16.9 not all that much,
8.9 or, nothing at all?
0.4 (Don't know)
0.3 (Refusal/Not answered)

Q610 *[DamNxtYr]*
How likely do you think it is that you will **damage your health** as a result of your job in the next 12 months? Do you think it is ... READ OUT ...
%
2.4 ...very likely,
10.6 fairly likely,
40.6 not very likely,
45.1 or, not at all likely?
1.0 (Don't know)
0.3 (Refusal/Not answered)

Q611 *[PrevDam]*
How much do you feel you yourself can do to prevent your health being damaged by your work ... READ OUT ...
%
35.1 ... a great deal,
32.6 a fair amount,
20.1 not all that much,
11.6 or, nothing at all?
0.3 (Don't know)
0.3 (Refusal/Not answered)

N = 1876

Understanding of public policy

N = 3287

ASK ALL

Q612 *[Propr100]*
The next few questions are about some important issues in Britain today, and I'll ask you to give an answer out of 100. If you are not sure about the number, please give your best guess.

Of every 100 adults who have an operation in hospital, about how many do you think pay for their operation themselves or through private medical insurance?

Median: 25

%
3.6 (Don't know)
0.2 (Refusal/Not answered)

Q613 *[PrPen100]*
Of every 100 adults in work now, about how many do you think will rely on a private occupational or personal pension for most of their income when they retire?

IF ASKED STAKEHOLDER PENSIONS ARE **PRIVATE** PENSIONS

Median: 55

%
3.8 (Don't know)
0.2 (Refusal/Not answered)

Q614 *[ViCri100]*
Of every 100 crimes recorded by the police, about how many do you think involve violence or the threat of violence?

Median: 50

%
2.5 (Don't know)
0.2 (Refusal/Not answered)

Q615 *[PrSch100]*
Of every 100 pupils in secondary education, about how many do you think are in fee-paying private schools?

Median: 20

%
6.1 (Don't know)
0.2 (Refusal/Not answered)

Q616 *[HiPay100]*
Of every 100 adults in work now, about how many do you think are paid more than £40,000 a year?

Median: 25

%
5.0 (Don't know)
0.2 (Refusal/Not answered)

N = 3287

Q617 *[ChPov100]*
Of every 100 children under 16 in Britain, about how many do you think live in poverty?

Median: 25

%
4.4 (Don't know)
0.2 (Refusal/Not answered)

VERSION A AND B: ASK ALL

Q618 *[BlAsi100]*
Of every 100 people in Britain today, about how many do you think are black or Asian?

Median: 30

%
3.3 (Don't know)
0.2 (Refusal/Not answered)

VERSION C: ASK ALL

N = 1642

Q619 *[Car100]*
Of every 100 adults in Britain, about how many do you think own or have regular use of a car?

Median: 80

%
0.8 (Don't know)
0.2 (Refusal/Not answered)

ASK ALL WITH ODD SERIAL NUMBERS

Q620 *[NHSTax1p]*
CARD G1
Would you be in favour of or against an extra 1p in the pound on income tax if the money was set aside and spent only on the **NHS**? **On average** it would mean around £100 more a year for every tax payer.

Q621 *[UBTax1p]*
CARD G1 AGAIN
Now suppose the money was **instead** spent only on **unemployment benefits**? (Would you be in favour of or against an extra 1p in the pound on income tax for this?)

Q622 *[SchTax1p]*
CARD G1 AGAIN
Now suppose the money was **instead** spent only on **schools**? (Would you be in favour of or against an extra 1p in the pound on income tax for this?)

Q623 *[PtrTax1p]*
CARD G1 AGAIN
Now suppose the money was **instead** spent only on **public transport**? (Would you be in favour of or against an extra 1p in the pound on income tax for this?)

Q624 [PenTax1p]
CARD G1 AGAIN
Now suppose the money was **instead** spent only on **pensions**?
(Would you be in favour of or against an extra 1p in the pound on income tax for this?)

Q625 [PolTax1p]
CARD G1 AGAIN
Now suppose the money was **instead** spent only on **policing**?
(Would you be in favour of or against an extra 1p in the pound on income tax for this?)

N = 1642

	[NHSTax1p]	[UBTax1p]	[SchTax1p]
	%	%	%
Strongly in favour	41.0	2.1	18.9
In favour	42.7	14.1	54.3
Neither in favour nor against	7.7	16.1	13.0
Against	5.9	47.6	10.7
Strongly against	1.7	18.9	2.1
(Don't know)	0.6	0.9	0.6
(Refusal/Not answered)	0.3	0.3	0.3

	[PtrTax1p]	[PenTax1p]	[PolTax1p]
	%	%	%
Strongly in favour	8.1	19.0	12.6
In favour	34.4	46.4	48.6
Neither in favour nor against	21.3	17.5	19.6
Against	30.1	14.8	15.5
Strongly against	4.8	1.8	2.8
(Don't know)	1.0	0.3	0.6
(Refusal/Not answered)	0.3	0.3	0.3

Q626 [NHSInc1p]
CARD G2
Now suppose the government **actually did** increase the basic rate of income tax by 1p in the pound and set it aside just for spending on the **NHS**, how much do you think this would improve the NHS?

Q627 [UBInc1p]
CARD G2 AGAIN
And how much do you think a 1p increase set aside for **unemployment benefits** would improve them?

Q628 [SchInc1p]
CARD G2 AGAIN
And how much do you think a 1p increase set aside for **schools** would improve them?

Q629 [PtrInc1p]
CARD G2 AGAIN
And how much do you think a 1p increase set aside for **public transport** would improve it?

Q630 [PenInc1p]
CARD G2 AGAIN
And how much do you think a 1p increase set aside for **pensions** would improve them?

Q631 [PolInc1p]
CARD G2 AGAIN
And how much do you think a 1p increase set aside for **policing** would improve it?

N = 1642

	[NHSInc1p]	[UBInc1p]	[SchInc1p]
	%	%	%
A great deal	16.8	8.4	13.2
Quite a bit	50.2	39.0	54.5
Not much	28.1	39.3	27.7
Not at all	3.0	8.7	2.5
(Don't know)	1.7	4.3	1.9
(Refusal/Not answered)	0.3	0.3	0.3

	[PtrInc1p]	[PenInc1p]	[PolInc1p]
	%	%	%
A great deal	10.9	13.4	9.8
Quite a bit	40.8	48.5	46.9
Not much	37.5	32.7	36.0
Not at all	7.1	2.7	4.6
(Don't know)	3.4	2.4	2.4
(Refusal/Not answered)	0.3	0.3	0.3

ASK ALL WITH EVEN SERIAL NUMBERS

N = 1645

Q632 [NHSTax3p]
CARD G3
Would you be in favour of or against an extra 3p in the pound on income tax if the money was set aside and spent only on the **NHS**? **On average** it would mean around £300 more a year for every tax payer.

Q633 [UBTax3p]
CARD G3 AGAIN
Now suppose the money was **instead** spent only on **unemployment benefits**? (Would you be in favour of or against an extra 3p in the pound on income tax for this?)

N = 1645

Q634 [SchTax3p]
CARD G3 AGAIN
Now suppose the money was **instead** spent only on **schools**?
(Would you be in favour of or against an extra 3p in the pound on income tax for this?)

Q635 [PtrTax3p]
CARD G3 AGAIN
Now suppose the money was **instead** spent only on **public transport**? (Would you be in favour of or against an extra 3p in the pound on income tax for this?)

Q636 [PenTax3p]
CARD G3 AGAIN
Now suppose the money was **instead** spent only on **pensions**?
(Would you be in favour of or against an extra 3p in the pound on income tax for this?)

Q637 [PolTax3p]
CARD G3 AGAIN
Now suppose the money was **instead** spent only on **policing**?
(Would you be in favour of or against an extra 3p in the pound on income tax for this?)

	[NHSTax3p]	[UBTax3p]	[SchTax3p]
	%	%	%
Strongly in favour	24.5	1.8	11.5
In favour	44.3	9.2	49.1
Neither in favour nor against	11.9	14.4	15.6
Against	14.5	48.9	18.9
Strongly against	4.1	24.9	3.9
(Don't know)	0.5	0.7	0.8
(Refusal/Not answered)	0.2	0.2	0.2

	[PtrTax3p]	[PenTax3p]	[PolTax3p]
	%	%	%
Strongly in favour	4.7	13.2	8.9
In favour	26.7	43.5	41.2
Neither in favour nor against	22.5	17.8	20.8
Against	37.7	20.9	23.3
Strongly against	7.5	3.7	5.1
(Don't know)	0.7	0.7	0.6
(Refusal/Not answered)	0.2	0.2	0.2

Q638 [NHSInc3p]
CARD G4
Now suppose the government **actually did** increase the basic rate of income tax by 3p in the pound and set it aside just for spending on the **NHS**, how much do you think this would improve the NHS?

N = 1645

Q639 [UBInc3p]
CARD G4 AGAIN
And how much do you think a 3p increase set aside for **unemployment benefits** would improve them?

Q640 [SchInc3p]
CARD G4 AGAIN
And how much do you think a 3p increase set aside for **schools** would improve them?

Q641 [PtrInc3p]
CARD G4 AGAIN
And how much do you think a 3p increase set aside for **public transport** would improve it?

Q642 [PenInc3p]
CARD G4 AGAIN
And how much do you think a 3p increase set aside for **pensions** would improve them?

Q643 [PolInc3p]
CARD G4 AGAIN
And how much do you think a 3p increase set aside for **policing** would improve it?

	[NHSInc3p]	[UBInc3p]	[SchInc3p]
	%	%	%
A great deal	20.6	11.9	18.7
Quite a bit	48.7	39.0	53.1
Not much	25.6	36.9	23.4
Not at all	3.4	8.7	2.9
(Don't know)	1.5	3.2	1.7
(Refusal/Not answered)	0.2	0.2	0.2

	[PtrInc3p]	[PenInc3p]	[PolInc3p]
	%	%	%
A great deal	13.0	16.7	14.4
Quite a bit	40.6	53.4	46.8
Not much	36.4	25.4	31.5
Not at all	7.3	2.5	5.2
(Don't know)	2.6	1.9	2.0
(Refusal/Not answered)	0.2	0.2	0.2

ASK ALL
Q644 [SpenMost]
CARD G5
Here are some areas of government spending. Look through the card and pick out the one area that you think has the **largest** amount of money spent on it at the moment.
Please read through the whole list before deciding.

N = 3287

N = 3287

Q645 [SpenNext]
CARD G5 AGAIN
And tell me which one you think has the **next largest** amount spent on it at the moment.

Q646 [SpenLast]
CARD G5 AGAIN
And which area do you think has the **smallest** amount of money spent on it at the moment.

	[SpenMost]	[SpenNext]	[SpenLast]
	%	%	%
Education	7.7	20.6	2.8
Defence	18.1	13.0	3.2
Health	27.1	24.1	5.6
Housing	1.1	2.5	10.4
Public transport	0.8	1.4	7.9
Roads	1.8	2.5	15.0
Police and prisons	3.3	6.4	2.5
Social security benefits	31.2	18.0	1.7
Help for industry	0.8	2.2	16.1
Overseas aid	3.7	3.8	30.6
(Don't know)	4.2	5.4	3.9
(Refusal/Not answered)	0.3	0.3	0.3

Q647 [SocBMost]
CARD G6
Here are some of the areas covered by social security spending. Look through the card and pick out the one area that you think has the **largest** amount of money spent on it at the moment.

Q648 [SocBNext]
CARD G6 AGAIN
And tell me which one you think has the **next largest** amount spent on it at the moment.

Q649 [SocBLast]
CARD G6 AGAIN
And which area do you think has the **smallest** amount of money spent on it at the moment.

	[SocBMost]	[SocBNext]	[SocBLast]
	%	%	%
Retirement pensions	26.9	19.2	23.5
Child benefits	10.3	21.1	13.4
Benefits for the unemployed	42.6	26.0	3.4
Benefits for disabled people	3.9	8.3	38.7
Benefits for single parents	12.3	20.5	16.6
(Don't know)	3.8	4.6	4.0
(Refusal/Not answered)	0.3	0.3	0.3

N = 1108

VERSION C: ASK ALL

Q650 [HarmTra1]
CARD G7
Imagine making a 300 mile journey in Britain. Which of the ways of making this journey do you think would do the most harm to the environment **per person travelling**?

Q651 [HarmTra2]
CARD G7 AGAIN
And which do you think would do the **least** harm to the environment **per person travelling**?

	[HarmTra1]	[HarmTra2]
	%	%
Car	75.0	3.6
Coach	6.7	3.5
Train	1.8	65.7
Aeroplane	14.6	25.3
(Don't know)	1.6	1.6
(Refusal/Not answered)	0.4	0.4

N = 2179

VERSIONS A AND B: ASK ALL

Q652 [PrejNow]
Do you think there is generally more racial prejudice in Britain now than there was 5 years ago, less, or about the same amount?

Q654 [PrejFut]
Do you think there will be more, less, or about the same amount of racial prejudice in Britain in 5 years time compared with now?

	[PrejNow]	[PrejFut]
	%	%
More now	52.2	49.3
Less now	13.0	19.3
About the same	34.6	26.8
Other (WRITE IN)	0.2	0.9
(Don't know)	1.4	3.2
(Refusal/Not answered)	0.5	0.5

Q656 [SRPrej]
%   How would you describe yourself ... READ OUT ...
2.4   ... as very prejudiced against people of other races,
22.7 a little prejudiced,
73.3 or, not prejudiced at all?
0.8   Other (WRITE IN)
0.3   (Don't know)
0.6   (Refusal/Not answered)

N = 2179

Education

N = 1101

VERSION A: ASK ALL

Q659 [EdSpend1]
CARD H1
Now some questions about education.
Which of the groups on this card, if any, would be your
highest priority for **extra** government spending on education?

IF ANSWER GIVEN AT

Q660 [EdSpend2]
CARD H1 AGAIN
And which is your next highest priority?

	[EdSpend1]	[EdSpend2]
	%	%
Nursery or pre-school children	10.2	2.7
Primary school children	22.7	10.8
Secondary school children	29.2	23.5
Less able children with special needs	22.2	27.6
Students at colleges or universities	13.0	18.5
(None of these)	0.8	16.4
(Don't know)	1.5	0.1
(Refusal/Not answered)	0.5	0.5

VERSION A: ASK ALL

Q661 [PrimImp1]
CARD H2
Here are a number of things that some people think would
improve education in our schools.
Which do you think would be the **most** useful one for improving
the education of children in **primary** schools - aged (5-11/5
-12) years? Please look at the whole list before deciding.

IF ANSWER GIVEN AT [PrimImp1]

Q663 [PrimImp2]
CARD H2 AGAIN
And which do you think would be the **next** most useful one for
children in **primary** schools?

N = 1101

	[PrimImp1]	[PrimImp2]
	%	%
More information available about individual schools	1.6	1.9
More linke between prents and schools	7.7	1.3
More resources for buildings, books and equipment	14.2	8.7
Better quality teachers	17.2	24.7
Small class sizes	40.9	17.3
More emphasis on exams and tests	0.9	23.5
More emphasis on developing the child's skills and interests	13.2	1.7
Better leadership within individual schools	1.4	17.7
Other (WRITE IN)	1.0	3.0
(Don't know)	1.4	0.2
(Refusal/Not answered)	0.5	0.2

VERSION A: ASK ALL

Q665 [SecImp1]
CARD H3
And which do you think would be the **most** useful thing for improving the education of children in **secondary** schools - aged (11-18/12-18) years?

IF ANSWER GIVEN AT [SecImp1]
Q667 [SecImp2]
CARD H3 AGAIN
And which do you think would be the **next** most useful one for children in **secondary** schools?

	[SecImp1]	[SecImp2]
	%	%
More information available about individual schools	1.0	2.2
More links between parents and schools	4.1	1.2
More resources for buildings, books and equipment	14.7	5.9
Better quality teachers	24.3	17.8
Smaller class sizes	26.8	16.6
More emphasis on exams and tests	3.3	18.4
More emphasis on developing the child's skills and interests	11.0	3.6
More training and preparation for jobs	9.6	14.6
Better leadership within individual schools	2.0	15.5
Other (WRITE IN)	1.1	3.0
(Don't know)	1.8	0.9
(Refusal/Not answered)	0.5	0.2

N = 1101

VERSION A: ASK ALL

Q669 [SchSelec]
CARD H4
Which of the following statements comes closest to your views about what kind of **secondary** school children should go to?

%
45.4 Children should go to a different kind of secondary school, according to how well they do at primary school
51.8 All children should go to the same kind of secondary school, no matter how well or badly they do at primary school
2.2 (Don't know)
0.6 (Refusal/Not answered)

Q670 [HEFeeNow]
CARD H5
I'm now going to ask you what you think about university or college students paying towards the costs of their tuition - either while they are studying or after they have finished. Firstly, students and their families paying towards the costs of their tuition **while they are studying**.
Which of the views on this card comes closest to what you think about that?

%
7.2 All students or their families should pay towards their tuition costs while they are studying
57.6 Some students or their families should pay towards their tuition costs while they are studying, depending on their circumstances
33.1 No students or their families should pay towards their tuition costs while they are studying
1.6 (Don't know)
0.5 (Refusal/Not answered)

Q671 [HEFeeAft]
CARD H6
And what about students paying back some of the costs of their tuition **after they have finished studying**?
Which of the views on this card comes closest to what you think about that?

%
16.1 All students should pay back some tuition costs after they have finished studying
47.0 Some students should pay back some tuition costs after they have finished studying, depending on their circumstances
34.9 No students should pay back tuition costs after they have finished studying
1.5 (Don't know)
0.5 (Refusal/Not answered)

Classification

N = 3287

Housing and local area

ASK ALL

Q746 *[Tenure1]*
Does your household own or rent this accommodation?
PROBE IF NECESSARY
IF OWNS: Outright or on a mortgage? IF RENTS: From whom?
%
27.5 Owns outright
43.8 Buying on mortgage
12.9 Rents: local authority
0.1 Rents: New Town Development Corporation
4.6 Rents: Housing Association
1.1 Rents: property company
0.6 Rents: employer
0.8 Rents: other organisation
5.6 Rents: relative
0.6 Rents: other individual
0.6 Rents: Housing Trust
0.3 Rent free, squatting
0.7 Other (WRITE IN)
0.1 (Don't know)
0.7 (Refusal/Not answered)

Q749 *[ResPres]*
Can I just check, would you describe the place where you live
as ... READ OUT ...
%
8.4 ...a big city,
25.8 the suburbs or outskirts of a big city,
44.0 a small city or town,
18.8 a country village,
1.9 or, a farm or home in the country?
0.5 (Other answer (WRITE IN))
0.1 (Don't know)
0.5 (Refusal/Not answered)

IN ENGLAND: ASK ALL

N = 2786

Q751 *[RLvElsE]*
Have you ever lived anywhere other than England for more than
a year?
IF YES: Where was that? PROBE TO IDENTIFY CORRECT CODE
ELSEWHERE IN UK = SCOTLAND, WALES, N. IRELAND, CHANNEL
ISLANDS, ISLE OF MAN
%
74.0 No - have never lived anywhere outside England for more than a
year
5.3 Yes - elsewhere in UK
15.6 Yes - outside UK
4.4 Yes - elsewhere in UK and outside UK
- (Don't know)
0.6 (Refusal/Not answered)

Q752 *[LivAreE]*
How long have you lived in the (town/city/village) where you
live now?
PROBE FOR BEST ESTIMATE
ENTER **TOTAL** NUMBER OF YEARS IN TOWN/CITY/VILLAGE
FOR LESS THAN ONE YEAR, CODE 0
%
Median: 20 years
- (Don't know)
0.6 (Refusal/Not answered)

Religion, national identity and race

ASK ALL

Q757 *[Religion]*
Do you regard yourself as belonging to any particular religion?
IF YES: Which?
CODE ONE ONLY - DO NOT PROMPT

%
41.2 No religion
4.7 Christian - no denomination
10.7 Roman Catholic
29.4 Church of England/Anglican
1.0 Baptist
2.4 Methodist
3.8 Presbyterian/Church of Scotland
0.2 Other Christian
0.7 Hindu
0.7 Jewish
1.5 Islam/Muslim
0.7 Sikh
0.2 Buddhist
0.3 Other non-Christian
0.2 Free Presbyterian
0.0 Brethren
0.5 United Reform Church (URC)/Congregational
1.3 Other Protestant
0.1 Refusal
- (Don't know)
0.5 (Not answered)

IF NOT REFUSED AT [RelRFW]
Q760 *[FamRelig]*
In what religion, if any, were you brought up?
PROBE IF NECESSARY: What was your family's religion?
CODE ONE ONLY - DO NOT PROMPT

%
12.1 No religion
6.1 Christian - no denomination
14.1 Roman Catholic
47.1 Church of England/Anglican
1.7 Baptist
4.9 Methodist
6.5 Presbyterian/Church of Scotland
0.2 Other Christian
0.8 Hindu
0.9 Jewish
1.5 Islam/Muslim
0.7 Sikh
0.2 Buddhist
0.1 Other non-Christian
0.2 Free Presbyterian
0.1 Brethren
0.7 United Reform Church (URC)/Congregational
1.6 Other Protestant
0.1 Refused
- (Don't know)
0.5 (Not answered)

IF RELIGION GIVEN AT [Religion] OR AT [FamRelig]
Q765 *[ChAttend]*
Apart from such special occasions as weddings, funerals and baptisms, how often nowadays do you attend services or meetings connected with your religion?
PROBE AS NECESSARY.

%
10.7 Once a week or more
2.2 Less often but at least once in two weeks
5.0 Less often but at least once a month
9.9 Less often but at least twice a year
5.1 Less often but at least once a year
3.9 Less often than once a year
50.4 Never or practically never
0.6 Varies too much to say
- (Don't know)
0.5 (Refusal/Not answered)

Education

ASK ALL
Q796 *[RPrivEd]*
Have you ever attended a fee-paying, **private** primary or
secondary school in the United Kingdom?
`PRIVATE' PRIMARY OR SECONDARY SCHOOLS INCLUDE:
* INDEPENDENT SCHOOLS
* SCHOLARSHIPS AND ASSISTED PLACES AT FEE-PAYING SCHOOLS
THEY EXCLUDE:
* DIRECT GRANT SCHOOLS (UNLESS FEE-PAYING)
* VOLUNTARY-AIDED SCHOOLS
* GRANT-MAINTAINED (`OPTED OUT') SCHOOLS
* NURSERY SCHOOLS
%
10.8 Yes
88.6 No
- (Don't know)
0.6 (Refusal/Not answered)

IF NO CHILDREN IN HOUSEHOLD (AS GIVEN AT HOUSEHOLD GRID)
Q798 *[OthChld3]*
Have you ever been responsible for bringing up any children of
school age, including stepchildren?
%
31.7 Yes
27.4 No
- (Don't know)
0.3 Refusal/Not answered)

**IF CHILDREN IN HOUSEHOLD (AS GIVEN AT HOUSEHOLD GRID) OR 'yes'
AT [OthChld3]**
Q797 *[ChPrivEd]*
And (have any of your children / has your child) ever attended
a fee-paying, **private** primary or secondary school in the
United Kingdom?
`PRIVATE' PRIMARY OR SECONDARY SCHOOLS INCLUDE:
* INDEPENDENT SCHOOLS
* SCHOLARSHIPS AND ASSISTED PLACES AT FEE-PAYING SCHOOLS
THEY EXCLUDE:
* DIRECT GRANT SCHOOLS (UNLESS FEE-PAYING)
* VOLUNTARY-AIDED SCHOOLS
* GRANT-MAINTAINED (`OPTED OUT') SCHOOLS
* NURSERY SCHOOLS
8.7 Yes
57.8 No
- (Don't know)
0.5 (Refusal/Not answered)

ASK ALL
Q775-CARD J1
Q786 Please say which, if any, of the words on this card describes
the way you think of **yourself**. Please choose as many or as few
as apply.
PROBE: Any other?
% Multicoded (Maximum of 8 codes)
64.2 British   *[NatBrit]*
54.8 English   *[NatEng]*
12.4 European   *[NatEuro]*
2.2 Irish   *[NatIrish]*
0.7 Northern Irish   *[NatNI]*
10.4 Scottish   *[NatScot]*
0.2 Ulster   *[NatUlst]*
5.5 Welsh   *[NatWelsh]*
2.5 Other answer (WRITE IN) *[NatOth]*
0.7 (None of these)   *[NatNone]*
1.2 **EDIT ONLY:** OTHER - ASIAN MENTIONED *[NatAsia]*
0.6 **EDIT ONLY:** OTHER - AFRICAN /CARIBBEAN MENTIONED *[NatAfric]*
0.0 (Don't know)
0.6 (Refusal/Not answered)

IF MORE THAN ONE ANSWER GIVEN AT [NationU]
Q787 *[BNationU]*
CARD J1 AGAIN
And if you had to choose, which one **best** describes the way you
think of yourself?

ASK ALL
Q790 *[RaceOri2]*
CARD J2
% To which of these groups do you consider you belong?
0.6 BLACK: of African origin
1.3 BLACK: of Caribbean origin
0.1 BLACK: of other origin (WRITE IN)
1.5 ASIAN: of Indian origin
0.6 ASIAN: of Pakistani origin
0.1 ASIAN: of Bangladeshi origin
0.2 ASIAN: of Chinese origin
0.6 ASIAN: of other origin (WRITE IN)
92.3 WHITE: of any European origin
0.8 WHITE: of other origin (WRITE IN)
0.6 MIXED ORIGIN (WRITE IN)
0.7 OTHER (WRITE IN)
0.1 (Don't know)
0.6 (Refusal/Not answered)

N = 3287

Q800 [TEA2]
How old were you when you completed your continuous full-time education?
PROBE IF NECESSARY
'STILL AT SCHOOL' - CODE 95
'STILL AT COLLEGE OR UNIVERSITY' - CODE 96
'OTHER ANSWER' - CODE 97 AND WRITE IN
Median: 16 years
%
0.1 (Still at school)
2.0 (Still at college)
0.3 (Other answer)
0.2 (Don't know)
0.6 (Refusal/Not answered)

Q803 [SchQual]
CARD J3
Have you passed any of the examinations on this card?
%
63.4 Yes
35.9 No
0.1 (Don't know)
0.6 (Refusal/Not answered)

N = 3287

IF 'yes' AT [SchQual]
Q804-[SchQFW]
Q807 CARD J3 AGAIN Please tell me which sections of the card they are in?
PROBE : Any other sections?
CODE ALL THAT APPLY
% Multicoded (Maximum of 4 codes)
27.1 **Section 1:**
GCSE Grades D-G
CSE Grades 2-5
GCE O-level Grades D-E or 7-9   [EdQual1]
Scottish (SCE) Ordinary Bands D-E
Scottish Standard Grades 4-7
School leaving certificate (no grade)
46.5 **Section 2:**
GCSE Grades A-C
CSE Grade 1
GCE O-level Grades A-C or 1-6
School Certificate or Matriculation   [EdQual2]
Scottish SCE Ordinary Bands A-C or pass
Scottish Standard Grades 1-3 or Pass
Scottish School Leaving Certificate Lower Grade
SUPE
21.4 **Section 3:**
GCE A-level, S-level, AS-level
Scottish Higher Grades
Scottish Higher-Still
Scottish SCE/SLC/SUPE at Higher Grade   [EdQual3]
Scottish Higher School Certificate
Certificate of Sixth Year Studies
Northern Ireland Senior Certificate
2.5 **Section 4:**
Overseas school leaving exam or certificate   [EdQual4]
-   (Don't know)
0.7 (Refusal/Not answered)

ASK ALL
Q808 [PSchQual]
CARD J4
And have you passed any of the exams or got any of the qualifications on **this** card?
%
57.3 Yes
41.9 No
0.1 (Don't know)
0.6 (Refusal/Not answered)

IF 'yes' AT [PSchQual]   N = 3287

Q833-CARD J4 AGAIN Which ones? PROBE: Which others?

Q859 PROBE FOR CORRECT LEVEL,

% Multicoded (Maximum of 23 codes)

2.4	**Modern** apprenticeship **completed**	[EdQual26]
4.8	Other recognised trade apprenticeship **completed**	[EdQual27]
6.3	RSA/OCR - Certificate	[EdQual28]
0.6	RSA/OCR - (First) Diploma	[EdQual29]
1.4	RSA/OCR - Advanced Diploma	[EdQual30]
0.6	RSA/OCR - Higher Diploma	[EdQual31]
1.9	Other clerical, commercial qualification	[EdQual32]
6.7	City&Guilds Certif - Part I	[EdQual22]
5.7	City&Guilds Certif - Craft/ Intermediate/ Ordinary/ Part I	[EdQual23]
3.8	City&Guilds Certif - Advanced/ Final/ Part III	[EdQual24]
1.6	City&Guilds Certif - Full Technological/ Part IV	[EdQual25]
5.4	BTEC/EdExcel/BEC/TEC General/Ordinary National Certif (ONC) or Diploma (OND)	[EdQual10]
5.5	BTEC/EdExcel/BEC/TEC Higher/Higher National Certifate (HNC) or Diploma (HND)	[EdQual11]
2.6	NVQ/SVQ Lev 1/GNVQ/GSVQ Foundation lev	[EdQual17]
4.4	NVQ/SVQ Lev 2/GNVQ/GSVQ Intermediate lev	[EdQual18]
2.9	NVQ/SVQ Lev 3/GNVQ/GSVQ Advanced lev	[EdQual19]
0.8	NVQ/SVQ Lev 4	[EdQual20]
0.2	NVQ/SVQ Lev 5	[EdQual21]
4.9	Teacher training qualification	[EdQual12]
2.9	Nursing qualification	[EdQual13]
5.7	Other technical or business qualification/ certificate	[EdQual14]
15.7	Univ/CNAA degree/diploma	[EdQual15]
7.0	Other recognised academic or vocational qual (WRITE IN)	[EdQual16]
0.0	(Don't kow)	
0.7	(Refusal/Not answered)	

ASK ALL

Q861 [Internet]

Does anyone have access to the Internet or World Wide Web from this address?

%
44.2 Yes
55.2 No
- (Don't know)
0.6 (Refusal/Not answered)

Q862 [WWUse]

Do you yourself ever use the Internet or World Wide Web for any reason (other than your work)?   N = 3287

%
42.8 Yes
56.6 No
- (Don't know)
0.6 (Refusal/Not answered)

IF 'yes' AT [WWWUse]

Q863 [WWWHrsWk]

How many **hours** a week on average do you spend using the Internet or World Wide Web (other than for your work)?

INTERVIEWER: ROUND UP TO NEAREST HOUR

Median: 2 hours

%
0.0 (Don't know)
0.6 (Refusal/Not answered)

Recall vote

IN ENGLAND: ASK ALL   N = 2786

Q864 [Vote97]

May I just check, thinking back to the **last** general election - that is the one in **1997** - do you remember which party you voted for then or perhaps you didn't vote in that election?

IF 'YES': Which party was that?

IF NECESSARY, SAY: The one where Tony Blair won against John Major?

IF 'CAN'T REMEMBER', CODE 'DON'T KNOW' (Ctrl + K)

DO NOT PROMPT

%
25.0 Did not vote/Not eligible / Too young to vote
22.3 Yes - Conservative
37.4 Yes - Labour
10.8 Yes - Liberal Democrat
0.0 Yes - Plaid Cymru
0.6 Yes - Scottish National Party
0.2 Yes - Green Party
0.4 Yes - Referendum Party
2.4 Other (WRITE IN)
1.0 (Don't know)
- (Not answered)

Partner's job details

ASK ALL MARRIED OR LIVING AS MARRIED (AT [MarStat2])

Q878 [SEconAct] **(Frequencies refer to highest answer on the list)**
CARD J5
Which of these descriptions applied to what your (husband/wife/partner) was doing last week, that is the seven days ending last Sunday?
PROBE: Which others? CODE ALL THAT APPLY
Multicoded (Maximum of 11 codes)

%
0.4 In full-time education (not paid for by employer, including on vacation)
0.1 On government training/employment programme
63.7 In paid work (or away temporarily) for at least 10 hours in week
0.2 Waiting to take up paid work already accepted
1.1 Unemployed and registered at a benefit office
0.3 Unemployed, not registered, but actively looking for a job (of at least 10 hrs a week)
0.3 Unemployed, wanting a job (of at least 10 hrs per week) but not actively looking for a job
3.5 Permanently sick or disabled
18.4 Wholly retired from work
10.4 Looking after the home
0.7 (Doing something else) (WRITE IN)
- (Don't know)
0.9 (Refusal/Not answered)

ASK ALL MARRIED OR LIVING AS MARRIED (AT [MarStat2]) AND PARTNER IS NOT WORKING OR WAITING TO TAKE UP WORK

N = 767

Q879 [SLastJob]
How long ago did (he/she) last have a paid job of at least 10 hours a week?
GOVERNMENT PROGRAMS/SCHEMES DO NOT COUNT AS 'PAID JOBS'.

%
8.7 Within past 12 months
23.8 Over 1, up to 5 years ago
23.1 Over 5, up to 10 years ago
21.7 Over 10, up to 20 years ago
15.5 Over 20 years ago
3.9 Never had a paid job of 10+ hours a week
0.7 (Don't know)
2.6 (Refusal/Not answered)

N = 2123

ASK ALL WHERE PARTNER'S JOB DETAILS ARE BEING COLLECTED[1]

N = 299

Q880 [Title] **(NOT ON DATAFILE)**
Now I want to ask you about your (husband/wife/partner)'s (present/future) job.
What (is his/her job?/ will that job be?)
PROBE IF NECESSARY: What is the name or title of the job?
Open Question (Maximum of 80 characters)

Q881 [TypeWk] **(NOT ON DATAFILE)**
What kind of work (do/will) (he/she) do most of the time?
IF RELEVANT: What materials/machinery (do/will) (he/she) use?
Open Question (Maximum of 80 characters)

Q882 [Train] **(NOT ON DATAFILE)**
What training or qualifications are needed for that job?
Open Question (Maximum of 80 characters)

Q883 [PSuper2]
(Does/Will) (he/she) directly supervise or (is/will) (he/she) (be) directly responsible for the work of any other people?
%
41.4 Yes
55.8 No
- (Don't know)
2.8 (Refusal/Not answered)

IF 'yes' AT [Super2]
Q884 [PMany]
How many?
Median: 6 people (of those supervising any)
%
5.9 (Don't know)
3.2 (Refusal/Not answered)

Q886 [PEmploye]
In your (husband/wife/partner)'s (main) job (is/will) (he/she) (be) ... READ OUT ...
%
79.7 ... an employee,
17.8 or self-employed?
- (Don't know)
2.4 (Refusal/Not answered)

---

[1] Partner's job details are collected if respondent is **not** working or waiting to take up work, but partner **is** working or waiting to take up work.

ASK ALL WHERE PARTNER'S JOB DETAILS ARE BEING COLLECTED AND PARTNER IS EMPLOYEE   N = 246

Q888 [PSupman2]
% Can I just check, (is/will) (he/she) (be) ... READ OUT ...
28.3 ...a manager,
12.7 a foreman or supervisor,
55.2 or not?
0.5 (Don't know)
3.4 (Refusal/Not answered)

Q889 [POcSect2]
CARD J6
Which of the types of organisation on this card (does he/she work / will he/she be working) for?
% PRIVATE SECTOR FIRM OR COMPANY Including, for example, limited
70.4 companies and PLCs
3.4 NATIONALISED INDUSTRY OR PUBLIC CORPORATION Including, for example, the Post Office and the BBC
20.1 OTHER PUBLIC SECTOR EMPLOYER
Incl eg: - Central govt/ Civil Service/ Govt Agency
- Local authority/ Local Educ Auth (incl 'opted out' schools)
- Universities
- Health Authority / NHS hospitals / NHS Trusts/ GP surgeries
- Police / Armed forces
2.3 CHARITY/ VOLUNTARY SECTOR Including, for example, charitable companies, churches, trade unions
0.9 Other answer (WRITE IN)
- (Don't know)
2.9 (Refusal/Not answered)

ASK ALL WHERE PARTNER'S JOB DETAILS ARE BEING COLLECTED (NOT ON Datafile)   N = 299

Q891 [EmpMake]
IF EMPLOYEE: What does (his/her) employer make or do at the place where (he/she) (usually works/will usually work) (from)?
IF SELF-EMPLOYED: What (does/will) (he/she) make or do at the place where (he/she) usually (works/will work) (from)?
Open Question (Maximum of 80 characters)

Q897 [PEmpWork]   N = 299
IF EMPLOYEE: Including (himself/herself), how many people are employed at the place where (he/she) usually (works/will work) (from)?
IF SELF-EMPLOYED: (Does/Will) (he/she) have any employees?
IF YES: PROBE FOR CORRECT PRECODE.
% (No employees/ DO NOT USE IF EMPLOYEE)
16.7 Under 10
13.2 10-24
15.8 25-99
22.7 100-499
13.0 500 or more
4.1 (Don't know)
2.8 (Refusal/Not answered)

ASK ALL WHO ARE MARRIED/LIVING AS MARRIED AND PARTNER IS IN PAID WORK   N = 1353

Q938 [SPartFul]
% Is the job ... READ OUT ...
78.0 .. full-time - that is, 30 or more hours per week,
21.8 or, part-time?
0.0 (Don't know)
0.2 (Refusal/Not answered)

Income

ASK ALL   N = 3287
Q951 [AnyBN3]
CARD J7
Do you (or your husband/wife/partner) receive any of the state benefits or tax credits on this card at present?
%
59.2 Yes
40.1 No
0.0 (Don't know)
0.7 (Refusal/Not answered)

IF 'yes' AT [AnyBN3]

N = 3287

Q975 - CARD J7 AGAIN
Q992 Which ones? PROBE: Any others?
Multicoded (Maximum of 20 codes)

%		
20.9	State retirement pension (National Insurance)	[BenefOAP]
0.6	War Pension (War Disablement Pension or War Widows Pension)	[BenefWar]
1.3	Widow's Benefits (Widow's Pension and Widowed Mother's Allowance)	[BenefWid]
2.4	Jobseeker's Allowance/ Unemployment Benefit / Income Support for the Unemployed	[BenefUB]
6.6	Income Support (other than for unemployment)/ Minimum Income Guarantee for pensioners	[BenefIS]
27.3	Child Benefit (formerly Family Allowance)	[BenefCB]
3.7	Child Tax Credit	[BenefCTC]
0.6	Childcare Tax Credit	[BenefCCT]
1.1	One Parent Benefit	[BenefOP]
3.7	Working Families Tax Credit/ Family Credit	[BenefFC]
7.5	Housing Benefit (Rent Rebate)	[BenefHB]
8.8	Council Tax Benefit (or Rebate)	[BenefCT]
5.3	Incapacity Benefit / Sickness Benefit / Invalidity Benefit	[BenefInc]
0.3	Disabled Person's Tax Credit/ Disability Working Allowance	[BenefDWA]
5.4	Disability Living Allowance (for people under 65)	[BenefDLA]
2.0	Attendance Allowance (for people aged 65+)	[BenefAtA]
0.7	Severe Disablement Allowance	[BenefSev]
1.2	Invalid Care Allowance	[BenefICA]
0.7	Industrial Injuries Disablement Benefit	[BenefInd]
0.4	Other state benefit (WRITE IN)	[BenefOth]
-	(Don't know)	
0.7	(Refusal/Not answered)	

ASK ALL

N = 3287

Q994 [MainInc]
CARD J8
Which of these is the **main** source of income for you (and your husband/wife/partner) at present?

%	
62.9	Earnings from employment (own or spouse / partner(s)
9.1	Occupational pension(s) - from previous employer(s)
12.6	State retirement or widow's pension(s)
1.9	Jobseeker's Allowance/ Unemployment benefit
4.4	Income Support/ Minimum Income Guarantee for pensioners
3.2	Invalidity, sickness or disabled pension or benefit(s)
0.5	Other state benefit (WRITE IN)
1.6	Interest from savings or investments
0.6	Student grant, bursary or loans
1.6	Dependent on parents/other relatives
0.7	Other main source (WRITE IN)
0.1	(Don't know)
0.7	(Refusal/Not answered)

ASK ALL WHO ARE NOT WHOLLY RETIRED AND MALE AGED 65 OR UNDER OR FEMALE AGED 60 OR UNDER

N = 2477

Q997 [PenXpct1]
CARD J9
When you have retired and have stopped doing paid work, where do you think **most** of your income will come from?
INTERVIEWER: IF RESPONDENT SAYS `SPOUSE/ PARTNER'S COMPANY PENSION', CODE AS `A COMPANY PENSION'.
SIMILARLY FOR STATE AND PERSONAL PENSIONS.

Q999 [PenXpct2]
CARD J9 AGAIN
And which do you think will be your **second most important** source of income?
INTERVIEWER: IF RESPONDENT SAYS `SPOUSE/ PARTNER'S COMPANY PENSION', CODE AS `A COMPANY PENSION'.
SIMILARLY FOR STATE AND PERSONAL PENSIONS.

	[PenXpct1]	[PenXpct2]
	%	%
State retirement pension	25.3	31.2
A company pension	34.1	13.4
A personal pension	28.3	13.3
Other savings or investments	8.4	27.7
From somewhere else (WRITE IN)	0.7	1.3
(None)	-	8.3
Earnings from job/still working	0.2	0.5
(Don't know)	2.6	3.7
(Refusal/Not answered)	0.6	0.6

ASK ALL

Q1001 [HHIncome]

CARD J10

Which of the letters on this card represents the total income of your household from **all** sources **before tax**?

Please just tell me the letter.

NOTE: INCLUDES INCOME FROM BENEFITS, SAVINGS, ETC.

N = 3287

ASK ALL IN PAID WORK (AT [REconAct])

Q1002 [REarn]

CARD J10 AGAIN

Which of the letters on this card represents your **own** gross or total **earnings**, before deduction of income tax and national insurance?

N = 1876

	[HHIncome]	[REarn]
	%	%
Less than £3,999	2.4	4.9
£4,000-£5,999	6.9	6.5
£6,000-£7,999	5.8	5.4
£8,000-£9,999	5.4	6.0
£10,000-£11,999	4.4	7.7
£12,000-£14,999	5.7	10.6
£15,000-£17,999	5.6	10.1
£18,000-£19,999	3.9	5.1
£20,000-£22,999	5.5	6.7
£23,000-£25,999	4.5	8.1
£26,000-£28,999	4.4	4.6
£29,000-£31,999	4.3	3.2
£32,000-£34,999	4.0	2.5
£35,000-£37,999	3.7	2.3
£28,000-£40,999	3.2	2.1
£41,000-£43,999	2.5	0.9
£44,000-£46,999	2.1	0.9
£47,000-£49,999	2.2	0.5
£50,000-£52,999	1.7	0.4
£53,000 or more	8.0	3.6
Refused information	6.8	6.3
(Don't know)	6.8	1.5
(Not answered)		0.1

ASK ALL

Q1003 [CarOwn]

Do you, or does anyone else in your household, own or have the regular use of a car or van?

%

79.7 Yes

19.7 No

- (Don't know)

0.5 (Refusal/Not answered)

N = 3287

Administration

ASK ALL

Q1005 [PhoneX]

% Is there a telephone in (your part of) this accommodation?

95.9 Yes

3.6 No

- (Don't know)

0.5 (Refusal/Not answered)

N = 3287

IF 'Yes' AT [PhoneX]

Q1006 [PhoneBck]

A few interviews on any survey are checked by a supervisor to make sure that people are satisfied with the way the interview was carried out. In case my supervisor needs to contact you, it would be helpful if we could have your telephone number.

ADD IF NECESSARY: Your 'phone number will **not** be passed to anyone outside the National Centre. .

IF NUMBER GIVEN, WRITE ON THE ARF

NOTE: YOU WILL BE ASKED TO KEY IN THE NUMBER IN THE ADMIN BLOCK

%

91.3 Number given

4.6 Number refused

- (Don't know)

0.5 (Refusal/Not answered)

ASK ALL

Q1007 [ComeBac2]

Sometime in the next year, we may be doing a follow up survey and may wish to contact you again. Could you give us the address or phone number of someone who knows you well, just in case we have difficulty in getting in touch with you.

IF NECESSARY, PROMPT: Perhaps a relative or friend who is unlikely to move?

WRITE IN DETAILS ON ARF

%

40.9 Information given

55.0 Information not given (other than code 3)

3.7 DO NOT PROMPT: Outright refusal ever to take part again

- (Don't know)

0.4 (Not answered)

VERSION B

Drugs

VERSION B: ASK ALL

N = 1077

Q673 [HerCrime]
CARD H1
I'd like to ask you some questions about illegal drug use in Britain. First, thinking about the drug **heroin**, how much do you agree or disagree that...
... heroin is a cause of crime and violence?

Q674 [HeroinOK]
CARD H1 AGAIN
(How much do you agree or disagree that ...)
heroin isn't nearly as damaging to users as some people think?

Q675 [HerLegAd]
CARD H1 AGAIN
(How much do you agree or disagree that ...)
if you legalise heroin many more people will become addicts?

Q676 [HerUsePr]
CARD H1 AGAIN
(How much do you agree or disagree that ...)
people should **not** be prosecuted for possessing small amounts of heroin for their own use?

Q677 [HerSelPr]
CARD H1 AGAIN
(How much do you agree or disagree that ...)
people who **sell** heroin should always be prosecuted?

	[HerCrime]	[HeroinOK]	[HerLegAd]
	%	%	%
Agree strongly	60.3	2.3	31.7
Agree	33.8	8.2	41.8
Neither agree nor disagree	2.7	5.0	11.0
Disagree	1.3	42.3	11.6
Disagree strongly	0.4	37.2	1.9
(Don't know)	0.9	4.4	1.4
(Refusal/Not answered)	0.6	0.6	0.6

N = 1077

	[HerUsePr]	[HerSelPr]
Agree strongly	2.0	73.1
Agree	11.9	23.7
Neither agree nor disagree	7.3	0.7
Disagree	51.3	0.6
Disagree strongly	25.9	1.0
(Don't know)	0.9	0.3
(Refusal/Not answered)	0.6	0.6

Q678 [HerLegal]
CARD H2
Which of these statements comes closest to your own view?
%
1.4 Taking heroin should be legal, without restrictions
9.8 Taking heroin should be legal, but it should only be available from licensed shops
86.7 Taking heroin should remain illegal
0.6 (Don't know)
- (Refusal/Not answered)

Q679 [CanCrime]
CARD H3
Now thinking about the drug **cannabis**. How much do you agree or disagree that...
cannabis is a cause of crime and violence?

Q680 [CannabOK]
CARD H3 AGAIN
(How much do you agree or disagree that ...)
cannabis isn't nearly as damaging as some people think?

Q681 [CanLegAd]
CARD H3 AGAIN
(How much do you agree or disagree that ...)
if you legalise cannabis many more people will become addicts?

Q682 [CanUsePr]
CARD H3 AGAIN
(How much do you agree or disagree that ...)
people should **not** be prosecuted for possessing small amounts of cannabis for their own use?

Q683 [CanSelPr]
CARD H3 AGAIN
(How much do you agree or disagree that ...)
people who **sell** cannabis should always be prosecuted?

N = 1077

	[CanCrime]	[CannabOK]	[CanLegAd]
	%	%	%
Agree strongly	14.0	4.9	11.2
Agree	30.7	41.2	40.0
Neither agree nor disagree	18.8	15.2	13.3
Disagree	27.0	27.7	28.8
Disagree strongly	5.6	6.3	3.8
(Don't know)	3.3	4.1	2.2
(Refusal/Not answered)	0.6	0.6	0.6

	[CanUsePr]	[CanSelPr]
	%	%
Agree strongly	8.7	28.6
Agree	43.4	41.2
Neither agree nor disagree	9.5	10.1
Disagree	28.7	16.4
Disagree strongly	7.4	2.0
(Don't know)	1.5	1.1
(Refusal/Not answered)	0.7	0.7

Q684 [CanLegal]
CARD H4

% Which of these statements comes closest to your own view?

6.2 Taking cannabis should be legal, without restrictions
45.2 Taking cannabis should be legal, but it should only be
available from licensed shops
46.1 Taking cannabis should remain illegal
1.7 (Don't know)
0.7 (Refusal/Not answered)

Q685 [CanSelf]
Have you yourself **ever tried** cannabis?

Q686 [DrgFamly]
And as far as you know, have any of your friends or family
ever used illegal drugs?

	[CanSelf]	[DrgFamly]
	%	%
Yes	24.7	38.8
No	74.5	59.1
(Don't know)	-	1.4
(Refusal/Not answered)	0.9	0.8

Q687 [ECrime]
CARD H5
Now thinking about the drug **ecstasy**. How much do you agree or
disagree
that...
ecstasy is a cause of crime and violence?

N = 1077

Q688 [EOK]
CARD H5 AGAIN
(How much do you agree or disagree that ...)
ecstasy isn't nearly as damaging as some people think?

Q689 [ELegAd]
CARD H5 AGAIN
(How much do you agree or disagree that ...)
if you legalise ecstasy many more people will become addicts?

Q690 [EUsePr]
CARD H5 AGAIN
(How much do you agree or disagree that ...)
people should **not** be prosecuted for possessing small amounts
of ecstasy for their own use?

Q691 [ESelPr] *
CARD H5 AGAIN
(How much do you agree or disagree that ...)
people who **sell** ecstasy should always be prosecuted?

	[ECrime]	[EOK]	[ElegAd]
	%	%	%
Agree strongly	29.2	1.5	27.3
Agree	31.7	5.6	45.6
Neither agree nor disagree	14.9	8.8	9.2
Disagree	17.2	47.3	12.0
Disagree strongly	1.2	31.2	4.0
(Don't know)	5.1	4.9	0.7
(Refusal/Not answered)	0.7	0.7	0.7

	[EUsePr]	[ESelPr]
	%	%
Agree strongly	1.5	54.0
Agree	14.8	36.1
Neither agree nor disagree	7.5	2.9
Disagree	50.0	2.5
Disagree strongly	22.9	1.7
(Don't know)	2.5	2.0
(Refusal/Not answered)	0.7	0.7

Q692 [ELegal]
CARD H6

% Which of these statements comes closest to your own view?

1.0 Taking ecstasy should be legal, without restrictions
8.3 Taking ecstasy should be legal, but it should only be
available from licensed shops
88.0 Taking ecstasy should remain illegal
2.0 (Don't know)
0.7 (Refusal/Not answered)

N = 1077

Q693-   CARD H7
Q698 This card shows a list of illegal drugs. Which drugs, if any, do you think can make people feel **relaxed**? Please choose as many or as few as you like and if you don't know, please just say so.
      CODE ALL THAT APPLY

%   Multicoded (Maximum of 6 codes)
4.8   Amphetamine (speed)   [RelaxSpe]
62.0 Cannabis   [RelaxCan]
8.8   Cocaine (coke)   [RelaxCok]
8.7   Ecstasy (E)   [RelaxE]
13.2 Heroin   [RelaxHer]
10.5 LSD (acid)   [RelaxLSD]
2.2   (All of these)   [RelaxAll]
2.0   (None of these)   [RelaxNon]
27.2 (Don't know)
0.7   (Refusal/Not answered)

Q699-CARD H7 AGAIN
Q704 And which, if any, do you think can make people feel **energetic**?
      (Again please choose as many or as few as you like and if you don't know, please just say so).
      CODE ALL THAT APPLY

%   Multicoded (Maximum of 6 codes)
56.3 Amphetamine (speed)   [EnergSpe]
1.2   Cannabis   [EnergCan]
19.0 Cocaine (coke)   [EnergCok]
52.1 Ecstasy (E)   [EnergE]
4.9   Heroin   [EnergHer]
19.8 LSD (acid)   [EnergLSD]
0.6   (All of these)   [EnergAll]
1.3   (None of these)   [EnergNon]
23.4 (Don't know)
0.7   (Refusal/Not answered)

N = 1077

Q705-CARD H7 AGAIN
Q710 Which drugs, if any, do you think can make people **hallucinate**?
      (Again please choose as many or as few as you like and if you don't know, please just say so).
      CODE ALL THAT APPLY

%   Multicoded (Maximum of 6 codes)
8.3   Amphetamine (speed)   [HalluSpe]
6.8   Cannabis   [HalluCan]
12.6 Cocaine (coke)   [HalluCok]
25.2 Ecstasy (E)   [HalluE]
24.9 Heroin   [HalluHer]
66.0 LSD (acid)   [HalluLSD]
3.2   (All of these)   [HalluAll]
0.6   (None of these)   [HalluNon]
17.6 (Don't know)
0.7   (Refusal/Not answered)

Q711-CARD H8
Q713 This card shows a list of legal and illegal drugs. Please can you read through the whole list and pick the three drugs which you think are the most harmful to **frequent** users?
      PROBE: Which others?
      ENTER UP TO THREE ANSWERS

%   Multicoded (Maximum of 3 codes)
31.5 Alcohol   [DrHrmAlc]
7.1   Amphetamine (speed)   [DrHrmSpe]
5.4   Cannabis   [DrHrmCan]
29.3 Cocaine (coke)   [DrHrmCok]
47.1 Crack cocaine   [DrHrmCra]
24.5 Ecstasy (E)   [DrHrmE]
63.5 Heroin   [DrHrmHer]
15.0 LSD (acid)   [DrHrmLSD]
1.8   Magic mushrooms   [DrHrmMMu]
33.9 Tobacco   [DrHrmTob]
12.3 Tranquillisers and sleeping pills   [DrHrmTra]
3.0   (All equally harmful/not harmful)   [DrHrmEq]
5.3   (Don't know)
0.8   (Refusal/Not answered)

Q714 [CanMed]
CARD H9
Some people with serious illnesses say that cannabis helps to relieve their symptoms. Do you think that doctors should be allowed to prescribe cannabis for these people?

N = 1077

	%
Definitely should	46.4
Probably should	39.9
Probably should not	4.1
Definitely should not	4.0
(Depends on results of medical trials)	2.7
(Don't know)	2.1
(Refusal/Not answered)	0.7

VERSION B: ASK ALL WITH ODD SERIAL NUMBER

Q715 [AlcDriv1]
CARD H10
How much do you agree or disagree that...
... people should never drive after drinking alcohol, even if they've only had one or two drinks?

N = 553

Q716 [DrgDriv1]
CARD H10 AGAIN
(And how much do you agree or disagree that...)
... people should never drive after taking cannabis, even if they've only had a small amount?

	[AlcDriv1]	[DrgDriv1]
	%	%
Agree strongly	54.1	49.4
Agree	30.0	32.8
Neither agree nor disagree	5.5	7.0
Disagree	8.6	4.5
Disagree strongly	1.0	0.4
(Don't know)	0.4	5.4
(Refusal/Not answered)	0.4	0.4

VERSION B: ASK ALL WITH EVEN SERIAL NUMBER

N = 524

Q717 [DrgDriv2]
CARD H10
How much do you agree or disagree that...
... people should never drive after taking cannabis, even if they've only had a small amount?

Q718 [AlcDriv2]
CARD H10 AGAIN
(And how much do you agree or disagree that...)
... people should never drive after drinking alcohol, even if they've only had one or two drinks?

N = 524

	[DrgDrive2]	[AlcDriv2]
	%	%
Agree strongly	59.0	60.0
Agree	29.8	26.9
Neither agree nor disagree	4.1	3.9
Disagree	1.6	7.3
Disagree strongly	1.0	0.2
(Don't know)	3.5	0.5
(Refusal/Not answered)	1.1	1.1

VERSION C

Transport

VERSION C: ASK ALL

Q722 [TransCar]
(May I just check...) ... do you, or does anyone in your household, own or have the regular use of a car or a van?
IF 'YES' PROBE FOR WHETHER RESPONDENT, OR OTHER PERSON(S) ONLY, OR BOTH
%
28.0 Yes, respondent only
17.0 Yes, other(s) only
36.3 Yes, both
18.4 No
- (Don't know)
0.4 (Refusal/Not answered)

IF 'yes' AT [TransCar]
Q723 [NumbCars]
% How many vehicles in all?
45.1 One
28.9 Two
5.2 Three
1.8 Four
0.3 Five or more
- (Don't know)
0.4 (Refusal/Not answered)

VERSION C: ASK ALL
Q724 [TrfPb6U]
CARD H1
Now thinking about traffic and transport problems, how serious a problem for you is congestion on motorways?

Q725 [TrfPb9U]
CARD H1 AGAIN
(And how serious a problem for you is ...)
traffic congestion in towns and cities?

	[TrfPb6U]	[TrfPb9U]
	%	%
A very serious problem	12.4	20.9
A serious problem	18.5	31.5
Not a very serious problem	33.0	28.7
Not a problem at all	35.5	18.4
(Don't know)	0.2	0.2
(Refusal/Not answered)	0.4	0.4

IF 'yes, respondent', 'yes,both', DON'T KNOW OR REFUSAL AT [TransCar]
Q726 [GetAbB1]
CARD H2
I am going to read out some of the things that might get people to **cut down** on the number of car journeys they take. For each one, please tell me what effect, if any, this might have on how much **you yourself** use the car to get about.
..gradually doubling the cost of petrol over the next ten years.

Q727 [GetAbB2]
CARD H2 AGAIN
(What effect, if any, might this have on how much **you yourself** use the car)
..greatly improving **long distance** rail and coach services?

Q728 [GetAbB3]
CARD H2 AGAIN
(What effect, if any, might this have on how much **you yourself** use the car)
..greatly improving the reliability of **local** public transport?

Q729 [GetAbB4]
CARD H2 AGAIN
(What effect, if any, might this have on how much **you yourself** use the car)
..charging all motorists around £2 each time they enter or drive through a city or town centre at peak times?

Q730 [GetAbB5]
CARD H2 AGAIN
(What effect, if any, might this have on how much **you yourself** use the car)
..charging £1 for every 50 miles motorists travel on motorways?

Q731 [GetAbB6]
CARD H2 AGAIN
(What effect, if any, might this have on how much **you yourself** use the car)
...making parking penalties and restrictions much more severe?

Q732 [GetAbB7]
CARD H2 AGAIN
(What effect, if any, might this have on how much **you yourself** use the car)
..special cycle lanes on roads around here?

Q733 [GetBOth1]
CARD H3
Now suppose that the two things on this card were done **at the same time**. What effect, if any, might this have on how much you yourself use the car? First, charging motorists £2 for entering town centres at peak times **but at the same time** greatly improving the reliability of local public transport?

Q734 [GetBOth2]
CARD H4
And what about charging motorists £1 for every 50 miles on motorways **but at the same time** greatly improving long distance rail and coach services?

N = 1108

	[GetABB1]	[GetABB2]	[GetABB3]
	%	%	%
Might use car even more	0.9	0.9	0.9
Might use car a little less	19.5	19.2	19.3
Might use car quite a bit less	15.1	14.1	17.8
Might give up using car	6.3	2.7	4.8
It would make no difference	22.3	27.0	21.3
(Don't know)	0.1	0.5	0.3
(Refusal/Not answered)	0.4	0.4	0.4

	[GetABB4]	[GetABB5]	[GetABB6]
	%	%	%
Might use car even more	0.5	0.5	0.1
Might use car a little less	13.6	13.4	13.4
Might use car quite a bit less	13.3	9.0	10.1
Might give up using car	4.3	2.9	1.9
It would make no difference	32.4	38.1	38.6
(Don't know)	0.3	0.5	0.2
(Refusal/Not answered)	0.4	0.4	0.4

	[GetABB7]	[GetBOth1]	[GetBOth2]
	%	%	%
Might use car even more	0.2	0.3	0.3
Might use car a little less	7.4	17.9	16.4
Might use car quite a bit less	4.6	19.7	14.1
Might give up using car	1.4	5.6	4.0
It would make no difference	50.5	20.5	29.3
(Don't know)	0.2	0.4	0.3
(Refusal/Not answered)	0.4	0.4	0.4

Q735 **[Drive]**
VERSION C: ASK ALL
May I just check, do you yourself drive a car at all these days?

N = 1108

%
69.2 Yes
30.4 No
-    (Don't know)
0.4 (Refusal/Not answered)

IF 'yes' AT [drive]
Q736 [Travel1]
CARD H5
How often nowadays do you **usually** travel ...by car as a driver?

VERSION C: ASK ALL
Q737 [Travel2]
CARD H5 AGAIN
(How often nowadays do you **usually**) ...travel by car as a passenger?

Q738 [Travel3]
CARD H5 AGAIN
(How often nowadays do you **usually**) ...travel by local bus?

Q739 [Travel4]
CARD H5 AGAIN
(How often nowadays do you **usually**) ...travel by train?

	[Travel1]	[Travel2]	[Travel3]	[Travel4]
	%	%	%	%
Every day or nearly every day	46.0	9.4	5.0	1.5
2-5 days a week	17.0	25.7	11.1	2.3
Once a week	3.2	22.2	7.5	3.1
Less often but at least once a month	1.8	17.1	10.7	12.1
Less often than that	0.6	12.9	14.0	35.3
Never nowadays	0.6	12.3	51.3	45.2
(Don't know)	-	-	-	0.1
(Refusal/Not answered)	0.4	0.4	0.4	0.4

ASK THOSE WHO HAVE A CAR AND TRAVEL EVERY DAY BY CAR AND ODD SERIAL NUMBER

N = 249

Q740 [CutQrt1]
CARD H6
Suppose you were forced for some reason to cut around **a quarter** of your regular car trips? How inconvenient would you find it?
Please choose your answer from this card

Q741 [CutHalf1]
CARD H6 AGAIN
Suppose you were forced for some reason to cut **as many as a
half** of your regular car trips. How inconvenient would you
find it?

Please choose your answer from this card

N = 249

**ASK THOSE WHO HAVE A CAR AND TRAVEL EVERY DAY BY
CAR AND EVEN SERIAL NUMBER**

Q742 [CutHalf2]
CARD H6
Suppose you were forced for some reason to cut **half** of your
regular car trips.
How inconvenient would you find it?
Please choose your answer from this card

N = 247

Q743 [CutQrt2]
CARD H6 AGAIN
Suppose you were forced for some reason to cut only around a
quarter of your regular car trips?
How inconvenient would you find it?
Please choose your answer from this card

	[CutQrt1]	[CutHalf1]	[CutHalf2]	[CutQrt2]
	%	%	%	%
Not at all inconvenient	2.5	2.0	2.9	3.8
Not very inconvenient	10.9	4.2	9.9	15.5
Fairly inconvenient	27.9	12.0	19.1	28.1
Very inconvenient	57.6	80.6	67.6	52.1
(Don't know)	-	-	-	-
(Refusal/Not answered)	1.1	1.1	0.4	0.4

National Centre for Social Research

Head Office
35 Northampton Square
London EC1V 0AX
Telephone 020 7250 1866
Fax 020 7250 1524

Operations Department
100 Kings Road, Brentwood
Essex CM14 4LX
Telephone 01277 200 600
Fax 01277 263 578

Charity No. 258538

A

P.2060   Pink team

BRITISH SOCIAL ATTITUDES 2001

Summer 2001

SELF-COMPLETION QUESTIONNAIRE

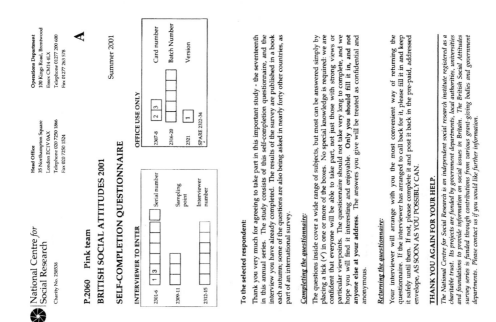

INTERVIEWER TO ENTER

2301-6 | 1 | 3 | Serial number

2309-11   Sampling point

2312-15   Interviewer number

OFFICE USE ONLY

2307-8 | 2 | 3 | Card number

2316-20   Batch Number

2321 | 1 | Version

SPARE 2322-34

To the selected respondent:

Thank you very much for agreeing to take part in this important study - the seventeenth in this annual series. The study consists of this self-completion questionnaire, and the interview you have already completed. The results of the survey are published in a book each autumn; some of the questions are also being asked in nearly forty other countries, as part of an international survey.

Completing the questionnaire:

The questions inside cover a wide range of subjects, but most can be answered simply by placing a tick (✓) in one or more of the boxes. No special knowledge is required: we are confident that everyone will be able to take part, not just those with strong views or particular viewpoints. The questionnaire should not take very long to complete, and we hope you will find it interesting and enjoyable. **Only you should fill it in, and not anyone else at your address.** The answers you give will be treated as confidential and anonymous.

Returning the questionnaire:

Your interviewer will arrange with you the most convenient way of returning the questionnaire. If the interviewer has arranged to call back for it, please fill it in and keep it safely until then. If not, please complete it and post it back in the pre-paid, addressed envelope, AS SOON AS YOU POSSIBLY CAN.

THANK YOU AGAIN FOR YOUR HELP.

The National Centre for Social Research is an independent social research institute registered as a charitable trust. Its projects are funded by government departments, local authorities, universities and foundations to provide information on social issues in Britain. The British Social Attitudes survey series is funded through contributions from various grant-giving bodies and government departments. Please contact us if you would like further information.

1

[MoneyGo]
1. Which one of these two statements comes closest to your own view?

PLEASE TICK ONE BOX ONLY

%

If the money is there, I find it just goes 23.6

OR I always try to keep some money in hand for emergencies 72.8

Can't choose 3.0

(Refusal/Not answered) 0.6

[NevBorro]
2. And which of these two statements comes closest to your own view?

PLEASE TICK ONE BOX ONLY

%

People should never borrow money 10.5

OR There is nothing wrong with borrowing money as long as you can manage the repayments 87.1

Can't choose 2.0

(Refusal/Not answered) 0.4

[MoneyRef]
3. And which of these two statements comes closest to your own view?

PLEASE TICK ONE BOX ONLY

%

Young people should spend their money while they are young and worry about saving for retirement when they are older 18.8

OR Young people should start saving for their retirement as soon as they can even if they have to cut back on other things 66.3

Can't choose 14.4

(Refusal/Not answered) 0.5

4. Please tick one box for each statement to show how much you agree or disagree with it.

PLEASE TICK ONE BOX ON EACH LINE	Agree strongly	Agree	Neither agree nor disagree	Disagree	Disagree strongly	Can't choose	(NA)
[CredPlan] a. Credit makes it easier for people to plan their finances	% 3.3	32.8	24.6	28.1	6.0	2.2	3.0
[BoroHard] b. It should be made much harder to borrow money even if this means that more people can't get credit	% 8.3	38.7	21.3	23.8	2.4	2.6	2.8
[CredSpnd] c. Credit encourages people to spend far more money than they can really afford to	% 32.2	51.1	9.6	4.3	0.5	0.8	1.5

2

5. How much do you agree or disagree with each of these statements?

PLEASE TICK ONE BOX ON EACH LINE	Agree strongly	Agree	Neither agree nor disagree	Disagree	Disagree strongly	Can't choose	(NA)
[FalsCont] a. A lot of false benefit claims are a result of confusion rather than dishonesty	% 3.1	18.0	21.7	41.1	10.2	3.4	2.5
[CheatPov] b. The reason that some people on benefit cheat the system is that they don't get enough to live on	% 6.2	30.2	17.6	32.3	8.6	3.0	2.2

[GovBen]
6. Which is it more important for the government to do?

PLEASE TICK ONE BOX ONLY

%

To get people to claim benefits to which they are entitled 34.1

OR To stop people claiming benefits to which they are not entitled 55.7

Can't choose 9.3

(Refusal/Not answered) 0.9

7. From what you know or have heard, please tick a box for each of the items below to show whether you think the National Health Service in your area is, on the whole, satisfactory or in need of improvement.

PLEASE TICK ONE BOX ON EACH LINE	In need of a lot of improvement	In need of some improvement	Satisfactory	Very good	(NA)
[HSArea3] a. Being able to choose which GP to see	% 9.7	28.2	51.0	8.9	2.2
[HSArea4] b. Quality of medical treatment by GPs	% 6.6	23.3	50.7	17.1	2.3
[HSArea7] c. General condition of hospital buildings	% 17.7	39.4	33.5	6.7	2.7
[HSArea9] d. Staffing level of nurses in hospitals	% 35.5	44.0	15.9	1.8	2.8
[HSArea10] e. Staffing level of doctors in hospitals	% 34.0	44.5	16.6	1.7	3.1
[HSArea11] f. Quality of medical treatment in hospitals	% 12.2	39.4	37.2	8.3	3.0
[HSArea12] g. Quality of nursing care in hospitals	% 12.1	34.9	36.9	12.5	3.7
[HSArea13] h. Waiting areas in accident and emergency departments in hospitals	% 30.4	37.1	27.2	2.2	3.1
[HSArea14] i. Waiting areas for out-patients in hospitals	% 20.5	38.3	35.2	2.7	3.3
[HSArea15] j. Waiting areas at GPs' surgeries	% 6.8	21.8	57.2	11.5	2.7

OFFICE USE ONLY

3

8. In the last twelve months, have you or a close family member ...

PLEASE TICK ONE BOX ON EACH LINE

N = 1899

	Yes, just me	Yes, not me but close family member	Yes, both	No, neither	(DK)	(NA)
[GPUseSC] a. ... visited an NHS GP?	% 21.9	15.5	54.3	6.3	-	2.1
[OutPUsSC] b. ... been an out-patient in an NHS hospital?	% 20.5	26.5	14.7	35.1	-	3.2
[InPUsSC] c. ... been an in-patient in an NHS hospital?	% 11.0	19.6	3.0	60.8	-	5.6
[VIstUsSC] d. ... visited a patient in an NHS hospital?	% 17.5	12.4	26.3	39.3	-	4.4
[PrivUsSC] e. ... had any medical treatment as a private patient?	% 6.2	5.2	2.3	82.5	-	3.8
[PrDnUsSC] f. ... had any dental treatment as a private patient?	% 9.3	7.6	11.1	69.0	-	3.0
[NHDnUsSC] g. ... had any dental treatment as an NHS patient?	% 13.3	14.2	29.2	41.0	-	2.3

9. Please tick one box to show how much you agree or disagree with each of these statements.

PLEASE TICK ONE BOX ON EACH LINE

N = 2821

	Agree strongly	Agree	Neither agree nor disagree	Disagree	Disagree strongly	Can't choose	(NA)
[WestLoth] a. Now that Scotland has its own parliament, Scottish MPs should no longer be allowed to vote in the House of Commons on laws that only affect England	% 18.6	37.9	18.3	11.6	1.8	10.5	1.4
[EngRgDev] b. Now that Scotland has its own Parliament and Wales its own Assembly, every English region should have its own elected assembly too.	% 4.9	23.6	25.4	25.9	6.7	11.9	1.7

10. [VoteDuty] Which of these statements comes closest to your view about general elections?

PLEASE TICK ONE BOX ONLY

In a general election ...

%

It's not really worth voting	11.0
People should vote only if they care who wins	22.9
It's everyone's duty to vote	64.9
(Refusal/Not answered)	1.2

4

N = 1899

11. [RIJbSex]
a. How often do you think that employers in Britain refuse a job to an applicant only because of his or her sex?

PLEASE TICK ONE BOX ONLY

%

A lot	11.2
Sometimes	62.7
Hardly ever	15.1
Can't choose	10.3
(Refusal/Not answered)	0.7

[RWRJbSx]
b. Do you think they would be right or wrong to refuse a job to an applicant only because of his or her sex?

PLEASE TICK ONE BOX ONLY

%

Always right	0.9
Usually right	7.8
Neither right nor wrong	16.7
Usually wrong	37.1
Always wrong	28.0
Can't choose	8.8
(Refusal/Not answered)	0.7

12. [RIJbAge]
a. And how often do you think that employers in Britain refuse a job to an applicant only because he or she is aged over 50?

PLEASE TICK ONE BOX ONLY

%

A lot	57.8
Sometimes	36.2
Hardly ever	1.9
Can't choose	3.5
(Refusal/Not answered)	0.6

[RWRJbAg]
b. Do you think they would be right or wrong to refuse a job to an applicant only because he or she is aged over 50?

PLEASE TICK ONE BOX ONLY

%

Always right	0.6
Usually right	3.3
Neither right nor wrong	12.5
Usually wrong	48.0
Always wrong	31.1
Can't choose	3.8
(Refusal/Not answered)	0.6

OFFICE USE ONLY

5

OFFICE USE ONLY

N = 1899

[RUbDis]
13a. And how often do you think that employers in Britain refuse a job to an applicant only because he or she has a disability?

PLEASE TICK ONE BOX ONLY

	%
A lot	32.4
Sometimes	55.7
Hardly ever	4.8
Can't choose	6.5
(Refusal/Not answered)	0.6

[RWRF-JbDi]
b. Do you think they would be right or wrong to refuse a job to an applicant only because he or she has a disability?

PLEASE TICK ONE BOX ONLY

	%
Always right	0.8
Usually right	5.9
Neither right nor wrong	18.2
Usually wrong	47.2
Always wrong	20.7
Can't choose	6.5
(Refusal/Not answered)	0.7

[RUbBlck]
14a. And how often do you think that employers in Britain refuse a job to an applicant only because he or she is black or Asian?

PLEASE TICK ONE BOX ONLY

	%
A lot	19.7
Sometimes	55.8
Hardly ever	15.0
Can't choose	8.7
(Refusal/Not answered)	0.8

[RWRLbBl]
b. Do you think they would be right or wrong to refuse a job to an applicant only because he or she is black or Asian?

PLEASE TICK ONE BOX ONLY

	%
Always right	1.0
Usually right	2.1
Neither right nor wrong	13.5
Usually wrong	32.1
Always wrong	44.5
Can't choose	6.1
(Refusal/Not answered)	0.6

6

OFFICE USE ONLY

N = 1899

[RUbGay]
15a. And how often do you think that employers in Britain refuse a job to an applicant only because he or she is gay or lesbian?

PLEASE TICK ONE BOX ONLY

	%
A lot	7.8
Sometimes	45.9
Hardly ever	31.2
Can't choose	14.4
(Refusal/Not answered)	0.7

[RWRLbGy]
b. Do you think they would be right or wrong to refuse a job to an applicant only because he or she is gay or lesbian?

PLEASE TICK ONE BOX ONLY

	%
Always right	1.0
Usually right	3.3
Neither right nor wrong	15.5
Usually wrong	32.6
Always wrong	37.8
Can't choose	9.3
(Refusal/Not answered)	0.6

[RUbReli]
16a. And how often do you think that employers in Britain refuse a job to an applicant only because of his or her religion?

PLEASE TICK ONE BOX ONLY

	%
A lot	2.0
Sometimes	27.4
Hardly ever	61.7
Can't choose	6.2
(Refusal/Not answered)	0.6

[RWRLbRl]
b. Do you think they would be right or wrong to refuse a job to an applicant only because of his or her religion?

PLEASE TICK ONE BOX ONLY

	%
Always right	0.4
Usually right	1.2
Neither right nor wrong	11.5
Usually wrong	33.6
Always wrong	46.6
Can't choose	6.1
(Refusal/Not answered)	0.5

7

N = 2821

17. How much do you think that you and people you know are at risk from injury or damage to their health...

PLEASE TICK ONE BOX ON EACH LINE

		A great deal	A fair amount	Not very very much	Not at all	(DK)	OFFICE USE ONLY (NA)
a.	[RiskHome] ...at home?	% 5.7	27.2	55.3	8.1	.	3.7
b.	[RiskWork] ...at work?	% 8.0	39.8	42.1	5.1	.	5.0
c.	[RiskRoad] ...on the roads?	% 39.9	45.8	10.7	0.8	.	2.8

18. From the following list, please tick one box for each item to show how important you personally think this is in a job :

PLEASE TICK ONE BOX ON EACH LINE

		Very important	Fairly important	Not very important	Not at all important	(DK)	(NA)
a.	[JbImSec2] ...job security?	% 70.6	25.4	2.1	0.4	.	1.5
b.	[JbImHIn2] ...high income?	% 19.2	65.8	11.8	0.7	.	2.6
c.	[JbImInd2] ...an interesting job?	% 59.4	35.1	3.1	0.3	.	2.0
d.	[JbImUse2] ...a job that is useful to society?	% 25.2	47.5	22.0	3.0	.	2.3
e.	[JbImSafe] ...a job where there is very little risk of injury or damage to one's health?	% 45.5	36.5	13.0	3.1	.	1.9

19. [TaxVAT]
One of the sources of government money is income tax. Do you think that the government gets more of its money from income tax, more of its money from other sources such as VAT or taxes on businesses, or does it get about the same amount from each?

PLEASE TICK ONE BOX ONLY

%
Much more from income tax 25.0
A bit more from income tax 20.4
The same from each 15.9
A bit more from other sources 11.8
Much more from other sources 9.6
Can't choose 16.0
(Refusal/Not answered) 1.3

8

N = 2821

OFFICE USE ONLY

20a. [TaxPaySh]
Do you think that people with high incomes **should** pay a larger share of their income in various taxes than those with low incomes, the same share, or a smaller share?

PLEASE TICK ONE BOX ONLY

%
Much larger share 11.2
Larger share 54.8
The same share 28.8
Smaller share 0.9
Much smaller share 0.2
Can't choose 3.7
(Refusal/Not answered) 0.5

b. [TaxPayDo]
And do you think that people with high incomes **do** pay a larger share of their income in various taxes than those with low incomes, the same share, or a smaller share?

PLEASE TICK ONE BOX ONLY

%
Much larger share 7.9
Larger share 55.6
The same share 21.0
Smaller share 5.9
Much smaller share 1.3
Can't choose 7.7
(Refusal/Not answered) 0.7

21a. [ChngNHS]
Which of the following statements about the NHS comes closest to your own view?

PLEASE TICK ONE BOX ONLY

%
Changing the way the NHS is run would do a great deal to improve it 25.3
OR Changing the way it is run is not enough, the NHS also needs a lot more money 69.2
Can't choose 5.0
(Refusal/Not answered) 0.5

b. [ChngSch]
And which of the following statements about schools comes closest to your own view?

PLEASE TICK ONE BOX ONLY

%
Changing the way schools are run would do a great deal to improve them 26.0
OR Changing the way they are run is not enough, schools also need a lot more money 65.9
Can't choose 7.6
(Refusal/Not answered) 0.5

9

[ChngPTr]
21c. And which of the following statements about public transport comes closest to your own view?

*PLEASE TICK **ONE** BOX ONLY*

	%
Changing the way public transport is run would do a great deal to improve it	38.0
Changing the way it is run is not enough, public transport needs a lot more money	52.0
Can't choose	9.4
(Refusal/Not answered)	0.6

OR

[ChngPol]
d. And which of the following statements about police forces comes closest to your own view?

*PLEASE TICK **ONE** BOX ONLY*

	%
Changing the way police forces are run would do a great deal to improve them	36.4
Changing the way police forces are run is not enough, they also need a lot more money	52.2
Can't choose	10.9
(Refusal/Not answered)	0.5

OR

22. Please tick a box to show how much you trust ...

*PLEASE TICK **ONE** BOX ON EACH LINE*

		A great deal	Quite a bit	Not much	Not at all	Can't choose	(NA)
[TrSpend1]	a. ... governments of any party to spend taxpayers' money wisely for the benefit of everyone?	8.7	24.4	49.9	11.4	4.6	1.0
[TrSpend2]	b. ... NHS hospitals to spend their money wisely for the benefit of their patients?	11.5	44.4	33.5	5.9	3.7	1.1
[TrSpend3]	c. ... private hospitals to spend their money wisely for the benefit of their patients?	13.7	42.9	24.0	6.8	11.0	1.7
[TrSpend4]	d. ... state schools to spend their money wisely for the benefit of their pupils?	14.8	50.1	24.7	2.9	6.3	1.2

23. And please tick a box to show how much you trust ...

*PLEASE TICK **ONE** BOX ON EACH LINE*

		A great deal	Quite a bit	Not much	Not at all	Can't choose	(NA)
[TrSpend5]	a. ... private fee-paying schools to spend their money wisely for the benefit of their pupils?	18.2	48.3	15.7	2.2	14.0	1.5
[TrSpend6]	b. ... local councils to spend their money wisely for the benefit of local people?	8.1	30.6	47.3	9.6	3.3	1.0
[TrSpend7]	c. ... private pension companies to spend their money wisely for the benefit of their pensioners?	10.4	39.8	33.9	6.3	8.1	1.6
[TrSpend8]	d. ... the state pension scheme to spend its money wisely for the benefit of pensioners?	9.9	35.3	38.8	7.1	7.4	1.5
[TrSpend9]	e. ... police forces to spend their money wisely for the benefit of llocal people?	8.9	42.6	34.7	5.9	6.7	1.1

10

24. From what you know or have heard, please tick one box on each line to show how well you think state secondary schools nowadays ...

*PLEASE TICK **ONE** BOX ON EACH LINE*

		Very well	Quite well	Not very well	Not at all well	(DK)	(NA)
[StatSec1]	a. ... prepare young people for work?	4.5	44.6	44.0	4.2	-	2.8
[StatSec2]	b. ... teach young people basic skills such as reading, writing and maths?	12.2	61.2	20.6	4.2	-	1.8
[StatSec3]	c. ... bring out young people's natural abilities?	4.0	43.8	43.2	6.6	-	2.3

25. Here are some qualities that students may have developed by the time they leave university. In your view how important is it that universities aim to develop such qualities in their students?

*PLEASE TICK **ONE** BOX ON EACH LINE*

		Essential	Very important	Fairly important	Not very important	Not at all important	Can't choose	(NA)
[UniQual1]	a. Self-confidence	34.2	43.9	16.3	1.1	0.5	1.9	2.1
[UniQual2]	b. How to live among people from different backgrounds	21.0	43.9	26.9	3.8	0.8	1.9	1.6
[UniQual3]	c. Skills and knowledge which will help them get a good job	38.3	48.4	9.0	1.0	-	1.6	1.6
[UniQual4]	d. A readiness to challenge other people's ideas	14.3	34.7	39.2	6.8	0.6	2.4	2.1
[UniQual5]	e. An ability to speak and write clearly	48.4	37.3	10.2	0.5	0.1	1.5	2.1
[UniQual6]	f. Knowledge that equips people for life in general	38.4	38.7	15.9	2.1	0.7	2.3	1.9

OFFICE USE ONLY

11

26. How much do you think universities in general actually develop these qualities in their students?

PLEASE TICK ONE BOX ON EACH LINE

N = 947

		Very much a lot	Quite much	Not very at all	Hardly choose	Can't choose (NA)	OFFICE USE ONLY
[UniDvQf1]		%					
a.	Self-confidence	9.7	57.6	20.2	2.9	7.7	1.9
[UniDvQf2]		%					
b.	How to live among people from different backgrounds	9.6	50.3	26.0	4.4	7.8	1.8
[UniDvQf3]		%					
c.	Skills and knowledge which will help them get a good job	12.5	55.0	20.7	2.4	7.0	2.4
[UniDvQf4]		%					
d.	A readiness to challenge other people's ideas	8.5	50.7	25.9	3.2	9.5	2.3
[UniDvQf5]		%					
e.	An ability to speak and write clearly	15.4	48.4	23.5	3.6	7.0	2.0
[UniDvQf6]		%					
f.	Knowledge that equips people for life in general	10.0	41.0	33.3	6.2	7.8	1.7

27. Please tick one box to show how much you agree or disagree with each of these statements:

PLEASE TICK ONE BOX ON EACH LINE

		Agree strongly	Agree	Neither agree nor disagree	Disagree	Disagree strongly	Can't choose	OFFICE USE ONLY (NA)
[UniPrWk]		%						
a.	A university education prepares people for the world of work	6.0	36.7	32.6	18.2	1.9	2.5	2.1
[UniAnyAg]		%						
b.	Older people should be able to go to university as easily as younger people	27.9	57.4	7.9	2.3	0.1	1.8	2.4

28. Thinking now of people who didn't go to university when they left school. How important is it to give them financial help to go to university if they want to do so later in life?

PLEASE TICK ONE BOX ONLY

[UniMatW]

	%
Very important	41.0
Fairly important	44.4
Not very important	9.0
Not at all important	1.0
Can't choose	2.8
(Refusal/Not answered)	1.8

12

29. Please tick one box for each statement to show how much you agree or disagree with it.

PLEASE TICK ONE BOX ON EACH LINE

N = 2821

		Agree strongly	Agree	Neither agree nor disagree	Disagree	Disagree strongly	(DK)	OFFICE USE ONLY (NA)
[WelfHelp]		%						
a.	The welfare state encourages people to stop helping each other	3.9	24.5	34.4	32.2	3.0	-	2.0
[MoreWelf]								
b.	The government should spend more money on welfare benefits for the poor, even if it leads to higher taxes	6.5	36.8	29.6	22.9	2.7	-	1.5
[UnEmpJob]		%						
c.	Around here, most unemployed people could find a job if they really wanted one	16.1	47.2	19.0	14.7	1.5	-	1.6
[SocHelp]		%						
d.	Many people who get social security don't really deserve any help	5.4	27.0	29.9	31.5	4.1	-	2.0
[DoleFidl]		%						
e.	Most people on the dole are fiddling in one way or another	8.4	26.7	29.5	28.7	4.7	-	1.9
[WelfFeel]		%						
f.	If welfare benefits weren't so generous, people would learn to stand on their own two feet	8.6	30.6	23.7	30.2	5.3	-	1.6
[DamLives]		%						
g.	Cutting welfare benefits would damage too many people's lives	10.9	47.3	25.2	12.9	1.9	-	1.9
[ProudWlf]		%						
h.	The creation of the welfare state is one of Britain's proudest achievements	18.8	38.0	29.8	9.6	2.0	-	1.8

30. Please tick one box for each statement below to show how much you agree or disagree with it.

PLEASE TICK ONE BOX ON EACH LINE

		Agree strongly	Agree	Neither agree nor disagree	Disagree	Disagree strongly	(DK)	OFFICE USE ONLY (NA)
[Redistrb]		%						
a.	Government should redistribute income from the better-off to those who are less well off	8.2	29.4	27.8	28.3	4.9	-	1.4
[BigBusnN]		%						
b.	Big business benefits owners at the expense of workers	11.2	42.1	28.2	15.4	1.3	-	1.8
[Wealth]		%						
c.	Ordinary working people do not get their fair share of the nation's wealth	11.2	48.6	25.5	12.5	0.8	-	1.4
[RichLaw]		%						
d.	There is one law for the rich and one for the poor	20.1	37.4	22.4	17.2	1.6	-	1.2
[Indust4]		%						
e.	Management will always try to get the better of employees if it gets the chance	14.9	39.9	24.4	17.5	2.0	-	1.3

13

31. Please tick one box for each statement below to show how much you agree or disagree with it.

PLEASE TICK ONE BOX ON EACH LINE

N = 2821

	Agree strongly	Agree	Neither agree nor disagree	Disagree	Disagree strongly	(DK)	(NA)
[TradVals] a. Young people today don't have enough respect for traditional British values	% 20.9	46.9	21.5	8.6	0.7	-	1.5
[StifSent] b. People who break the law should be given stiffer sentences	% 31.3	47.9	14.1	4.9	0.6	-	1.2
[DeathApp] c. For some crimes, the death penalty is the most appropriate sentence	% 24.1	28.4	14.3	19.4	12.4	-	1.5
[Obey] d. Schools should teach children to obey authority	% 30.0	51.7	11.0	5.6	0.4	-	1.3
[WrongLaw] e. The law should always be obeyed, even if a particular law is wrong	% 7.9	33.4	31.6	22.5	3.1	-	1.5
[Censor] f. Censorship of films and magazines is necessary to uphold moral standards	% 20.0	44.1	17.8	12.9	3.7	-	1.5

[CrimeA]
32a. To help us plan better in future, please tell us about how long it took you to complete this questionnaire.

PLEASE TICK *ONE* BOX ONLY

N = 947

	%
Less than 15 minutes	30.3
Between 15 and 20 minutes	38.5
Between 21 and 30 minutes	19.3
Between 31 and 45 minutes	7.4
Between 46 and 60 minutes	1.8
Over one hour	1.9
(Refusal/Not answered)	0.8

b. And on what date did you fill in the questionnaire?

PLEASE WRITE IN: DATE   MONTH   2001

33. And lastly just a few details about yourself.

a. Are you .....   (✓)   Male   Female

b. What was your age last birthday?

PLEASE WRITE IN: YEARS

Thank you very much for your help

Please keep the completed questionnaire for the interviewer if he or she has arranged to call for it. Otherwise, please post it as soon as possible in the pre-paid envelope provided.

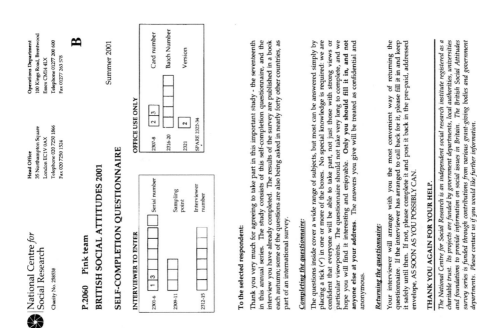

National Centre *for* **Social Research**

Charity No. 228838

Head Office
35 Northampton Square
London EC1V 0AX
Telephone 020 7250 1866
Fax 020 7250 1524

Operations Department
100 Kings Road, Brentwood
Essex CM14 4LX
Telephone 01277 200 600
Fax 01277 263 578

B

P.2060   Pink team

BRITISH SOCIAL ATTITUDES 2001   Summer 2001

SELF-COMPLETION QUESTIONNAIRE

INTERVIEWER TO ENTER

2301-6   1 3   Serial number

2309-11   Sampling
                       point

2312-15   Interviewer
                       number

OFFICE USE ONLY

2307-8   2 3   Card number

2316-20   Batch Number

2321   2   Version

SPARE 2322-34

To the selected respondent:

Thank you very much for agreeing to take part in this important study - the seventeenth in this annual series. The study consists of this self-completion questionnaire, and the interview you have already completed. The results of the survey are published in a book each autumn; some of the questions are also being asked in nearly forty other countries, as part of an international survey.

Completing the questionnaire:

The questions inside cover a wide range of subjects, but most can be answered simply by placing a tick (✓) in one or more of the boxes. No special knowledge is required: we are confident that everyone will be able to take part, not just those with strong views or particular viewpoints. The questionnaire should not take very long to complete, and we hope you will find it interesting and enjoyable. **Only you should fill it in, and not anyone else at your address.** The answers you give will be treated as confidential and anonymous.

Returning the questionnaire:

Your interviewer will arrange with you the most convenient way of returning the questionnaire. If the interviewer has arranged to call back for it, please fill it in and keep it safely until then. If not, please complete it and post it back in the pre-paid, addressed envelope, AS SOON AS YOU POSSIBLY CAN.

THANK YOU AGAIN FOR YOUR HELP.

The National Centre for Social Research is an independent social research institute registered as a charitable trust. Its projects are funded by government departments, local authorities, universities and foundations to provide information on social issues in Britain. The British Social Attitudes survey series is funded through contributions from various grant-giving bodies and government departments. Please contact us if you would like further information.

10

N = 952

Note: B1 to B23 are the same as A1 to A23 on Version A of the questionnaire.

[LegCan]
24. Please tick one box to show how much you agree or disagree with this statement.

"Smoking cannabis (marijuana) should be legalised."

PLEASE TICK ONE BOX ONLY

	%
Strongly agree	15.1
Just agree	25.5
Neither agree nor disagree	14.7
Just disagree	13.8
Strongly disagree	29.2
(Refusal/Not answered)	1.7

25. Here are some statements about illegal drugs, such as cannabis, cocaine and heroin.

PLEASE TICK ONE BOX ON EACH LINE	Agree strongly	Agree	Neither agree nor disagree	Disagree	Disagree strongly	Can't choose	(NA)
[DrugSc1] a. Doctors must be allowed to prescribe drugs for those who are addicted to them	% 4.4	21.3	18.8	32.0	16.2	4.7	2.7
[DrugSc3] b. Adults should be free to take any drug they wish	% 2.9	4.9	9.5	40.9	37.7	2.4	1.6
[DrugSc7] c. The best way to treat people who are addicted to drugs is to stop them from using drugs altogether	% 18.0	33.2	17.0	19.9	4.2	5.9	1.8
[DrugSc8] d. Taking illegal drugs can sometimes be beneficial	% 5.4	46.4	14.4	15.9	10.6	5.3	2.1
[DrugSc9] e. The use of illegal drugs always leads to addiction	% 16.1	25.7	16.5	25.6	9.2	5.1	1.8
[DrugSc12] f. Taking drugs is always morally wrong	% 16.9	27.7	21.3	23.8	6.8	2.1	1.4
[DrugSc13] g. All use of illegal drugs is misuse	% 17.2	29.8	16.3	25.6	6.2	2.7	2.3
[DrugSc14] h. We need to accept that using illegal drugs is a normal part of some people's lives	% 7.1	33.1	15.1	26.6	13.0	2.9	2.2
[DrNeedle] i. Drug users should be given clean needles to stop them getting diseases	% 16.0	46.9	13.4	11.3	6.3	4.3	1.9
[DrugInfo] j. Young people should be given information about how to use drugs more safely	% 24.3	29.3	10.6	18.0	12.3	3.4	2.2

12

N = 952

Note: B25 to B28 are the same as questions A29 to A31 on Version A of the questionnaire.

[QTimeB]
29a. To help us plan better in future, please tell us about how long it took you to complete this questionnaire.

PLEASE TICK ONE BOX ONLY

	%
Less than 15 minutes	31.1
Between 15 and 20 minutes	38.1
Between 21 and 30 minutes	19.4
Between 31 and 45 minutes	6.6
Between 46 and 60 minutes	2.2
Over one hour	1.5
(Refusal/Not answered)	1.2

Note: B29b to B30 are the same as questions A32b to A33 on Version A of the questionnaire.

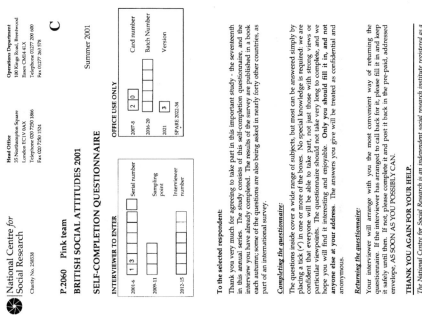

National Centre *for* Social Research

Charity No. 258538

Head Office
35 Northampton Square
London EC1V 0AX
Telephone 020 7250 1866
Fax 020 7250 1524

Operations Department
100 Kings Road, Brentwood
Essex CM14 4LX
Telephone 01277 200 600
Fax 01277 261 578

C

P.2060   **Pink team**

BRITISH SOCIAL ATTITUDES 2001   Summer 2001

SELF-COMPLETION QUESTIONNAIRE

INTERVIEWER TO ENTER

2001-6 1 3 ☐☐☐	Serial number
2009-11 ☐☐	Sampling point
2012-15 ☐☐☐☐	Interviewer number

OFFICE USE ONLY

2007-8 2 0	Card number
2016-20 ☐☐☐☐☐	Batch Number
2021 3	Version
SPARE 2022-34	

To the selected respondent:

Thank you very much for agreeing to take part in this important study - the seventeenth in this annual series. The study consists of this self-completion questionnaire, and the interview you have already completed. The results of the survey are published in a book each autumn; some of the questions are also being asked in nearly forty other countries, as part of an international survey.

Completing the questionnaire:

The questions inside cover a wide range of subjects, but most can be answered simply by placing a tick (✓) in one or more of the boxes. No special knowledge is required: we are confident that everyone will be able to take part, not just those with strong views or particular viewpoints. The questionnaire should not take very long to complete, and we hope you will find it interesting and enjoyable. **Only you should fill it in, and not anyone else at your address.** The answers you give will be treated as confidential and anonymous.

Returning the questionnaire:

Your interviewer will arrange with you the most convenient way of returning the questionnaire. If the interviewer has arranged to call back for it, please fill it in and keep it safely until then. If not, please complete it and post it back in the pre-paid, addressed envelope, AS SOON AS YOU POSSIBLY CAN.

THANK YOU AGAIN FOR YOUR HELP.

The National Centre for Social Research is an independent social research institute registered as a charitable trust. Its projects are funded by government departments, local authorities, universities and foundations to provide information on social issues in Britain. The British Social Attitudes survey series is funded through contributions from various grant-giving bodies and government departments. Please contact us if you would like further information.

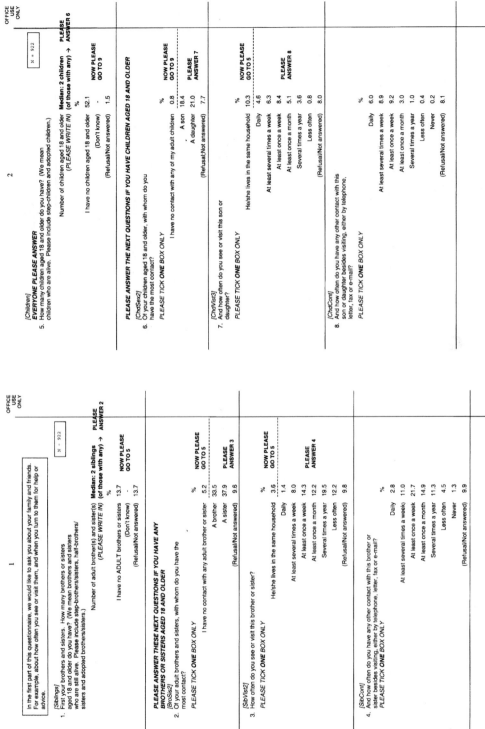

Page 1

OFFICE USE ONLY

N = 922

In the first part of this questionnaire, we would like to ask you about your family and friends. For example, about how often you see or visit them, and when you turn to them for help or advice.

[Siblings]

1. First your brothers and sisters. How many brothers or sisters aged 18 and older do you have? (We mean brothers and sisters who are still alive. Please include step-brothers/sisters, half-brothers/sisters and adopted brothers/sisters.)

Number of adult brother(s) and sister(s) (PLEASE WRITE IN) → **Median: 2 siblings** (of those with any) → **NOW PLEASE GO TO 5** / **PLEASE ANSWER 2**

%
- I have no ADULT brothers or sisters   13.7
- (Don't know)   -
- (Refusal/Not answered)   13.7

PLEASE ANSWER THESE NEXT QUESTIONS IF YOU HAVE ANY BROTHERS OR SISTERS AGED 18 AND OLDER

[BroSis2]

2. Of your adult brothers and sisters, with whom do you have the most contact?

PLEASE TICK ONE BOX ONLY

%
- I have no contact with any adult brother or sister   5.2   **NOW PLEASE GO TO 5**
- A brother   33.5
- A sister   37.9   **PLEASE ANSWER 3**
- (Refusal/Not answered)   9.6

[SibVist2]

3. How often do you see or visit this brother or sister?

PLEASE TICK ONE BOX ONLY

%
- He/she lives in the same household   3.6   **NOW PLEASE GO TO 5**
- Daily   1.4
- At least several times a week   8.0
- At least once a week   14.3
- At least once a month   12.2   **PLEASE ANSWER 4**
- Several times a year   19.5
- Less often   12.2
- (Refusal/Not answered)   9.8

[SibCont]

4. And how often do you have any other contact with this brother or sister besides visiting, either by telephone, letter, fax or e-mail?

PLEASE TICK ONE BOX ONLY

%
- Daily   2.8
- At least several times a week   11.0
- At least once a week   21.7
- At least once a month   14.9
- Several times a year   11.3
- Less often   4.5
- Never   1.3
- (Refusal/Not answered)   9.9

Page 2

OFFICE USE ONLY

2

N = 922

[Children]

EVERYONE PLEASE ANSWER

5. How many children aged 18 and older do you have? (We mean children who are still alive. Please include step-children and adopted children.)

Number of children aged 18 and older (PLEASE WRITE IN)   **Median: 2 children** (of those with any) → **PLEASE ANSWER 6**

%
- I have no children aged 18 and older   52.1   **NOW PLEASE GO TO 9**
- (Don't know)   -
- (Refusal/Not answered)   1.5

PLEASE ANSWER THE NEXT QUESTIONS IF YOU HAVE CHILDREN AGED 18 AND OLDER

[ChdSex2]

6. Of your children aged 18 and older, with whom do you have the most contact?

PLEASE TICK ONE BOX ONLY

%
- I have no contact with any of my adult children   0.8   **NOW PLEASE GO TO 9**
- A son   18.4
- A daughter   21.0   **PLEASE ANSWER 7**
- (Refusal/Not answered)   7.7

[ChdVist3]

7. And how often do you see or visit this son or daughter?

PLEASE TICK ONE BOX ONLY

%
- He/she lives in the same household   10.3   **NOW PLEASE GO TO 5**
- Daily   4.6
- At least several times a week   6.3
- At least once a week   8.4
- At least once a month   5.1   **PLEASE ANSWER 8**
- Several times a year   3.6
- Less often   0.8
- (Refusal/Not answered)   8.0

[ChdCont]

8. And how often do you have any other contact with this son or daughter besides visiting, either by telephone, letter, fax or e-mail?

PLEASE TICK ONE BOX ONLY

%
- Daily   6.0
- At least several times a week   8.9
- At least once a week   9.2
- At least once a month   3.0
- Several times a year   1.0
- Less often   0.4
- Never   0.2
- (Refusal/Not answered)   8.1

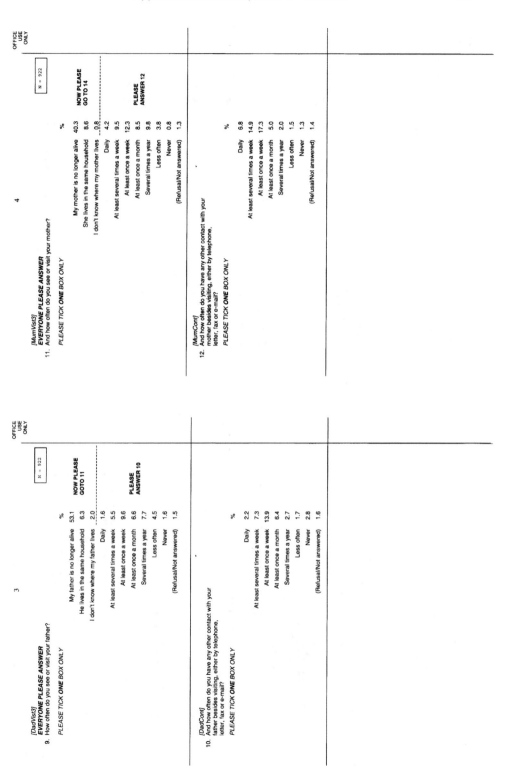

OFFICE USE ONLY

3

N = 922

[DadVist3]
EVERYONE PLEASE ANSWER
9. How often do you see or visit your father?

PLEASE TICK ONE BOX ONLY

	%	
My father is no longer alive	53.1	**NOW PLEASE GOTO 11**
He lives in the same household	6.3	
I don't know where my father lives	2.0	
Daily	1.6	**PLEASE ANSWER 10**
At least several times a week	5.5	
At least once a week	9.6	
At least once a month	6.6	
Several times a year	7.7	
Less often	4.5	
Never	1.6	
(Refusal/Not answered)	1.5	

[DadCont]
10. And how often do you have any other contact with your father besides visiting, either by telephone, letter, fax or e-mail?

PLEASE TICK ONE BOX ONLY

	%
Daily	2.2
At least several times a week	7.3
At least once a week	13.9
At least once a month	6.4
Several times a year	2.7
Less often	1.7
Never	2.8
(Refusal/Not answered)	1.6

OFFICE USE ONLY

4

N = 922

[MumVist3]
EVERYONE PLEASE ANSWER
11. And how often do you see or visit your mother?

PLEASE TICK ONE BOX ONLY

	%	
My mother is no longer alive	40.3	**NOW PLEASE GO TO 14**
She lives in the same household	8.6	
I don't know where my mother lives	0.8	
Daily	4.2	**PLEASE ANSWER 12**
At least several times a week	9.5	
At least once a week	12.3	
At least once a month	8.5	
Several times a year	9.8	
Less often	3.8	
Never	0.8	
(Refusal/Not answered)	1.3	

[MumCont]
12. And how often do you have any other contact with your mother besides visiting, either by telephone, letter, fax or e-mail?

PLEASE TICK ONE BOX ONLY

	%
Daily	6.8
At least several times a week	14.9
At least once a week	17.3
At least once a month	5.0
Several times a year	2.0
Less often	1.5
Never	1.3
(Refusal/Not answered)	1.4

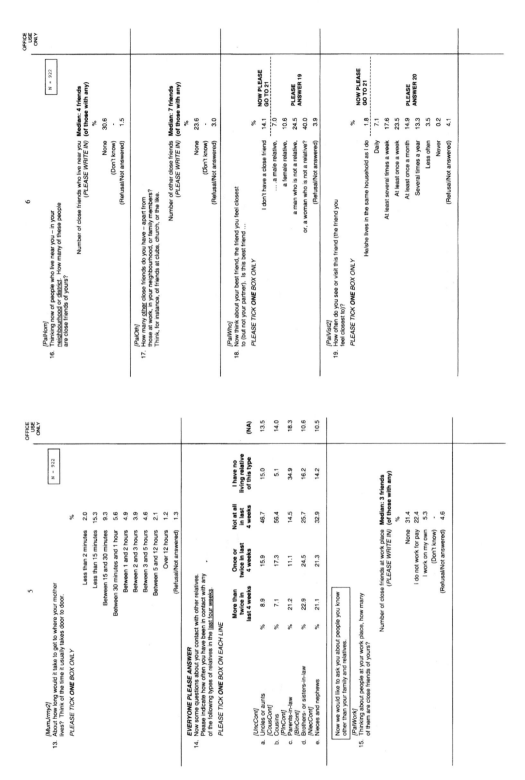

[Mum/rrmv2]
13. About how long would it take to get to where your mother lives? Think of the time it usually takes door to door.

PLEASE TICK ONE BOX ONLY

	%
Less than 2 minutes	2.0
Less than 15 minutes	15.3
Between 15 and 30 minutes	9.3
Between 30 minutes and 1 hour	5.6
Between 1 and 2 hours	4.9
Between 2 and 3 hours	3.9
Between 3 and 5 hours	4.6
Between 5 and 12 hours	2.1
Over 12 hours	1.2
(Refusal/Not answered)	1.3

EVERYONE PLEASE ANSWER

14. Now some questions about your contact with other relatives. Please indicate how often you have been in contact with any of the following types of relatives in the last four weeks.

PLEASE TICK ONE BOX ON EACH LINE

		More than twice in last 4 weeks	Once or twice in last 4 weeks	Not at all in last 4 weeks	I have no living relative of this type	(NA)
a. [UncCont]	Uncles or aunts	8.9	15.9	46.7	15.0	13.5
b. [CousCont]	Cousins	7.1	17.3	56.4	5.1	14.0
c. [PInCont]	Parents-in-law	21.2	11.1	14.5	34.9	18.3
d. [BInCont]	Brothers- or sisters-in-law	22.9	24.5	25.7	16.2	10.6
e. [NiecCont]	Nieces and nephews	21.1	21.3	32.9	14.2	10.5

(each row preceded by %)

Now we would like to ask you about people you know other than your family and relatives.

[PalWork]
15. Thinking about people at your work place, how many of them are close friends of yours?

Number of close friends at work place   **Median: 3 friends**
(PLEASE WRITE IN)   (of those with any)

	%
None	31.4
I do not work for pay	22.4
I work on my own	5.3
(Don't know)	-
(Refusal/Not answered)	4.6

6

[Pal/Hom]
16. Thinking now of people who live near you – in your neighbourhood or district. How many of these people are close friends of yours?

Number of close friends who live near you   **Median: 4 friends**
(PLEASE WRITE IN)   (of those with any)

	%
None	30.6
(Don't know)	-
(Refusal/Not answered)	1.5

[PalOth]
17. How many other close friends do you have – apart from those at work, in your neighbourhood, or family members? Think, for instance, of friends at clubs, church, or the like.

Number of other close friends   **Median: 7 friends**
(PLEASE WRITE IN)   (of those with any)

	%
None	23.6
(Don't know)	-
(Refusal/Not answered)	3.0

[PalWho]
18. Now think about your best friend, the friend you feel closest to (but not your partner). Is this best friend ...

PLEASE TICK ONE BOX ONLY

	%	
I don't have a close friend	14.1	NOW PLEASE GO TO 21
... a male relative,	7.0	
a female relative,	10.6	
a man who is not a relative,	24.5	PLEASE ANSWER 19
or, a woman who is not a relative?	40.0	
(Refusal/Not answered)	3.9	

[PalVist2]
19. How often do you see or visit this friend (the friend you feel closest to)?

PLEASE TICK ONE BOX ONLY

	%	
He/she lives in the same household as I do	1.8	NOW PLEASE GO TO 21
Daily	7.1	
At least several times a week	17.6	
At least once a week	23.5	
At least once a month	14.9	PLEASE ANSWER 20
Several times a year	13.3	
Less often	3.5	
Never	0.2	
(Refusal/Not answered)	4.1	

8

N = 922

22. Now we would like to ask you how you would get help in situations that anyone could find herself or himself in. First, suppose you had the 'flu and had to stay in bed for a few days and needed help around the house, with shopping and so on.

a. Who would you turn to first for help?

b. And who would you turn to second?

PLEASE TICK ONLY ONE AS YOUR FIRST CHOICE AND ONE AS YOUR SECOND CHOICE

	[HelpBed1] a. FIRST CHOICE %	[HelpBed2] b. SECOND CHOICE %
Husband, wife, partner	64.4	1.5
Mother	10.4	16.2
Father	1.0	6.2
Daughter	4.7	18.4
Daughter-in-law	0.3	1.4
Son	3.0	9.9
Son-in-law	0.1	0.3
Sister	1.7	6.5
Brother	1.0	2.7
Other blood relative	0.1	1.3
Other in-law relative	0.6	4.1
Close friend	3.8	13.4
Neighbour	1.7	6.4
Someone you work with	0.2	1.3
Someone you pay to help	0.4	0.5
Someone else	0.3	1.3
No-one	1.1	2.7
(Refusal/Not answered)	5.1	5.8

BEFORE GOING ON TO THE NEXT QUESTION, PLEASE CHECK TO SEE THAT YOU HAVE ONLY TICKED ONE FIRST CHOICE AND ONE SECOND CHOICE

7

N = 922

[PaiCont]

20. And how often do you have any other contact with this friend besides visiting, either by telephone, letter, fax or e-mail?

PLEASE TICK ONE BOX ONLY

	%
Daily	8.3
At least several times a week	20.0
At least once a week	26.9
At least once a month	12.8
Several times a year	6.6
Less often	3.0
Never	2.0
(Refusal/Not answered)	4.5

EVERYONE PLEASE ANSWER

21. People sometimes belong to different kinds of groups or associations. The list below contains different types of groups. For each type of group, please tick a box to say whether you have taken part in the activities of this group in the past 12 months.

PLEASE TICK ONE BOX ON EACH LINE

		I have taken part more than twice	I have taken part once or twice	I belong to such a group but never taken part	I do not belong to such a group	(NA)
a. A political party, club or association	[Partic1]	% 2.5	1.7	1.4	81.4	13.0
b. A trade union or professional association	[Partic2]	% 2.8	3.3	14.7	66.7	12.6
c. A church or other religious organisation	[Partic3]	% 14.6	4.5	5.9	64.0	11.0
d. A sports group, hobby or leisure club	[Partic4]	% 31.9	6.0	2.0	51.0	9.2
e. A charitable organisation or group	[Partic5]	% 11.0	3.1	2.7	70.5	12.8
f. A neighbourhood association or group	[Partic6]	% 4.1	3.7	3.1	75.2	14.0
g. Other associations or groups	[Partic7]	% 11.3	2.5	1.6	71.1	13.4

9

23. Suppose you needed to borrow a large sum of money.

a. Who would you turn to first for help?

b. And who would you turn to second?

PLEASE TICK ONLY ONE AS YOUR FIRST CHOICE AND ONE AS YOUR SECOND CHOICE

N = 922

	[HelpMny1] a. FIRST CHOICE %	[HelpMny2] b. SECOND CHOICE %
Husband, wife, partner	23.0	2.2
Mother	11.8	9.2
Father	8.1	9.4
Daughter	1.8	2.5
Son	2.0	4.9
Sister	1.1	3.6
Brother	2.8	4.3
Other blood relative	0.8	2.2
In-law relative	2.4	6.0
Close friend	1.1	4.3
Neighbour	-	0.1
Someone you work with	-	0.1
Employer	0.5	2.3
Government or social services agency	0.8	0.5
A bank or credit union	29.8	16.3
A private money lender	0.7	1.8
Someone else	0.4	1.9
No-one	9.0	20.2
(Refusal/Not answered)	3.9	20.2

BEFORE GOING ON TO THE NEXT QUESTION, PLEASE CHECK TO SEE THAT YOU HAVE ONLY TICKED ONE FIRST CHOICE AND ONE SECOND CHOICE

10

24. Suppose you felt just a bit down or depressed, and you wanted to talk about it.

a. Who would you turn to first for help?

b. And who would you turn to second?

PLEASE TICK ONLY ONE AS YOUR FIRST CHOICE AND ONE AS YOUR SECOND CHOICE

N = 922

	[HelpDpr1] a. FIRST CHOICE %	[HelpDpr2] b. SECOND CHOICE %
Husband, wife, partner	51.4	5.2
Mother	4.4	16.1
Father	0.2	1.9
Daughter	5.2	8.4
Son	0.7	5.4
Sister	3.9	7.5
Brother	1.9	3.3
Other blood relative	0.2	2.2
In-law relative	0.6	2.2
Close friend	20.6	24.1
Neighbour	0.2	2.0
Someone you work with	0.4	2.2
Priest or member of the clergy	0.1	0.7
Family doctor	2.1	5.2
A psychologist or another professional counsellor	0.5	0.5
A self-help group	0.1	0.2
Someone else	0.5	1.7
No-one	3.0	5.5
(Refusal/Not answered)	3.9	5.6

BEFORE GOING ON TO THE NEXT QUESTION, PLEASE CHECK TO SEE THAT YOU HAVE ONLY TICKED ONE FIRST CHOICE AND ONE SECOND CHOICE

11

25. During the past 12 months, how often have you done any of the following things for people you know personally, such as relatives, friends, neighbours or other acquaintances?

PLEASE TICK ONE BOX ON EACH LINE

N = 922

OFFICE USE ONLY

	More than once a week	Once a week	Once a month	At least two or three times in the past year	Once in the past year	Not at all in the past year	(NA)
[OthHelp] a. Helped someone outside of your household with housework or shopping	% 8.7	10.9	11.9	24.9	8.7	29.5	5.4
[OthLent] b. Lent quite a bit of money to another person	% 0.2	0.7	2.0	9.6	16.9	63.0	7.5
[OthChat] c. Spent time talking with someone who was a bit down or depressed	% 10.3	11.3	14.3	29.9	10.6	18.4	5.1
[OthJob] d. Helped somebody to find a job	% 1.3	0.8	1.3	14.3	19.4	54.9	8.0

26. [JobHow] There are many ways people hear about jobs – from other people, from advertisements or employment agencies, and so on. Please show how you first found out about work at your present employer.
IF YOU ARE NOT CURRENTLY WORKING FOR PAY, PLEASE THINK ABOUT YOUR LAST JOB.

PLEASE TICK ONE BOX ONLY

	%
I have never worked for pay	1.1
From parents, brothers or sisters	6.0
From other relatives	4.4
From a close friend	10.5
From an acquaintance	6.9
From a public employment agency or service	7.4
From a private employment agency or service	3.1
From a private employment agency	3.1
From a school or university placement office	3.7
From an advertisement or a sign	23.8
The employer contacted me about a job	6.1
I just called them or went there to ask for work	8.9
Some other way	7.8
(Refusal/Not answered)	7.2

12

27. People look for various things in a close friend and can differ on how important or not some things are for them. Please tick a box to say how important or not it is for close friends of yours to be each of the following:

PLEASE TICK ONE BOX ON EACH LINE

N = 922

OFFICE USE ONLY

	Extremely important	Very important	Fairly important	Not too important	Not at all important	(NA)
[FrndQul1] a. Someone who is intelligent and makes me think	% 10.4	18.7	31.5	23.6	8.9	7.0
[FrndQul2] b. Someone who helps me get things done	% 5.3	17.0	32.1	26.9	11.3	7.4
[FrndQul3] c. Someone who really understands me	% 23.3	35.3	23.8	8.5	3.9	5.3
[FrndQul4] d. Someone who is enjoyable company	% 43.1	36.3	12.2	1.6	1.6	5.2

28. Please tick a box on each line to indicate how much you agree or disagree with each of the following statements.

PLEASE TICK ONE BOX ON EACH LINE

	Agree strongly	Agree	Neither agree nor disagree	Disagree	Disagree strongly	Can't choose	(NA)
[HelpEldy] a. Adult children have a duty to look after their elderly parents	% 13.7	31.1	27.6	19.8	5.2	1.0	1.6
[HelpSlf1] b. You should take care of yourself and your family first before helping other people	% 24.9	45.1	15.9	10.2	1.1	1.3	1.4
[HelpFrnd] c. People who are better off should help friends who are less well off	% 4.4	28.9	34.2	24.1	3.7	2.4	2.4
[HelpSlf2] d. It is all right to develop friendships with people just because you know they can be of use to you	% 0.4	4.7	10.7	40.6	39.9	1.3	2.5

29. On the whole, do you think it should or should not be the government's responsibility to …

PLEASE TICK ONE BOX ON EACH LINE

	Definitely should be	Probably should be	Probably should not be	Definitely should not be	Can't choose	(NA)
[GovRes11] a. … provide childcare for everyone who wants it?	% 22.8	40.0	16.2	12.4	6.6	2.0
[GovResp4] b. … provide a decent standard of living for the old?	% 62.4	32.0	2.7	0.5	1.2	1.3

13

N = 922

[RUHappy]
30. If you were to consider your life in general these days, how happy or unhappy would you say you are, on the whole?

PLEASE TICK ONE BOX ONLY

	%
Very happy	33.1
Fairly happy	56.3
Not very happy	7.1
Not at all happy	1.4
Can't choose	0.8
(Refusal/Not answered)	1.2

[FeltDemd]
31. Do you feel that your family, relatives and/or friends make too many demands on you?

PLEASE TICK ONE BOX ONLY

	%
No, never	47.9
Yes, seldom	18.1
Yes, sometimes	26.7
Yes, often	4.7
Yes, very often	1.1
(Refusal/Not answered)	1.4

32. To what extent do you agree or disagree with the following statements?

PLEASE TICK ONE BOX ON EACH LINE

	Agree strongly	Agree	Neither agree nor disagree	Disagree	Disagree strongly	Can't choose	(NA)
a. [TrustFew] There are only a few people I can trust completely %	33.9	45.2	7.2	9.5	1.4	1.0	1.9
b. [TrustOth] Most of the time you can be sure that other people want the best for you %	5.3	50.2	27.9	10.6	1.4	2.1	2.5
c. [TrustNon] If you are not careful other people will take advantage of you %	15.6	47.2	17.5	14.6	1.4	0.7	3.0

[LiveArea2]
33. How long have you lived in the city, town or local community where you live now?

Median: since 1987 (other than since birth)

	%
Since birth	24.5
(Don't know)	-
(Refusal/Not answered)	1.4

14

N = 922

[LocGovEf]
34. Suppose you wanted the local government to bring about some improvement in your local community. How likely is it that you would be able to do something about it?

PLEASE TICK ONE BOX ONLY

	%
Very likely	3.7
Somewhat likely	15.7
Not very likely	51.6
Not at all likely	20.7
Don't know	7.0
(Refusal/Not answered)	1.3

Note: C36 to C42b are the same as questions A1 to A9 in version A of the questionnaire

20

[BusLink]
51. Are there bus services around here that link your neighbourhood with nearby shops and services?

PLEASE TICK ONE BOX ONLY

N = 922

	%	
Yes	89.5 →	PLEASE ANSWER 52
No	8.9 →	NOW PLEASE GO TO 53
(Refusal/Not answered)	1.7	

[BusServ1]
52. From what you know or have heard, please tick one box for each statement to show how much you agree or disagree that these buses generally …

PLEASE TICK ONE BOX ON EACH LINE

Katrina: I have got two sets of figures for BusServ1??

N = 841

	Agree strongly	Agree	Dis-agree	Dis-agree strongly	Vary too much to say	Can't choose	(NA)
a. … are clean and tidy? [BusServ1] %	1.6	55.2	15.0	2.3	6.9	13.2	4.0
b. … stop too far away from your home? [BusServ2] %	1.7	15.0	51.3	14.4	2.6	9.3	5.6
c. … are safe to travel in after dark? [BusServ3] %	2.6	42.9	21.7	6.8	3.9	16.7	5.4
d. … do not run often enough? [BusServ4] %	12.9	32.2	29.7	6.0	2.3	11.9	5.0
e. … cost too much? [BusServ5] %	12.5	33.6	29.7	3.2	1.6	13.4	6.1
f. … will take you where you mostly need to go? [BusServ6] %	3.3	56.6	17.7	5.6	2.4	9.9	4.6
g. … do the journey quickly enough? [BusServ7] %	1.3	52.0	20.8	4.8	3.0	13.1	5.0
h. … generally run on time? [BusServ8] %	2.2	43.3	24.5	8.0	2.8	15.3	4.0

EVERYONE PLEASE ANSWER
53. Please tick one box for each statement to show how much you agree or disagree.

PLEASE TICK ONE BOX ON EACH LINE

N = 922

	Agree strongly	Agree	Neither agree nor disagree	Disagree	Disagree strongly	Can't choose	(NA)
[BusNoOth] a. I would only travel somewhere by bus if I had no other way of getting there %	22.7	43.9	8.6	18.6	2.7	1.3	2.3
[Bus4Poor] b. Travelling by bus is mainly for people who can't afford anything better %	4.9	14.0	16.1	44.2	15.2	1.4	4.3

16

PLEASE TICK ONE BOX ON EACH LINE

N = 922

	Agree strongly	Agree	Neither agree nor disagree	Disagree	Disagree strongly	Can't choose	(NA)
[Proprep] 42c. Britain should introduce proportional representation, so that the number of MPs in the House of Commons each party gets matches more closely the number of votes each party gets %	13.7	32.9	20.8	11.7	4.0	13.7	3.3

Note: C43 is the same as question A9 in version A of the questionnaire

Note: C44 to C50 are the same as questions A17 to A23 in version A of the questionnaire

21

54. Please tick one box for each statement to show how much you agree or disagree.

PLEASE TICK ONE BOX ON EACH LINE

N = 922

	Agree strongly	Agree	Neither agree nor disagree	Disagree	Disagree strongly	Can't choose	(NA)
[CarTax.Hi] a. For the sake of the environment, car users should pay higher taxes [Motorway]	% 3.4	11.6	15.4	46.8	19.1	1.7	2.0
b. The government should build more motorways to reduce traffic congestion [CarConv]	% 8.4	29.5	22.2	29.1	5.1	3.8	2.0
c. Driving one's own car is too convenient to give up for the sake of the environment [BuildTra]	% 8.1	37.4	24.2	20.5	3.7	3.7	2.4
d. Building more roads just encourages more traffic [CutCars]	% 8.6	37.9	18.4	25.1	4.3	3.4	2.2

55a. How important do you think it is to cut down the number of cars on Britain's roads?

PLEASE TICK ONE BOX ONLY

	%
Very important	25.0
Fairly important	48.3
Not very important	15.2
Not at all important	5.0
Can't choose	4.8
(Refusal/Not answered)	1.7

[PImprLm]
b. And how important is it to improve public transport in Britain?

PLEASE TICK ONE BOX ONLY

	%
Very important	70.6
Fairly important	23.3
Not very important	2.9
Not at all important	0.5
Can't choose	1.1
(Refusal/Not answered)	1.6

22

56. Many people feel that public transport should be improved. Here are some ways of finding the money to do it. How much would you support or oppose each one, as a way of raising money to improve public transport?

PLEASE TICK ONE BOX ON EACH LINE

N = 922

	Strongly support	Support	Neither support nor oppose	Oppose	Strongly oppose	Can't choose	(NA)
[PImpr1] a. Gradually doubling the cost of petrol over the next ten years [PImpr2]	% 2.2	4.2	10.8	39.1	38.3	2.8	2.7
b. Charging all motorists around £2 each time they enter or drive through a city or town centre at peak times [PImpr3]	% 4.5	25.9	12.3	29.1	22.6	3.1	2.5
c. Cutting in half spending on new roads [PImpr4]	% 2.8	14.8	19.4	33.6	20.3	5.1	4.0
d. Cutting in half spending on maintenance of the roads we already have [PImpr5]r	% 0.9	4.3	9.8	47.4	30.3	3.7	3.7
e. Charging £1 for every 50 miles motorists travel on motorways [PImpr6]	% 2.7	23.5	14.0	32.7	21.2	3.3	2.8
f. increasing taxes like VAT that we all pay on goods and services [PImpr8]	% 0.7	8.4	11.6	42.9	30.7	2.9	2.7
g. Taxing employers for each car parking space they provide for their employees	% 3.6	18.1	16.4	33.3	21.0	5.0	2.5

57. Here are some things that could be done about traffic in residential streets that are not main roads. Please tick one box for each to show whether you would be in favour or not in favour.

PLEASE TICK ONE BOX ON EACH LINE

	Strongly in favour	In favour	Neither in favour nor against	Against	Strongly against	Can't choose	(NA)
[ResClose] a. Closing residential streets to through traffic [Res20mph]	% 11.5	34.4	22.9	19.5	6.0	3.3	2.5
b. Having speed limits of 20 miles per hour in residential streets [ResCross]	% 24.5	51.7	10.2	8.0	2.9	0.6	2.0
c. Making cars stop for people to cross residential streets even if they are not at a pedestrian crossing [ResBumps]	% 10.2	23.7	21.0	32.5	9.1	1.4	2.0
d. Having speed bumps to slow down traffic in residential streets	% 19.0	43.8	11.2	16.0	7.5	0.7	1.9

OFFICE USE ONLY

24

Note: C58 to C60 are the same as A29 to A31 in version A of the questionnaire.

[QtimeC]
61a. To help us plan better in future, please tell us about
       how long it took you to complete this questionnaire.

       *PLEASE TICK **ONE BOX** ONLY*   %

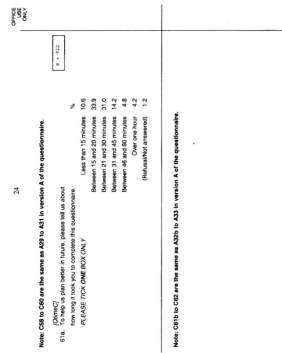

                                       Less than 15 minutes   10.6
                                Between 15 and 20 minutes   33.9
                                Between 21 and 30 minutes   31.0
                                Between 31 and 45 minutes   14.2
                                Between 46 and 60 minutes   4.8
                                            Over one hour   4.2
                                    (Refusal/Not answered)   1.2

N = 922

Note: C61b to C62 are the same as A32b to A33 in version A of the questionnaire.

Subject index